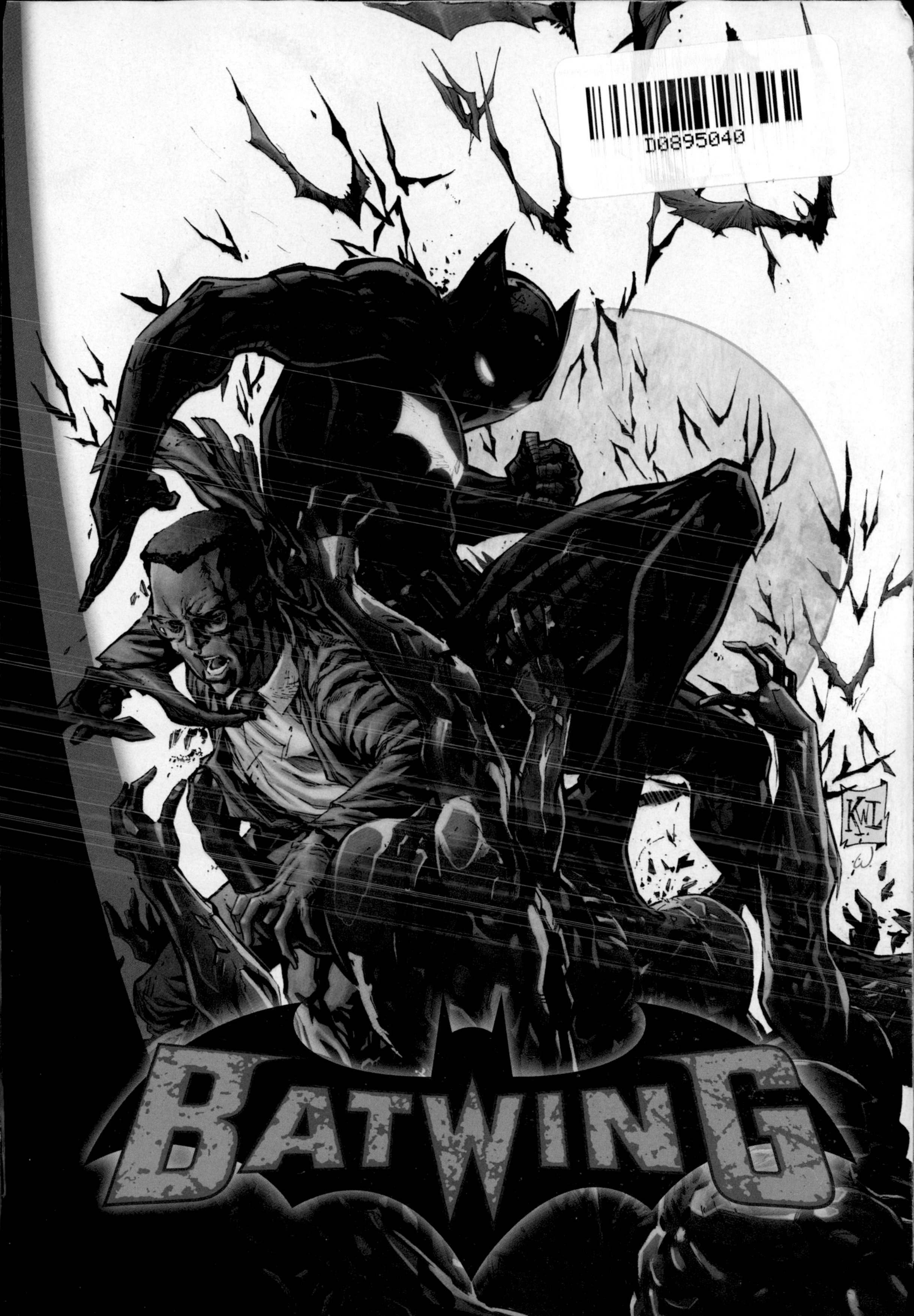
BATWING

VOLUME 4 W

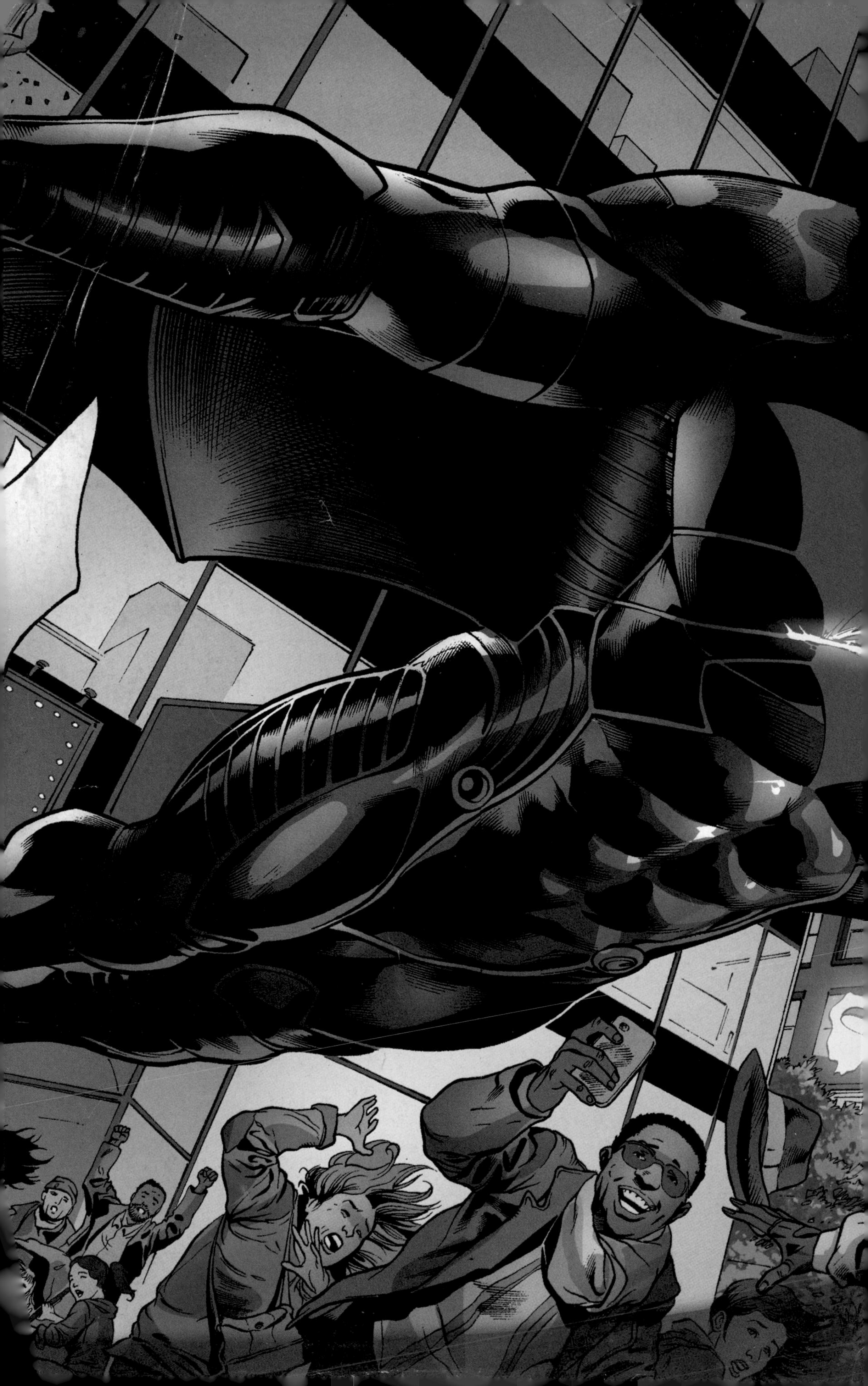

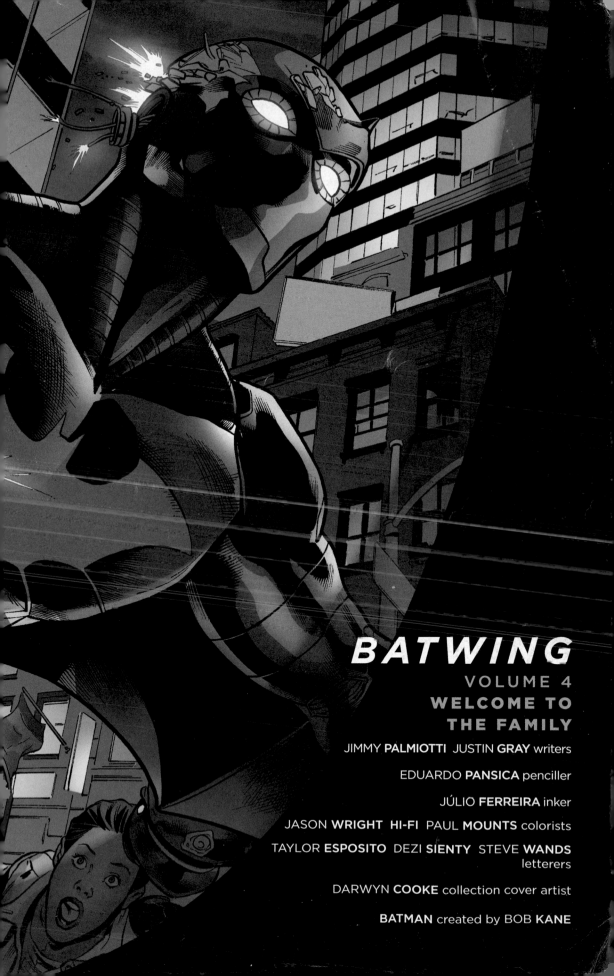

BATWING

VOLUME 4
WELCOME TO
THE FAMILY

JIMMY **PALMIOTTI** JUSTIN **GRAY** writers

EDUARDO **PANSICA** penciller

JÚLIO **FERREIRA** inker

JASON **WRIGHT** HI-FI PAUL **MOUNTS** colorists

TAYLOR **ESPOSITO** DEZI **SIENTY** STEVE **WANDS**
letterers

DARWYN **COOKE** collection cover artist

BATMAN created by BOB **KANE**

RACHEL GLUCKSTERN Editor – Original Series DARREN SHAN Assistant Editor – Original Series
ROWENA YOW Editor ROBBIN BROSTERMAN Design Director – Books
ROBBIN BROSTERMAN Publication Design

BOB HARRAS Senior VP – Editor-in-Chief, DC Comics

DIANE NELSON President DAN DIDIO & JIM LEE Co-Publishers
GEOFF JOHNS Chief Creative Officer
JOHN ROOD Executive VP – Sales, Marketing and Business Development
AMY GENKINS Senior VP – Business and Legal Affairs NAIRI GARDINER Senior VP – Finance
JEFF BOISON VP – Publishing Planning MARK CHIARELLO VP – Art Direction and Design
JOHN CUNNINGHAM VP – Marketing TERRI CUNNINGHAM VP – Editorial Administration
LARRY GANEM VP – Talent Relations & Services ALISON GILL Senior VP – Manufacturing and Operations
HANK KANALZ Senior VP – Vertigo and Integrated Publishing JAY KOGAN VP – Business and Legal Affairs, Publishing
JACK MAHAN VP – Business Affairs, Talent NICK NAPOLITANO VP – Manufacturing Administration
SUE POHJA VP – Book Sales FRED RUIZ VP – Manufacturing Operations
COURTNEY SIMMONS Senior VP – Publicity BOB WAYNE Senior VP – Sales

BATWING VOLUME 4: WELCOME TO THE FAMILY

DC Comics, 1700 Broadway, New York, NY 10019
A Warner Bros. Entertainment Company.
Printed by RR Donnelley, Owensville, MO, USA. 6/27/14. First Printing.
ISBN: 978-1-4012-4631-0

SUSTAINABLE
FORESTRY
INITIATIVE

Certified Chain of Custody
20% Certified Forest Content,
80% Certified Sourcing
www.sfiprogram.org
SFI-01042
APPLIES TO TEXT STOCK ONLY

Library of Congress Cataloging-in-Publication Data is Available

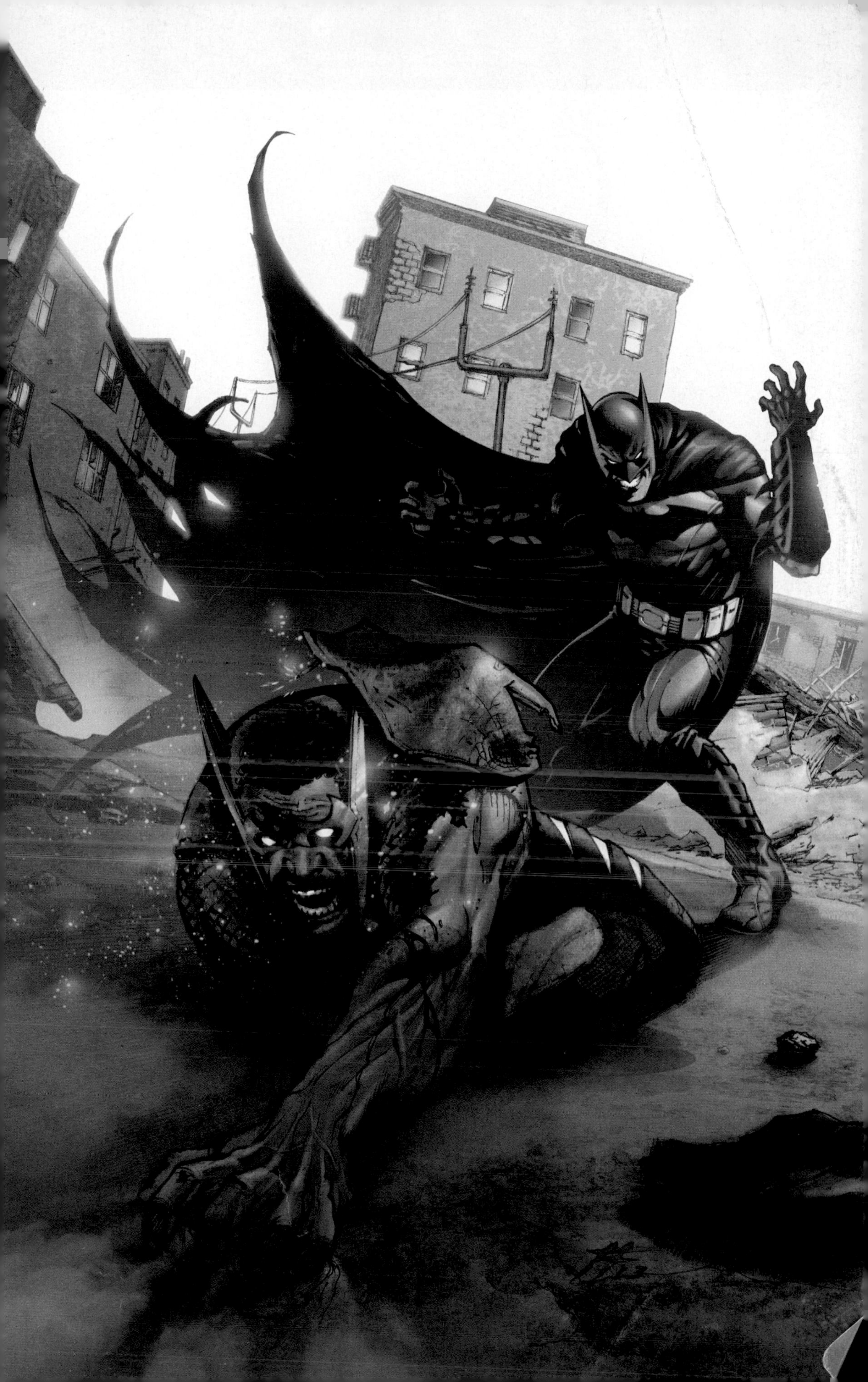

THE END OF THE BEGINNING
cover art by **FABRIZIO FIORENTINO**

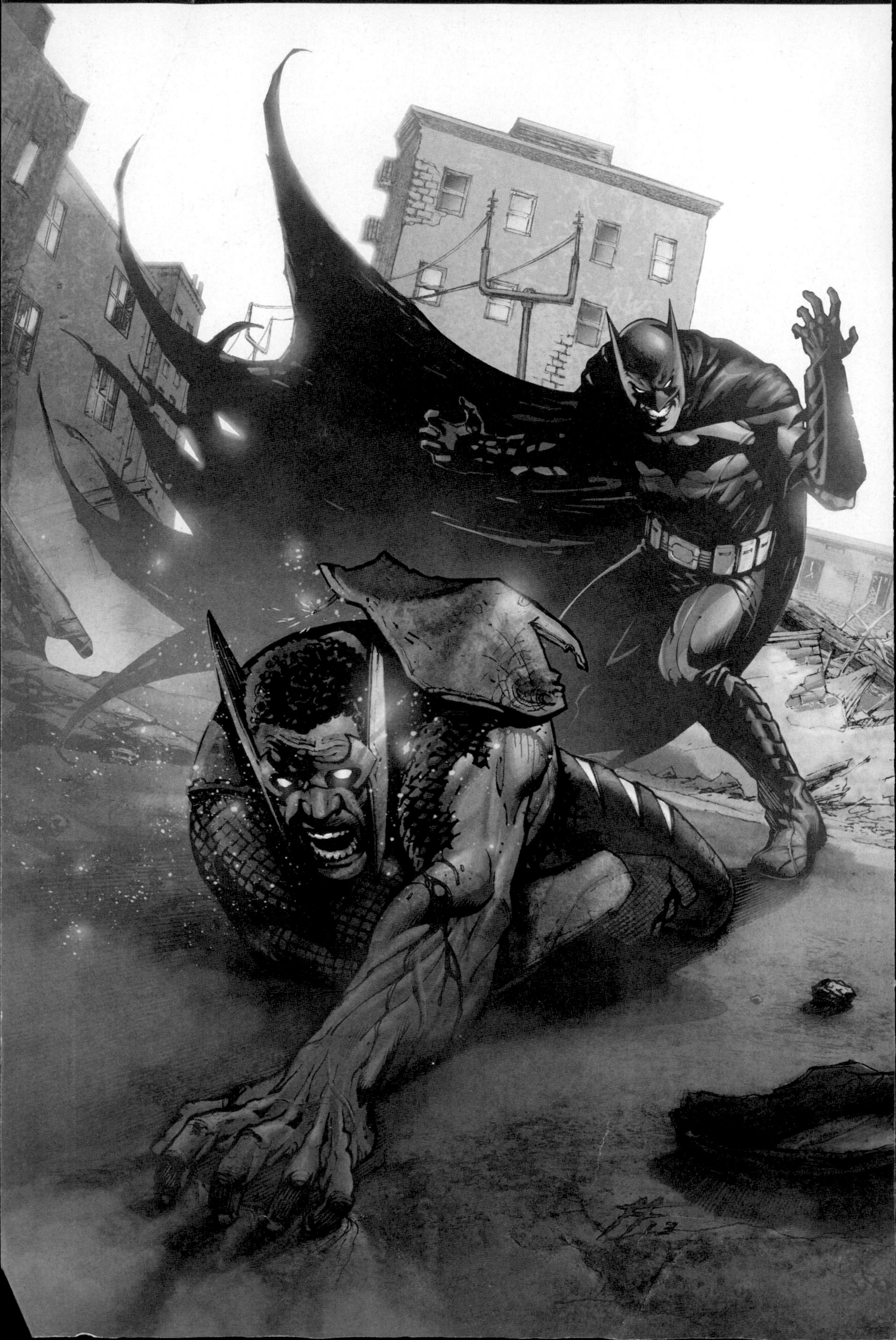

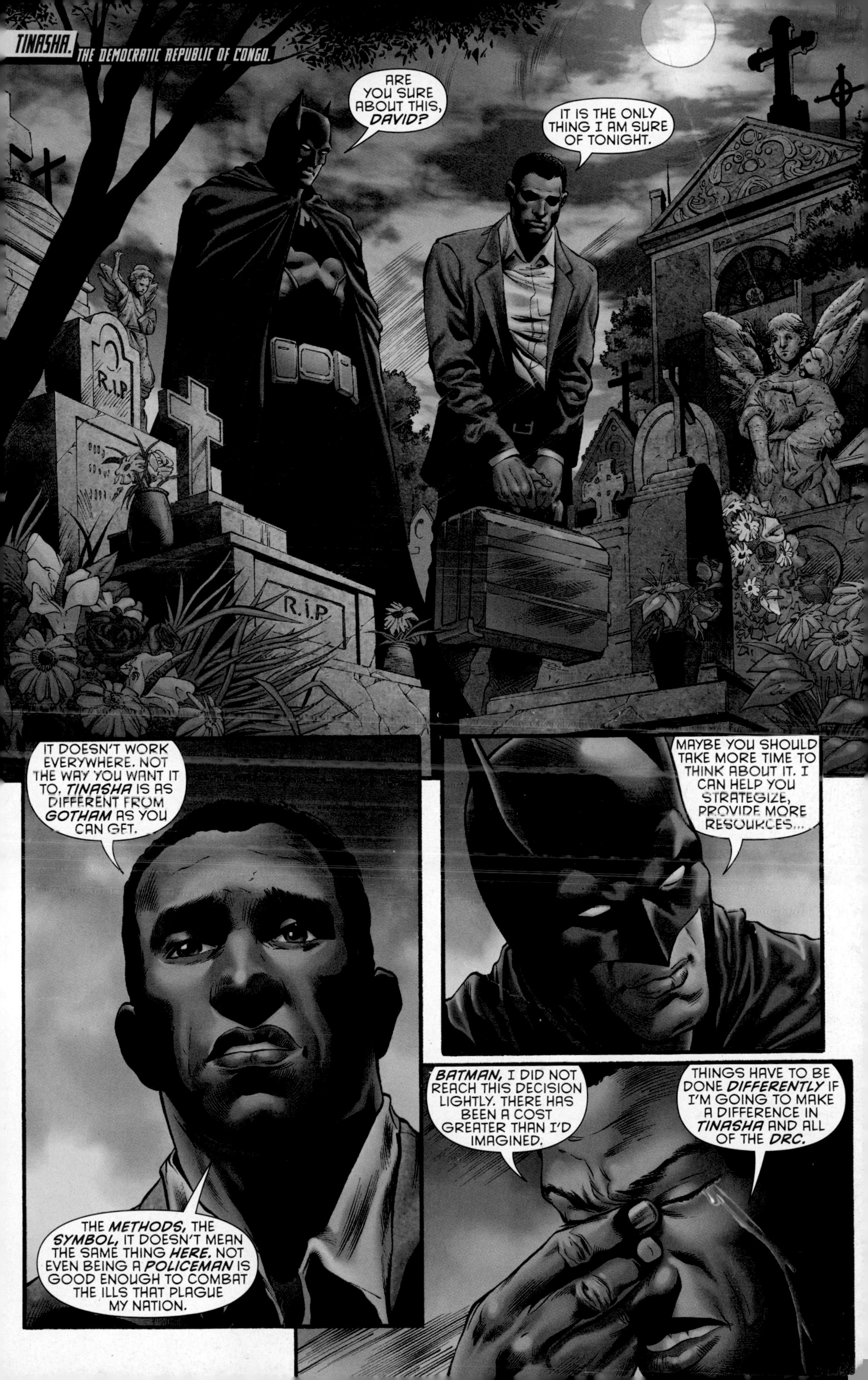
TINASHA. THE DEMOCRATIC REPUBLIC OF CONGO.
ARE YOU SURE ABOUT THIS, DAVID?
IT IS THE ONLY THING I AM SURE OF TONIGHT.
IT DOESN'T WORK EVERYWHERE. NOT THE WAY YOU WANT IT TO. TINASHA IS AS DIFFERENT FROM GOTHAM AS YOU CAN GET.
MAYBE YOU SHOULD TAKE MORE TIME TO THINK ABOUT IT. I CAN HELP YOU STRATEGIZE, PROVIDE MORE RESOURCES...
THE METHODS, THE SYMBOL, IT DOESN'T MEAN THE SAME THING HERE. NOT EVEN BEING A POLICEMAN IS GOOD ENOUGH TO COMBAT THE ILLS THAT PLAGUE MY NATION.
BATMAN, I DID NOT REACH THIS DECISION LIGHTLY. THERE HAS BEEN A COST GREATER THAN I'D IMAGINED.
THINGS HAVE TO BE DONE DIFFERENTLY IF I'M GOING TO MAKE A DIFFERENCE IN TINASHA AND ALL OF THE DRC.

A SEASON OF CHANGE

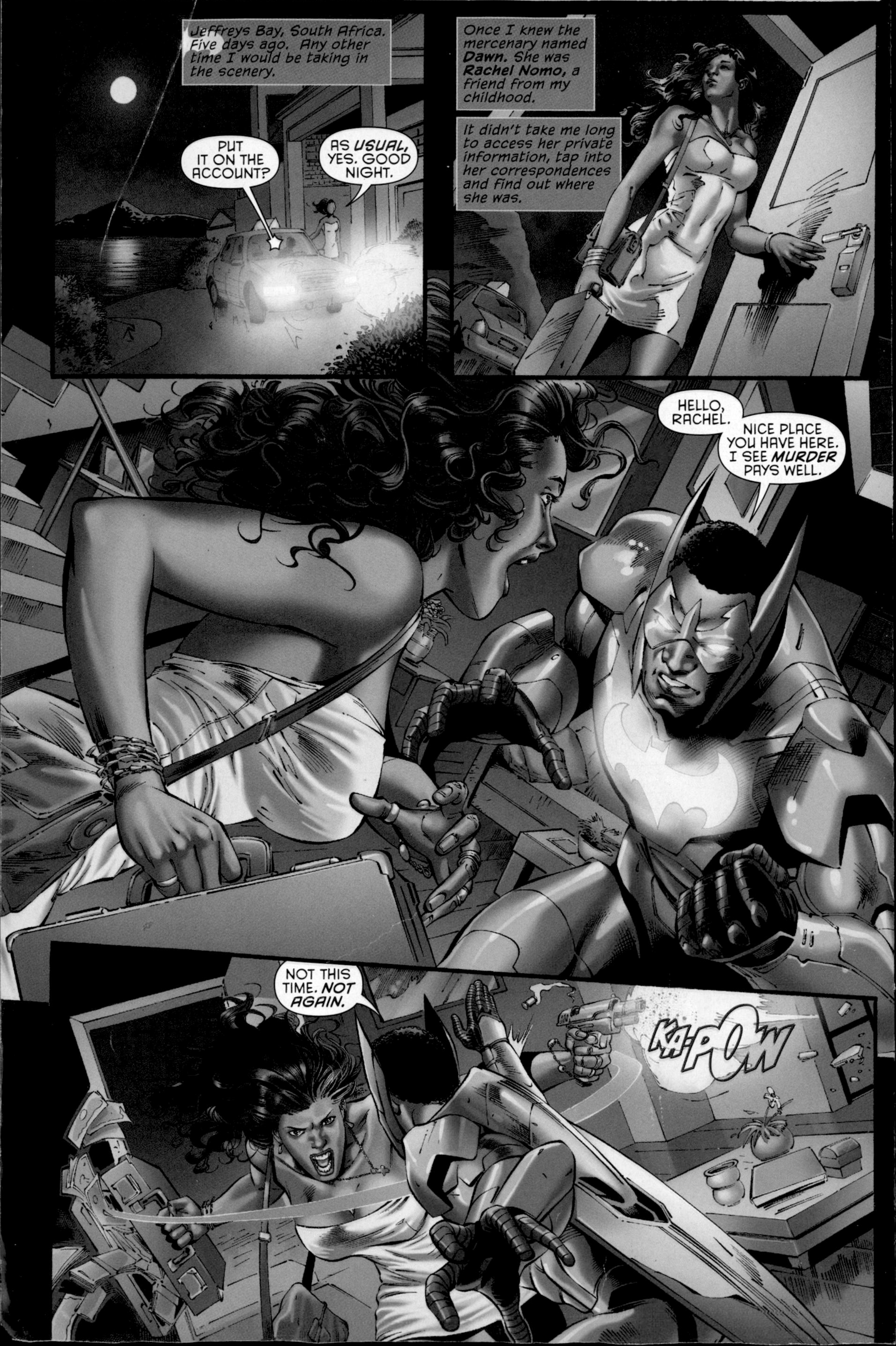

Jeffreys Bay, South Africa. Five days ago. Any other time I would be taking in the scenery.
PUT IT ON THE ACCOUNT?
AS USUAL, YES. GOOD NIGHT.
Once I knew the mercenary named Dawn. She was Rachel Nomo, a friend from my childhood.
It didn't take me long to access her private information, tap into her correspondences and find out where she was.
HELLO, RACHEL.
NICE PLACE YOU HAVE HERE. I SEE MURDER PAYS WELL.
NOT THIS TIME. NOT AGAIN.
KA-POW

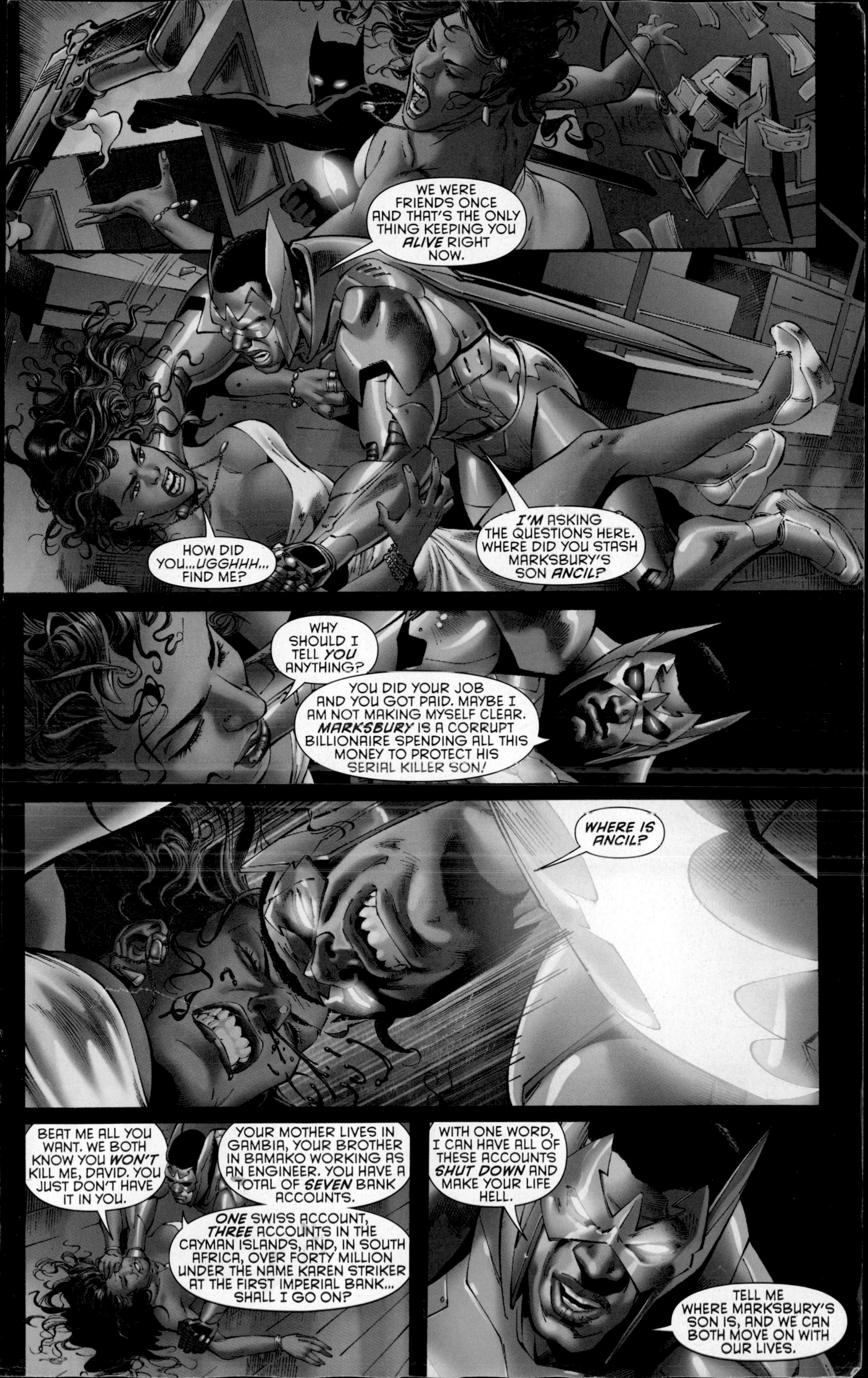
WE WERE FRIENDS ONCE AND THAT'S THE ONLY THING KEEPING YOU ALIVE RIGHT NOW.
HOW DID YOU...UGGHHH... FIND ME?
I'M ASKING THE QUESTIONS HERE. WHERE DID YOU STASH MARKSBURY'S SON ANCIL?
WHY SHOULD I TELL YOU ANYTHING?
YOU DID YOUR JOB AND YOU GOT PAID. MAYBE I AM NOT MAKING MYSELF CLEAR. MARKSBURY IS A CORRUPT BILLIONAIRE SPENDING ALL THIS MONEY TO PROTECT HIS SERIAL KILLER SON!
WHERE IS ANCIL?
BEAT ME ALL YOU WANT. WE BOTH KNOW YOU WON'T KILL ME, DAVID. YOU JUST DON'T HAVE IT IN YOU.
YOUR MOTHER LIVES IN GAMBIA, YOUR BROTHER IN BAMAKO WORKING AS AN ENGINEER. YOU HAVE A TOTAL OF SEVEN BANK ACCOUNTS.
ONE SWISS ACCOUNT, THREE ACCOUNTS IN THE CAYMAN ISLANDS, AND, IN SOUTH AFRICA, OVER FORTY MILLION UNDER THE NAME KAREN STRIKER AT THE FIRST IMPERIAL BANK... SHALL I GO ON?
WITH ONE WORD, I CAN HAVE ALL OF THESE ACCOUNTS SHUT DOWN AND MAKE YOUR LIFE HELL.
TELL ME WHERE MARKSBURY'S SON IS, AND WE CAN BOTH MOVE ON WITH OUR LIVES.

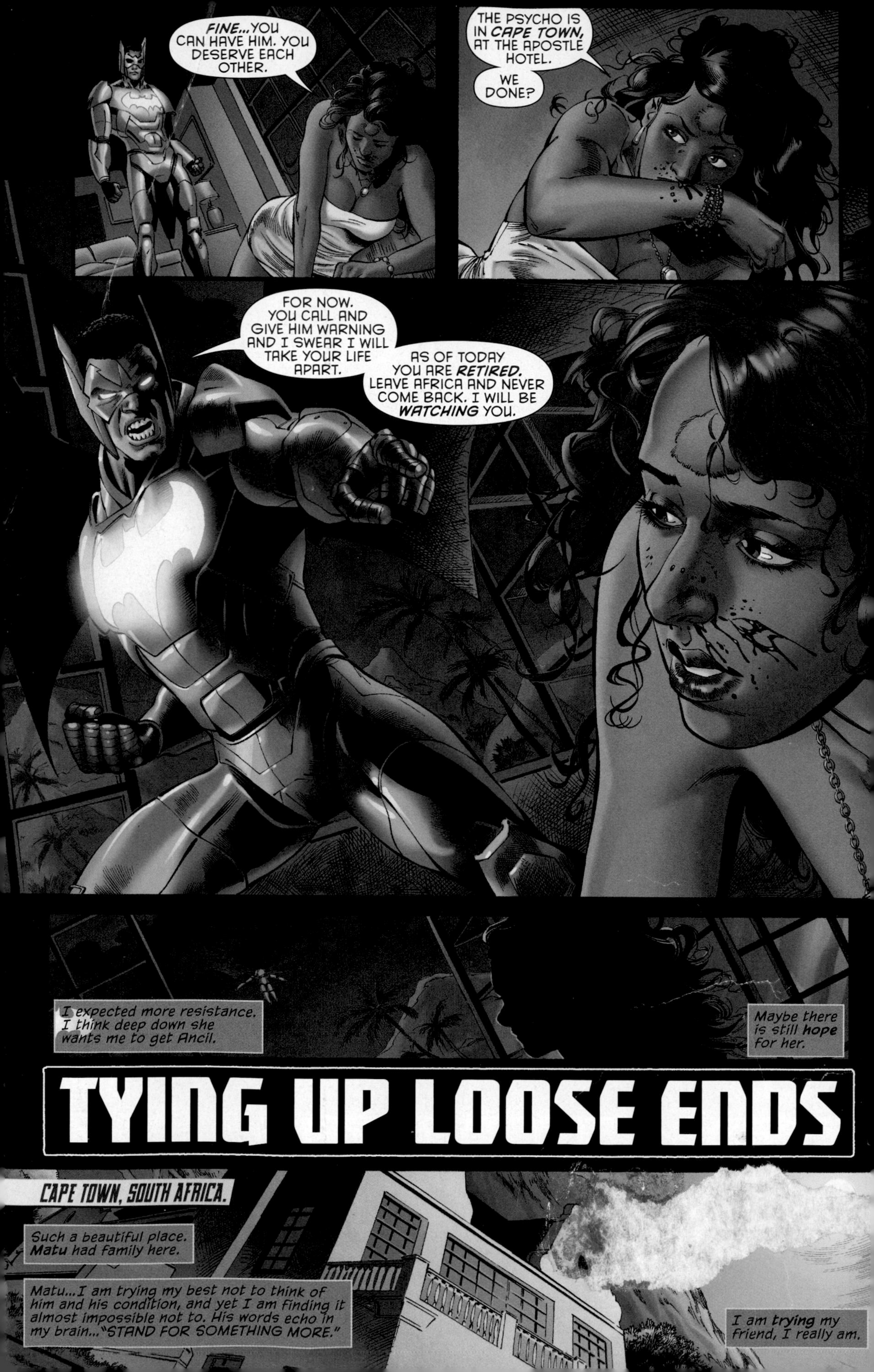
FINE...YOU CAN HAVE HIM. YOU DESERVE EACH OTHER.
THE PSYCHO IS IN CAPE TOWN, AT THE APOSTLE HOTEL.
WE DONE?
FOR NOW. YOU CALL AND GIVE HIM WARNING AND I SWEAR I WILL TAKE YOUR LIFE APART.
AS OF TODAY YOU ARE RETIRED. LEAVE AFRICA AND NEVER COME BACK. I WILL BE WATCHING YOU.
I expected more resistance. I think deep down she wants me to get Ancil.
Maybe there is still hope for her.
TYING UP LOOSE ENDS
CAPE TOWN, SOUTH AFRICA.
Such a beautiful place. Matu had family here.
Matu...I am trying my best not to think of him and his condition, and yet I am finding it almost impossible not to. His words echo in my brain..."STAND FOR SOMETHING MORE."
I am trying my friend, I really am.

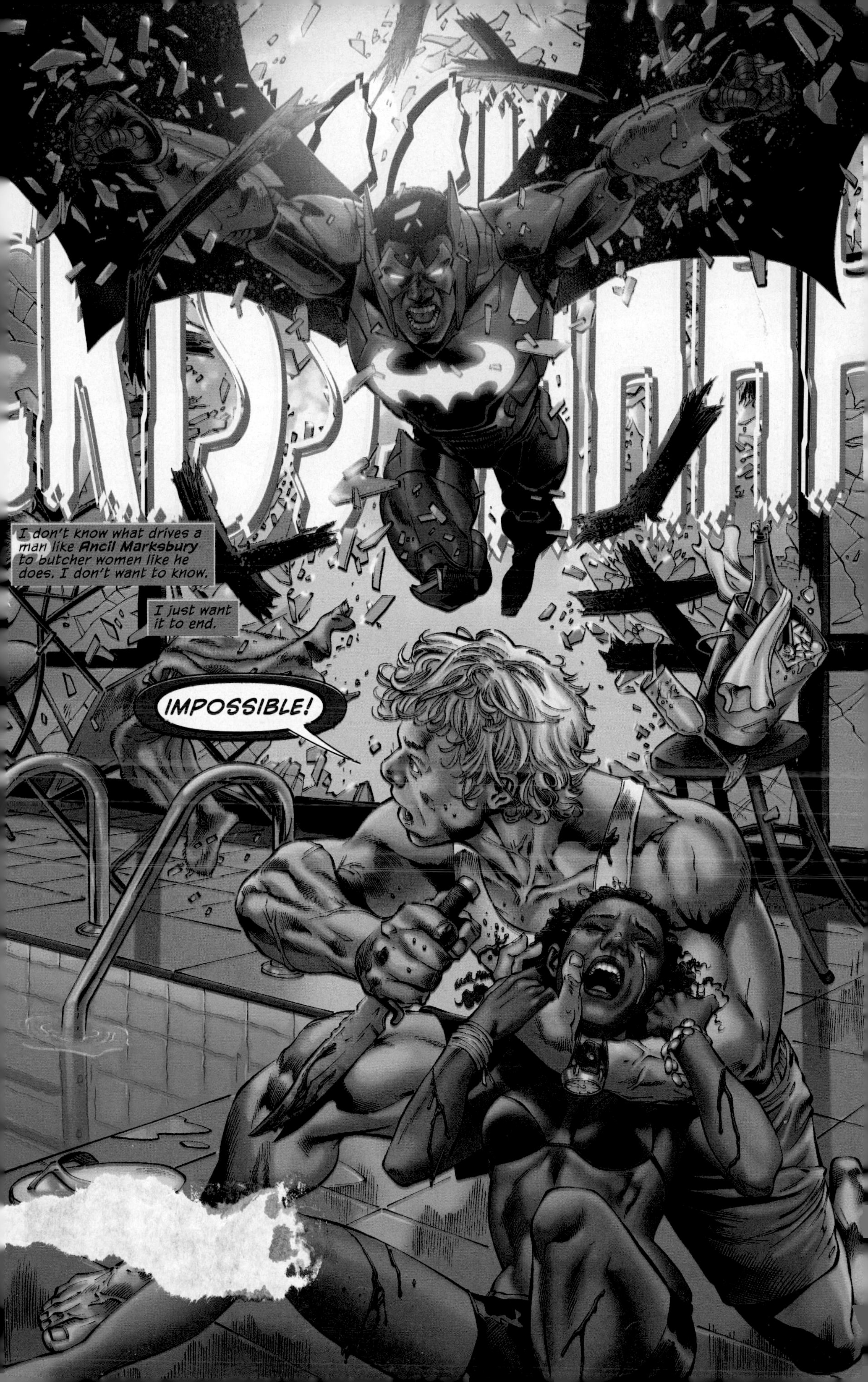
I don't know what drives a man like Ancil Marksbury to butcher women like he does. I don't want to know.
I just want it to end.
IMPOSSIBLE!

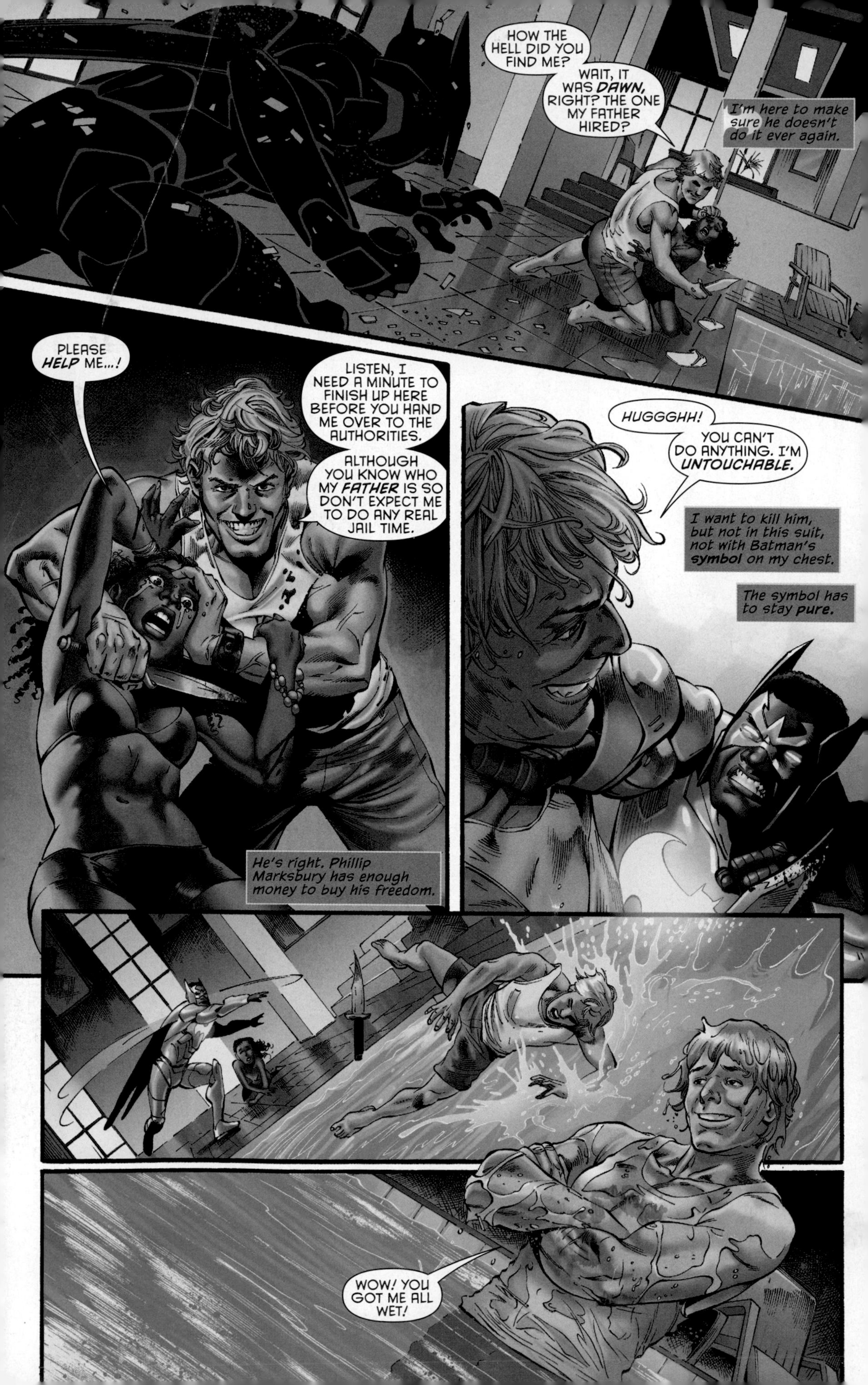
HOW THE HELL DID YOU FIND ME?
WAIT, IT WAS DAWN, RIGHT? THE ONE MY FATHER HIRED?
I'm here to make sure he doesn't do it ever again.
PLEASE HELP ME...!
LISTEN, I NEED A MINUTE TO FINISH UP HERE BEFORE YOU HAND ME OVER TO THE AUTHORITIES.
ALTHOUGH YOU KNOW WHO MY FATHER IS SO DON'T EXPECT ME TO DO ANY REAL JAIL TIME.
He's right. Phillip Marksbury has enough money to buy his freedom.
HUGGGHH!
YOU CAN'T DO ANYTHING. I'M UNTOUCHABLE.
I want to kill him, but not in this suit, not with Batman's symbol on my chest.
The symbol has to stay pure.
WOW! YOU GOT ME ALL WET!

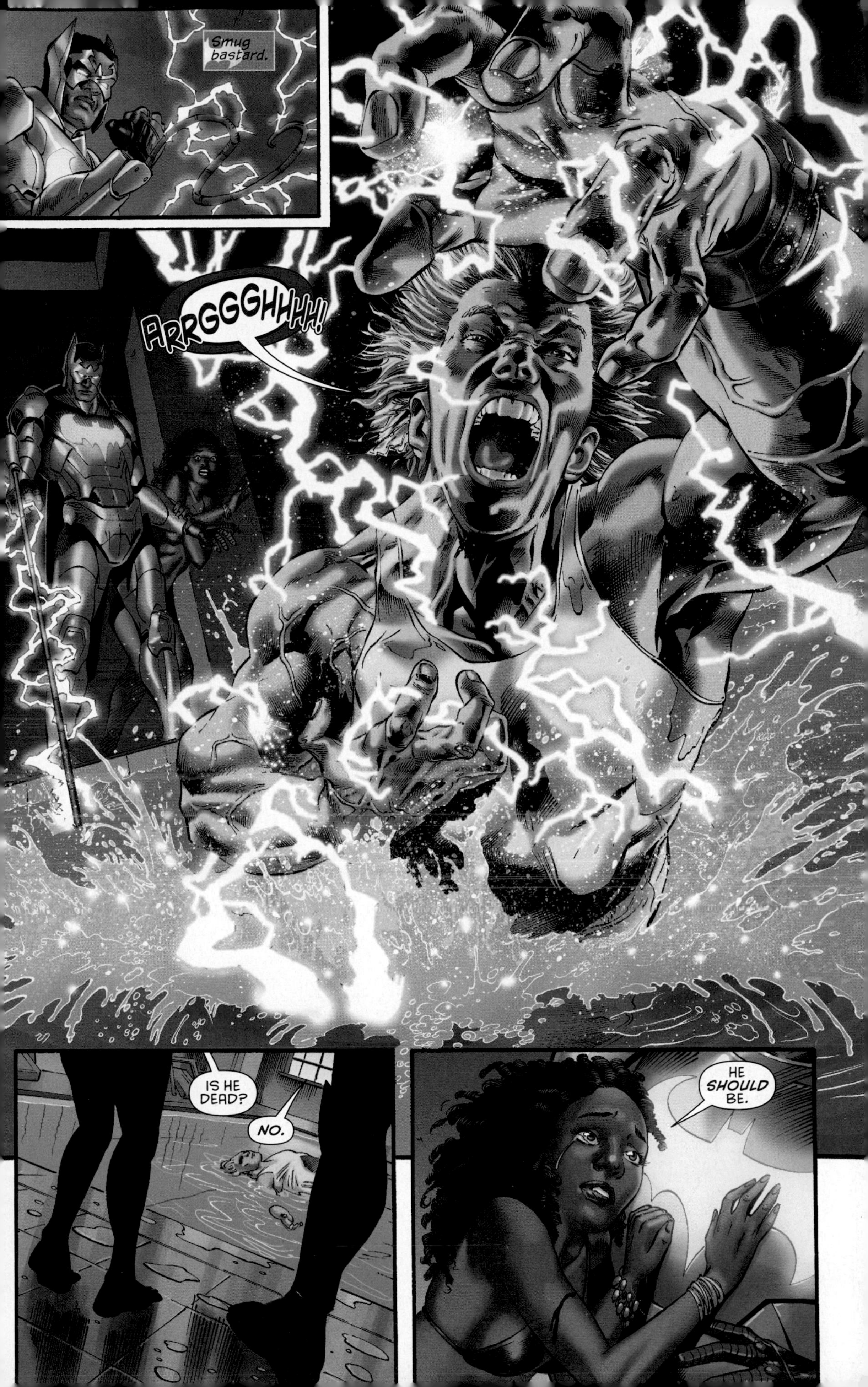
Smug bastard.
ARRGGGHHHH!
IS HE DEAD?
NO.
HE SHOULD BE.

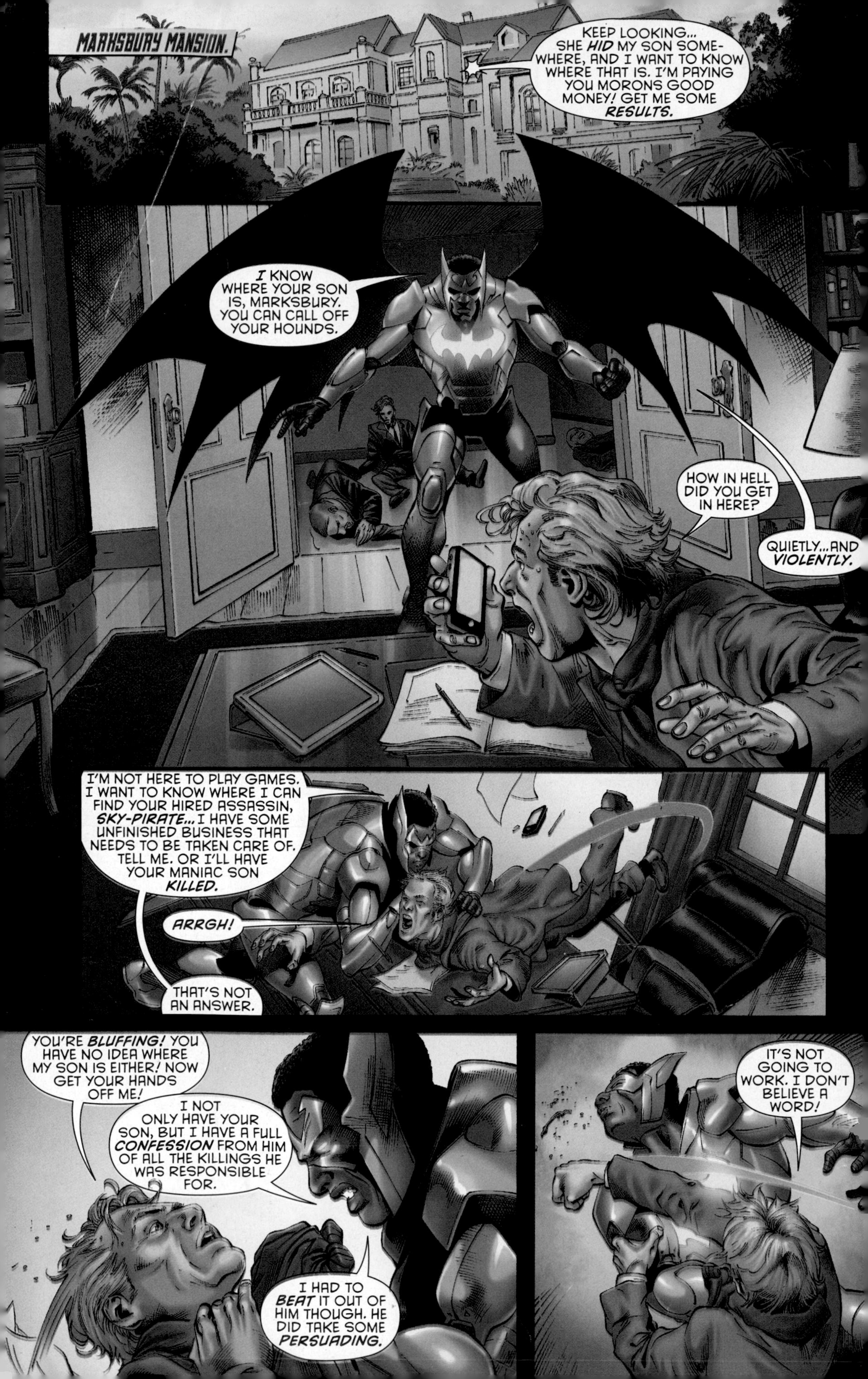
MARKSBURY MANSION.
KEEP LOOKING... SHE HID MY SON SOME-WHERE, AND I WANT TO KNOW WHERE THAT IS. I'M PAYING YOU MORONS GOOD MONEY! GET ME SOME RESULTS.
I KNOW WHERE YOUR SON IS, MARKSBURY. YOU CAN CALL OFF YOUR HOUNDS.
HOW IN HELL DID YOU GET IN HERE?
QUIETLY...AND VIOLENTLY.
I'M NOT HERE TO PLAY GAMES. I WANT TO KNOW WHERE I CAN FIND YOUR HIRED ASSASSIN, SKY-PIRATE... I HAVE SOME UNFINISHED BUSINESS THAT NEEDS TO BE TAKEN CARE OF. TELL ME. OR I'LL HAVE YOUR MANIAC SON KILLED.
ARRGH!
THAT'S NOT AN ANSWER.
YOU'RE BLUFFING! YOU HAVE NO IDEA WHERE MY SON IS EITHER! NOW GET YOUR HANDS OFF ME!
I NOT ONLY HAVE YOUR SON, BUT I HAVE A FULL CONFESSION FROM HIM OF ALL THE KILLINGS HE WAS RESPONSIBLE FOR.
I HAD TO BEAT IT OUT OF HIM THOUGH. HE DID TAKE SOME PERSUADING.
IT'S NOT GOING TO WORK. I DON'T BELIEVE A WORD!

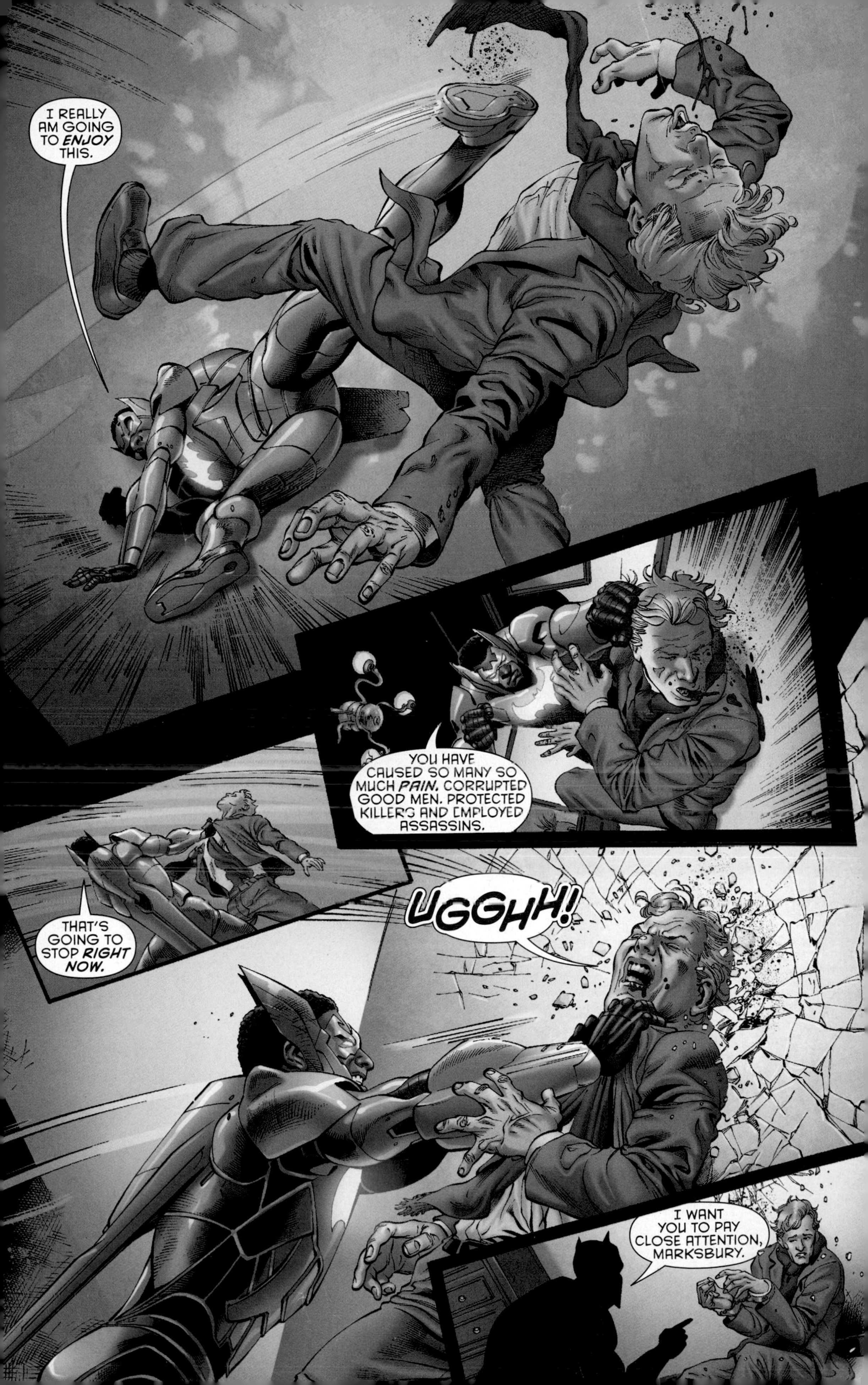
I REALLY AM GOING TO ENJOY THIS.
YOU HAVE CAUSED SO MANY SO MUCH PAIN. CORRUPTED GOOD MEN. PROTECTED KILLERS AND EMPLOYED ASSASSINS.
THAT'S GOING TO STOP RIGHT NOW.
UGGHH!
I WANT YOU TO PAY CLOSE ATTENTION, MARKSBURY.

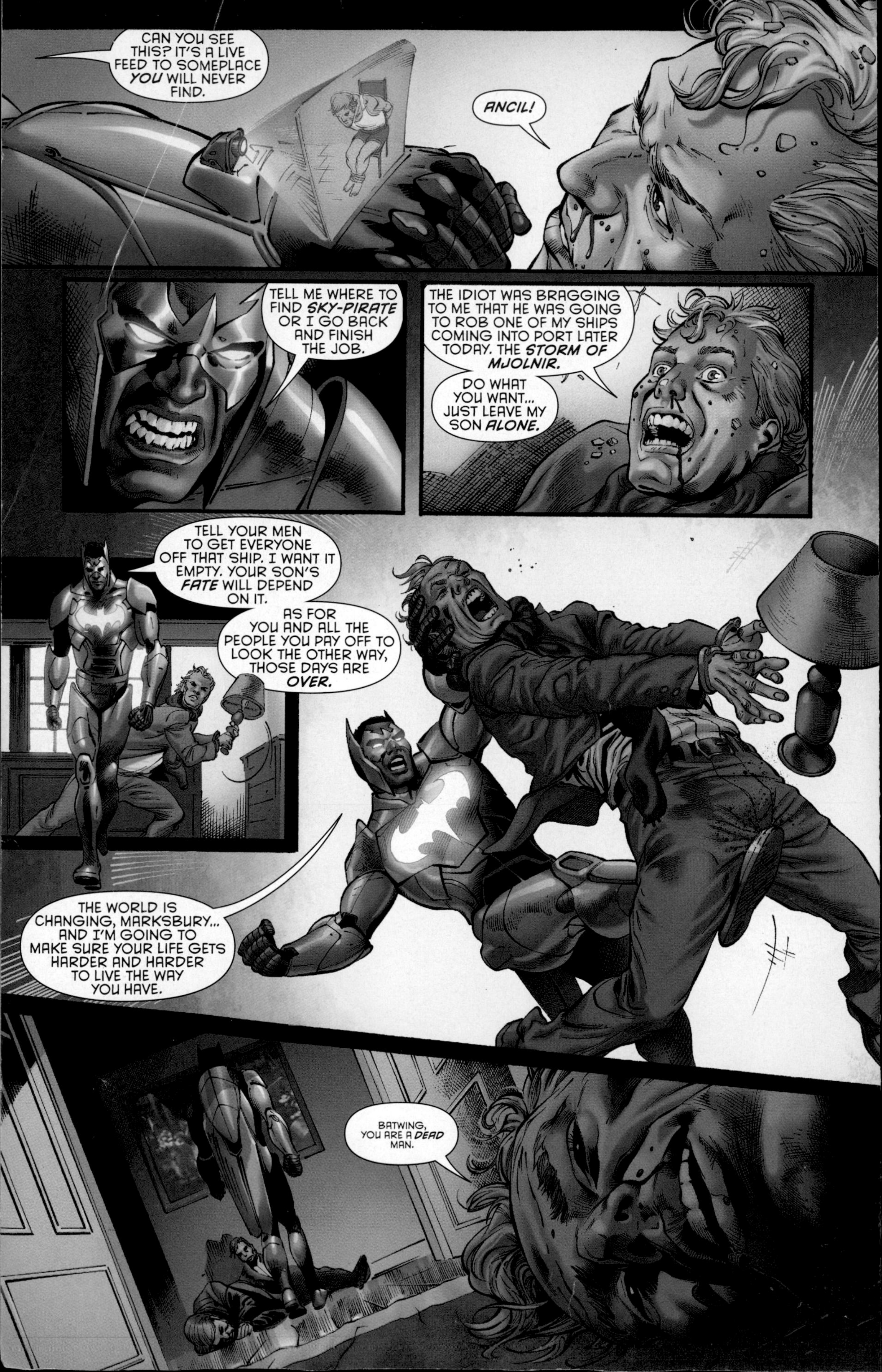
CAN YOU SEE THIS? IT'S A LIVE FEED TO SOMEPLACE YOU WILL NEVER FIND.
ANCIL!
TELL ME WHERE TO FIND SKY-PIRATE OR I GO BACK AND FINISH THE JOB.
THE IDIOT WAS BRAGGING TO ME THAT HE WAS GOING TO ROB ONE OF MY SHIPS COMING INTO PORT LATER TODAY. THE STORM OF MJOLNIR.
DO WHAT YOU WANT... JUST LEAVE MY SON ALONE.
TELL YOUR MEN TO GET EVERYONE OFF THAT SHIP. I WANT IT EMPTY. YOUR SON'S FATE WILL DEPEND ON IT.
AS FOR YOU AND ALL THE PEOPLE YOU PAY OFF TO LOOK THE OTHER WAY, THOSE DAYS ARE OVER.
THE WORLD IS CHANGING, MARKSBURY... AND I'M GOING TO MAKE SURE YOUR LIFE GETS HARDER AND HARDER TO LIVE THE WAY YOU HAVE.
BATWING, YOU ARE A DEAD MAN.

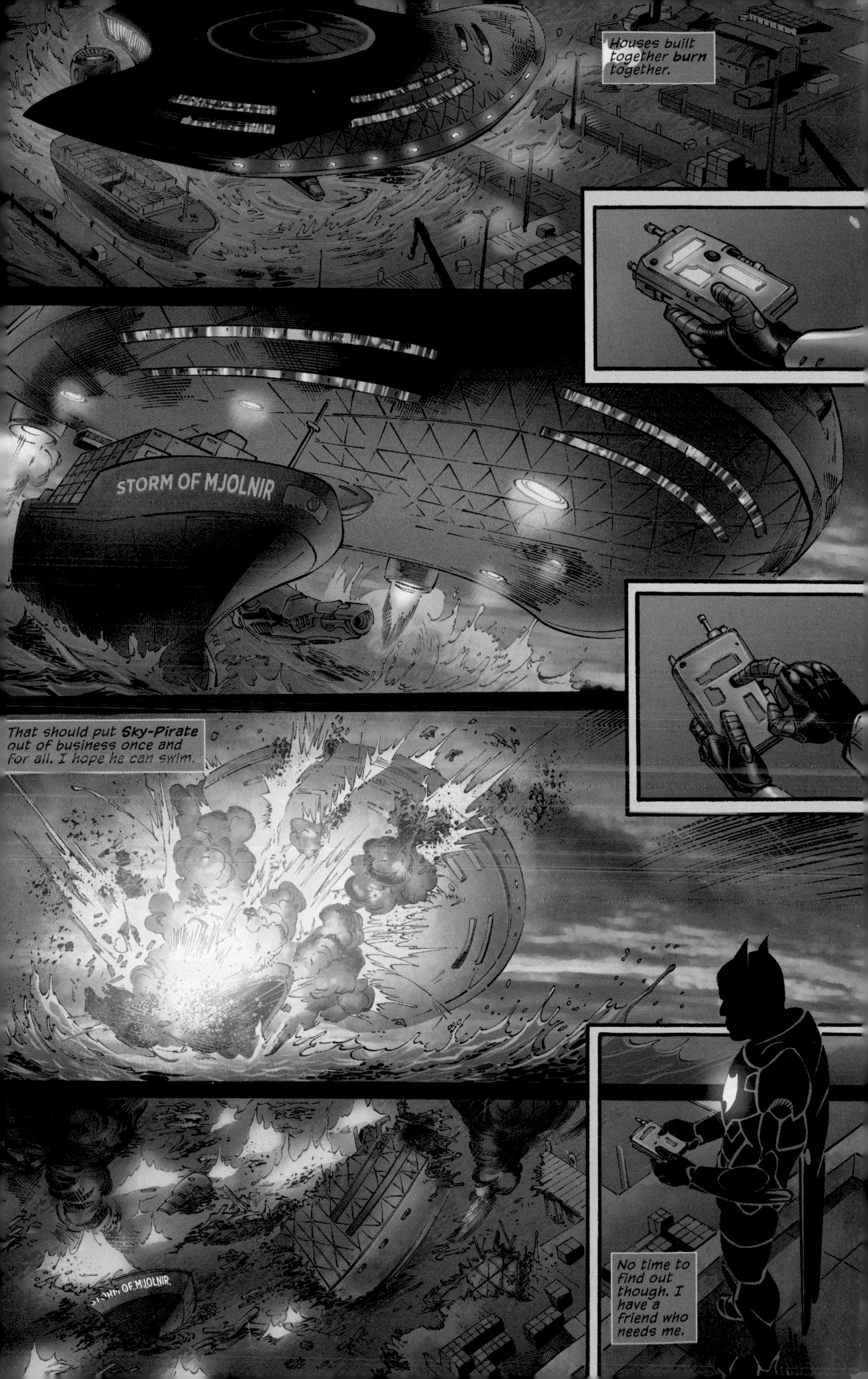
Houses built together burn together.
STORM OF MJOLNIR
That should put Sky-Pirate out of business once and for all. I hope he can swim.
STORM OF MJOLNIR
No time to find out though. I have a friend who needs me.

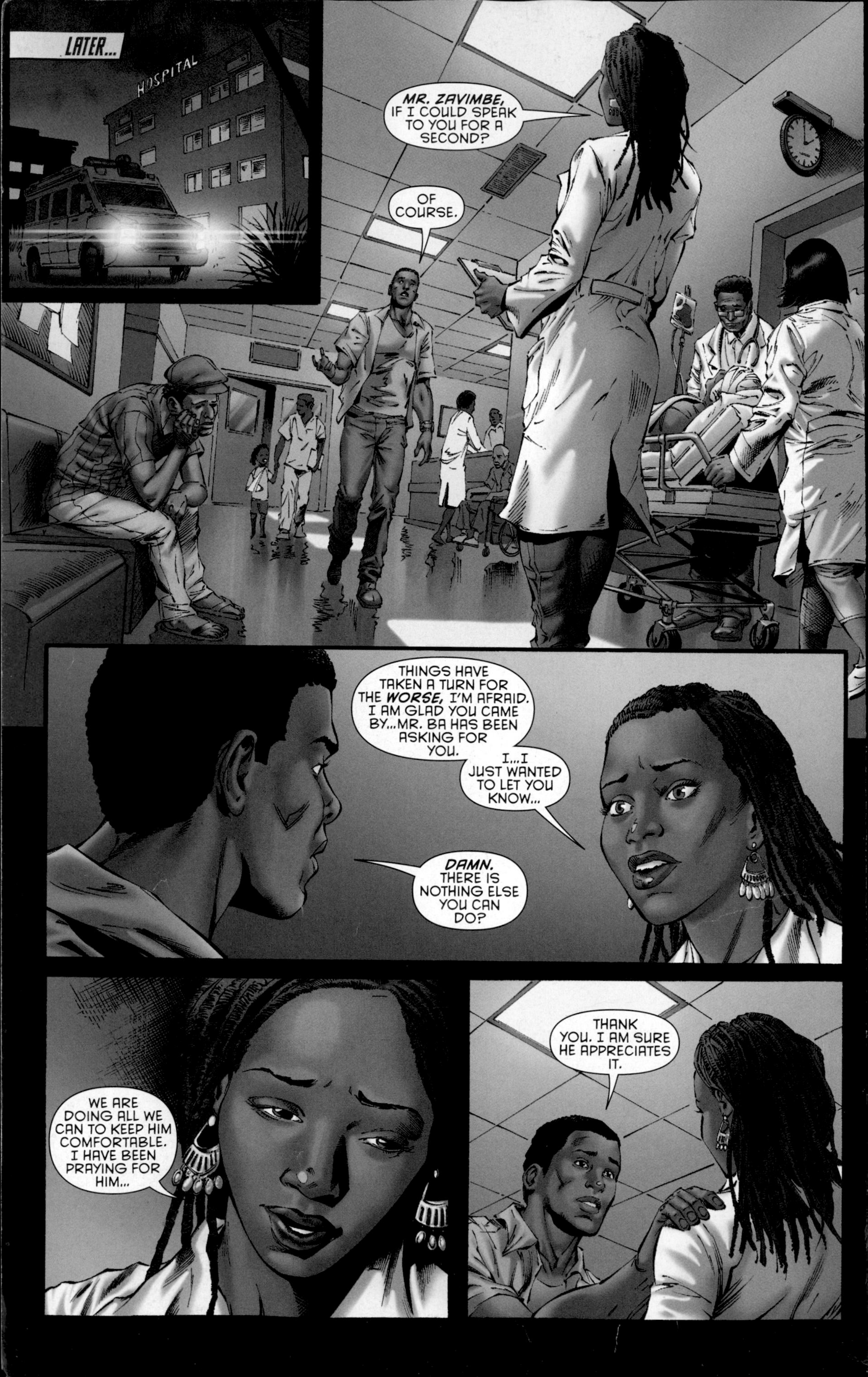
LATER...
HOSPITAL
MR. ZAVIMBE, IF I COULD SPEAK TO YOU FOR A SECOND?
OF COURSE.
THINGS HAVE TAKEN A TURN FOR THE WORSE, I'M AFRAID. I AM GLAD YOU CAME BY...MR. BA HAS BEEN ASKING FOR YOU.
I...I JUST WANTED TO LET YOU KNOW...
DAMN. THERE IS NOTHING ELSE YOU CAN DO?
WE ARE DOING ALL WE CAN TO KEEP HIM COMFORTABLE. I HAVE BEEN PRAYING FOR HIM...
THANK YOU. I AM SURE HE APPRECIATES IT.

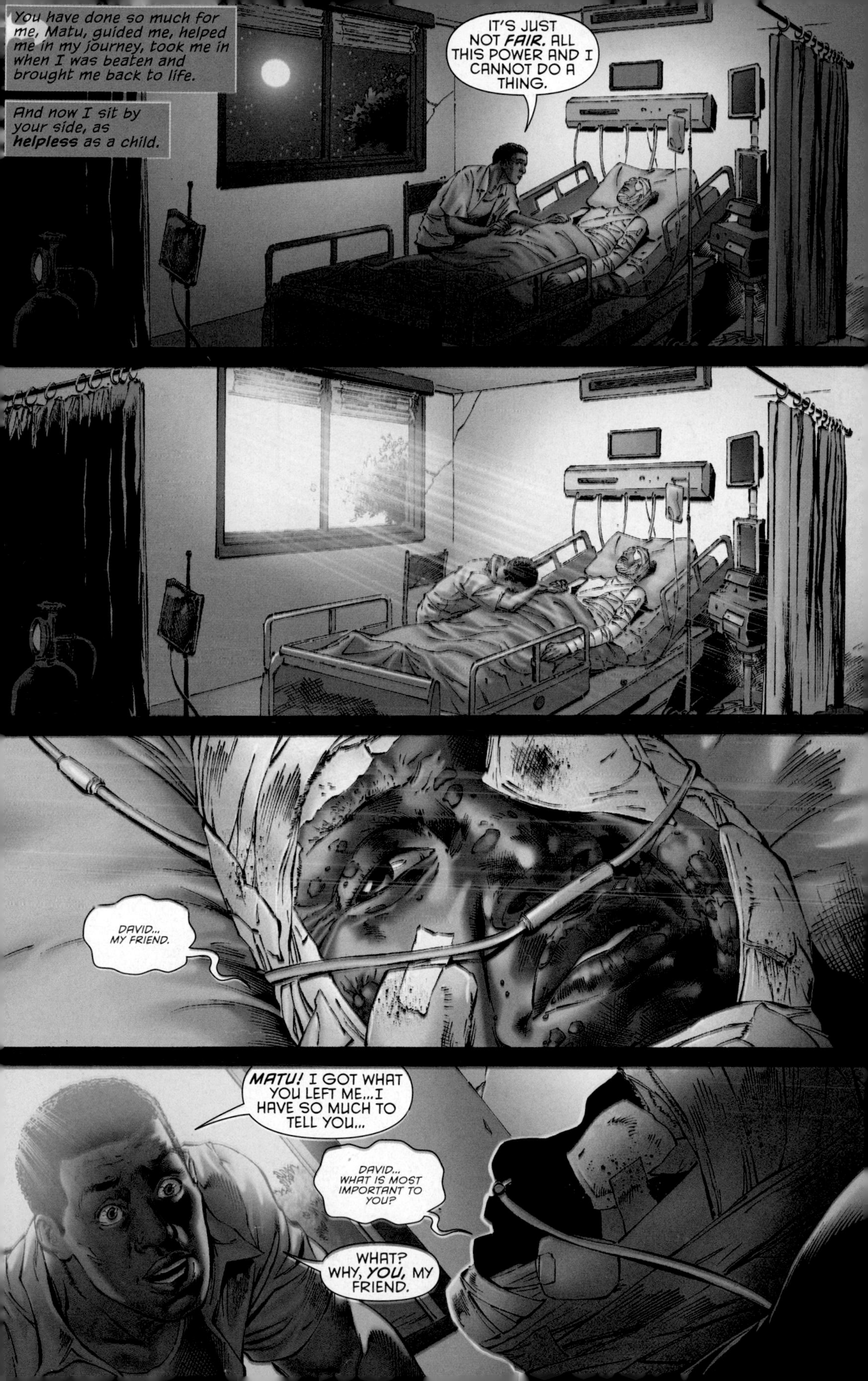
You have done so much for me, Matu, guided me, helped me in my journey, took me in when I was beaten and brought me back to life.
And now I sit by your side, as helpless as a child.
IT'S JUST NOT FAIR. ALL THIS POWER AND I CANNOT DO A THING.
DAVID... MY FRIEND.
MATU! I GOT WHAT YOU LEFT ME...I HAVE SO MUCH TO TELL YOU...
DAVID... WHAT IS MOST IMPORTANT TO YOU?
WHAT? WHY, YOU, MY FRIEND.

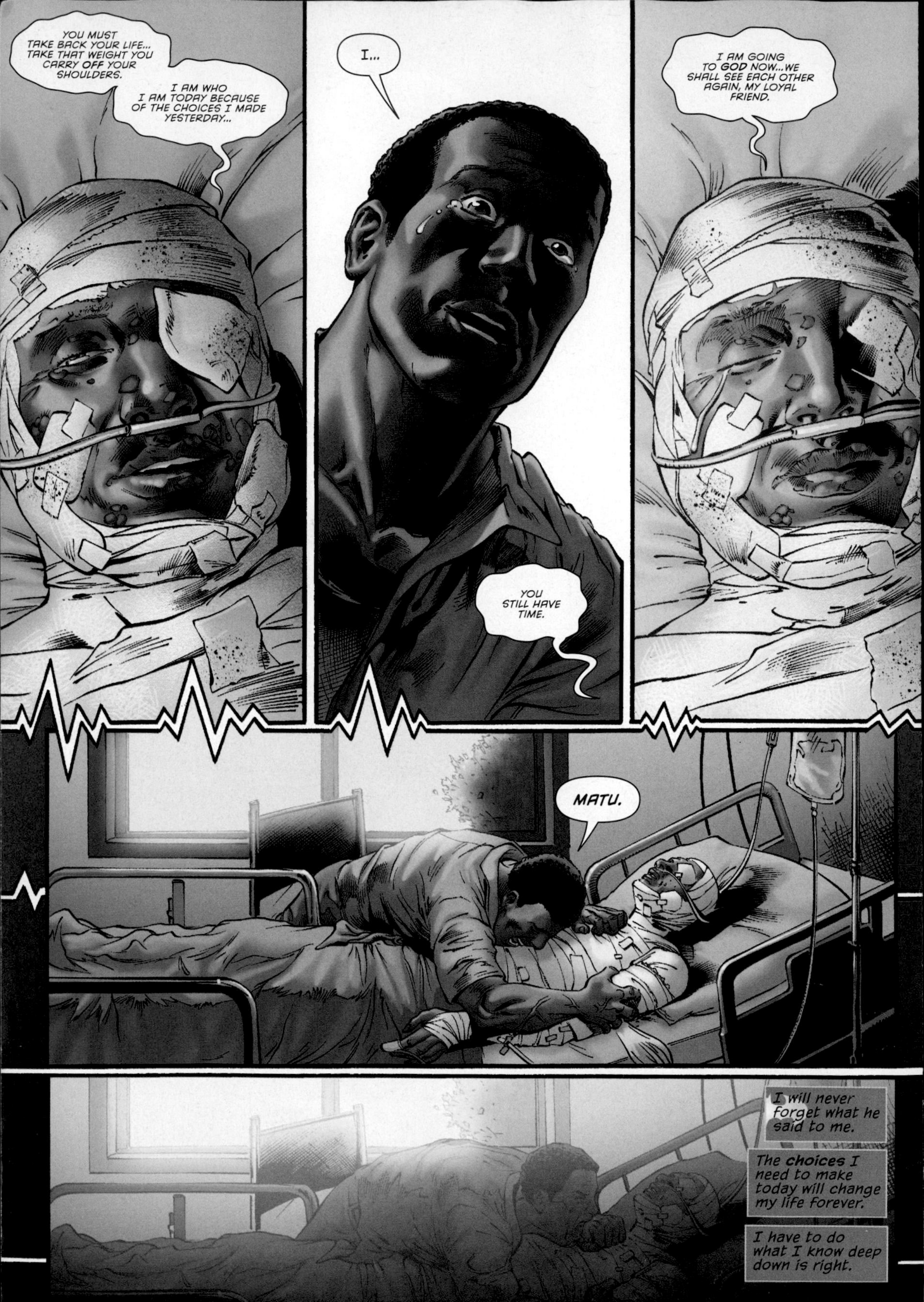
YOU MUST TAKE BACK YOUR LIFE... TAKE THAT WEIGHT YOU CARRY OFF YOUR SHOULDERS.
I AM WHO I AM TODAY BECAUSE OF THE CHOICES I MADE YESTERDAY...
I...
YOU STILL HAVE TIME.
I AM GOING TO GOD NOW...WE SHALL SEE EACH OTHER AGAIN, MY LOYAL FRIEND.
MATU.
I will never forget what he said to me.
The choices I need to make today will change my life forever.
I have to do what I know deep down is right.

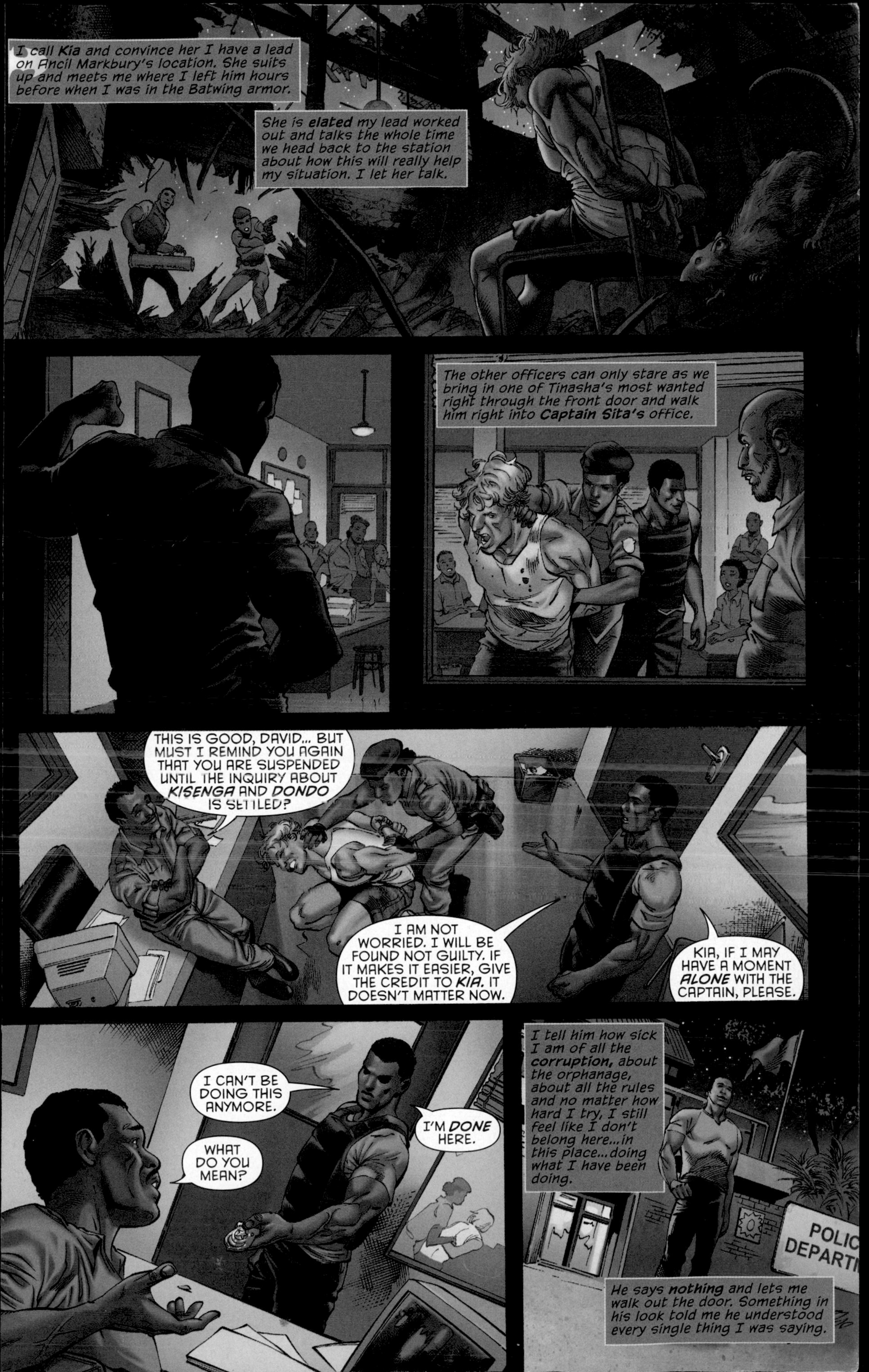
I call Kia and convince her I have a lead on Ancil Markbury's location. She suits up and meets me where I left him hours before when I was in the Batwing armor.
She is elated my lead worked out and talks the whole time we head back to the station about how this will really help my situation. I let her talk.
The other officers can only stare as we bring in one of Tinasha's most wanted right through the front door and walk him right into Captain Sita's office.
THIS IS GOOD, DAVID... BUT MUST I REMIND YOU AGAIN THAT YOU ARE SUSPENDED UNTIL THE INQUIRY ABOUT KISENGA AND DONDO IS SETTLED?
I AM NOT WORRIED. I WILL BE FOUND NOT GUILTY. IF IT MAKES IT EASIER, GIVE THE CREDIT TO KIA. IT DOESN'T MATTER NOW.
KIA, IF I MAY HAVE A MOMENT ALONE WITH THE CAPTAIN, PLEASE.
I CAN'T BE DOING THIS ANYMORE.
WHAT DO YOU MEAN?
I'M DONE HERE.
I tell him how sick I am of all the corruption, about the orphanage, about all the rules and no matter how hard I try, I still feel like I don't belong here...in this place...doing what I have been doing.
POLIC DEPARTI
He says nothing and lets me walk out the door. Something in his look told me he understood every single thing I was saying.

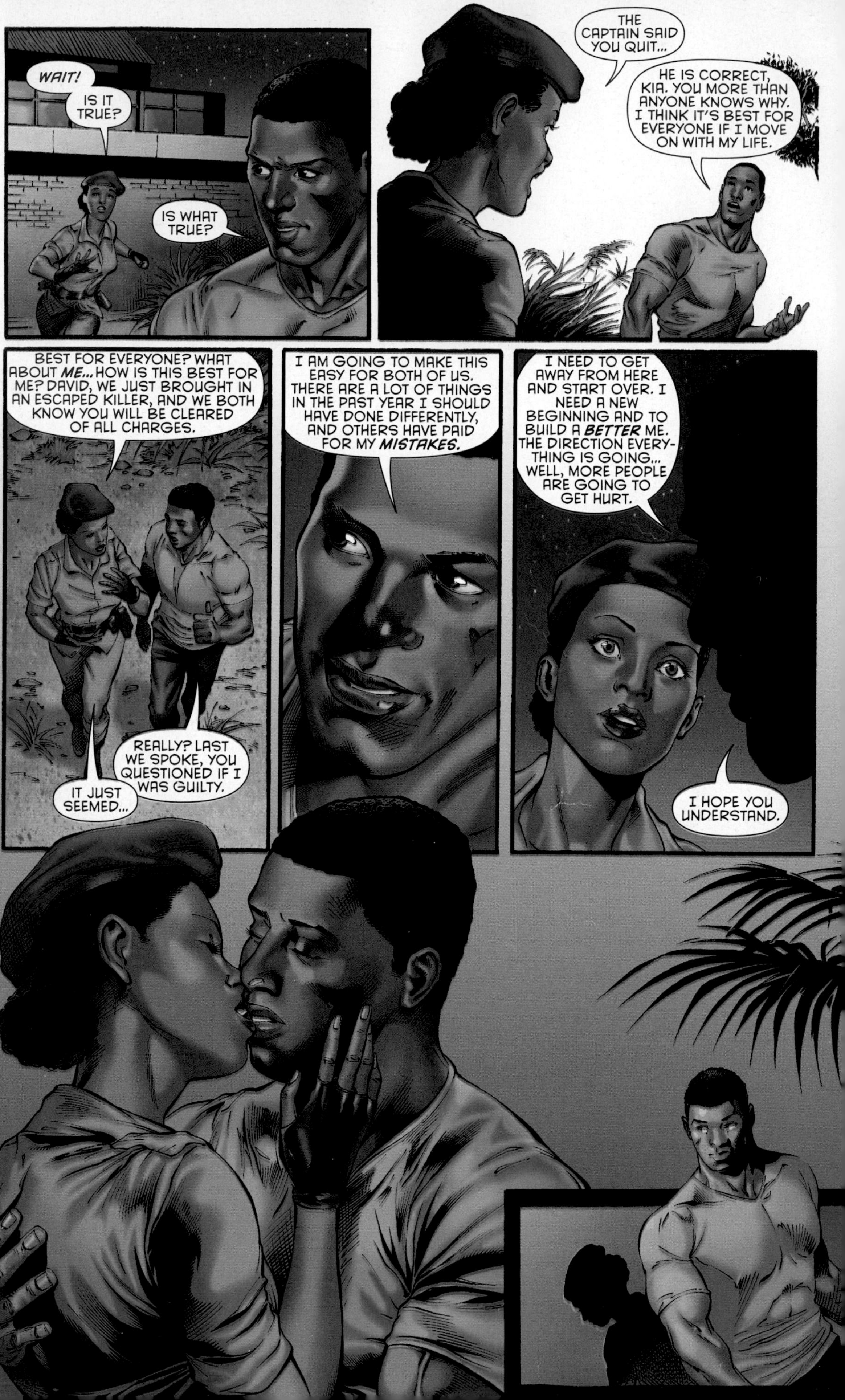
WAIT!
IS IT TRUE?
IS WHAT TRUE?
THE CAPTAIN SAID YOU QUIT...
HE IS CORRECT, KIA. YOU MORE THAN ANYONE KNOWS WHY. I THINK IT'S BEST FOR EVERYONE IF I MOVE ON WITH MY LIFE.
BEST FOR EVERYONE? WHAT ABOUT *ME*... HOW IS THIS BEST FOR ME? DAVID, WE JUST BROUGHT IN AN ESCAPED KILLER, AND WE BOTH KNOW YOU WILL BE CLEARED OF ALL CHARGES.
REALLY? LAST WE SPOKE, YOU QUESTIONED IF I WAS GUILTY.
IT JUST SEEMED...
I AM GOING TO MAKE THIS EASY FOR BOTH OF US. THERE ARE A LOT OF THINGS IN THE PAST YEAR I SHOULD HAVE DONE DIFFERENTLY, AND OTHERS HAVE PAID FOR MY *MISTAKES.*
I NEED TO GET AWAY FROM HERE AND START OVER. I NEED A NEW BEGINNING AND TO BUILD A *BETTER* ME. THE DIRECTION EVERYTHING IS GOING... WELL, MORE PEOPLE ARE GOING TO GET HURT.
I HOPE YOU UNDERSTAND.

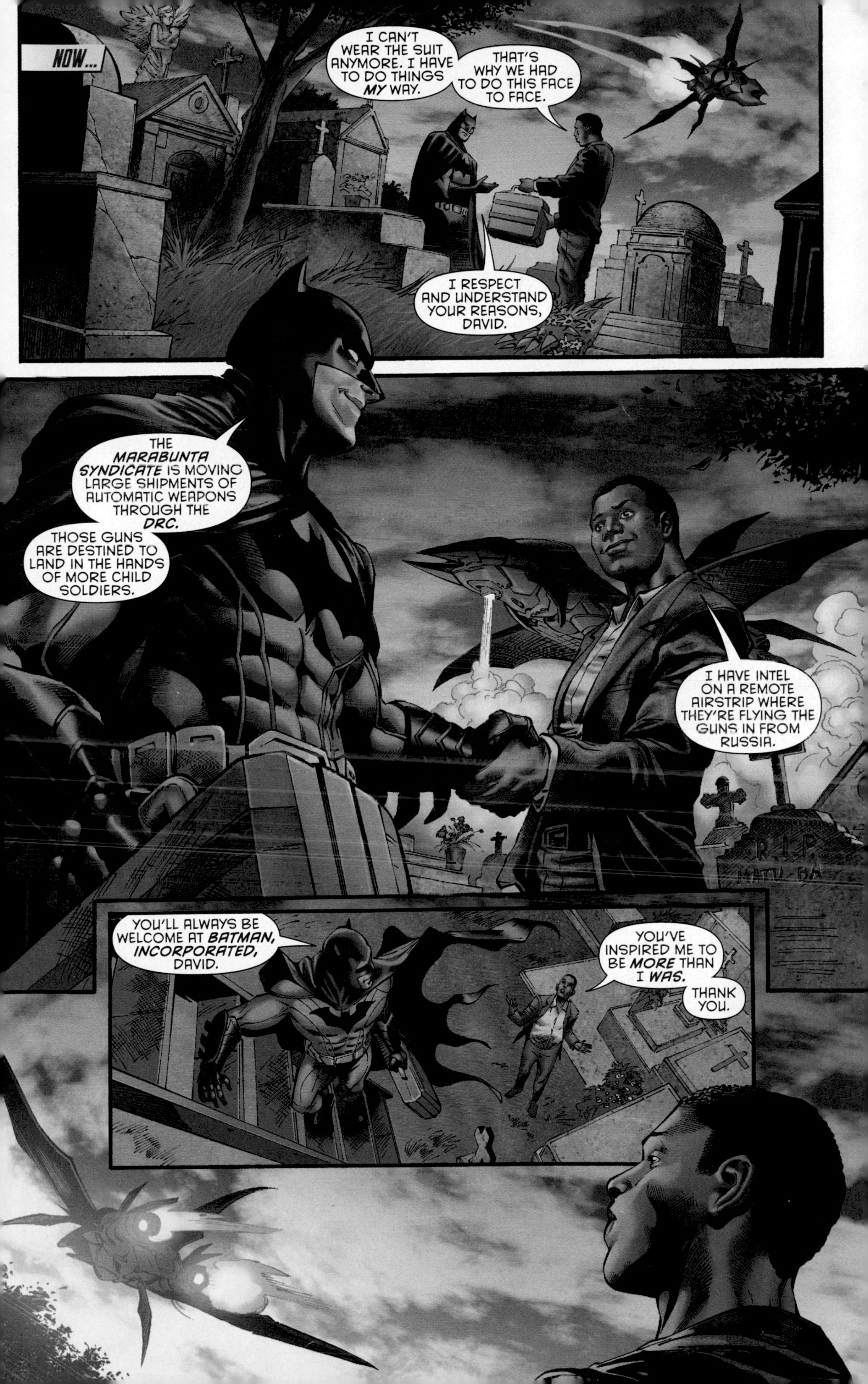
NOW...
I CAN'T WEAR THE SUIT ANYMORE. I HAVE TO DO THINGS MY WAY.
THAT'S WHY WE HAD TO DO THIS FACE TO FACE.
I RESPECT AND UNDERSTAND YOUR REASONS, DAVID.
THE MARABUNTA SYNDICATE IS MOVING LARGE SHIPMENTS OF AUTOMATIC WEAPONS THROUGH THE DRC.
THOSE GUNS ARE DESTINED TO LAND IN THE HANDS OF MORE CHILD SOLDIERS.
I HAVE INTEL ON A REMOTE AIRSTRIP WHERE THEY'RE FLYING THE GUNS IN FROM RUSSIA.
R.I.P.
YOU'LL ALWAYS BE WELCOME AT BATMAN, INCORPORATED, DAVID.
YOU'VE INSPIRED ME TO BE MORE THAN I WAS.
THANK YOU.

ALFRED, YOU'RE GOING TO LOVE THIS.

WHAT MAKES *THIS* ONE SO SPECIAL?

EVERYTHING. LUCIUS FOX OUTDID HIMSELF ON THE DESIGN.

SAFETY, MOBILITY, RETRACTABLE CAPE, IT HAS AN INTERIOR SKIN THAT MONITORS VITAL SIGNS AND PRODUCES MEDICAL REPAIR CAPABILITIES.

FOR INSTANCE, IF THE WEARER BREAKS HIS ARM, THE SUIT HARDENS AROUND THAT AREA HOLDING THE BONE IN PLACE AND ADMINISTERS A SHOT OF PAINKILLERS.

NEXT, YOU'LL TELL ME IT TURNS *INVISIBLE.*

INVISIBILITY IS LIMITED BY THE FACT THAT THE SUIT NEEDS TO BE BULLET-PROOF, BUT IT IS FUNCTIONAL IN LOW LIGHT AREAS.

IT HAS SENSORS THAT RELAY IMAGES OF WHAT'S BEHIND THE SUIT, GIVING THE ILLUSION OF INVISIBILITY, BUT YOU HAVE TO REMAIN STILL, OTHERWISE THERE'S A BLURRING EFFECT.

I'M IMPRESSED.

YOU SHOULD BE. THIS IS THE SAFEST AND SMARTEST SUIT FOX HAS EVER DESIGNED.

THE IRONY OF THAT IS NOT LOST ON ME.

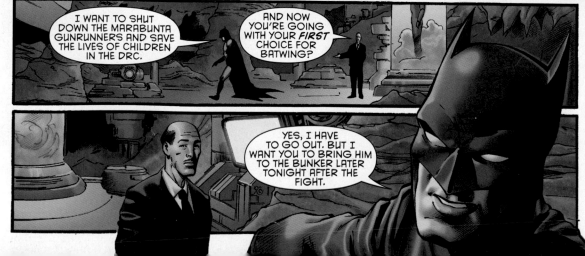

I WANT TO SHUT DOWN THE MARABUNTA GUNRUNNERS AND SAVE THE LIVES OF CHILDREN IN THE DRC.

AND NOW YOU'RE GOING WITH YOUR *FIRST* CHOICE FOR BATWING?

YES, I HAVE TO GO OUT. BUT I WANT YOU TO BRING HIM TO THE BUNKER LATER TONIGHT AFTER THE FIGHT.

I can still hear his voice in my head from the locker room before the fight.

SMASHMOUTH MMA! TONIGHT ONLY!

THIS IS RIDICULOUSLY DANGEROUS, AND I FORBID IT!

He either doesn't get it or doesn't want to get it.

I'VE BEEN TOURNAMENT FIGHTING SINCE I WAS SIXTEEN!

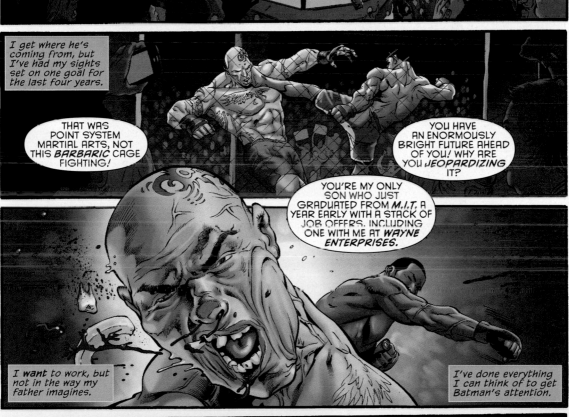

I get where he's coming from, but I've had my sights set on one goal for the last four years.

THAT WAS POINT SYSTEM MARTIAL ARTS, NOT THIS BARBARIC CAGE FIGHTING!

YOU HAVE AN ENORMOUSLY BRIGHT FUTURE AHEAD OF YOU! WHY ARE YOU JEOPARDIZING IT?

YOU'RE MY ONLY SON WHO JUST GRADUATED FROM M.I.T. A YEAR EARLY WITH A STACK OF JOB OFFERS. INCLUDING ONE WITH ME AT WAYNE ENTERPRISES.

I want to work, but not in the way my father imagines.

I've done everything I can think of to get Batman's attention.

I can't tell my father I secretly want to be part of Batman, Incorporated.

LADIES AND GENTLEMEN, FORTY-NINE SECONDS INTO THE FIRST ROUND, YOUR WINNER BY K.O....!

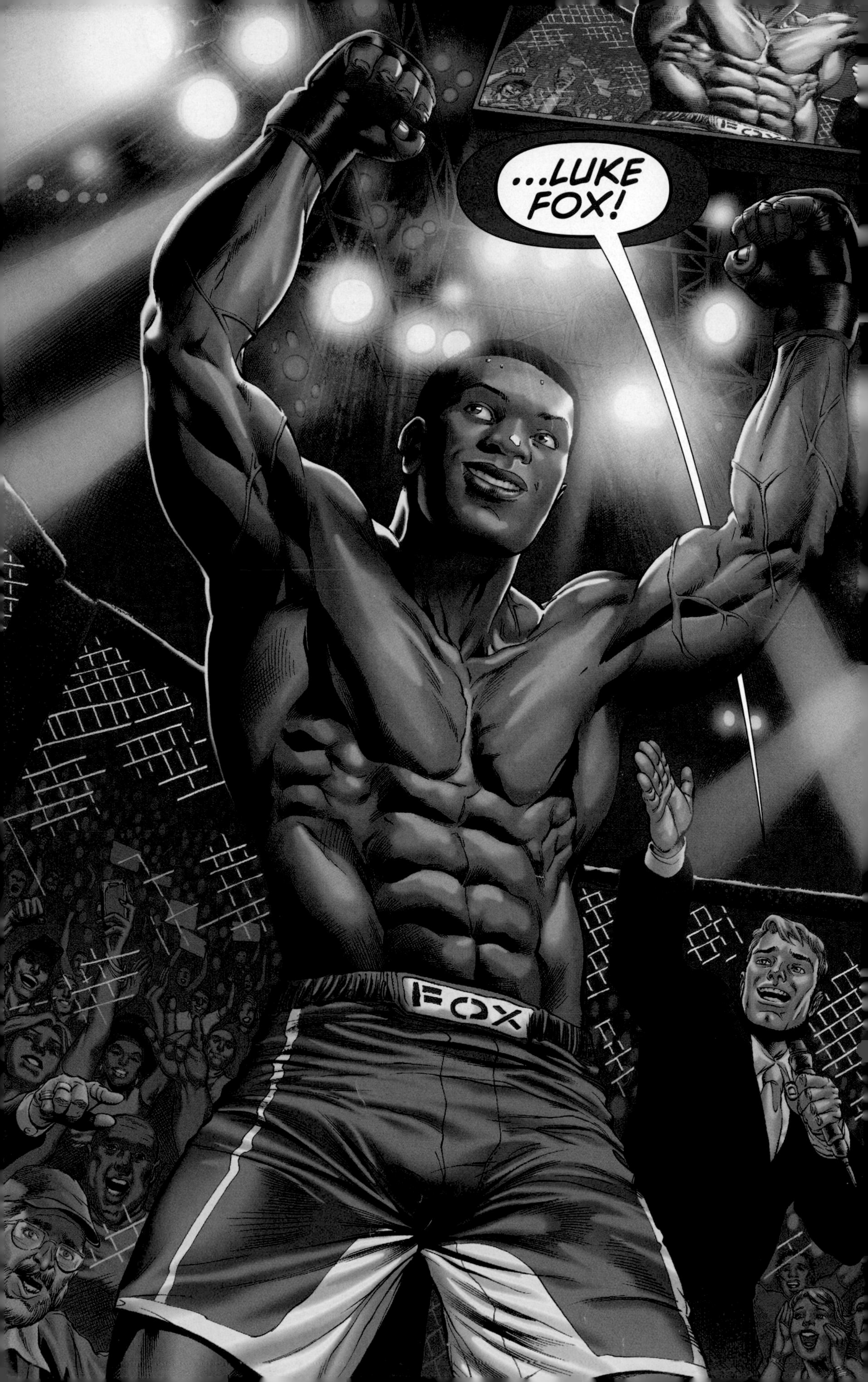
...LUKE FOX!
FOX

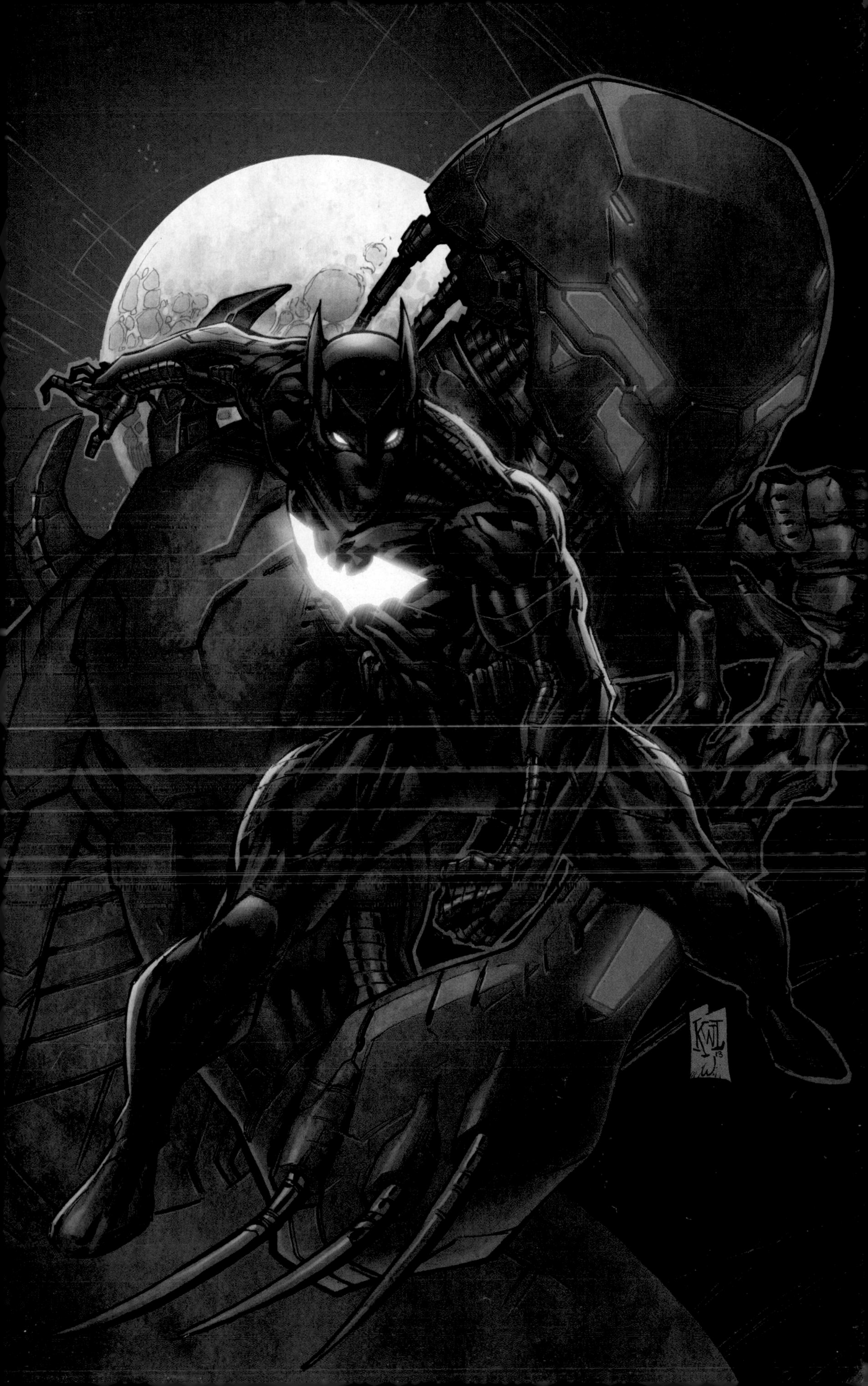

WELCOME TO THE FAMILY

cover art by **KEN LASHLEY & JASON WRIGHT**

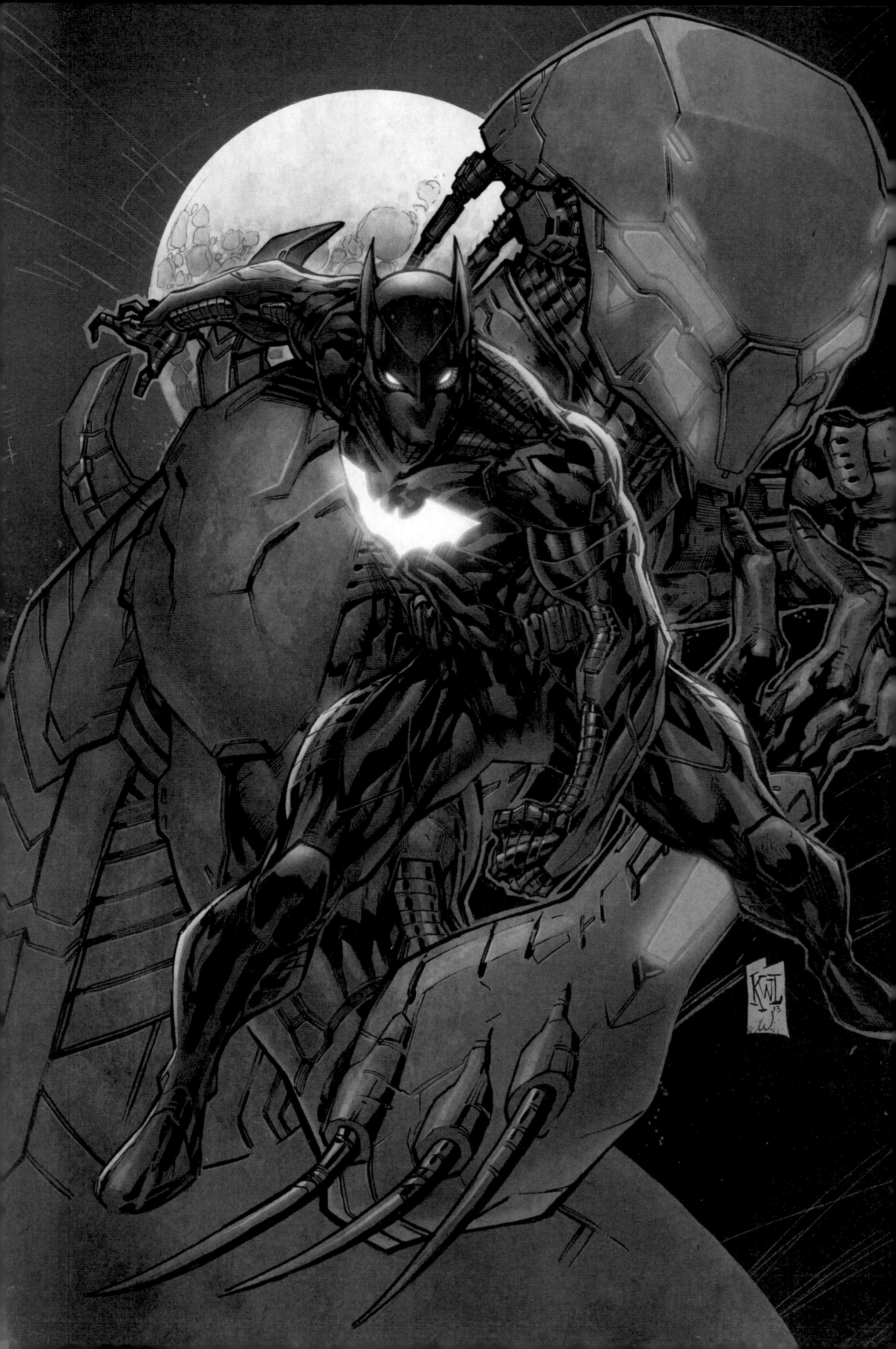

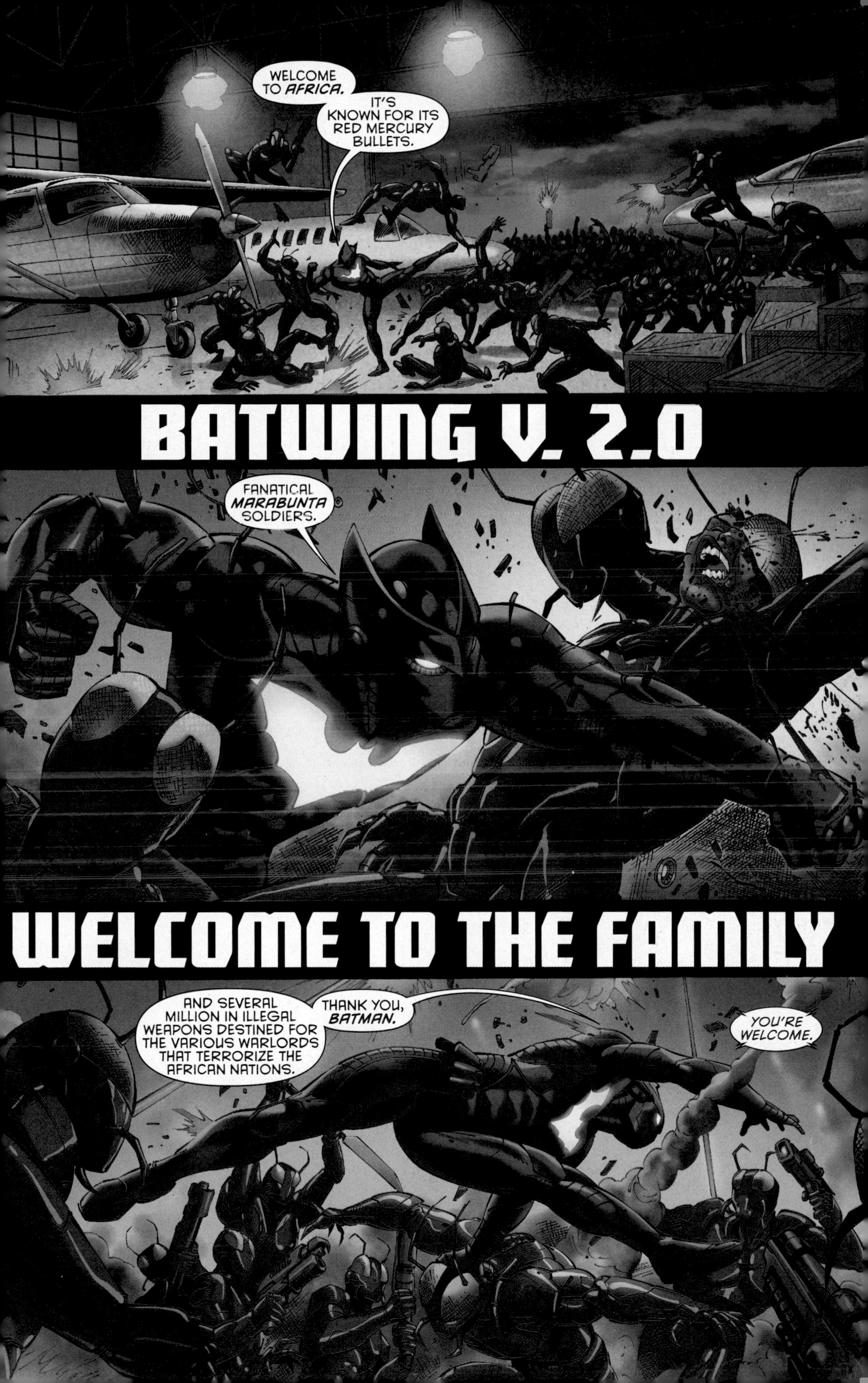
WELCOME TO AFRICA.
IT'S KNOWN FOR ITS RED MERCURY BULLETS.
BATWING V. 2.0
FANATICAL MARABUNTA SOLDIERS.
WELCOME TO THE FAMILY
AND SEVERAL MILLION IN ILLEGAL WEAPONS DESTINED FOR THE VARIOUS WARLORDS THAT TERRORIZE THE AFRICAN NATIONS.
THANK YOU, BATMAN.
YOU'RE WELCOME.

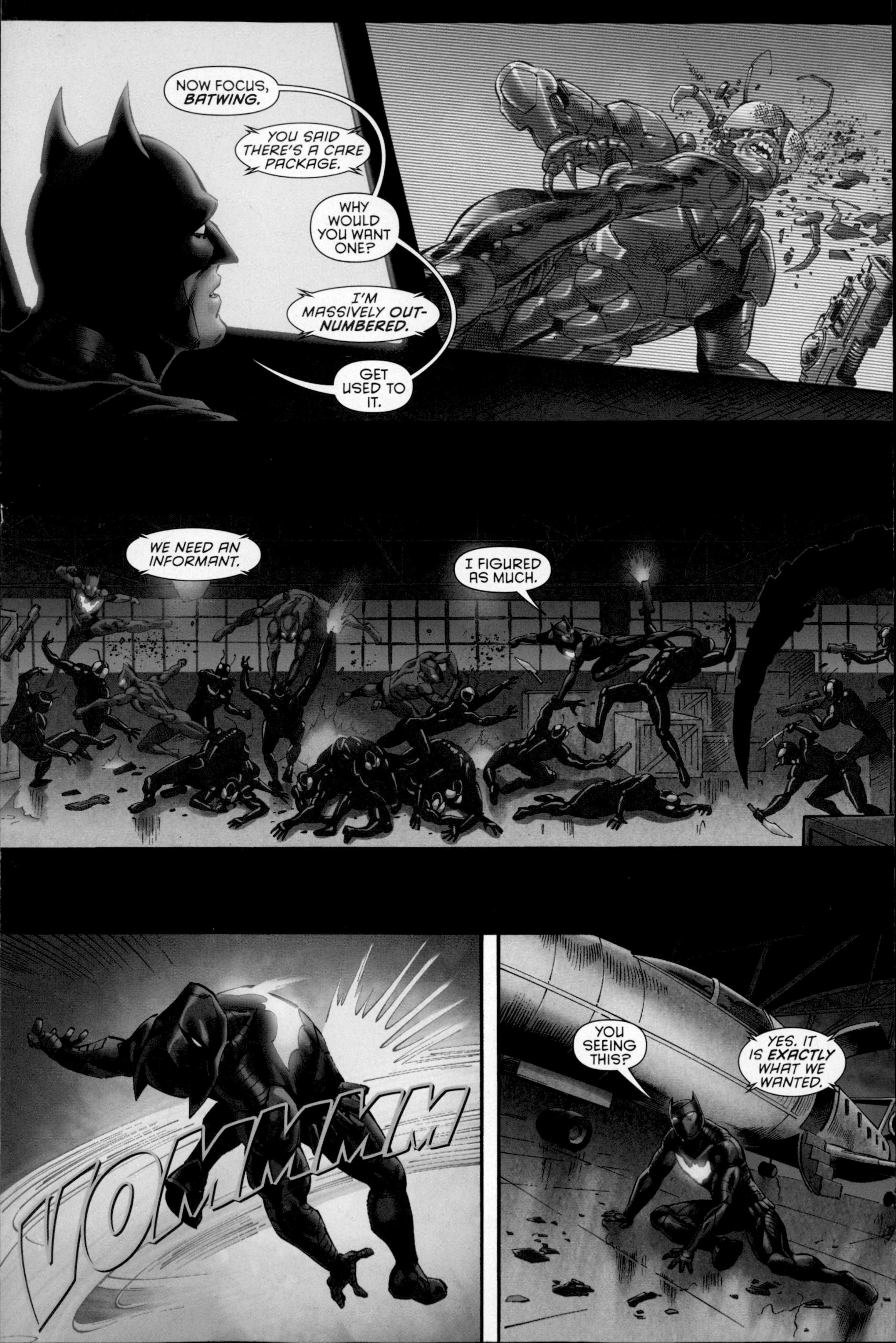
NOW FOCUS, BATWING.
YOU SAID THERE'S A CARE PACKAGE.
WHY WOULD YOU WANT ONE?
I'M MASSIVELY OUT-NUMBERED.
GET USED TO IT.
WE NEED AN INFORMANT.
I FIGURED AS MUCH.
VOMMMM
YOU SEEING THIS?
YES. IT IS EXACTLY WHAT WE WANTED.

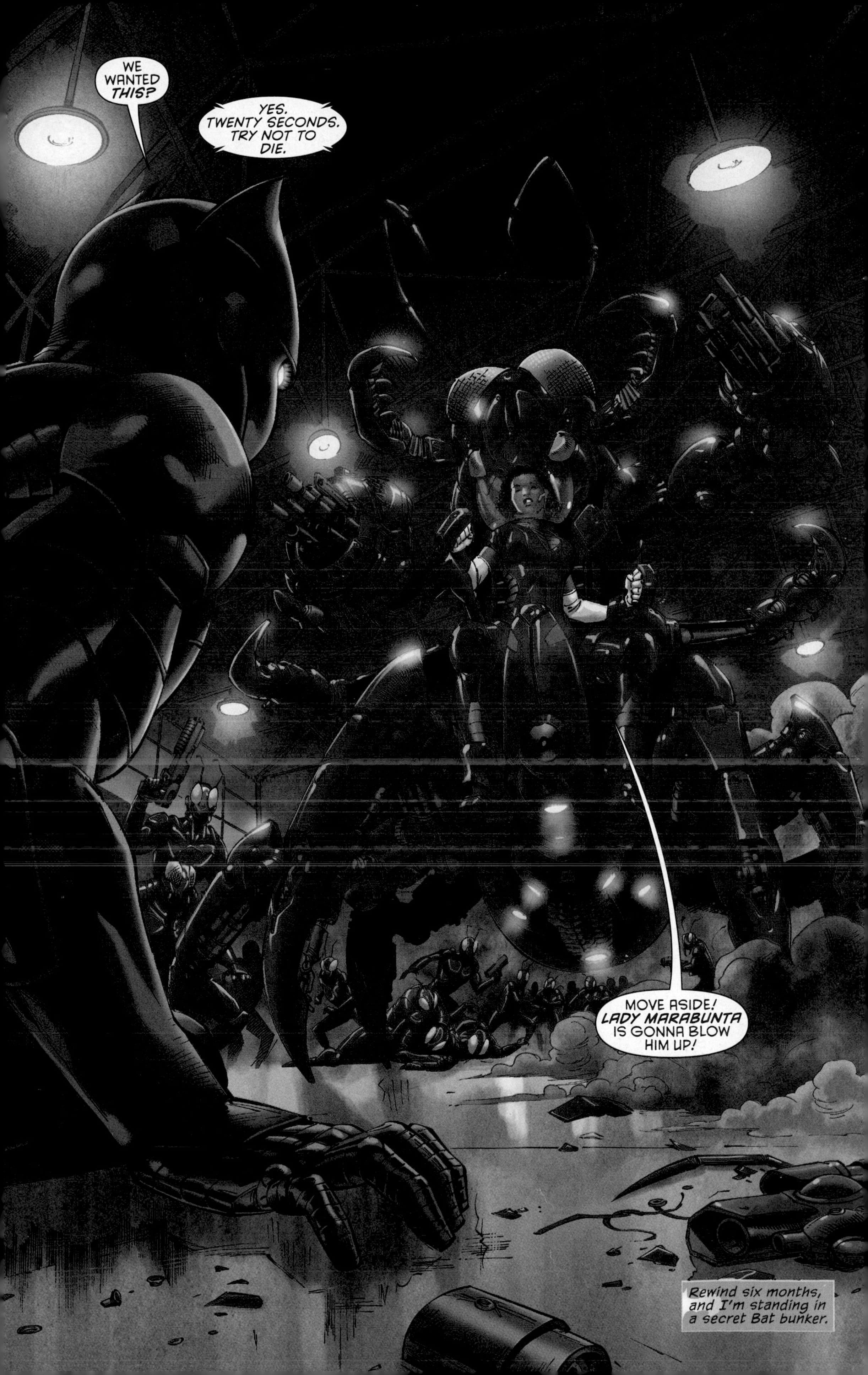
WE WANTED THIS?
YES. TWENTY SECONDS. TRY NOT TO DIE.
MOVE ASIDE! LADY MARABUNTA IS GONNA BLOW HIM UP!
Rewind six months, and I'm standing in a secret Bat bunker.

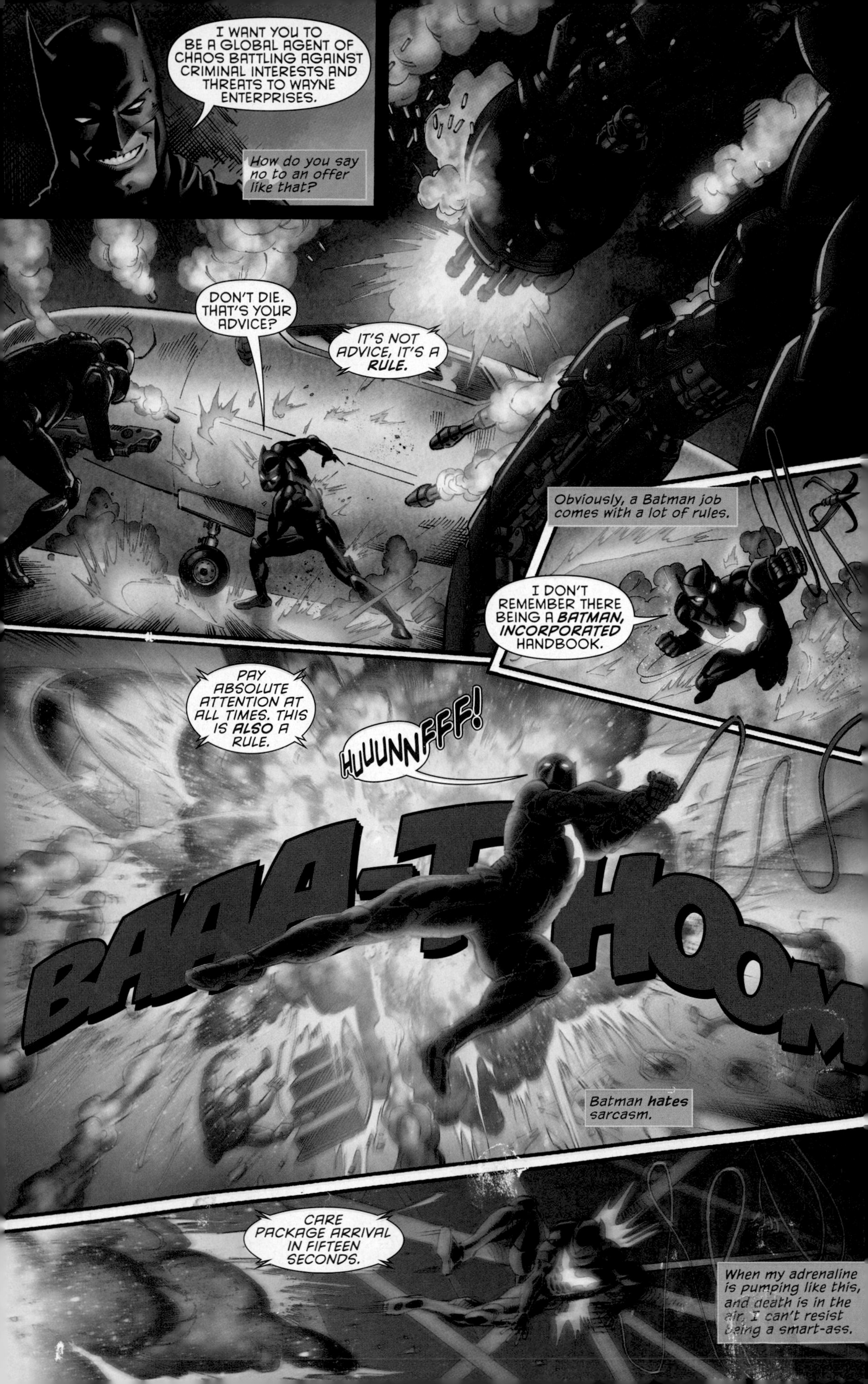

I WANT YOU TO BE A GLOBAL AGENT OF CHAOS BATTLING AGAINST CRIMINAL INTERESTS AND THREATS TO WAYNE ENTERPRISES.
How do you say no to an offer like that?
DON'T DIE. THAT'S YOUR ADVICE?
IT'S NOT ADVICE, IT'S A RULE.
Obviously, a Batman job comes with a lot of rules.
I DON'T REMEMBER THERE BEING A BATMAN, INCORPORATED HANDBOOK.
PAY ABSOLUTE ATTENTION AT ALL TIMES. THIS IS ALSO A RULE.
HUUUNNFFF!
BAAA-THOOM
Batman hates sarcasm.
CARE PACKAGE ARRIVAL IN FIFTEEN SECONDS.
When my adrenaline is pumping like this, and death is in the air, I can't resist being a smart-ass.

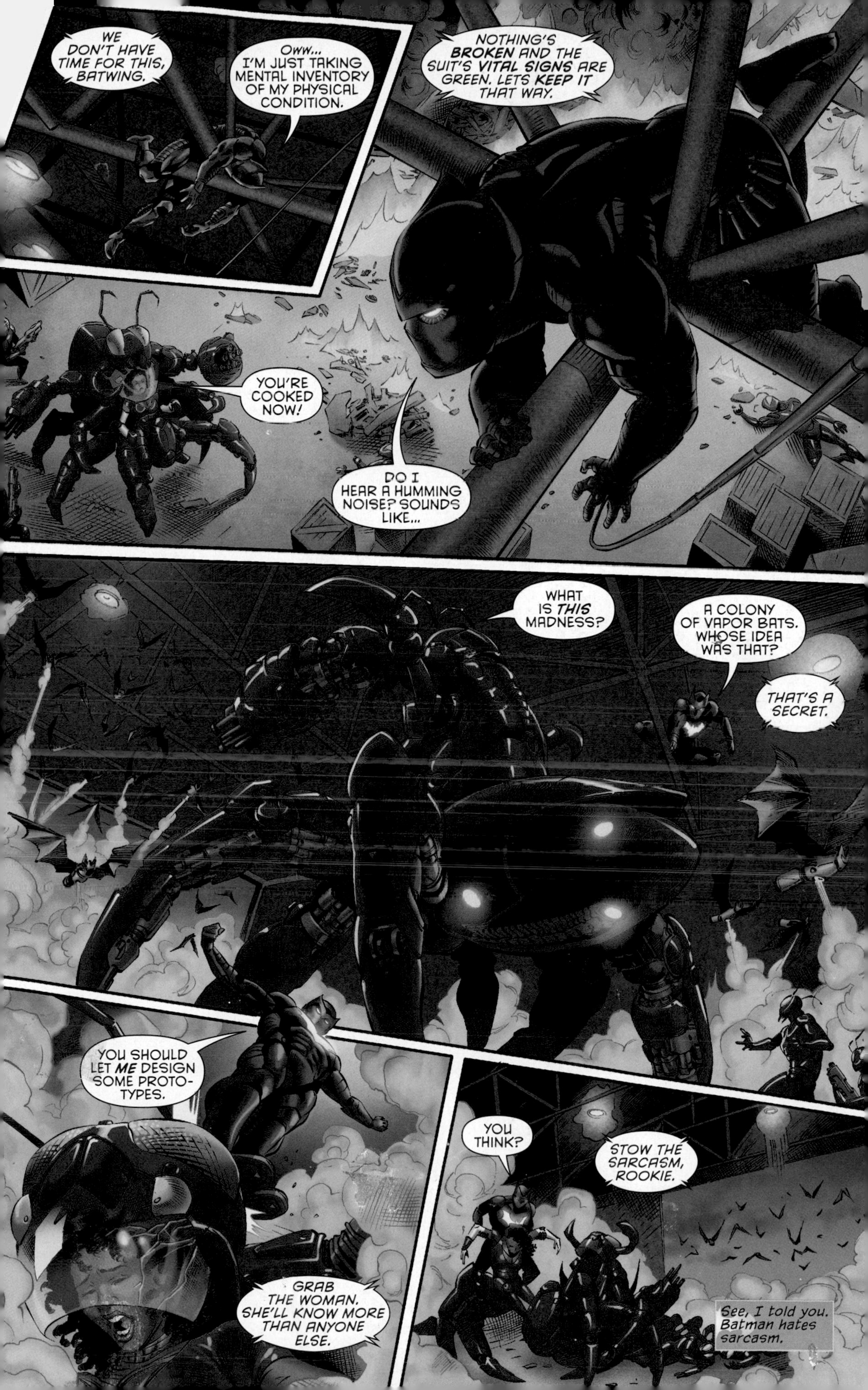
WE DON'T HAVE TIME FOR THIS, BATWING.
OWW... I'M JUST TAKING MENTAL INVENTORY OF MY PHYSICAL CONDITION.
NOTHING'S BROKEN AND THE SUIT'S VITAL SIGNS ARE GREEN. LETS KEEP IT THAT WAY.
YOU'RE COOKED NOW!
DO I HEAR A HUMMING NOISE? SOUNDS LIKE...
WHAT IS THIS MADNESS?
A COLONY OF VAPOR BATS. WHOSE IDEA WAS THAT?
THAT'S A SECRET.
YOU SHOULD LET ME DESIGN SOME PROTO-TYPES.
GRAB THE WOMAN. SHE'LL KNOW MORE THAN ANYONE ELSE.
YOU THINK?
STOW THE SARCASM, ROOKIE.
See, I told you. Batman hates sarcasm.

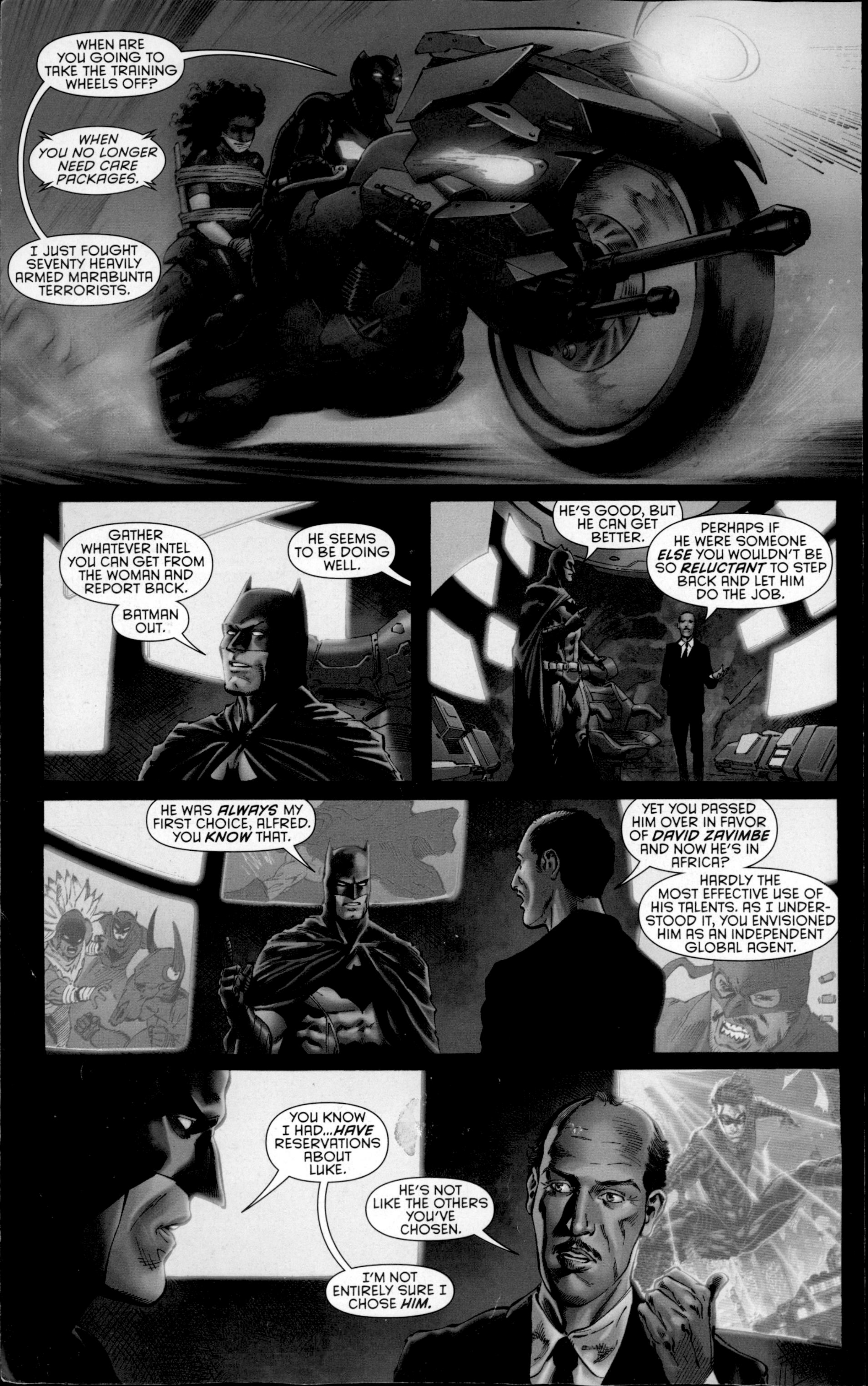
WHEN ARE YOU GOING TO TAKE THE TRAINING WHEELS OFF?
WHEN YOU NO LONGER NEED CARE PACKAGES.
I JUST FOUGHT SEVENTY HEAVILY ARMED MARABUNTA TERRORISTS.
GATHER WHATEVER INTEL YOU CAN GET FROM THE WOMAN AND REPORT BACK.
BATMAN OUT.
HE SEEMS TO BE DOING WELL.
HE'S GOOD, BUT HE CAN GET BETTER.
PERHAPS IF HE WERE SOMEONE ELSE YOU WOULDN'T BE SO RELUCTANT TO STEP BACK AND LET HIM DO THE JOB.
HE WAS ALWAYS MY FIRST CHOICE, ALFRED. YOU KNOW THAT.
YET YOU PASSED HIM OVER IN FAVOR OF DAVID ZAVIMBE AND NOW HE'S IN AFRICA?
HARDLY THE MOST EFFECTIVE USE OF HIS TALENTS. AS I UNDERSTOOD IT, YOU ENVISIONED HIM AS AN INDEPENDENT GLOBAL AGENT.
YOU KNOW I HAD...HAVE RESERVATIONS ABOUT LUKE.
HE'S NOT LIKE THE OTHERS YOU'VE CHOSEN.
I'M NOT ENTIRELY SURE I CHOSE HIM.

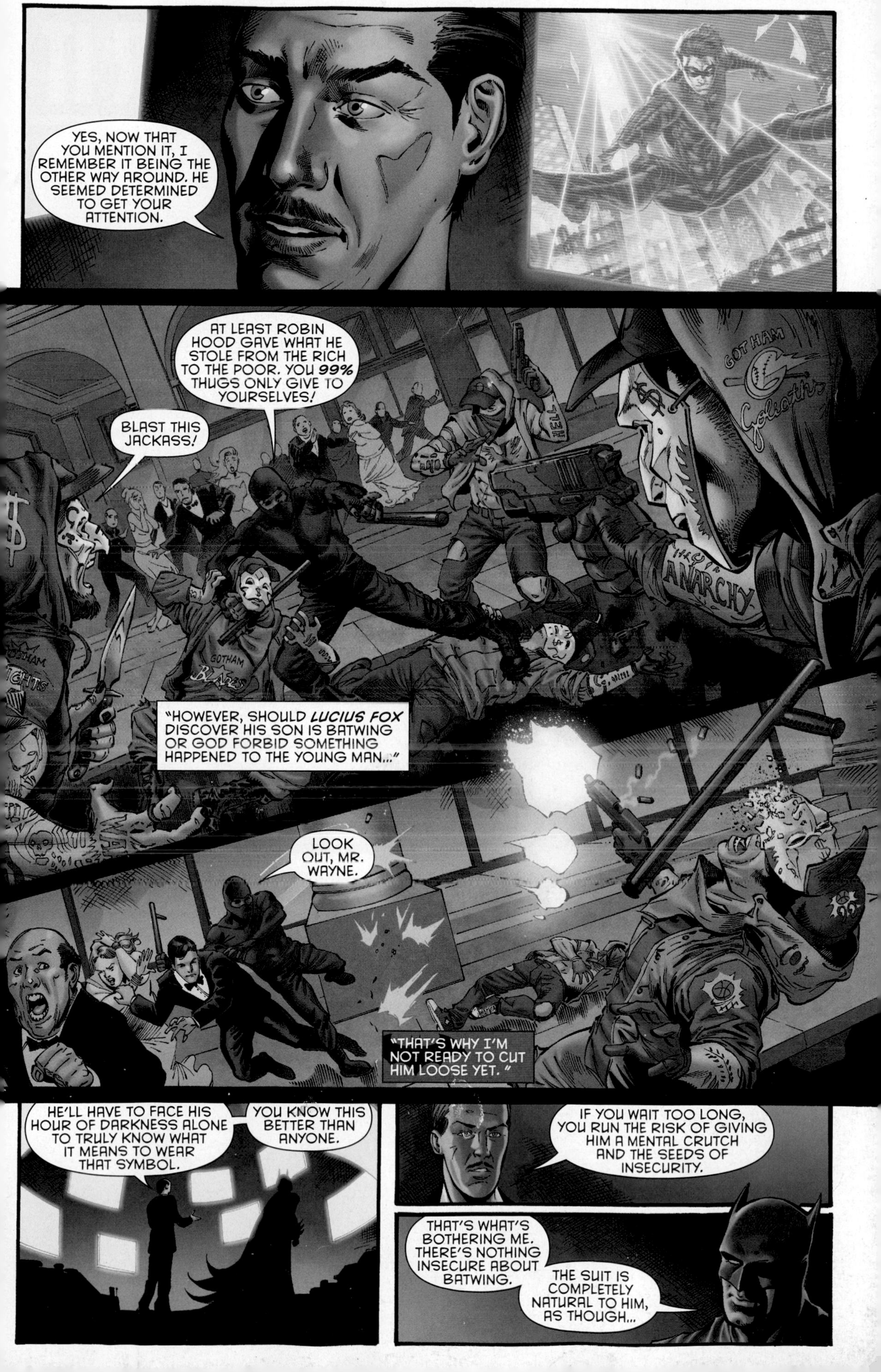
YES, NOW THAT YOU MENTION IT, I REMEMBER IT BEING THE OTHER WAY AROUND. HE SEEMED DETERMINED TO GET YOUR ATTENTION.
AT LEAST ROBIN HOOD GAVE WHAT HE STOLE FROM THE RICH TO THE POOR. YOU 99% THUGS ONLY GIVE TO YOURSELVES!
BLAST THIS JACKASS!
GOTHAM GOLIATHS
ANARCHY
GOTHAM BLADES
"HOWEVER, SHOULD LUCIUS FOX DISCOVER HIS SON IS BATWING OR GOD FORBID SOMETHING HAPPENED TO THE YOUNG MAN..."
LOOK OUT, MR. WAYNE.
"THAT'S WHY I'M NOT READY TO CUT HIM LOOSE YET."
HE'LL HAVE TO FACE HIS HOUR OF DARKNESS ALONE TO TRULY KNOW WHAT IT MEANS TO WEAR THAT SYMBOL.
YOU KNOW THIS BETTER THAN ANYONE.
IF YOU WAIT TOO LONG, YOU RUN THE RISK OF GIVING HIM A MENTAL CRUTCH AND THE SEEDS OF INSECURITY.
THAT'S WHAT'S BOTHERING ME. THERE'S NOTHING INSECURE ABOUT BATWING.
THE SUIT IS COMPLETELY NATURAL TO HIM, AS THOUGH...

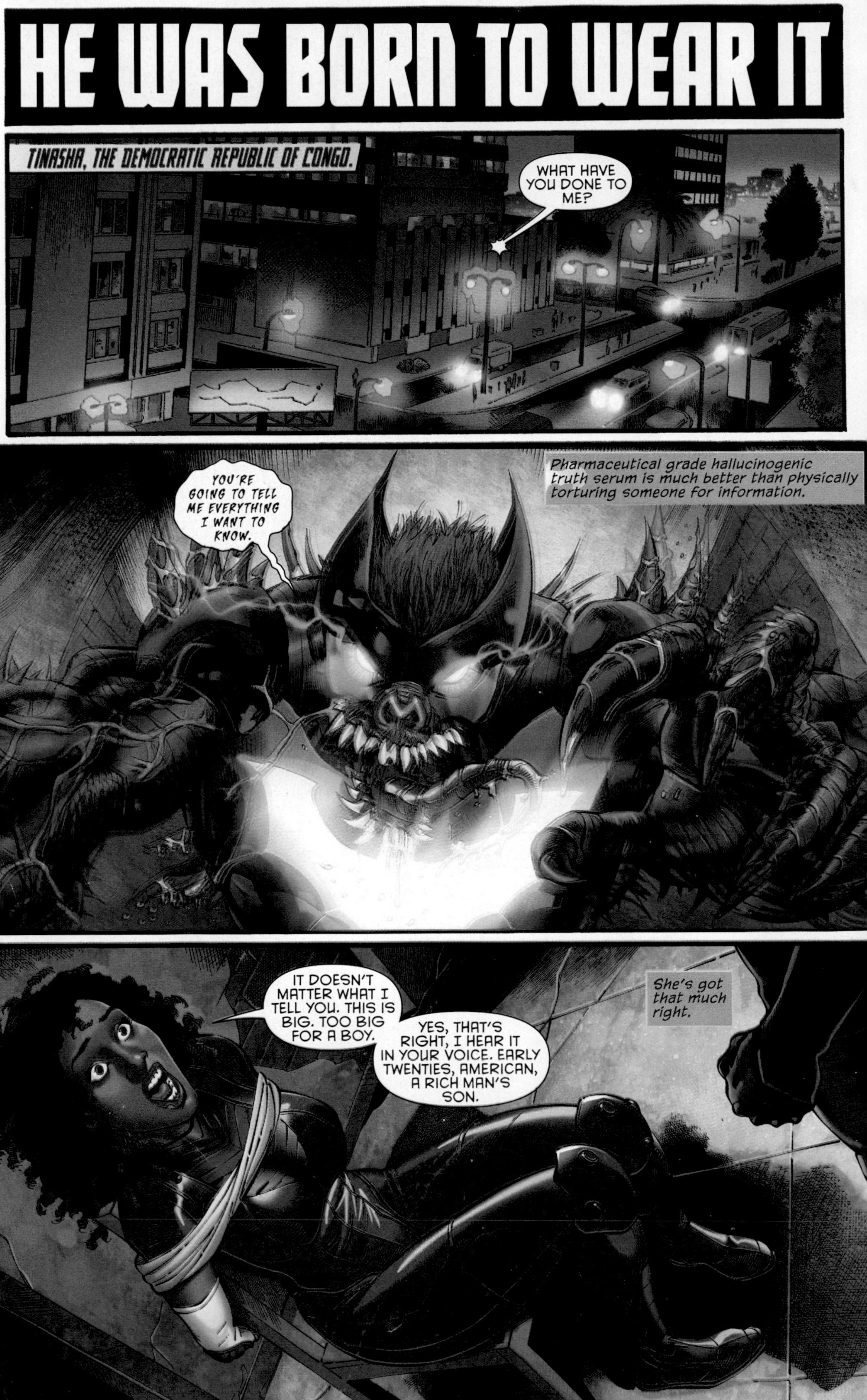
HE WAS BORN TO WEAR IT
TINASHA, THE DEMOCRATIC REPUBLIC OF CONGO.
WHAT HAVE YOU DONE TO ME?
YOU'RE GOING TO TELL ME EVERYTHING I WANT TO KNOW.
Pharmaceutical grade hallucinogenic truth serum is much better than physically torturing someone for information.
IT DOESN'T MATTER WHAT I TELL YOU. THIS IS BIG. TOO BIG FOR A BOY.
YES, THAT'S RIGHT, I HEAR IT IN YOUR VOICE. EARLY TWENTIES, AMERICAN, A RICH MAN'S SON.
She's got that much right.

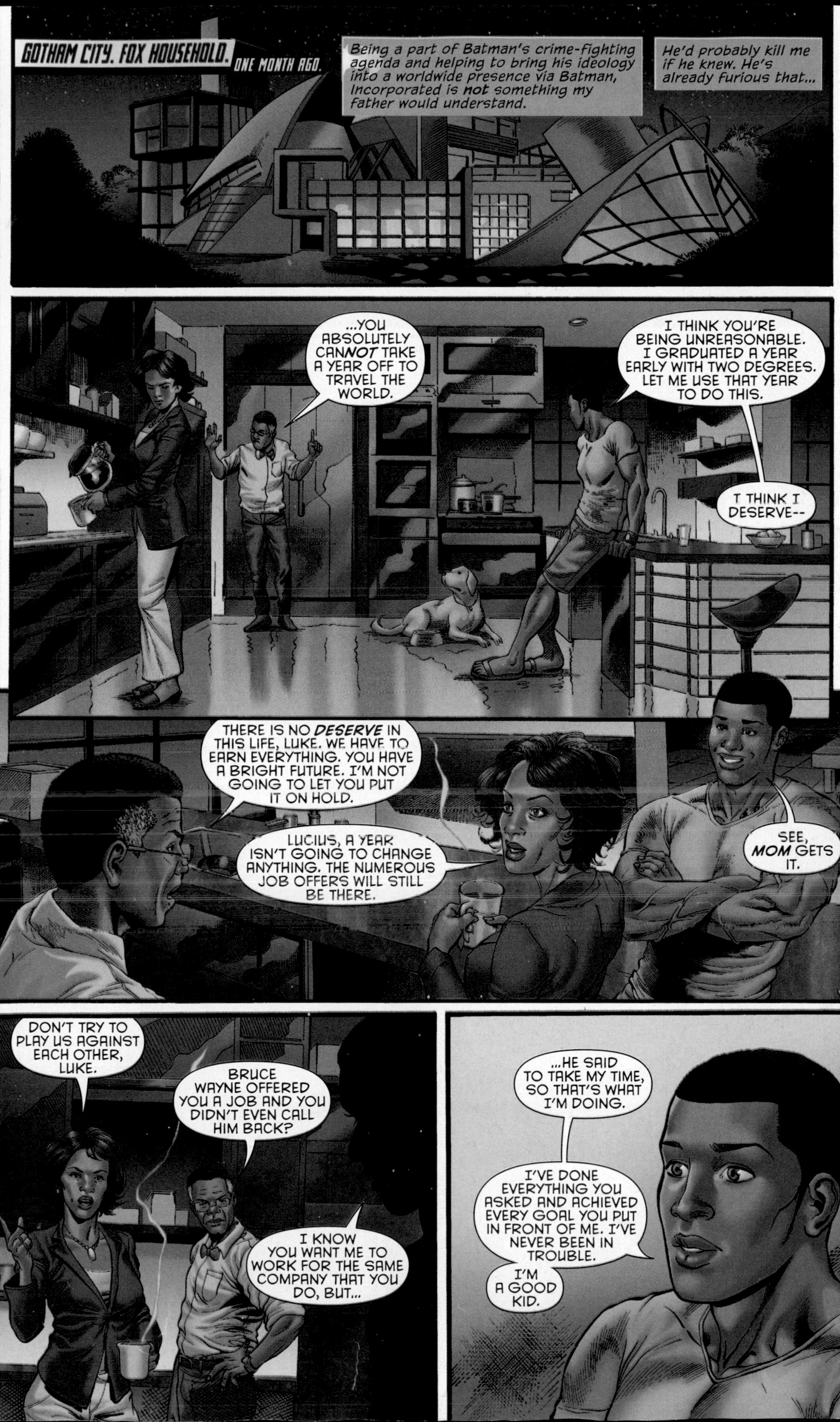
GOTHAM CITY. FOX HOUSEHOLD.
ONE MONTH AGO.
Being a part of Batman's crime-fighting agenda and helping to bring his ideology into a worldwide presence via Batman, Incorporated is not something my father would understand.
He'd probably kill me if he knew. He's already furious that...
...YOU ABSOLUTELY CANNOT TAKE A YEAR OFF TO TRAVEL THE WORLD.
I THINK YOU'RE BEING UNREASONABLE. I GRADUATED A YEAR EARLY WITH TWO DEGREES. LET ME USE THAT YEAR TO DO THIS.
I THINK I DESERVE--
THERE IS NO DESERVE IN THIS LIFE, LUKE. WE HAVE TO EARN EVERYTHING. YOU HAVE A BRIGHT FUTURE. I'M NOT GOING TO LET YOU PUT IT ON HOLD.
LUCIUS, A YEAR ISN'T GOING TO CHANGE ANYTHING. THE NUMEROUS JOB OFFERS WILL STILL BE THERE.
SEE, MOM GETS IT.
DON'T TRY TO PLAY US AGAINST EACH OTHER, LUKE.
BRUCE WAYNE OFFERED YOU A JOB AND YOU DIDN'T EVEN CALL HIM BACK?
I KNOW YOU WANT ME TO WORK FOR THE SAME COMPANY THAT YOU DO, BUT...
...HE SAID TO TAKE MY TIME, SO THAT'S WHAT I'M DOING.
I'VE DONE EVERYTHING YOU ASKED AND ACHIEVED EVERY GOAL YOU PUT IN FRONT OF ME. I'VE NEVER BEEN IN TROUBLE.
I'M A GOOD KID.

AND THAT'S HOW A RESPONSIBLE MAN *SHOULD* LIVE. YOU'RE SAYING YOU SHOULD BE REWARDED FOR NOT BEING A SCREW-UP? IS THIS WHAT YOU THINK?

I'M SORRY YOU HAD TO WORK YOUR WAY UP FROM THE STREETS FROM NOTHING--

LUCAS FOX, DON'T TALK BACK TO YOUR FATHER!

LET HIM TALK, TANYA. I'M CURIOUS TO SEE WHERE THIS IS GOING.

YOU DON'T *APPRECIATE* WHAT YOU HAVE. YOU WORK SO HARD ALL THE TIME AND YOU *NEVER* GO ANYWHERE, YOU NEVER TAKE MOM ON A VACATION.

YOU TREAT *ME*, *TIFF* AND *TAM* LIKE EMPLOYEES.

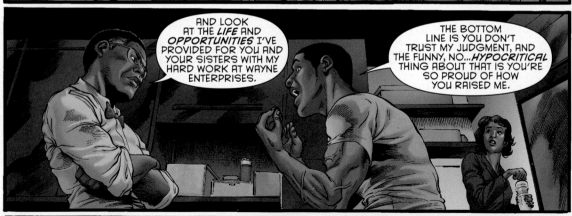

AND LOOK AT THE *LIFE* AND *OPPORTUNITIES* I'VE PROVIDED FOR YOU AND YOUR SISTERS WITH MY HARD WORK AT WAYNE ENTERPRISES.

THE BOTTOM LINE IS YOU DON'T TRUST MY JUDGMENT, AND THE FUNNY, NO...*HYPOCRITICAL* THING ABOUT THAT IS YOU'RE SO PROUD OF HOW YOU RAISED ME.

YOU WOULDN'T HAVE THAT CAR, OR YOUR APARTMENT--

I'M TWENTY-THREE AND I'M DOING IT WHETHER YOU LIKE IT OR NOT, DAD. I WAS HOPING FOR THE "LIKE" PART.

MAYBE WHEN I COME BACK, I'LL CREATE A STARTUP TECH COMPANY INSTEAD OF WORKING FOR SOMEONE ELSE.

Yes, so when Batman asked me to be a part of this operation, I had to have a cover story.

The truth is, being the only son in the Fox family doesn't leave a lot of room for self-exploration.

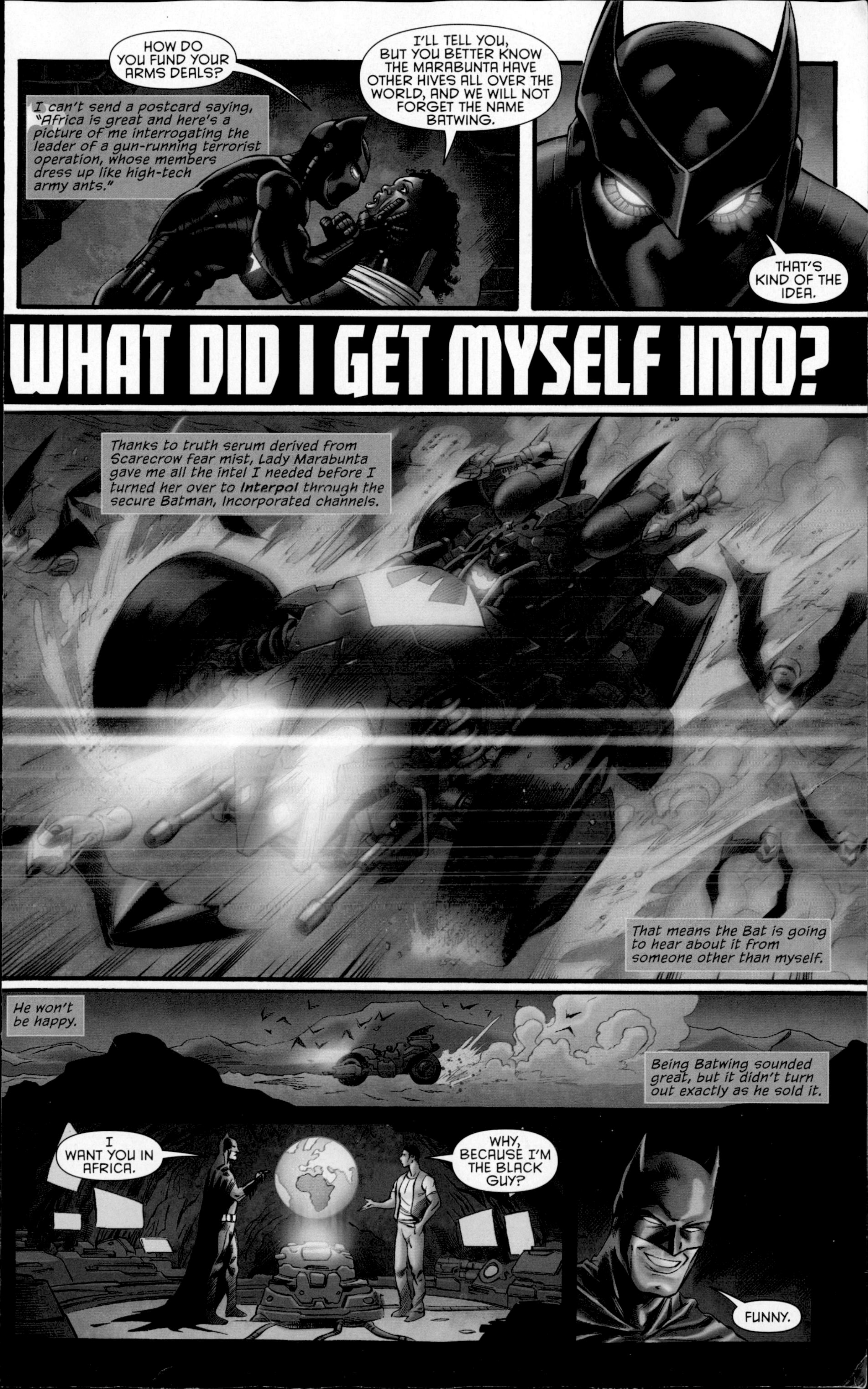
HOW DO YOU FUND YOUR ARMS DEALS?
I can't send a postcard saying, "Africa is great and here's a picture of me interrogating the leader of a gun-running terrorist operation, whose members dress up like high-tech army ants."
I'LL TELL YOU, BUT YOU BETTER KNOW THE MARABUNTA HAVE OTHER HIVES ALL OVER THE WORLD, AND WE WILL NOT FORGET THE NAME BATWING.
THAT'S KIND OF THE IDEA.
WHAT DID I GET MYSELF INTO?
Thanks to truth serum derived from Scarecrow fear mist, Lady Marabunta gave me all the intel I needed before I turned her over to Interpol through the secure Batman, Incorporated channels.
That means the Bat is going to hear about it from someone other than myself.
He won't be happy.
Being Batwing sounded great, but it didn't turn out exactly as he sold it.
I WANT YOU IN AFRICA.
WHY, BECAUSE I'M THE BLACK GUY?
FUNNY.

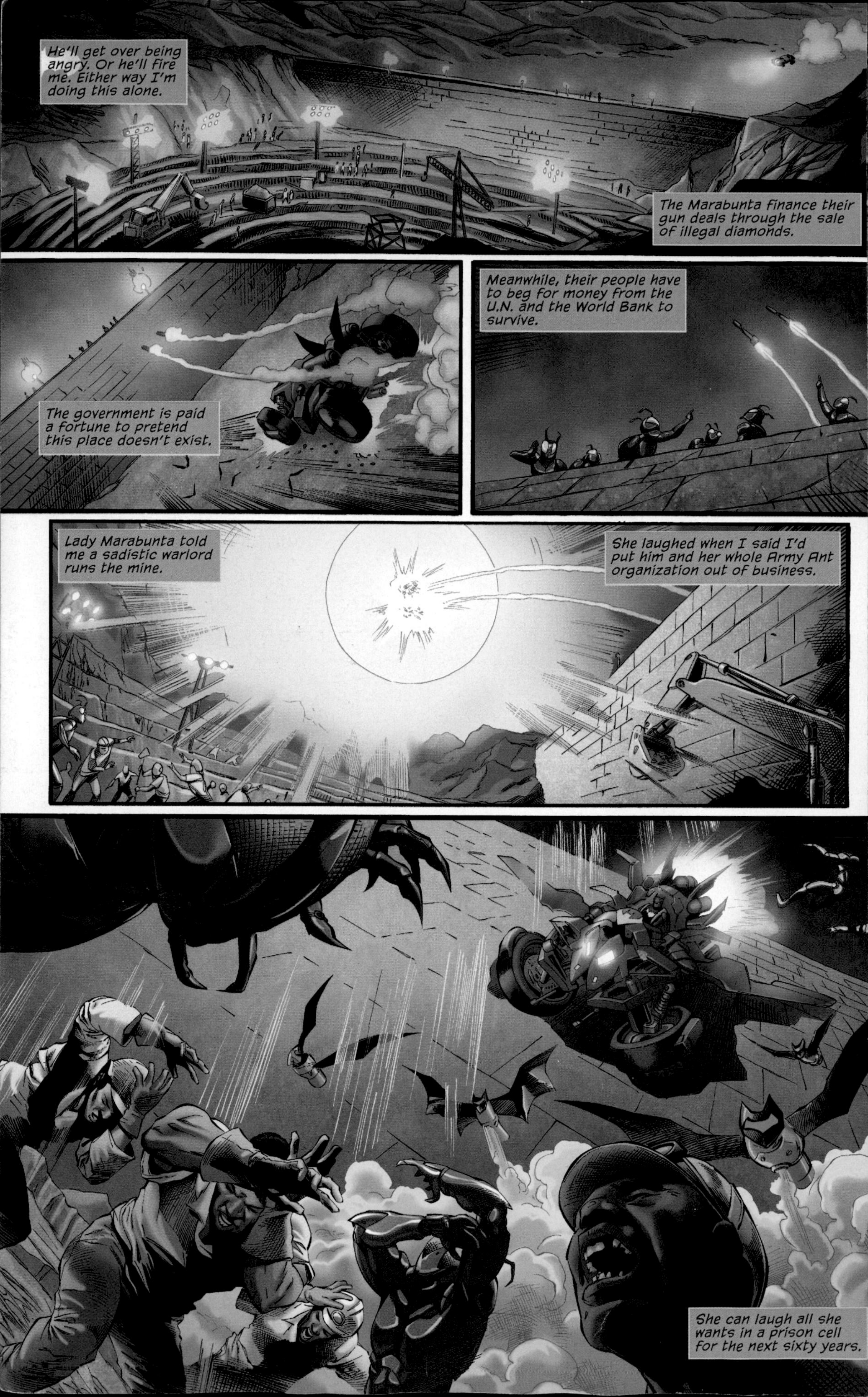
He'll get over being angry. Or he'll fire me. Either way I'm doing this alone.
The Marabunta finance their gun deals through the sale of illegal diamonds.
The government is paid a fortune to pretend this place doesn't exist.
Meanwhile, their people have to beg for money from the U.N. and the World Bank to survive.
Lady Marabunta told me a sadistic warlord runs the mine.
She laughed when I said I'd put him and her whole Army Ant organization out of business.
She can laugh all she wants in a prison cell for the next sixty years.

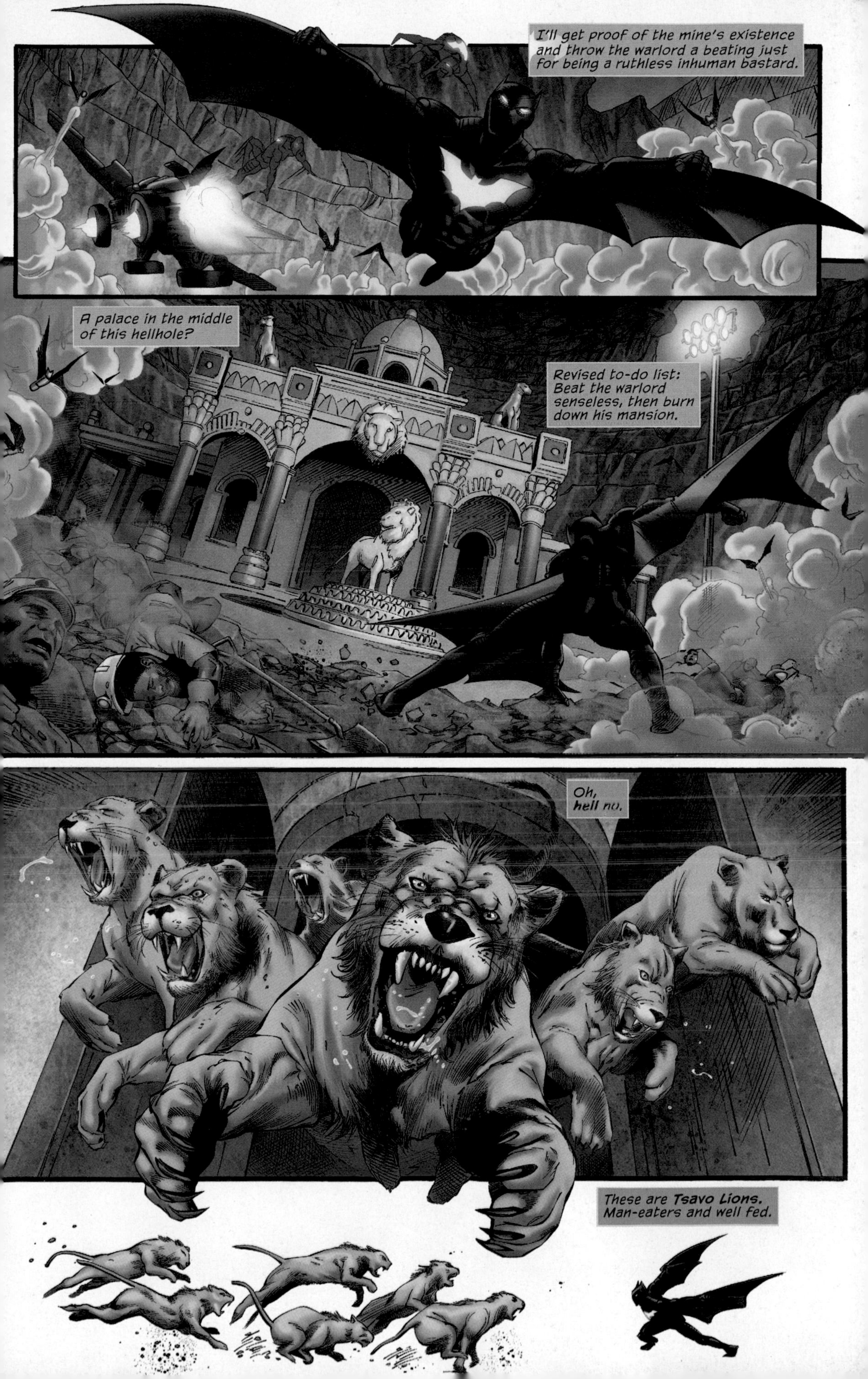
I'll get proof of the mine's existence and throw the warlord a beating just for being a ruthless inhuman bastard.
A palace in the middle of this hellhole?
Revised to-do list: Beat the warlord senseless, then burn down his mansion.
Oh, hell no.
These are Tsavo Lions. Man-eaters and well fed.

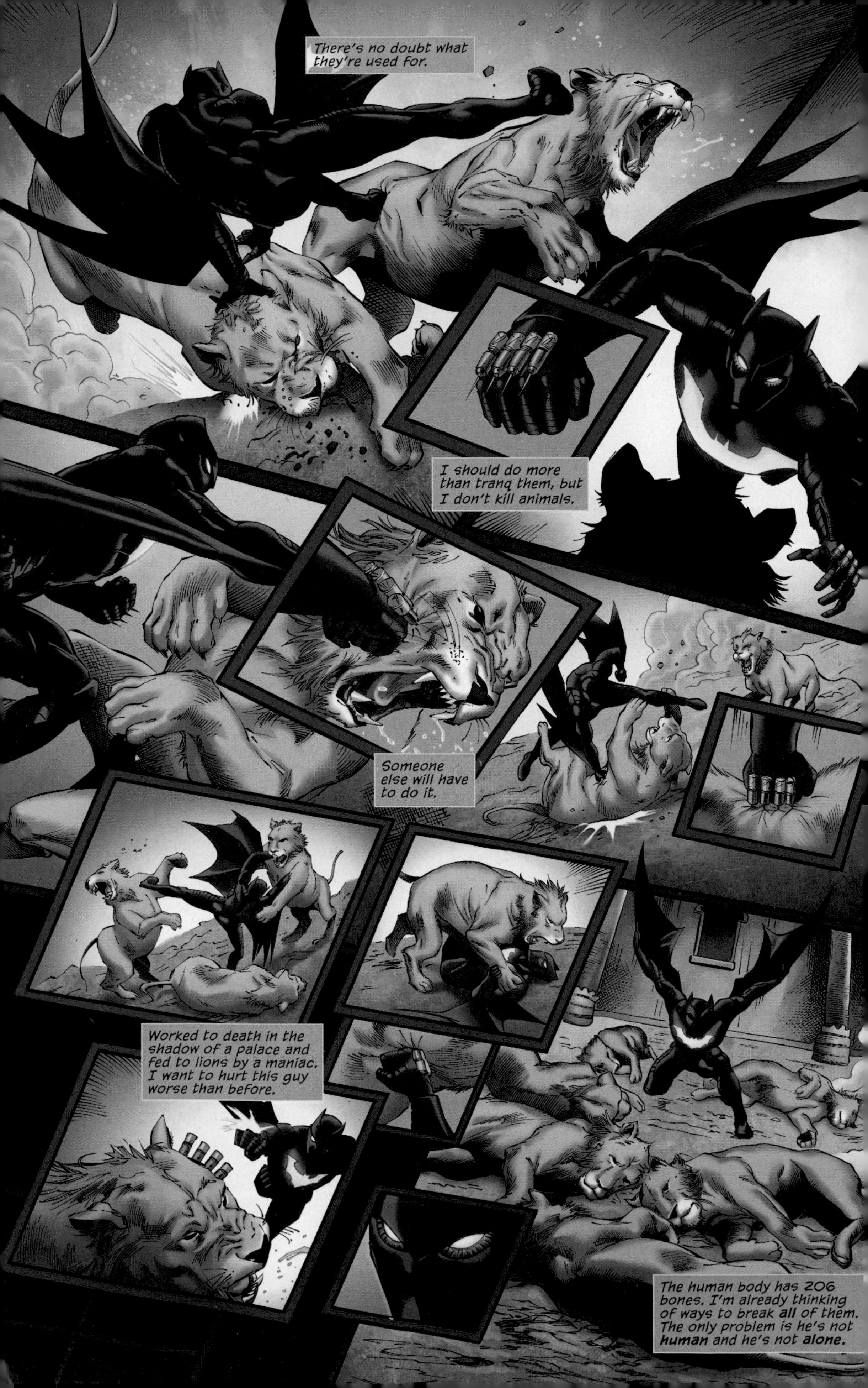
There's no doubt what they're used for.
I should do more than tranq them, but I don't kill animals.
Someone else will have to do it.
Worked to death in the shadow of a palace and fed to lions by a maniac. I want to hurt this guy worse than before.
The human body has 206 bones. I'm already thinking of ways to break **all** of them. The only problem is he's not **human** and he's not **alone.**

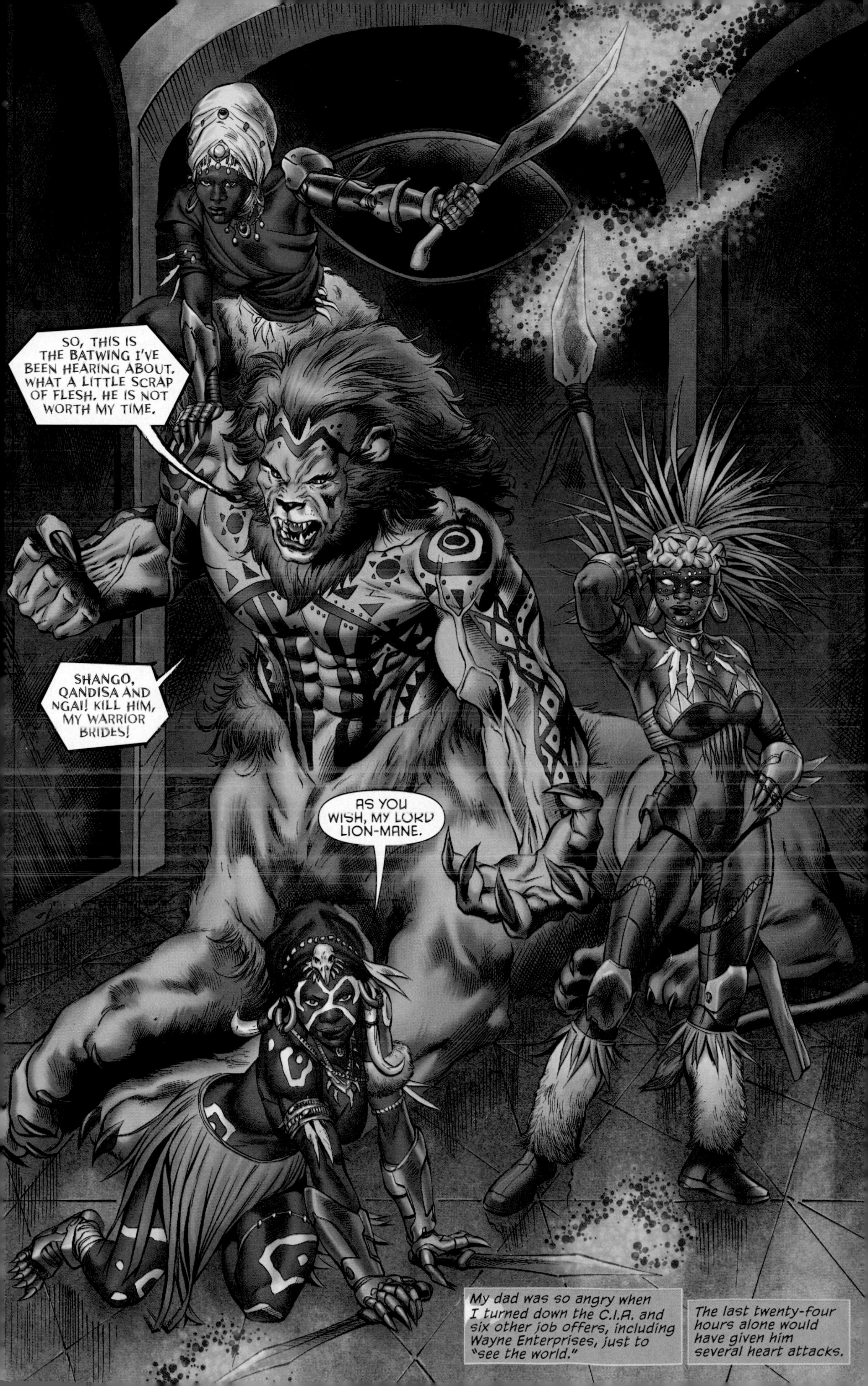
SO, THIS IS THE BATWING I'VE BEEN HEARING ABOUT. WHAT A LITTLE SCRAP OF FLESH. HE IS NOT WORTH MY TIME.
SHANGO, QANDISA AND NGAI! KILL HIM, MY WARRIOR BRIDES!
AS YOU WISH, MY LORD LION-MANE.
My dad was so angry when I turned down the C.I.A. and six other job offers, including Wayne Enterprises, just to "see the world."
The last twenty-four hours alone would have given him several heart attacks.

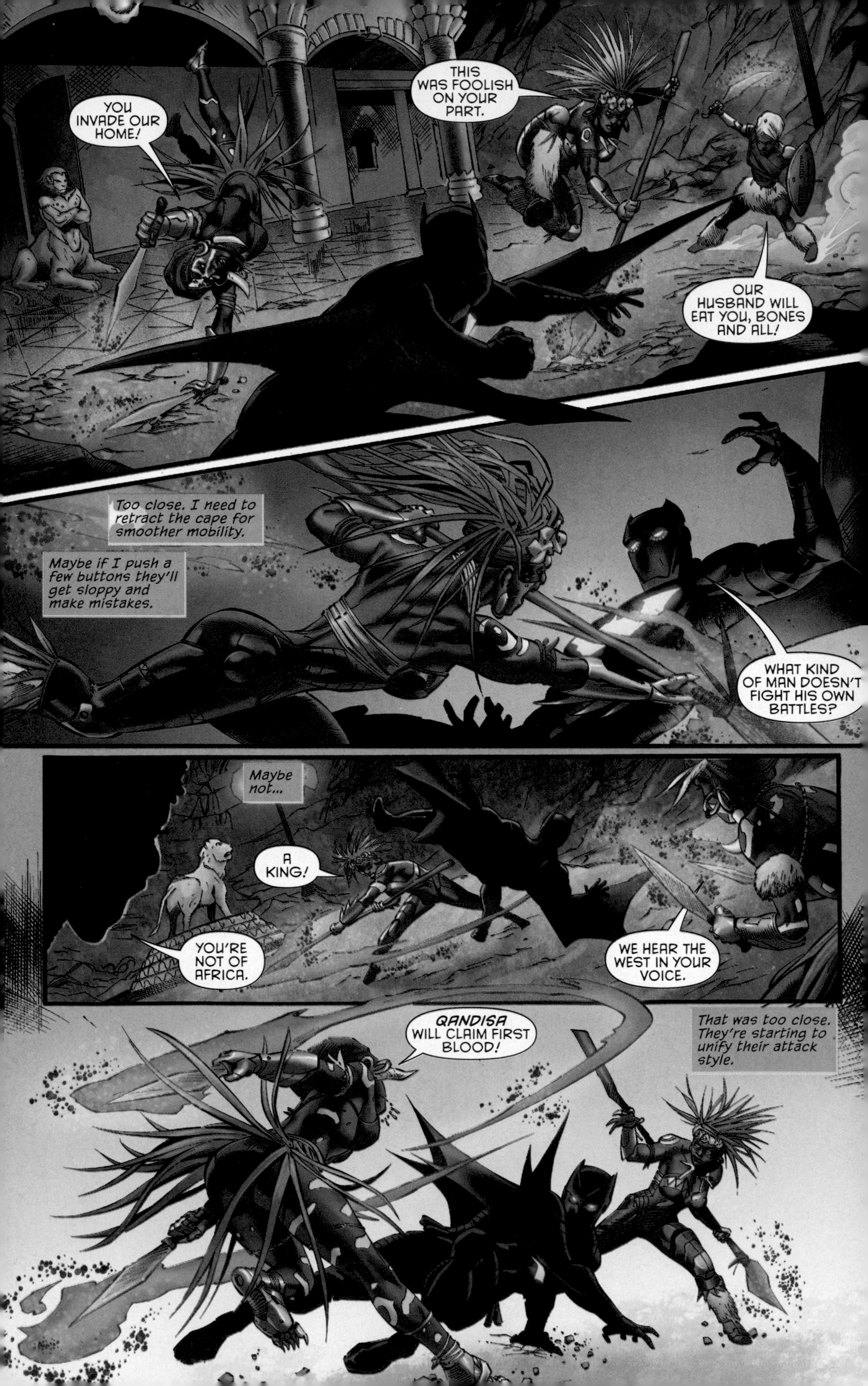
YOU INVADE OUR HOME!
THIS WAS FOOLISH ON YOUR PART.
OUR HUSBAND WILL EAT YOU, BONES AND ALL!
Too close. I need to retract the cape for smoother mobility.
Maybe if I push a few buttons they'll get sloppy and make mistakes.
WHAT KIND OF MAN DOESN'T FIGHT HIS OWN BATTLES?
Maybe not...
A KING!
YOU'RE NOT OF AFRICA.
WE HEAR THE WEST IN YOUR VOICE.
QANDISA WILL CLAIM FIRST BLOOD!
That was too close. They're starting to unify their attack style.

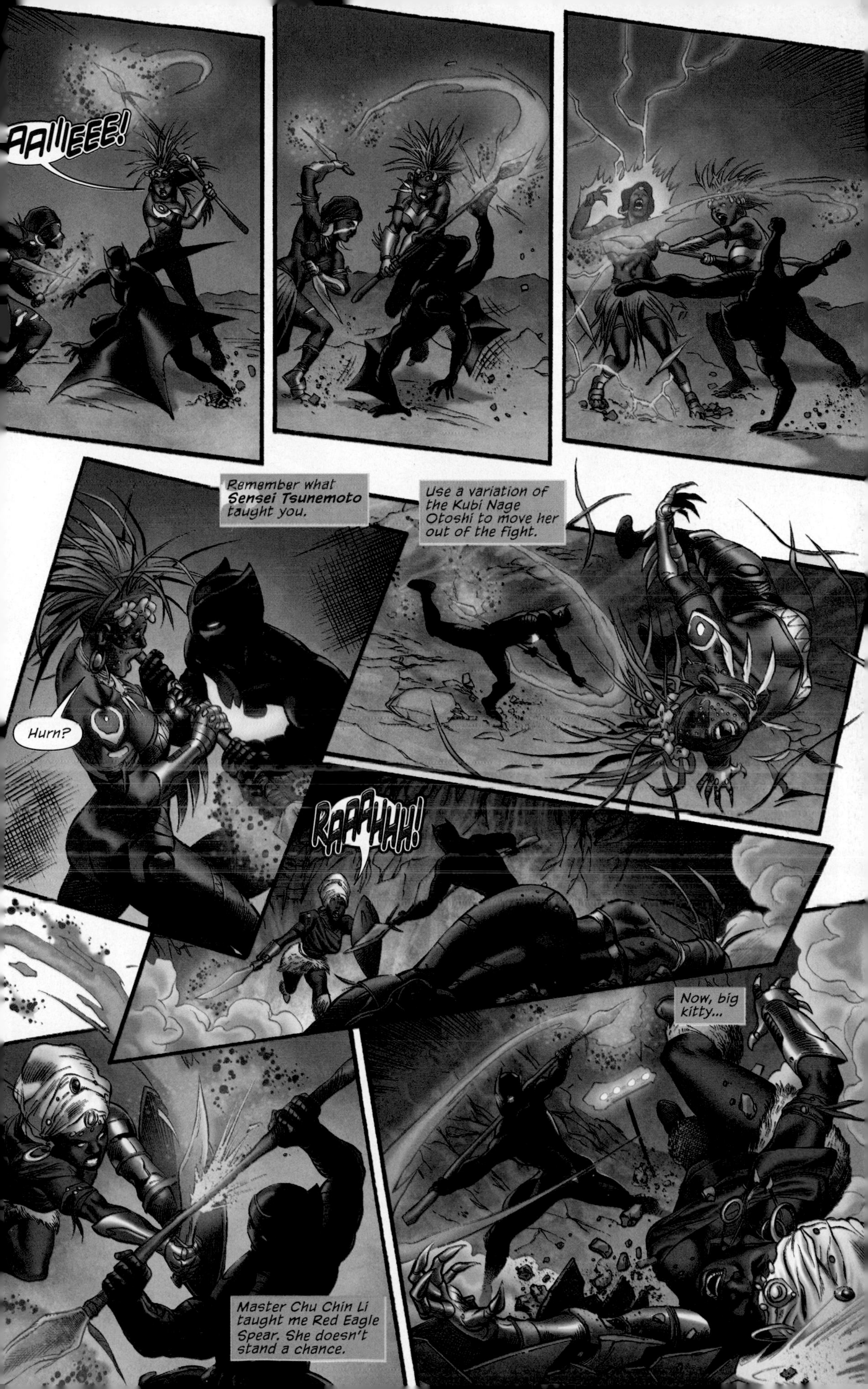
AAIIIEEE!
Remember what Sensei Tsunemoto taught you.
Use a variation of the Kubi Nage Otoshi to move her out of the fight.
Hurn?
RAAAHHH!
Master Chu Chin Li taught me Red Eagle Spear. She doesn't stand a chance.
Now, big kitty...

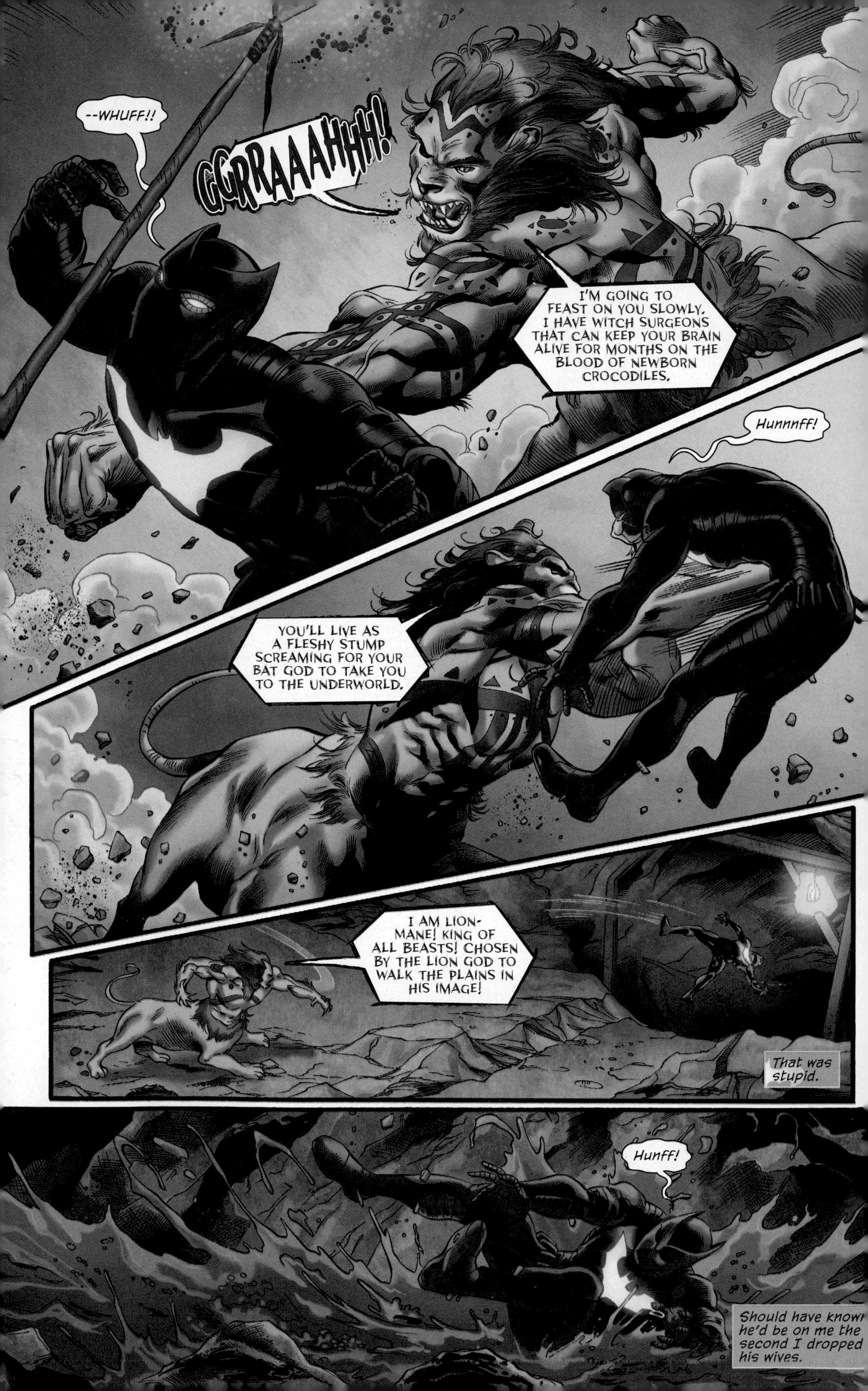

--WHUFF!!
GGRRAAAHHH!
I'M GOING TO FEAST ON YOU SLOWLY. I HAVE WITCH SURGEONS THAT CAN KEEP YOUR BRAIN ALIVE FOR MONTHS ON THE BLOOD OF NEWBORN CROCODILES.
Hunnnff!
YOU'LL LIVE AS A FLESHY STUMP SCREAMING FOR YOUR BAT GOD TO TAKE YOU TO THE UNDERWORLD.
I AM LION-MANE! KING OF ALL BEASTS! CHOSEN BY THE LION GOD TO WALK THE PLAINS IN HIS IMAGE!
That was stupid.
Hunff!
Should have known he'd be on me the second I dropped his wives.

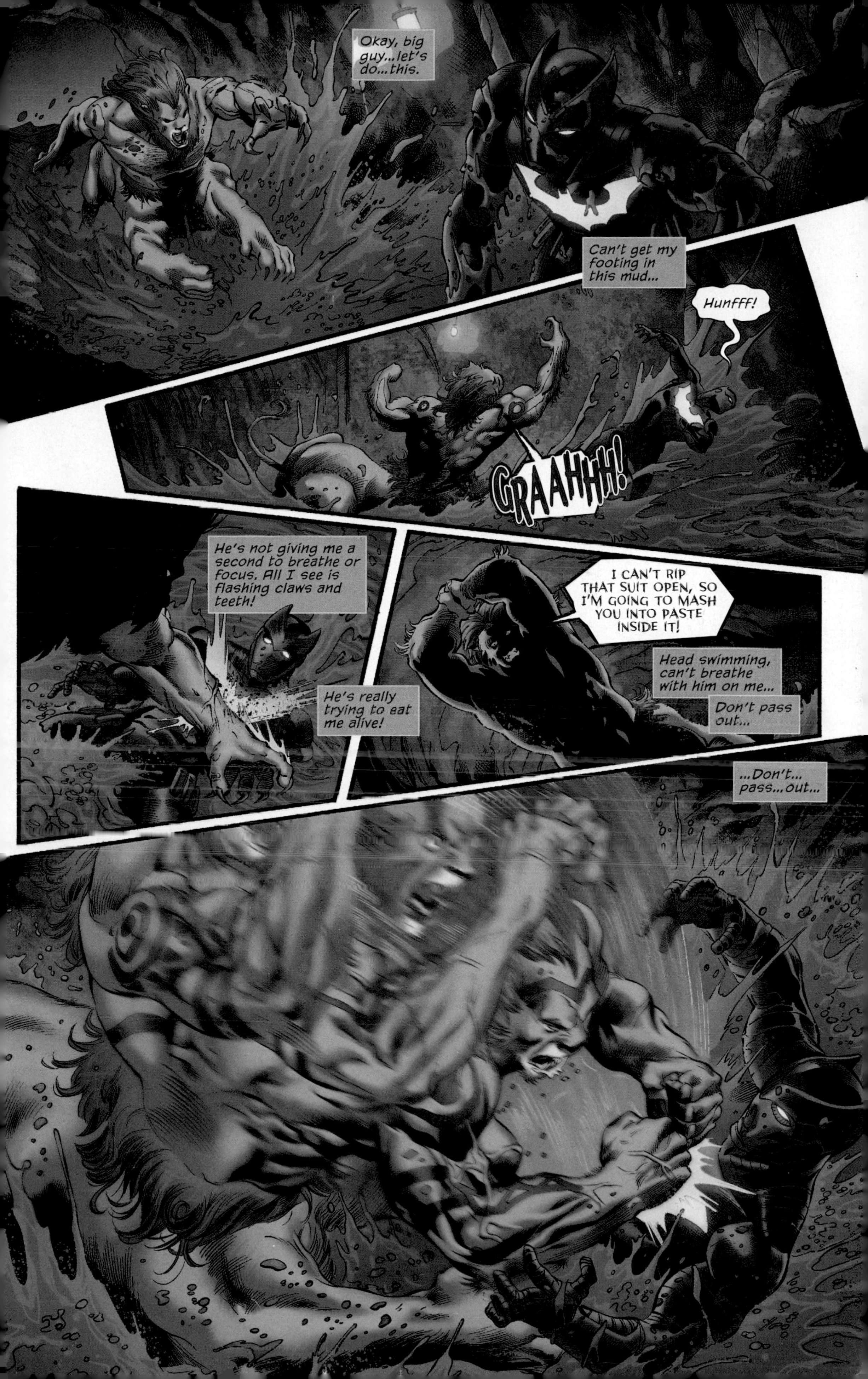
Okay, big guy...let's do...this.
Can't get my footing in this mud...
Hunfff!
GRAAHHH!
He's not giving me a second to breathe or focus. All I see is flashing claws and teeth!
He's really trying to eat me alive!
I CAN'T RIP THAT SUIT OPEN, SO I'M GOING TO MASH YOU INTO PASTE INSIDE IT!
Head swimming, can't breathe with him on me...
Don't pass out...
...Don't... pass...out...

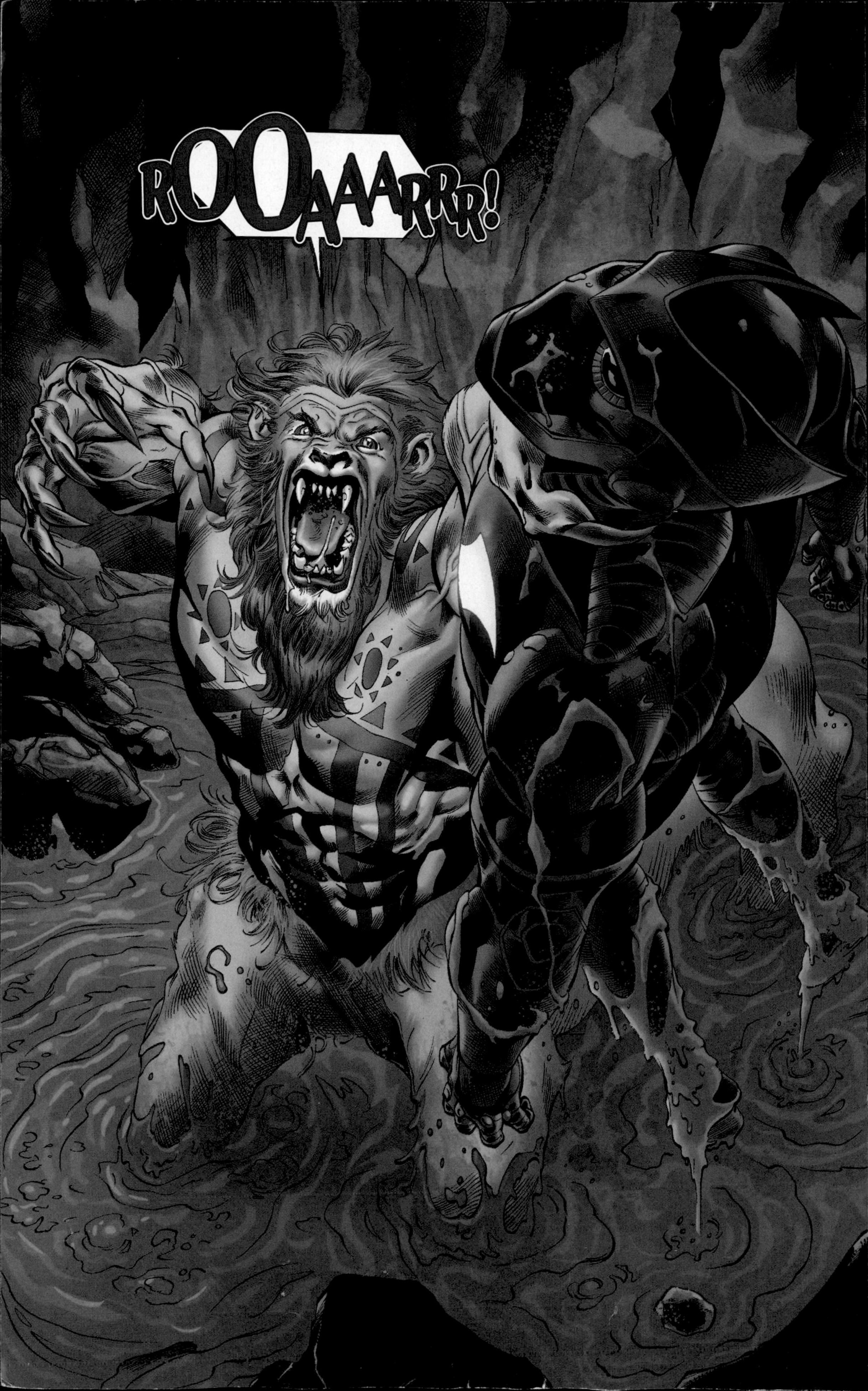
rOOAAAARRRR!

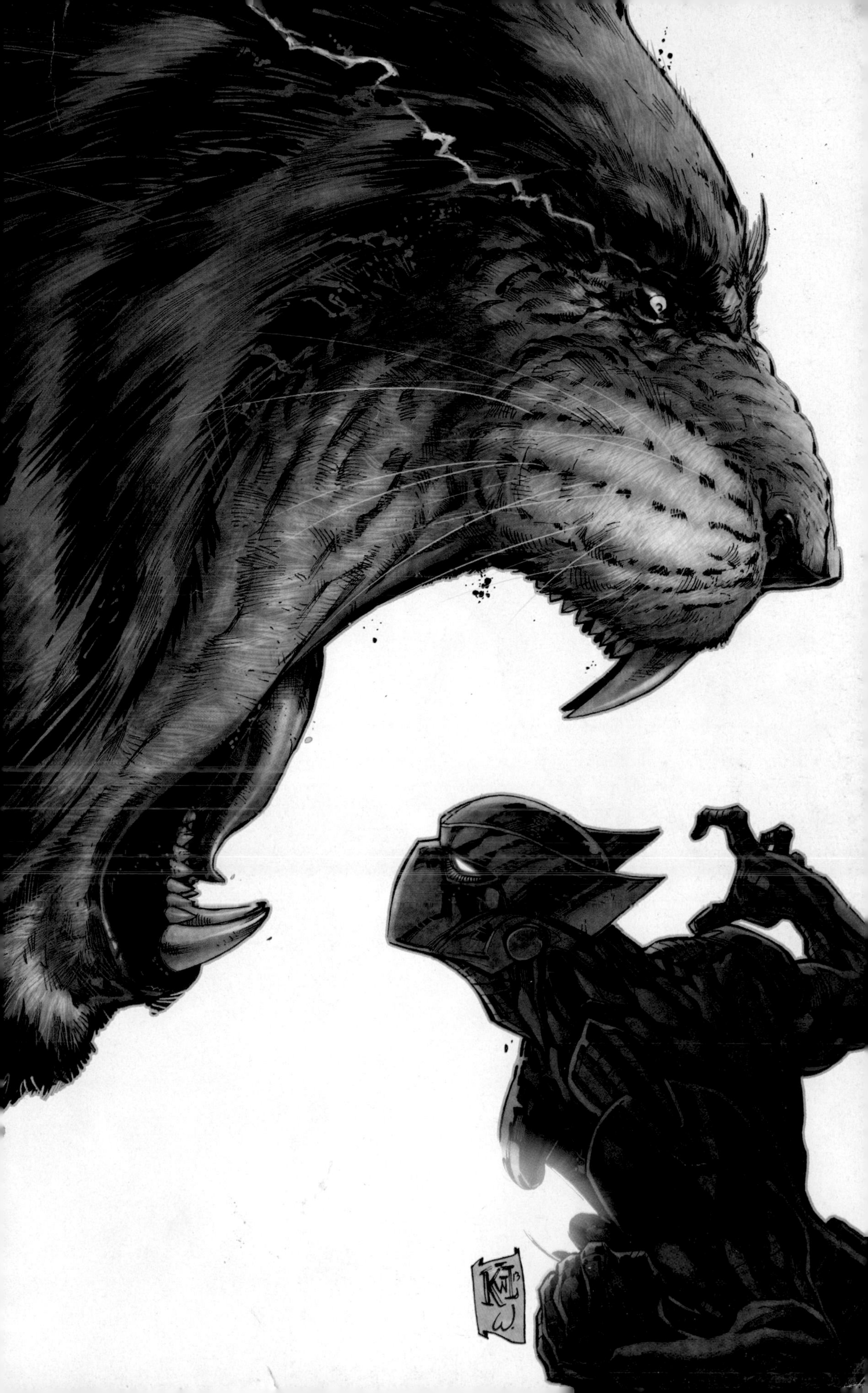

FANGS OF DOOM

cover art by **KEN LASHLEY & JASON WRIGHT**

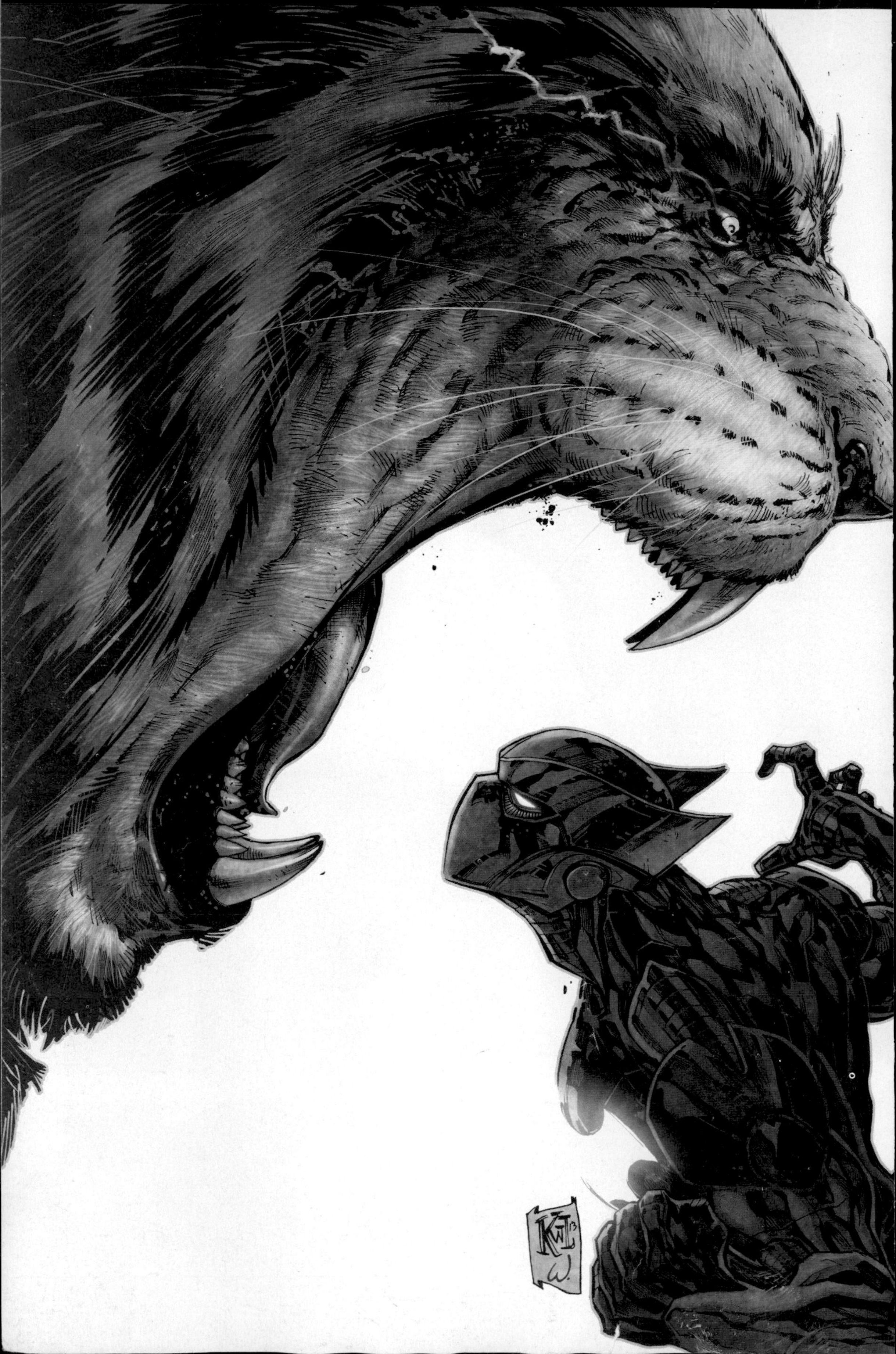
KWL 13
W.

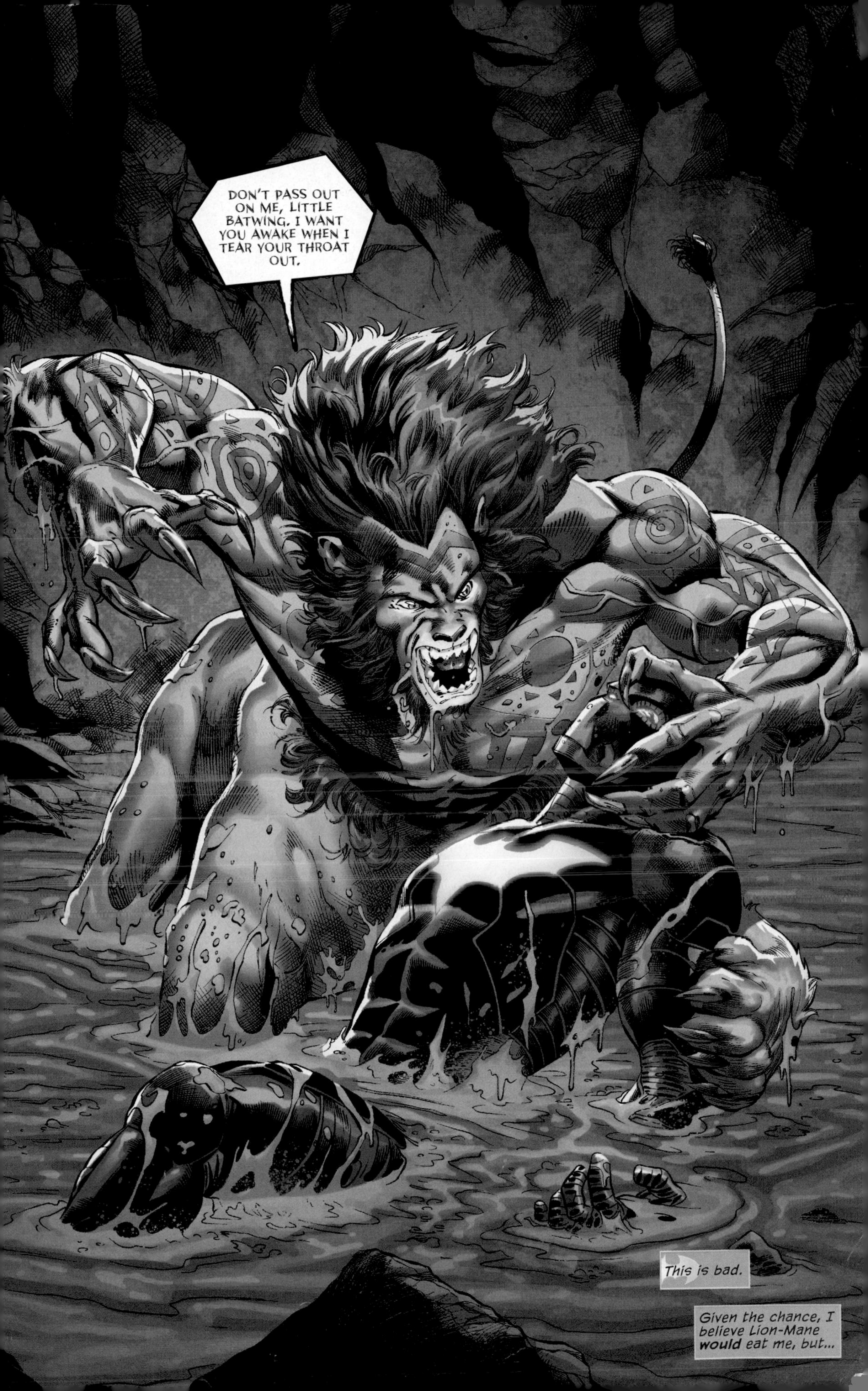
DON'T PASS OUT ON ME, LITTLE BATWING. I WANT YOU AWAKE WHEN I TEAR YOUR THROAT OUT.
This is bad.
Given the chance, I believe Lion-Mane **would** eat me, but...

...fifty thousand volts says that's not going to happen.

ZZZZZAAAAKKKK

JUST GIVE UP, LION-MANE.

THIS IS MY KINGDOM! I AM A GOD HERE!

THAT WAS A WARNING SHOT. BE A GOOD SIX-LEGGED-KITTY-THING AND SURRENDER TO THE PROPER AUTHORITIES.

I WAS REBORN AND TRANSFORMED BY THE CULT OF APEDAMAK TO WALK THE EARTH IN HIS VISAGE! IT IS HERE I WILL BUILD ISHTAR'S GATE AND UNLEASH A PLAGUE OF LIONS UPON ALL WHO THREATEN MY FOLLOWERS.

I CAN SEE WE'RE A FAN OF LONG-WINDED SPEECHES.

SILENCE

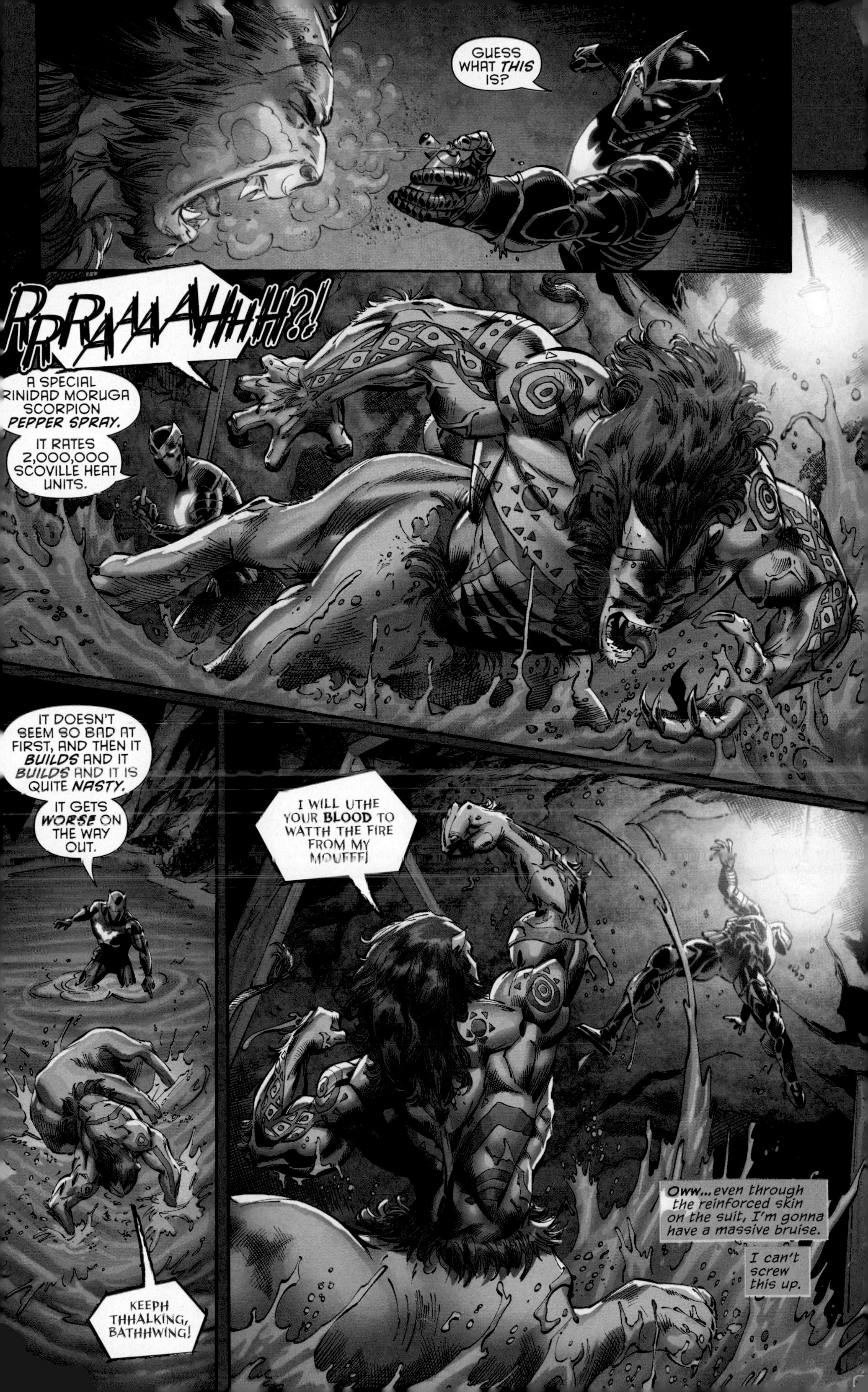
GUESS WHAT THIS IS?
RRRAAAAHHHH?!
A SPECIAL RINIDAD MORUGA SCORPION PEPPER SPRAY.
IT RATES 2,000,000 SCOVILLE HEAT UNITS.
IT DOESN'T SEEM SO BAD AT FIRST, AND THEN IT BUILDS AND IT BUILDS AND IT IS QUITE NASTY.
IT GETS WORSE ON THE WAY OUT.
KEEPH THHALKING, BATHHWING!
I WILL UTHE YOUR BLOOD TO WATTH THE FIRE FROM MY MOUFFF!
Oww...even through the reinforced skin on the suit, I'm gonna have a massive bruise.
I can't screw this up.

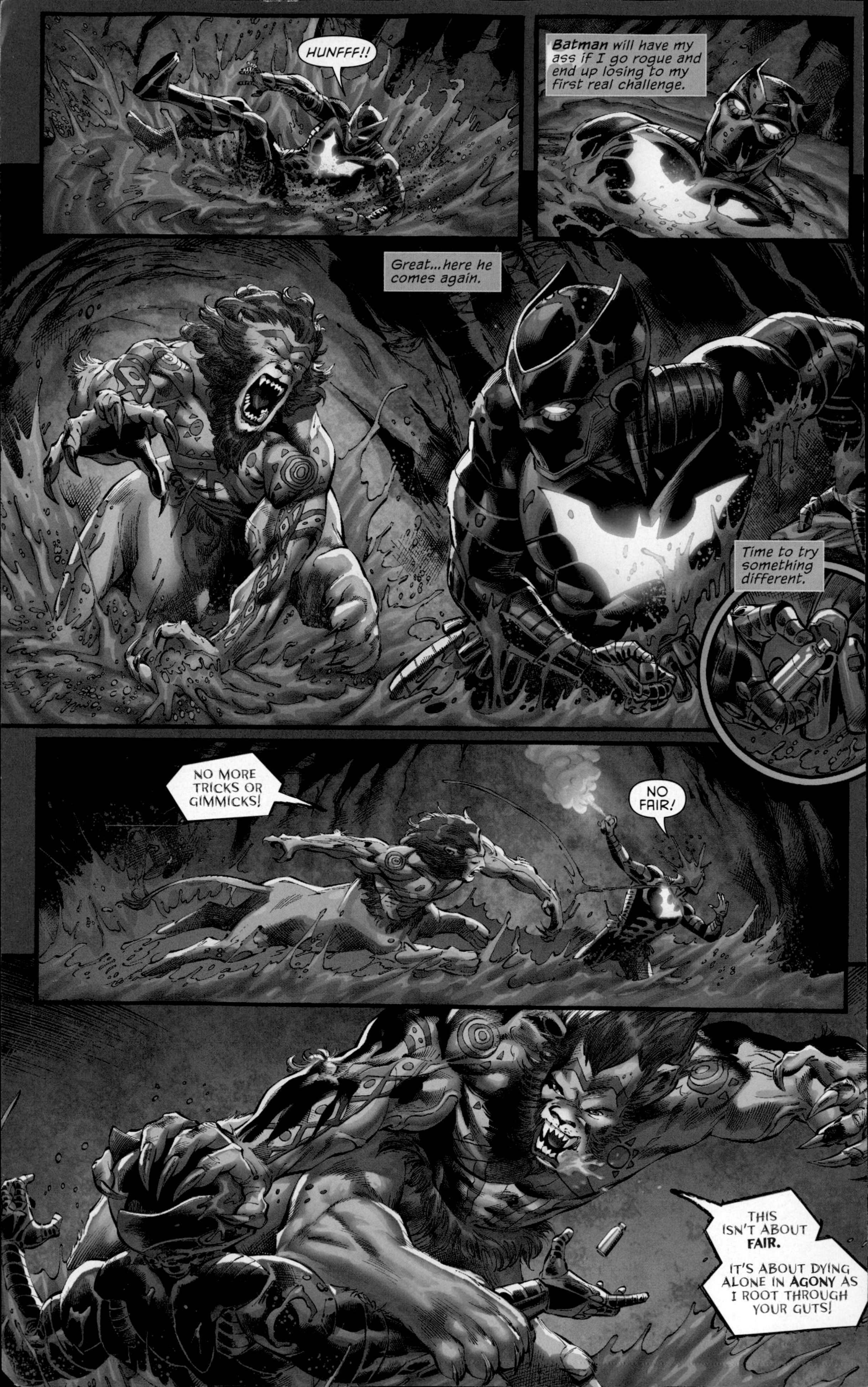
HUNFFF!!
Batman will have my ass if I go rogue and end up losing to my first real challenge.
Great...here he comes again.
Time to try something different.
NO MORE TRICKS OR GIMMICKS!
NO FAIR!
THIS ISN'T ABOUT FAIR.
IT'S ABOUT DYING ALONE IN AGONY AS I ROOT THROUGH YOUR GUTS!

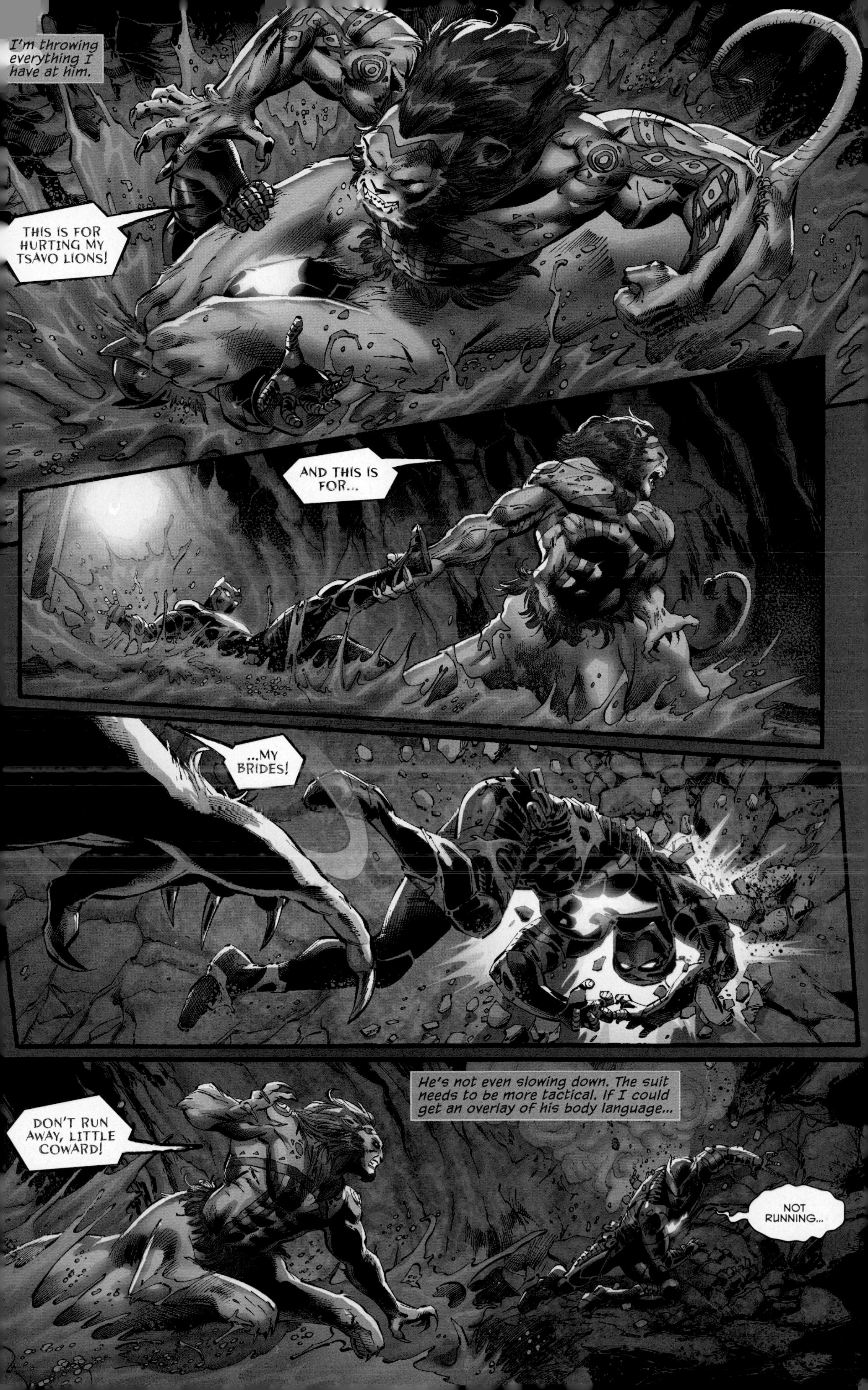
I'm throwing everything I have at him.
THIS IS FOR HURTING MY TSAVO LIONS!
AND THIS IS FOR...
...MY BRIDES!
He's not even slowing down. The suit needs to be more tactical. If I could get an overlay of his body language...
DON'T RUN AWAY, LITTLE COWARD!
NOT RUNNING...

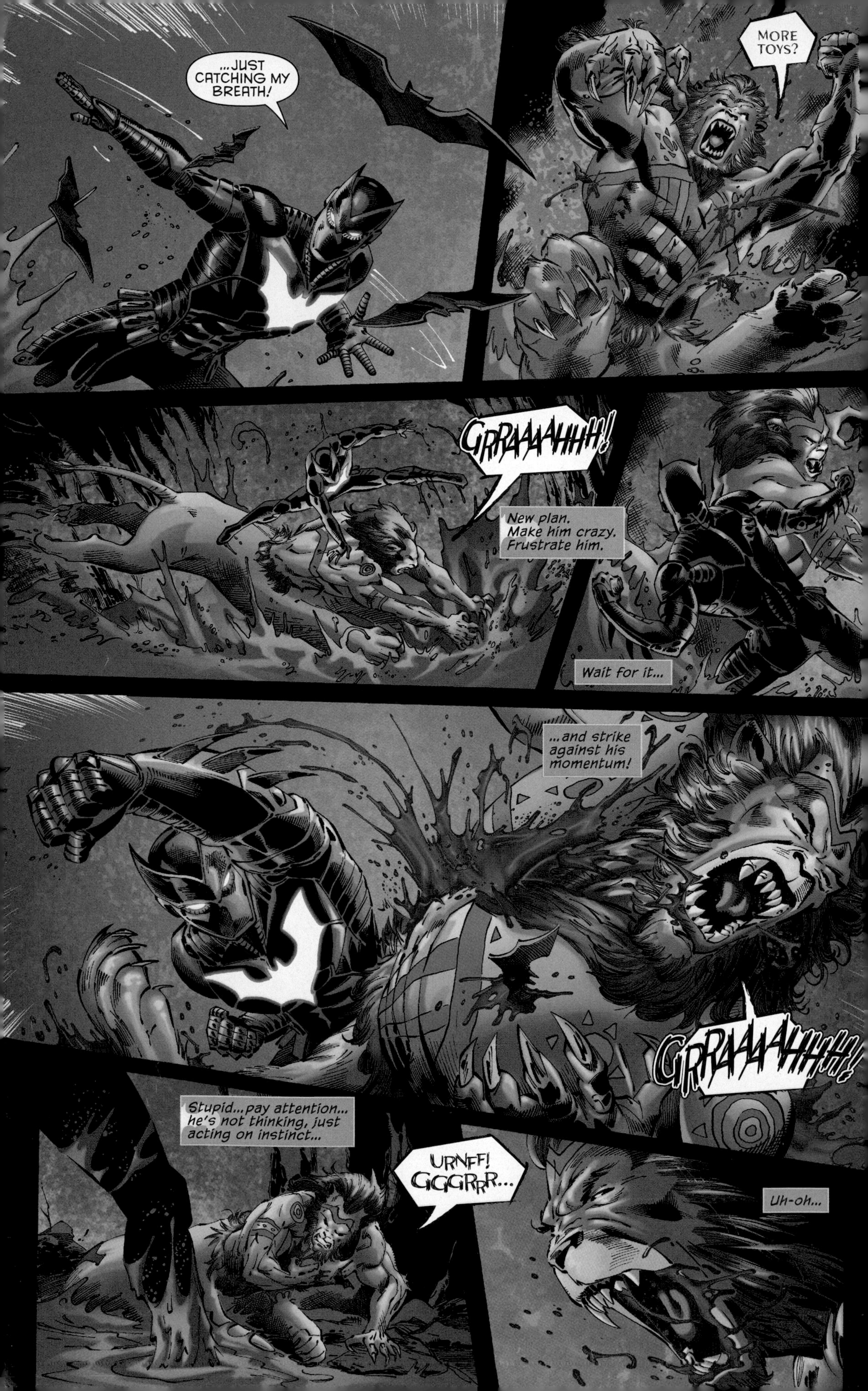
...JUST CATCHING MY BREATH!
MORE TOYS?
GRRAAAAHHH!
New plan. Make him crazy. Frustrate him.
Wait for it...
...and strike against his momentum!
GRRAAAAHHH!
Stupid...pay attention... he's not thinking, just acting on instinct...
URNFF! GGGRRR...
Uh-oh...

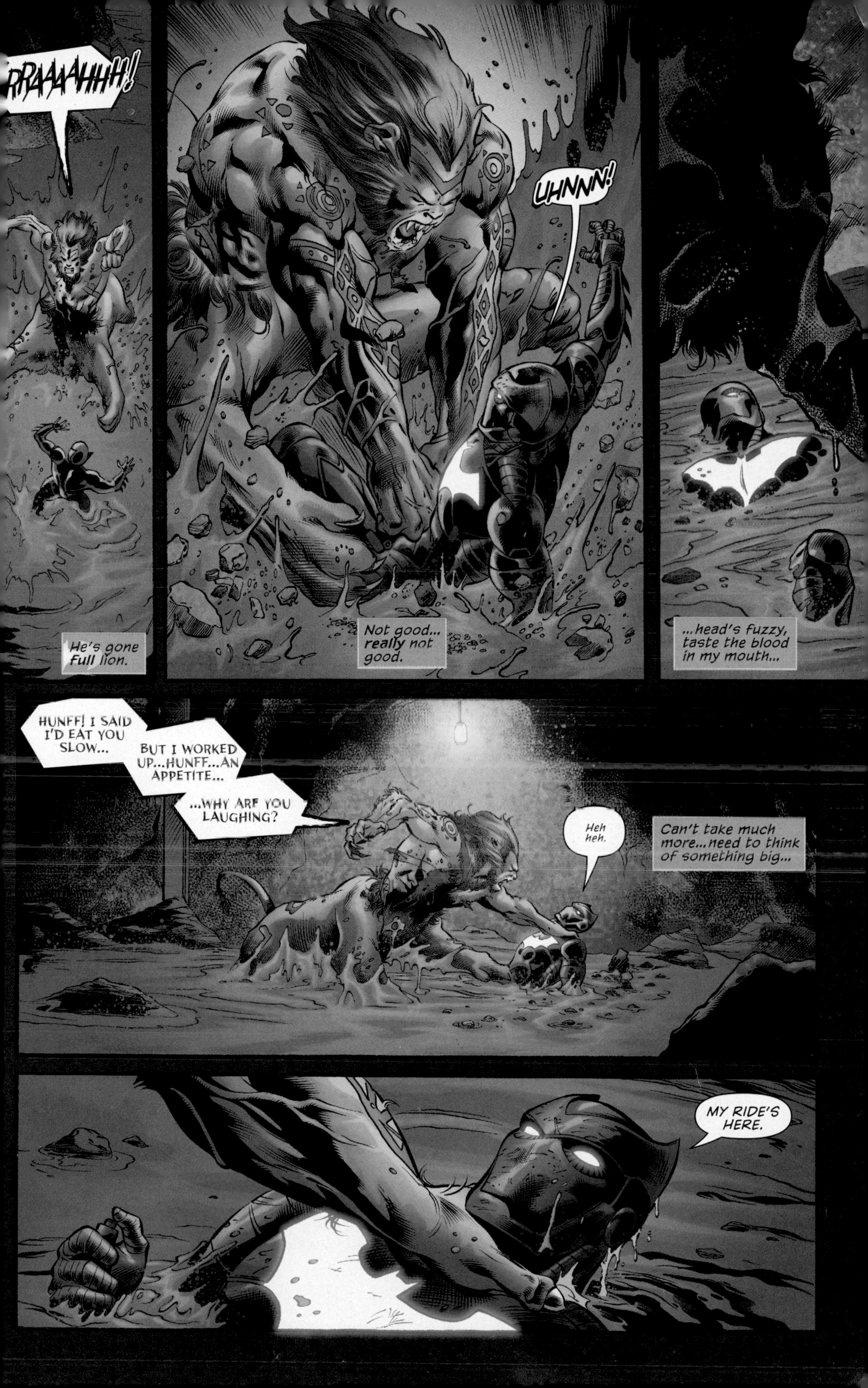
RRAAAAHHH!
He's gone full lion.
UHNNN!
Not good... really not good.
...head's fuzzy, taste the blood in my mouth...
HUNFF! I SAID I'D EAT YOU SLOW...
BUT I WORKED UP...HUNFF...AN APPETITE...
...WHY ARE YOU LAUGHING?
Heh heh.
Can't take much more...need to think of something big...
MY RIDE'S HERE.

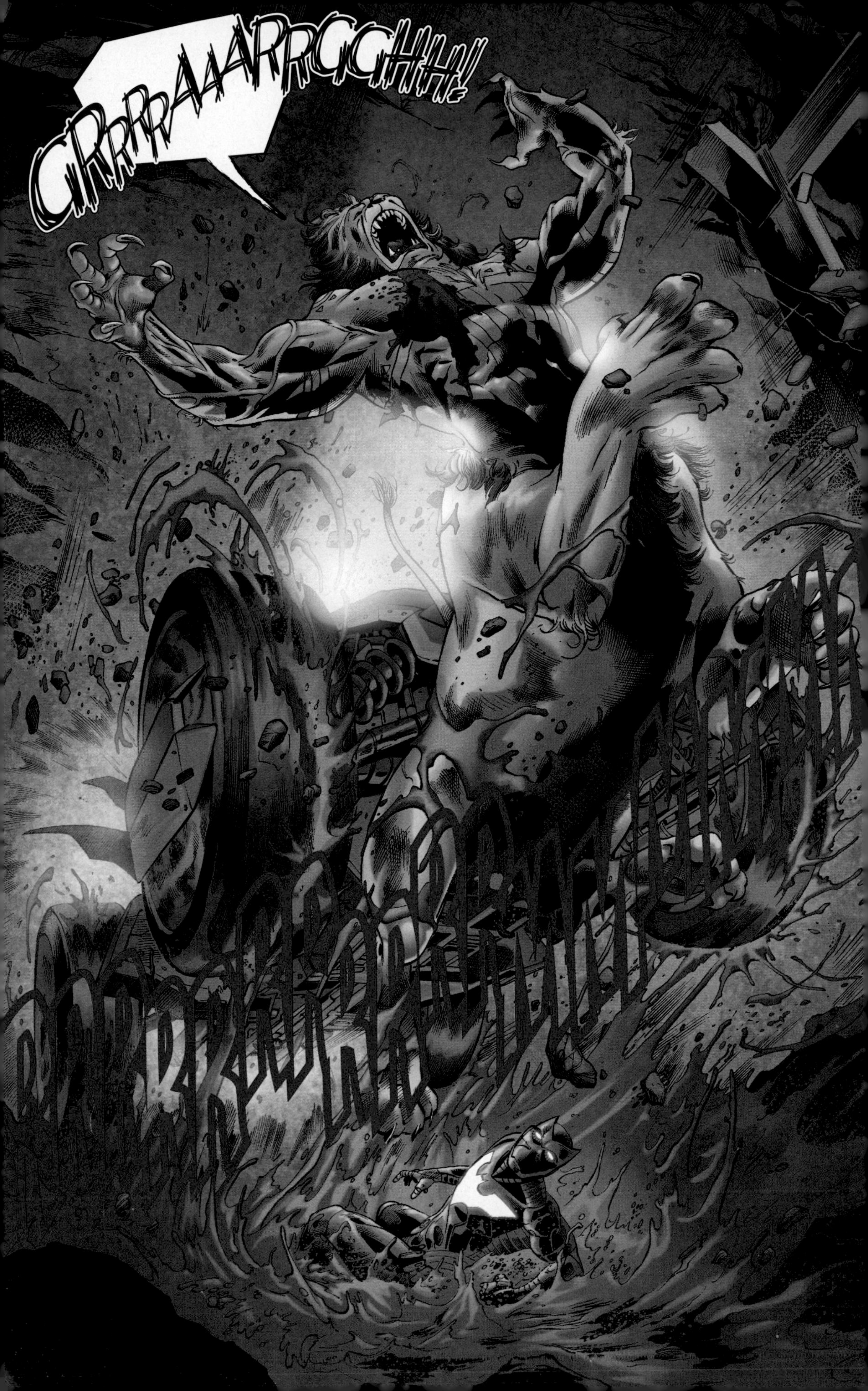
GRRRRAAARRGGHHH!

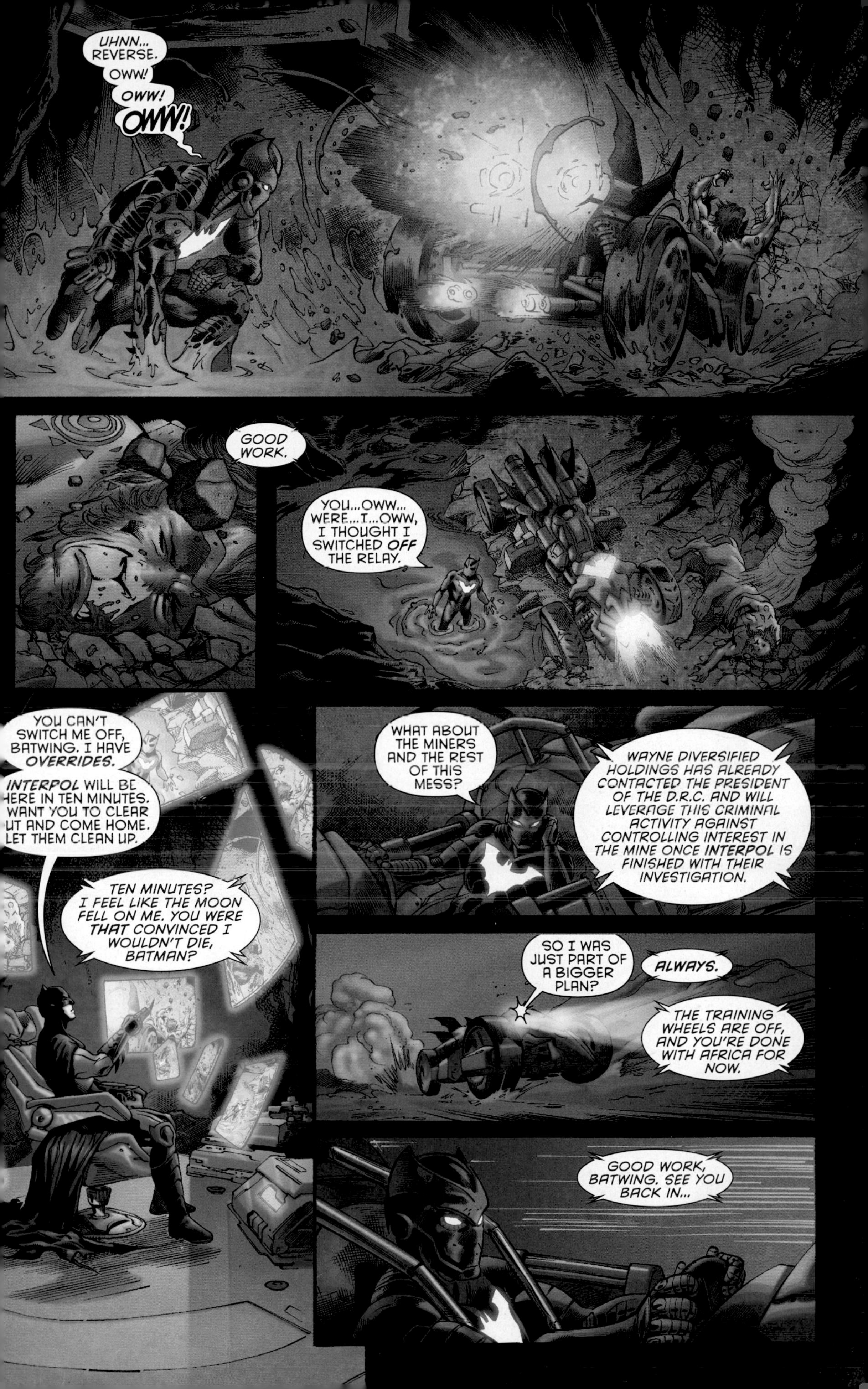
UHNN... REVERSE.
OWW!
OWW!
OWW!
GOOD WORK.
YOU...OWW... WERE...I...OWW, I THOUGHT I SWITCHED OFF THE RELAY.
YOU CAN'T SWITCH ME OFF, BATWING. I HAVE OVERRIDES.
INTERPOL WILL BE HERE IN TEN MINUTES. WANT YOU TO CLEAR UT AND COME HOME. LET THEM CLEAN UP.
TEN MINUTES? I FEEL LIKE THE MOON FELL ON ME. YOU WERE THAT CONVINCED I WOULDN'T DIE, BATMAN?
WHAT ABOUT THE MINERS AND THE REST OF THIS MESS?
WAYNE DIVERSIFIED HOLDINGS HAS ALREADY CONTACTED THE PRESIDENT OF THE D.R.C. AND WILL LEVERAGE THIS CRIMINAL ACTIVITY AGAINST CONTROLLING INTEREST IN THE MINE ONCE INTERPOL IS FINISHED WITH THEIR INVESTIGATION.
SO I WAS JUST PART OF A BIGGER PLAN?
ALWAYS.
THE TRAINING WHEELS ARE OFF, AND YOU'RE DONE WITH AFRICA FOR NOW.
GOOD WORK, BATWING. SEE YOU BACK IN...

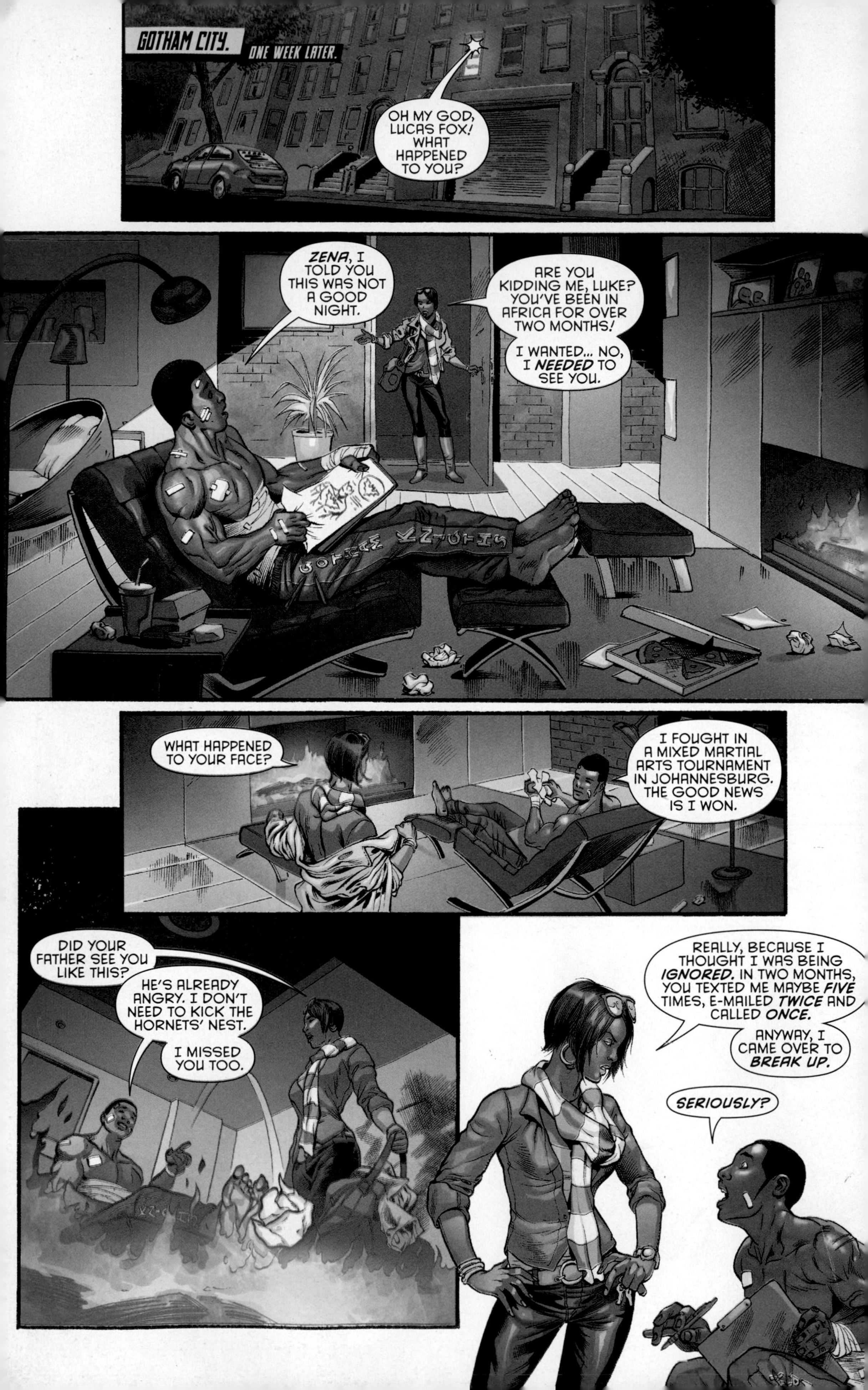
GOTHAM CITY.
ONE WEEK LATER.
OH MY GOD, LUCAS FOX! WHAT HAPPENED TO YOU?
ZENA, I TOLD YOU THIS WAS NOT A GOOD NIGHT.
ARE YOU KIDDING ME, LUKE? YOU'VE BEEN IN AFRICA FOR OVER TWO MONTHS!
I WANTED... NO, I NEEDED TO SEE YOU.
WHAT HAPPENED TO YOUR FACE?
I FOUGHT IN A MIXED MARTIAL ARTS TOURNAMENT IN JOHANNESBURG. THE GOOD NEWS IS I WON.
DID YOUR FATHER SEE YOU LIKE THIS?
HE'S ALREADY ANGRY. I DON'T NEED TO KICK THE HORNETS' NEST.
I MISSED YOU TOO.
REALLY, BECAUSE I THOUGHT I WAS BEING IGNORED. IN TWO MONTHS, YOU TEXTED ME MAYBE FIVE TIMES, E-MAILED TWICE AND CALLED ONCE.
ANYWAY, I CAME OVER TO BREAK UP.
SERIOUSLY?

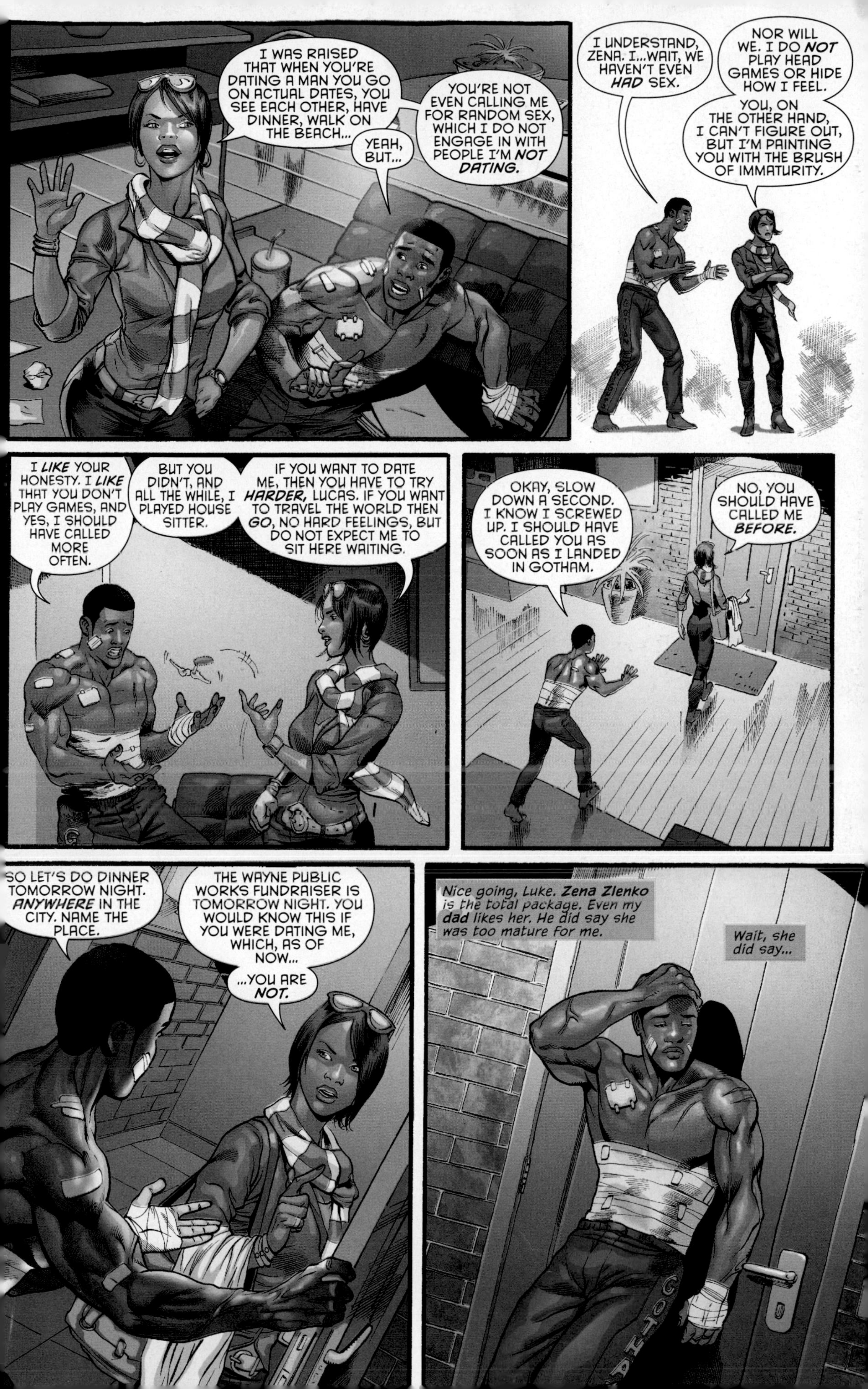
I WAS RAISED THAT WHEN YOU'RE DATING A MAN YOU GO ON ACTUAL DATES, YOU SEE EACH OTHER, HAVE DINNER, WALK ON THE BEACH...
YEAH, BUT...
YOU'RE NOT EVEN CALLING ME FOR RANDOM SEX, WHICH I DO NOT ENGAGE IN WITH PEOPLE I'M NOT DATING.
I UNDERSTAND, ZENA. I...WAIT, WE HAVEN'T EVEN HAD SEX.
NOR WILL WE. I DO NOT PLAY HEAD GAMES OR HIDE HOW I FEEL.
YOU, ON THE OTHER HAND, I CAN'T FIGURE OUT, BUT I'M PAINTING YOU WITH THE BRUSH OF IMMATURITY.
I LIKE YOUR HONESTY. I LIKE THAT YOU DON'T PLAY GAMES, AND YES, I SHOULD HAVE CALLED MORE OFTEN.
BUT YOU DIDN'T, AND ALL THE WHILE, I PLAYED HOUSE SITTER.
IF YOU WANT TO DATE ME, THEN YOU HAVE TO TRY HARDER, LUCAS. IF YOU WANT TO TRAVEL THE WORLD THEN GO, NO HARD FEELINGS, BUT DO NOT EXPECT ME TO SIT HERE WAITING.
OKAY, SLOW DOWN A SECOND. I KNOW I SCREWED UP. I SHOULD HAVE CALLED YOU AS SOON AS I LANDED IN GOTHAM.
NO, YOU SHOULD HAVE CALLED ME BEFORE.
SO LET'S DO DINNER TOMORROW NIGHT. ANYWHERE IN THE CITY. NAME THE PLACE.
THE WAYNE PUBLIC WORKS FUNDRAISER IS TOMORROW NIGHT. YOU WOULD KNOW THIS IF YOU WERE DATING ME, WHICH, AS OF NOW...
...YOU ARE NOT.
Nice going, Luke. Zena Zlenko is the total package. Even my dad likes her. He did say she was too mature for me.
Wait, she did say...

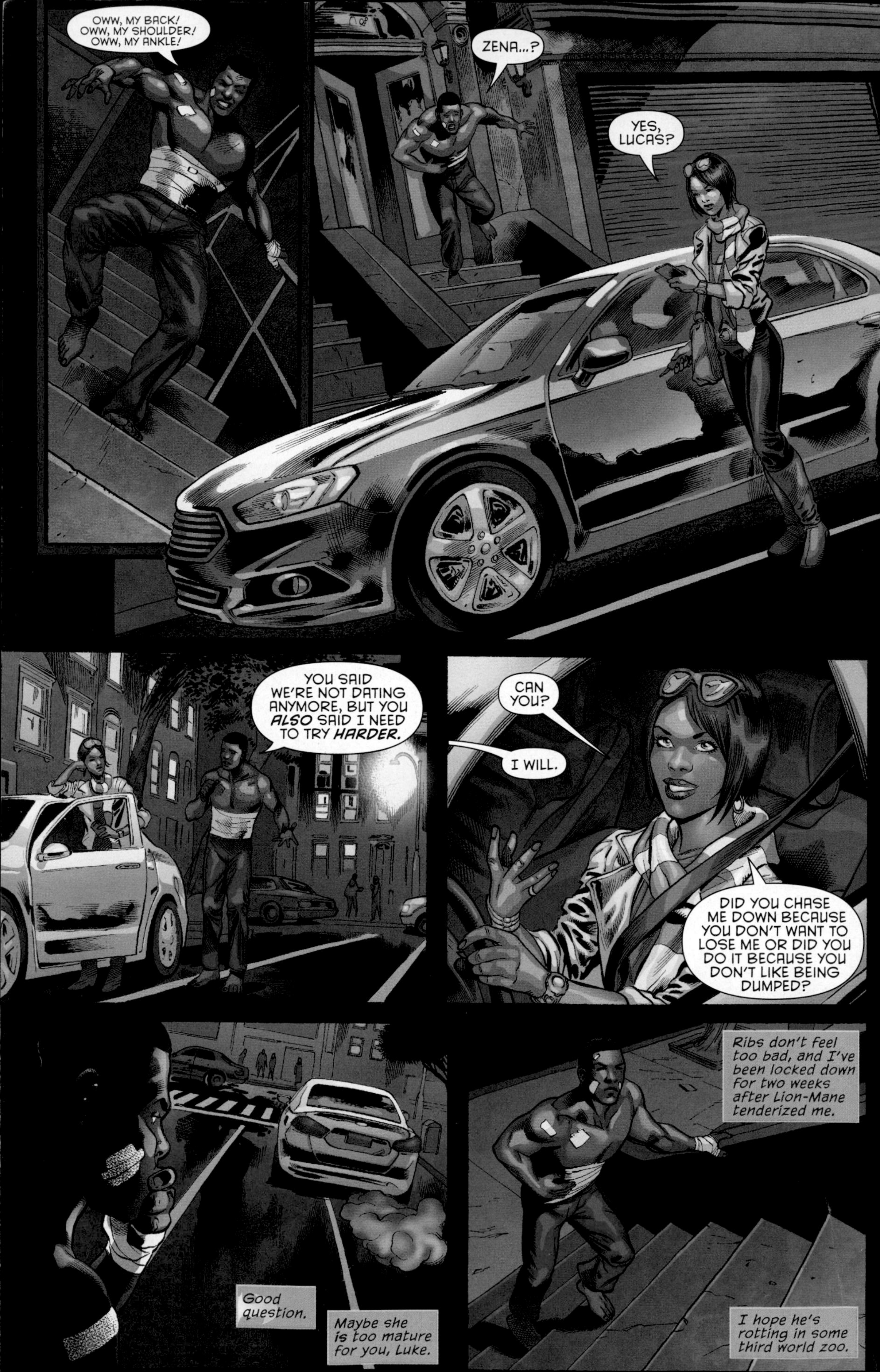
OWW, MY BACK! OWW, MY SHOULDER! OWW, MY ANKLE!
ZENA...?
YES, LUCAS?
YOU SAID WE'RE NOT DATING ANYMORE, BUT YOU *ALSO* SAID I NEED TO TRY *HARDER.*
CAN YOU?
I WILL.
DID YOU CHASE ME DOWN BECAUSE YOU DON'T WANT TO LOSE ME OR DID YOU DO IT BECAUSE YOU DON'T LIKE BEING DUMPED?
Good question.
Maybe she *is* too mature for you, Luke.
Ribs don't feel too bad, and I've been locked down for two weeks after Lion-Mane tenderized me.
I hope he's rotting in some third world zoo.

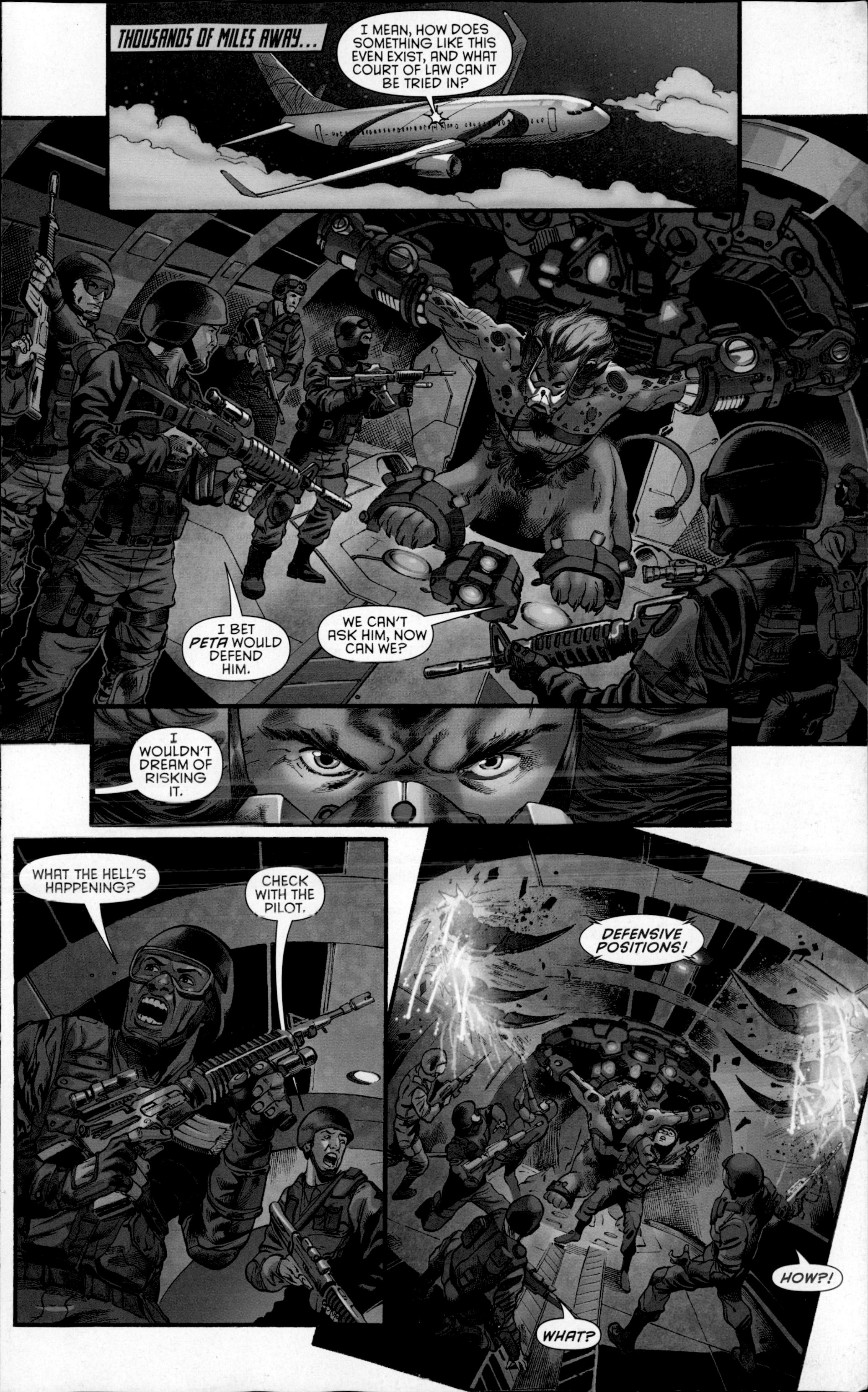
THOUSANDS OF MILES AWAY...
I MEAN, HOW DOES SOMETHING LIKE THIS EVEN EXIST, AND WHAT COURT OF LAW CAN IT BE TRIED IN?
I BET *PETA* WOULD DEFEND HIM.
WE CAN'T ASK HIM, NOW CAN WE?
I WOULDN'T DREAM OF RISKING IT.
WHAT THE HELL'S HAPPENING?
CHECK WITH THE PILOT.
DEFENSIVE POSITIONS!
HOW?!
WHAT?

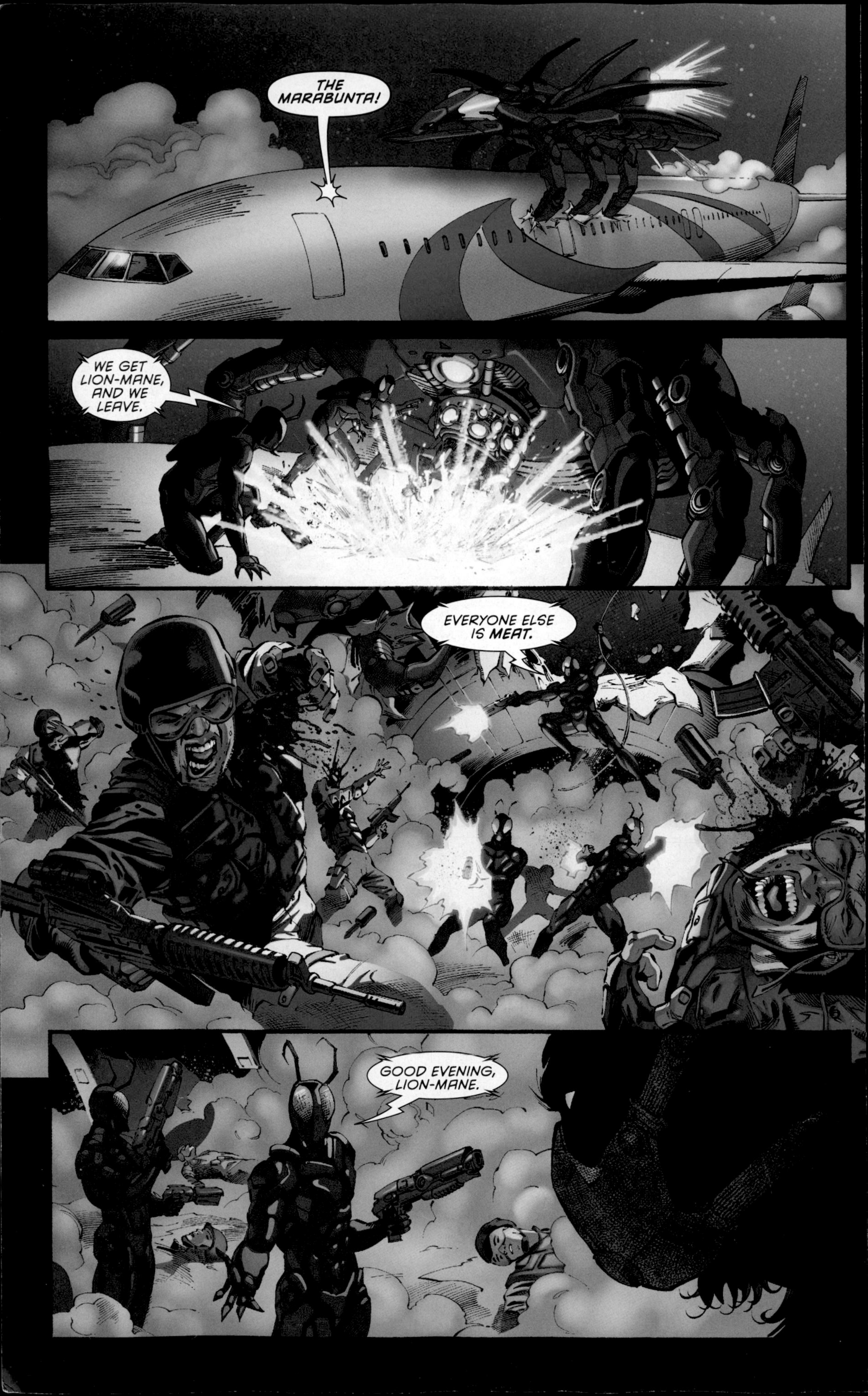
THE MARABUNTA!
WE GET LION-MANE, AND WE LEAVE.
EVERYONE ELSE IS MEAT.
GOOD EVENING, LION-MANE.

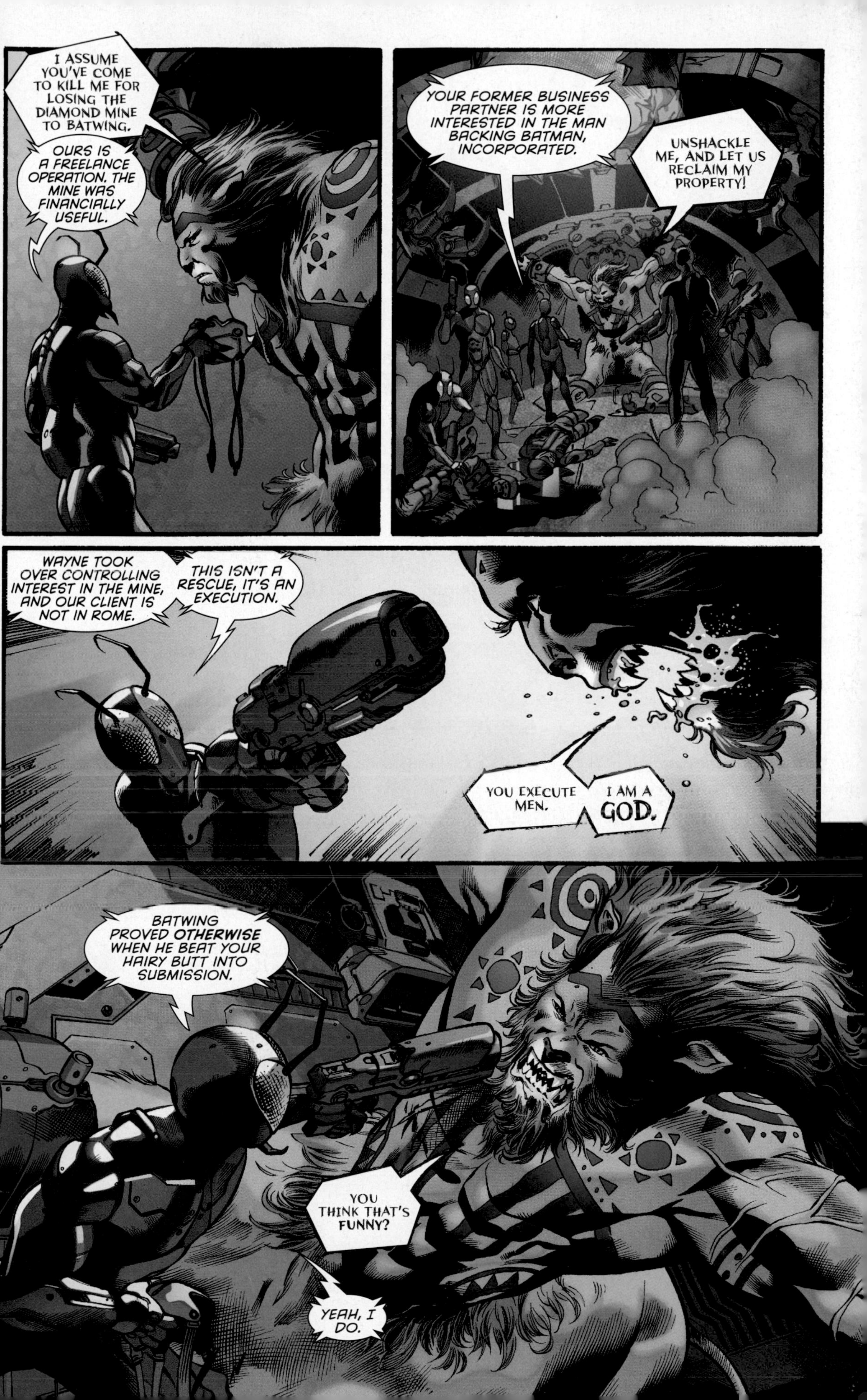
I ASSUME YOU'VE COME TO KILL ME FOR LOSING THE DIAMOND MINE TO BATWING.
OURS IS A FREELANCE OPERATION. THE MINE WAS FINANCIALLY USEFUL.
YOUR FORMER BUSINESS PARTNER IS MORE INTERESTED IN THE MAN BACKING BATMAN, INCORPORATED.
UNSHACKLE ME, AND LET US RECLAIM MY PROPERTY!
WAYNE TOOK OVER CONTROLLING INTEREST IN THE MINE, AND OUR CLIENT IS NOT IN ROME.
THIS ISN'T A RESCUE, IT'S AN EXECUTION.
YOU EXECUTE MEN.
I AM A GOD.
BATWING PROVED **OTHERWISE** WHEN HE BEAT YOUR HAIRY BUTT INTO SUBMISSION.
YOU THINK THAT'S **FUNNY?**
YEAH, I DO.

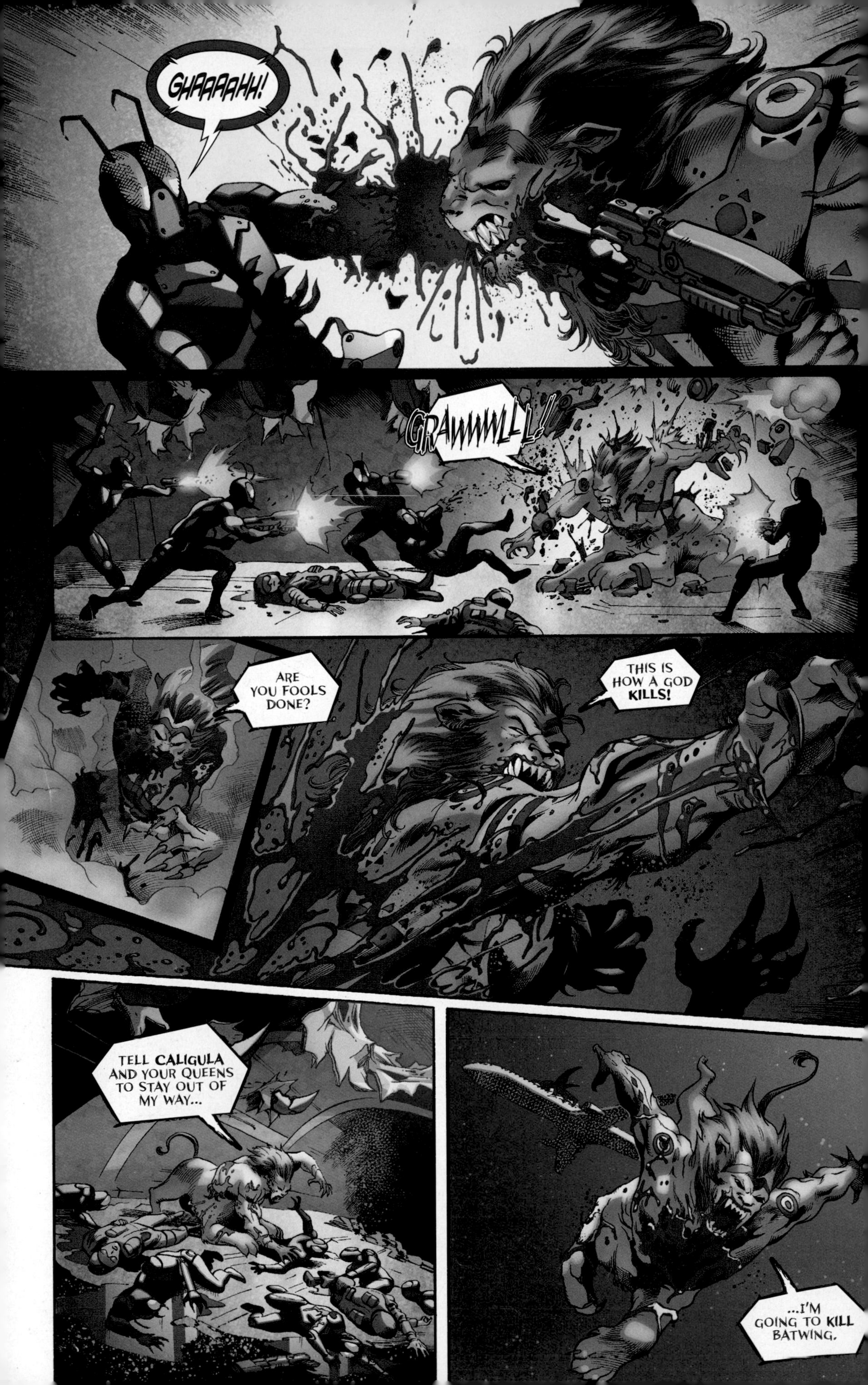
GHAAAAHH!
GRAWWWLLL!
ARE YOU FOOLS DONE?
THIS IS HOW A GOD KILLS!
TELL CALIGULA AND YOUR QUEENS TO STAY OUT OF MY WAY...
...I'M GOING TO KILL BATWING.

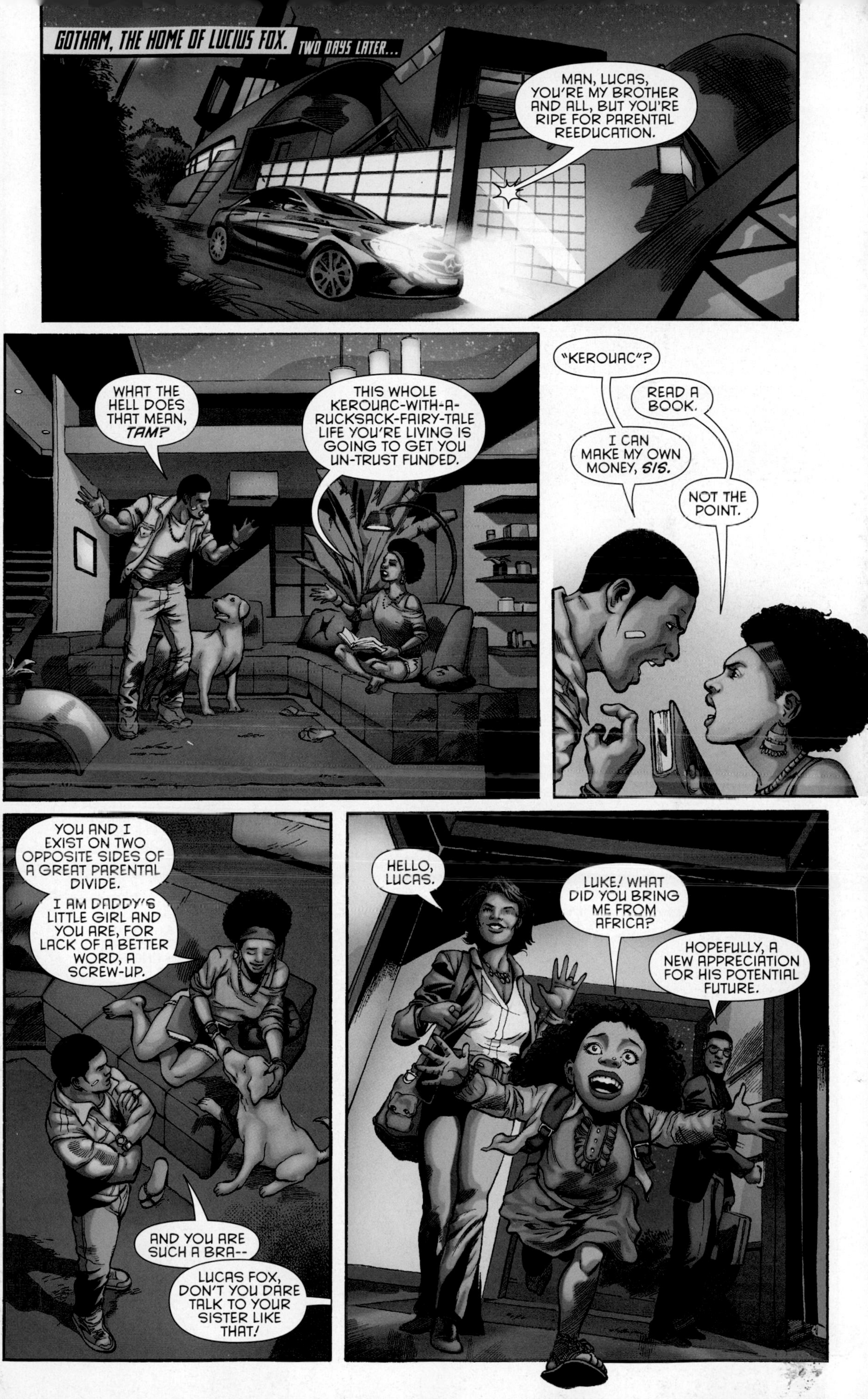
GOTHAM, THE HOME OF LUCIUS FOX.
TWO DAYS LATER...
MAN, LUCAS, YOU'RE MY BROTHER AND ALL, BUT YOU'RE RIPE FOR PARENTAL REEDUCATION.
WHAT THE HELL DOES THAT MEAN, TAM?
THIS WHOLE KEROUAC-WITH-A-RUCKSACK-FAIRY-TALE LIFE YOU'RE LIVING IS GOING TO GET YOU UN-TRUST FUNDED.
"KEROUAC"?
READ A BOOK.
I CAN MAKE MY OWN MONEY, SIS.
NOT THE POINT.
YOU AND I EXIST ON TWO OPPOSITE SIDES OF A GREAT PARENTAL DIVIDE.
I AM DADDY'S LITTLE GIRL AND YOU ARE, FOR LACK OF A BETTER WORD, A SCREW-UP.
AND YOU ARE SUCH A BRA--
LUCAS FOX, DON'T YOU DARE TALK TO YOUR SISTER LIKE THAT!
HELLO, LUCAS.
LUKE! WHAT DID YOU BRING ME FROM AFRICA?
HOPEFULLY, A NEW APPRECIATION FOR HIS POTENTIAL FUTURE.

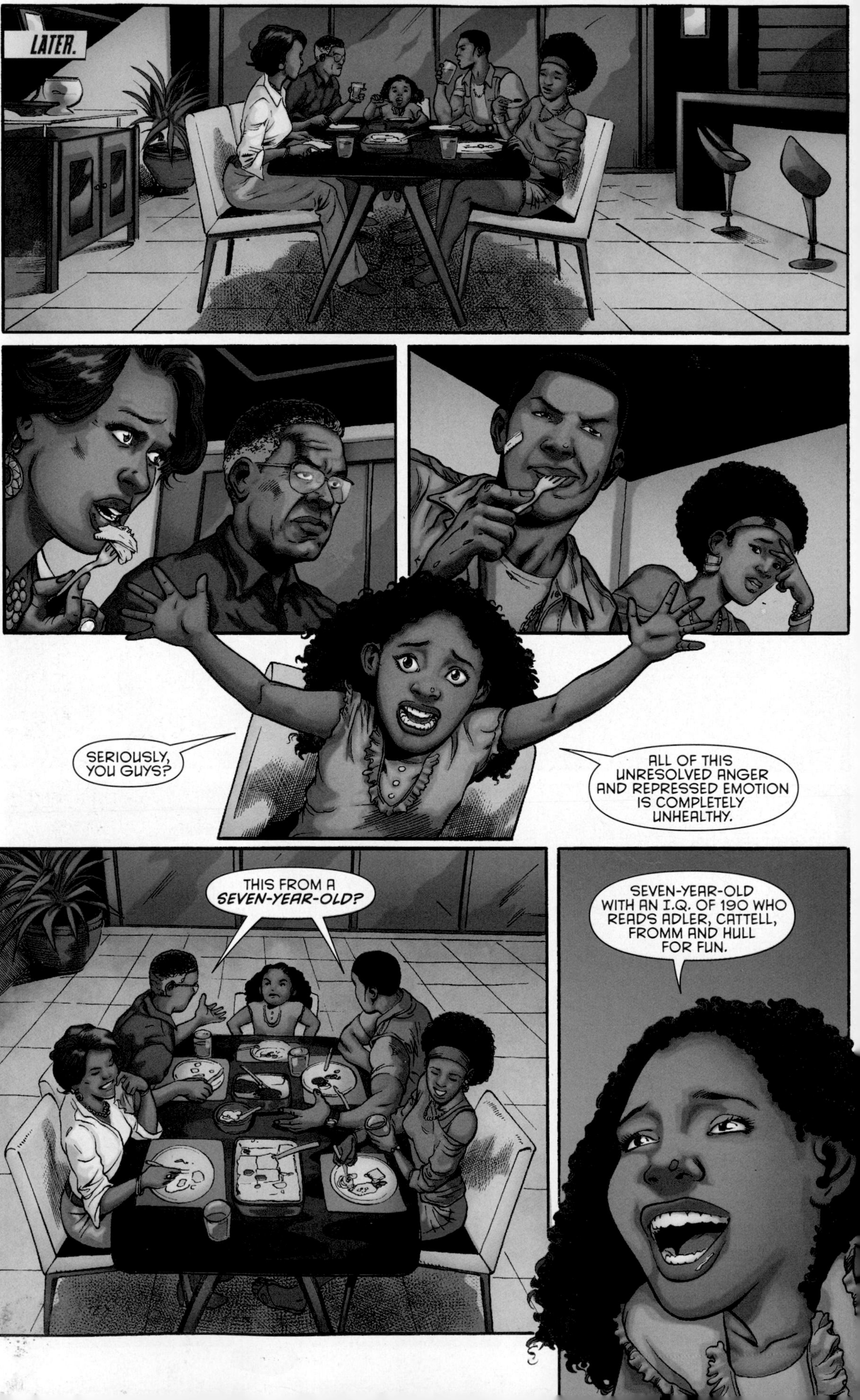

LATER.
SERIOUSLY, YOU GUYS?
ALL OF THIS UNRESOLVED ANGER AND REPRESSED EMOTION IS COMPLETELY UNHEALTHY.
THIS FROM A SEVEN-YEAR-OLD?
SEVEN-YEAR-OLD WITH AN I.Q. OF 190 WHO READS ADLER, CATTELL, FROMM AND HULL FOR FUN.

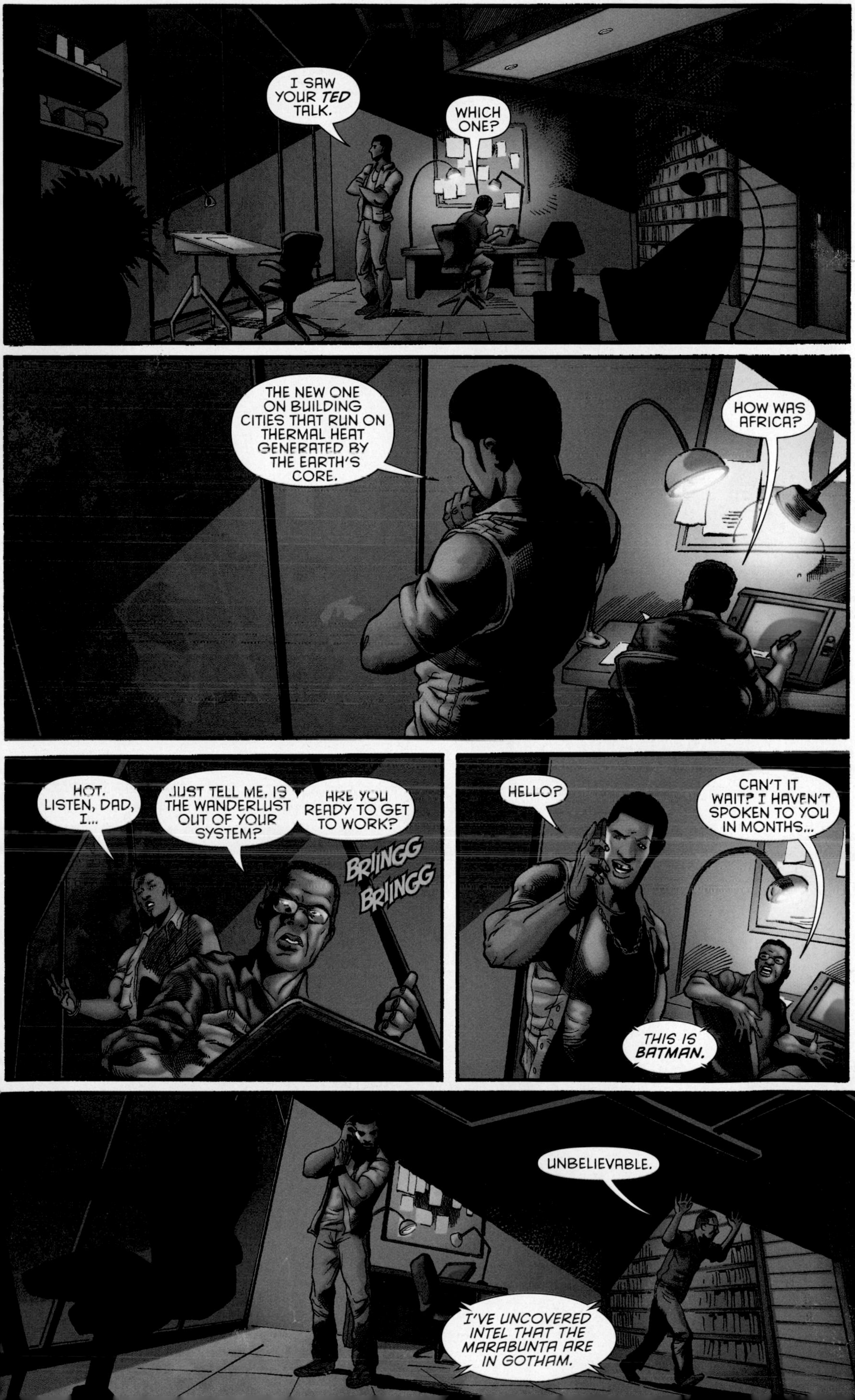

I SAW YOUR *TED* TALK.
WHICH ONE?
THE NEW ONE ON BUILDING CITIES THAT RUN ON THERMAL HEAT GENERATED BY THE EARTH'S CORE.
HOW WAS AFRICA?
HOT. LISTEN, DAD, I...
JUST TELL ME. IS THE WANDERLUST OUT OF YOUR SYSTEM?
ARE YOU READY TO GET TO WORK?
BRIINGG
BRIINGG
HELLO?
CAN'T IT WAIT? I HAVEN'T SPOKEN TO YOU IN MONTHS...
THIS IS ***BATMAN.***
UNBELIEVABLE.
I'VE UNCOVERED INTEL THAT THE MARABUNTA ARE IN GOTHAM.

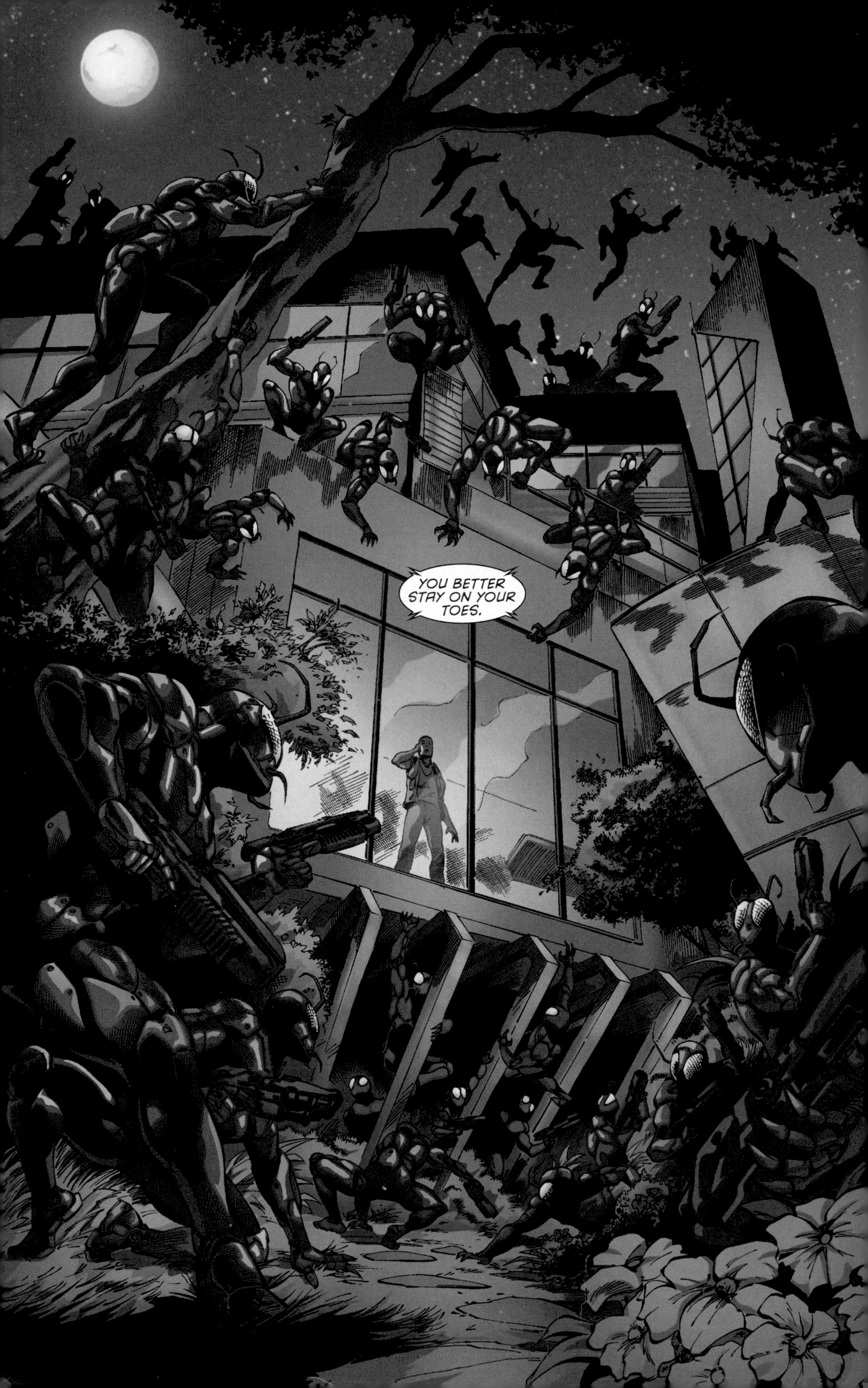
YOU BETTER STAY ON YOUR TOES.

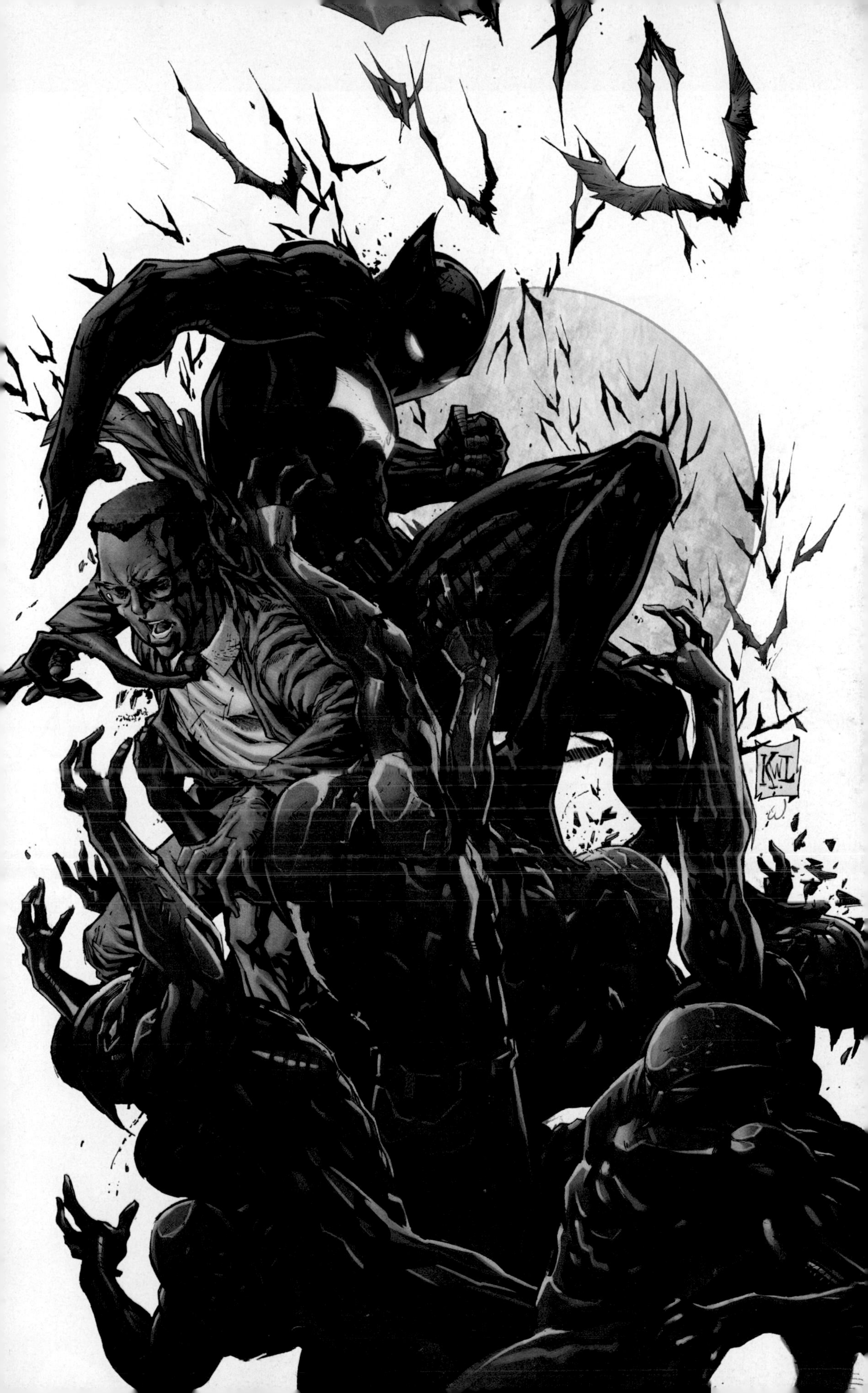

DADDY ISSUES
cover art by **KEN LASHLEY & JASON WRIGHT**

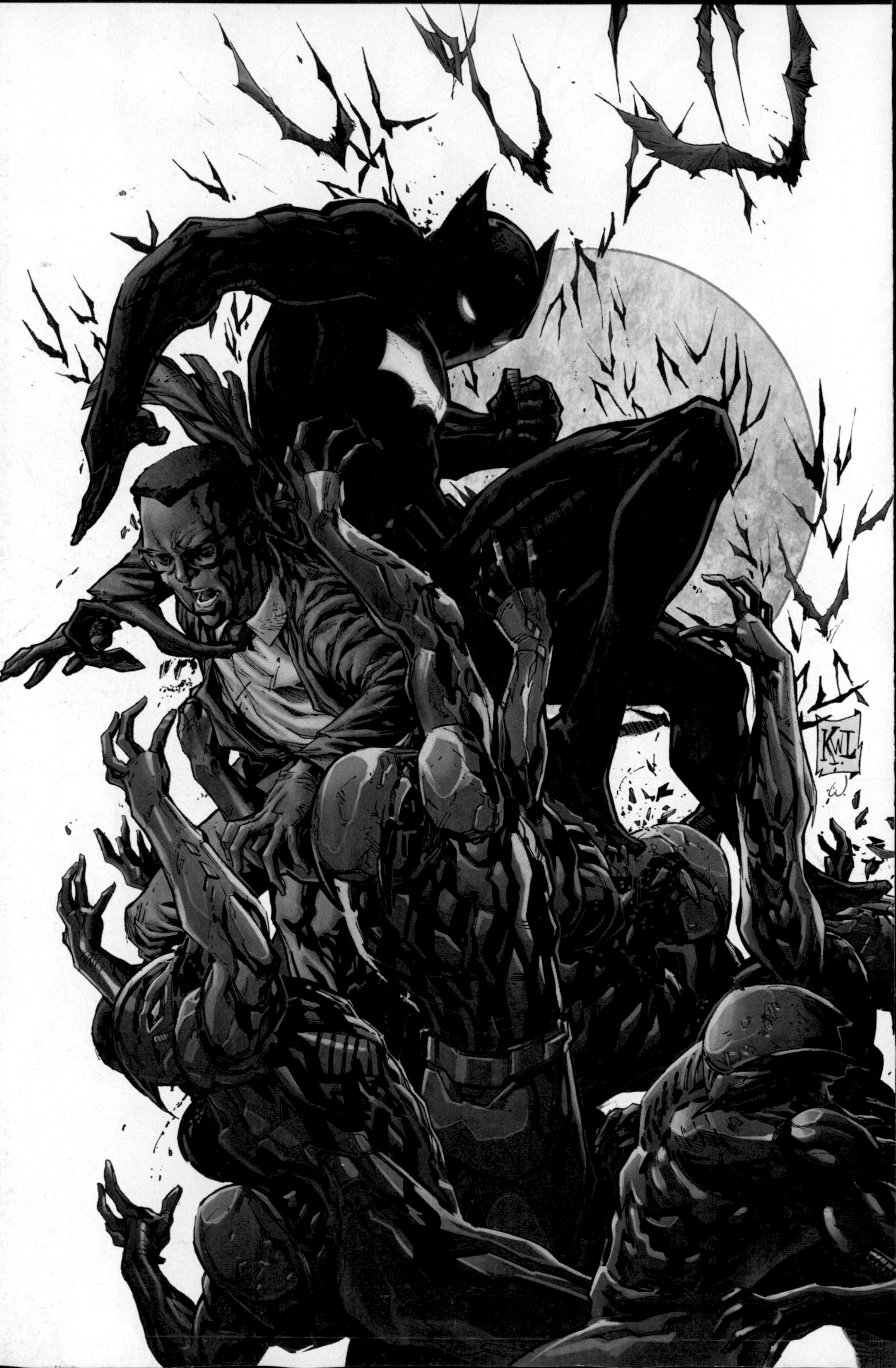

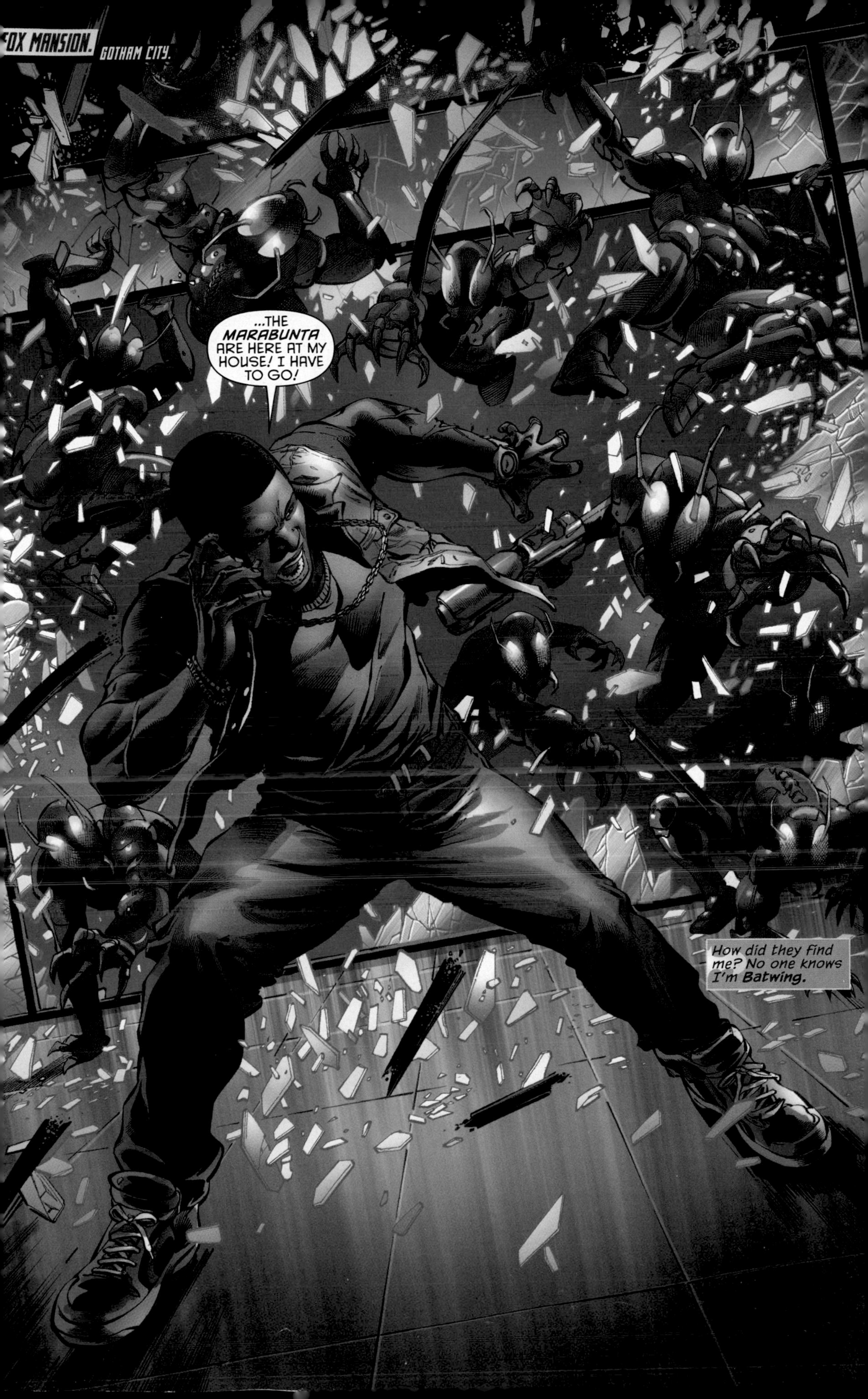
FOX MANSION. GOTHAM CITY.
...THE MARABUNTA ARE HERE AT MY HOUSE! I HAVE TO GO!
How did they find me? No one knows I'm Batwing.

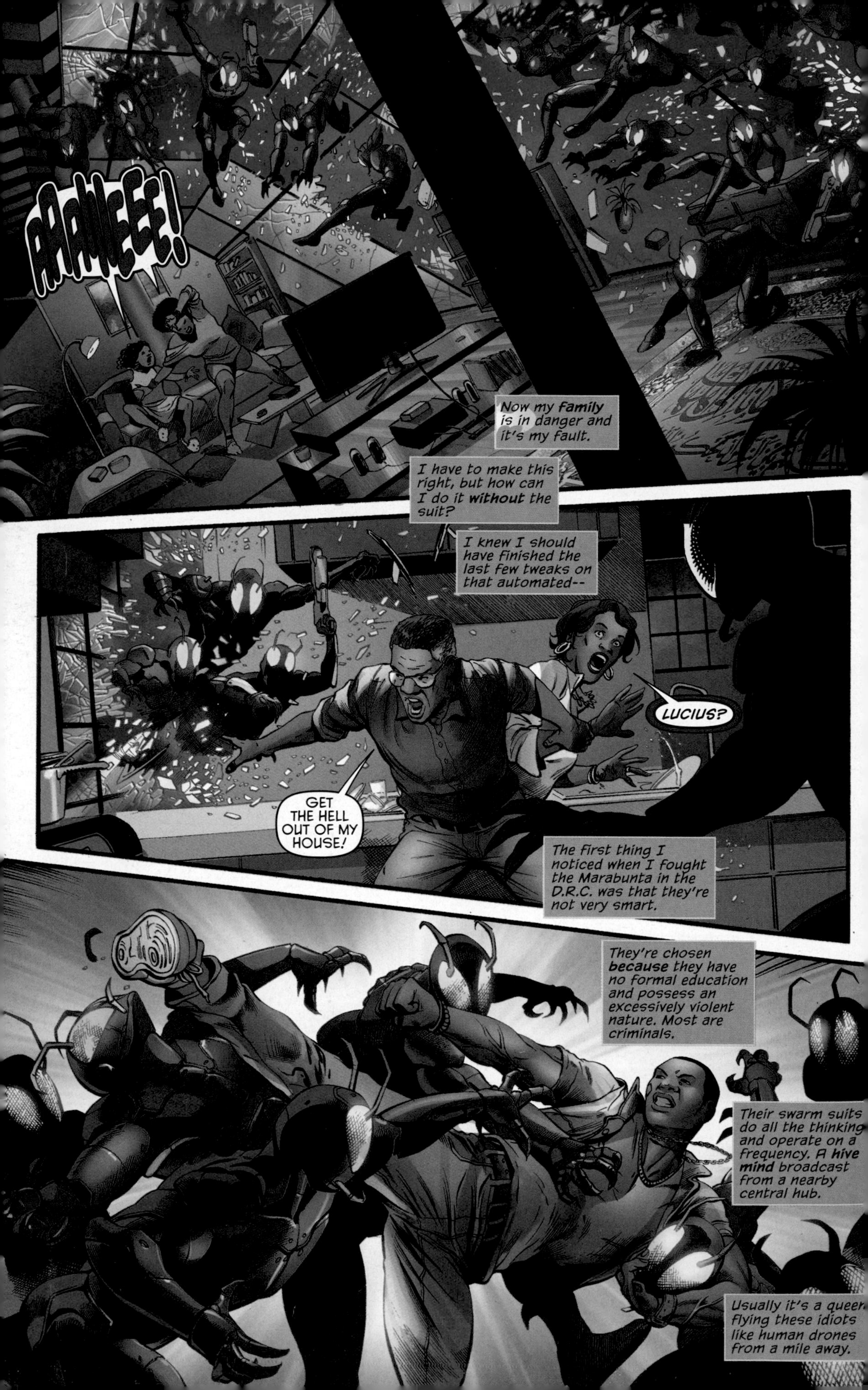
AAAHEEEE!
Now my family is in danger and it's my fault.
I have to make this right, but how can I do it without the suit?
I knew I should have finished the last few tweaks on that automated--
LUCIUS?
GET THE HELL OUT OF MY HOUSE!
The first thing I noticed when I fought the Marabunta in the D.R.C. was that they're not very smart.
They're chosen because they have no formal education and possess an excessively violent nature. Most are criminals.
Their swarm suits do all the thinking and operate on a frequency. A hive mind broadcast from a nearby central hub.
Usually it's a queen flying these idiots like human drones from a mile away.

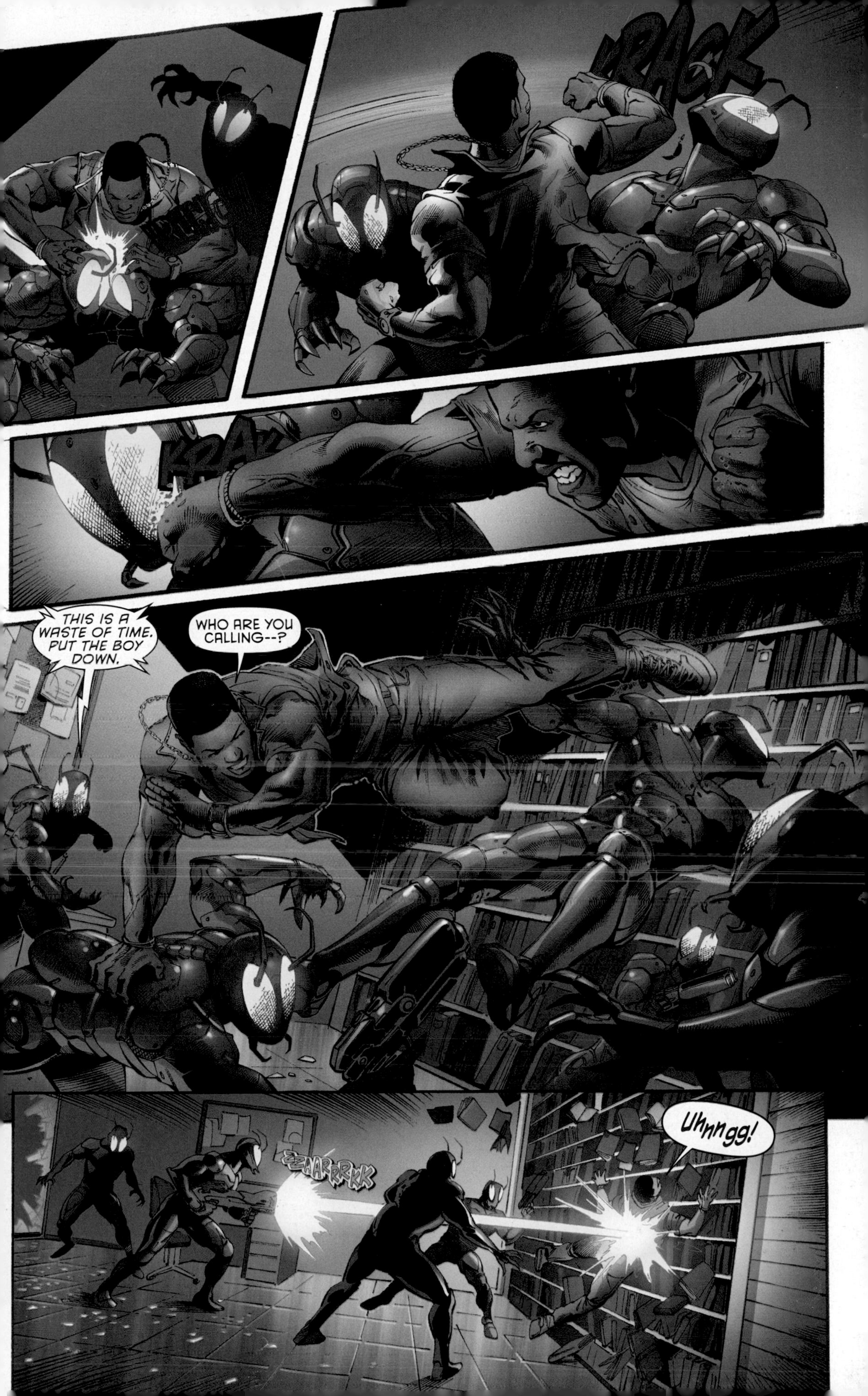

WRACK
KRAK
THIS IS A WASTE OF TIME. PUT THE BOY DOWN.
WHO ARE YOU CALLING--?
ZZAARRRKK
Uhnngg!

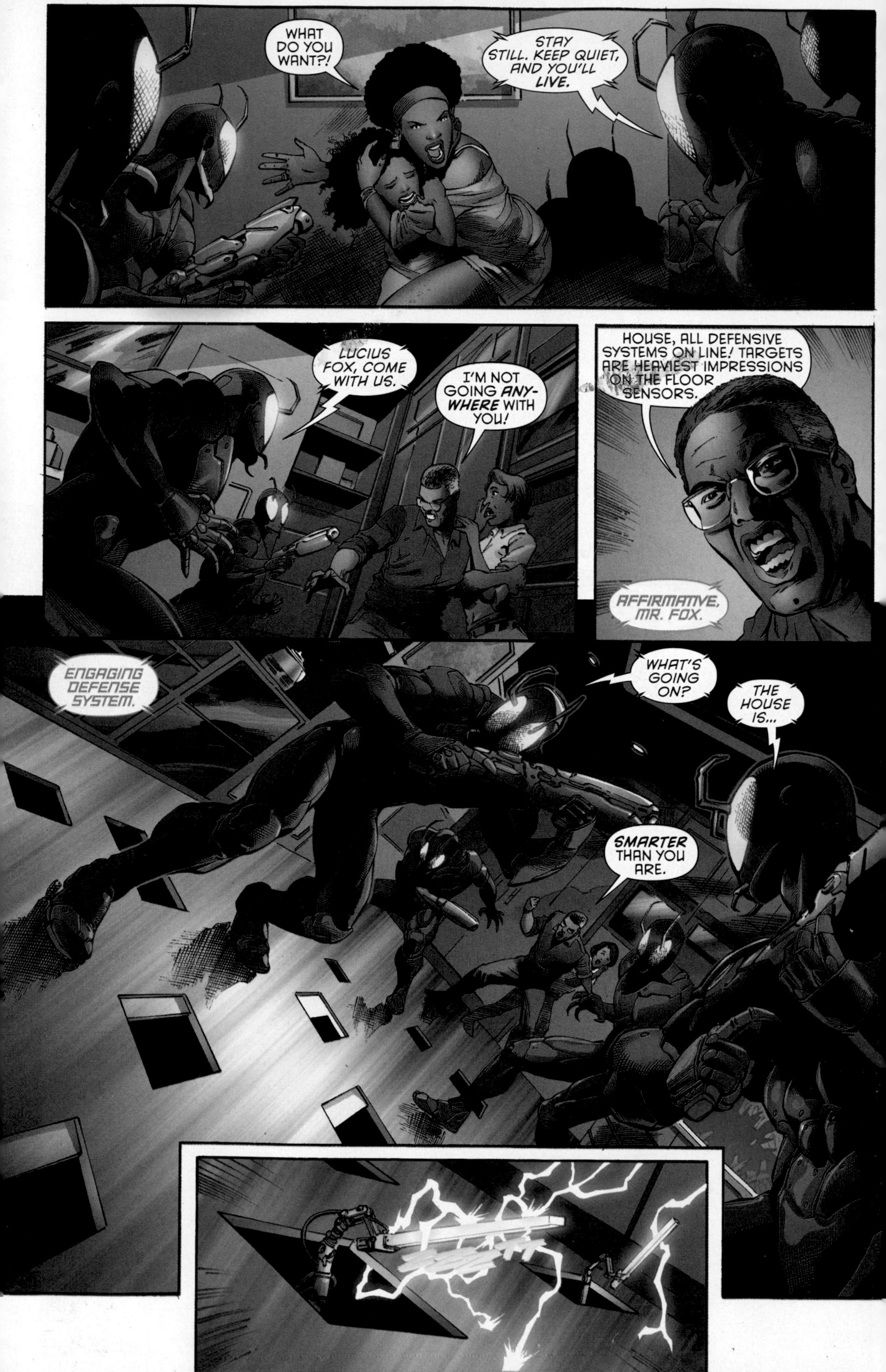
WHAT DO YOU WANT?!
STAY STILL. KEEP QUIET, AND YOU'LL LIVE.
LUCIUS FOX, COME WITH US.
I'M NOT GOING ANYWHERE WITH YOU!
HOUSE, ALL DEFENSIVE SYSTEMS ON LINE! TARGETS ARE HEAVIEST IMPRESSIONS ON THE FLOOR SENSORS.
AFFIRMATIVE, MR. FOX.
ENGAGING DEFENSE SYSTEM.
WHAT'S GOING ON?
THE HOUSE IS...
SMARTER THAN YOU ARE.

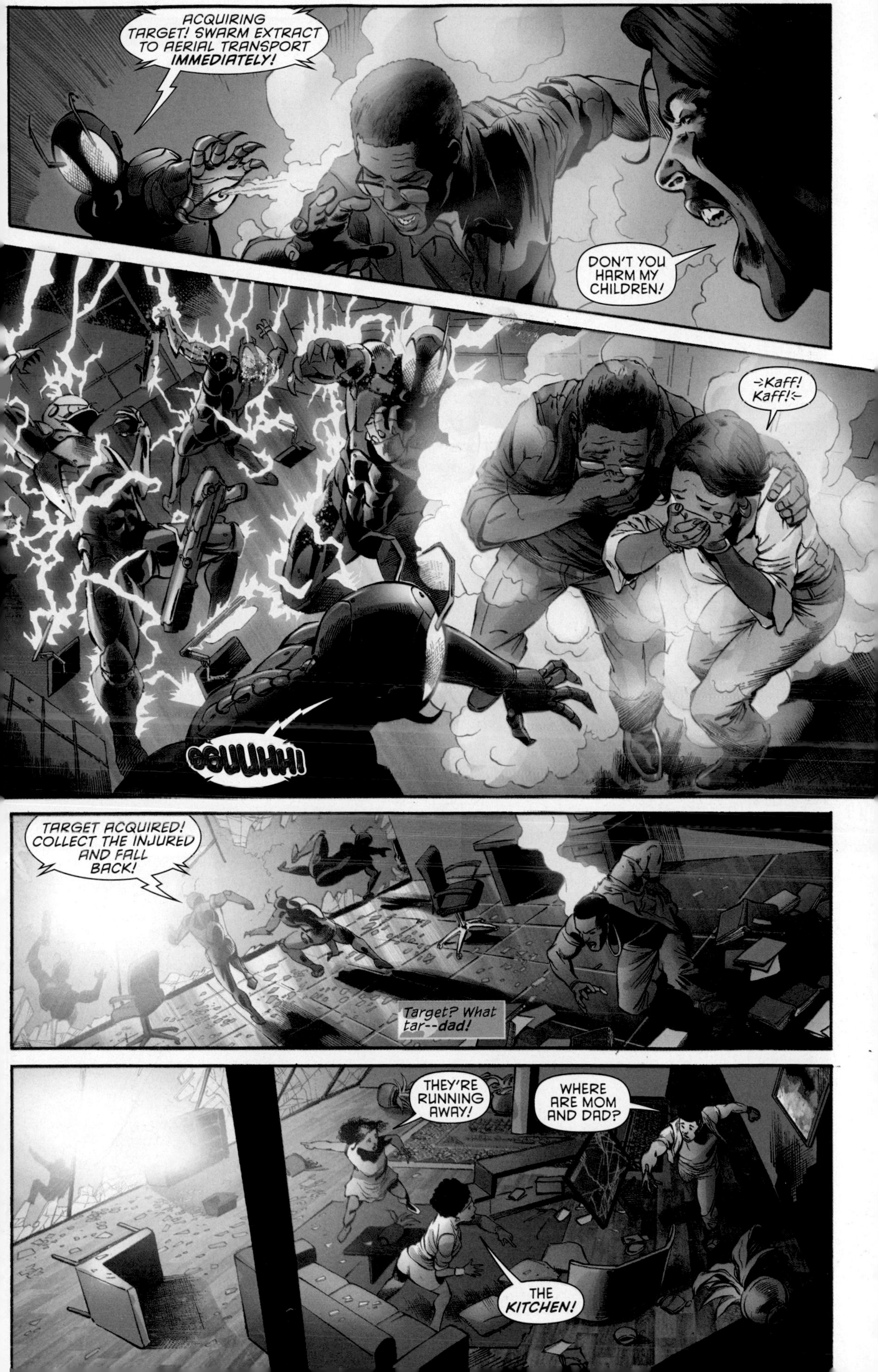
ACQUIRING TARGET! SWARM EXTRACT TO AERIAL TRANSPORT IMMEDIATELY!
DON'T YOU HARM MY CHILDREN!
Kaff! Kaff!
GSUUHH!
TARGET ACQUIRED! COLLECT THE INJURED AND FALL BACK!
Target? What tar--dad!
THEY'RE RUNNING AWAY!
WHERE ARE MOM AND DAD?
THE KITCHEN!

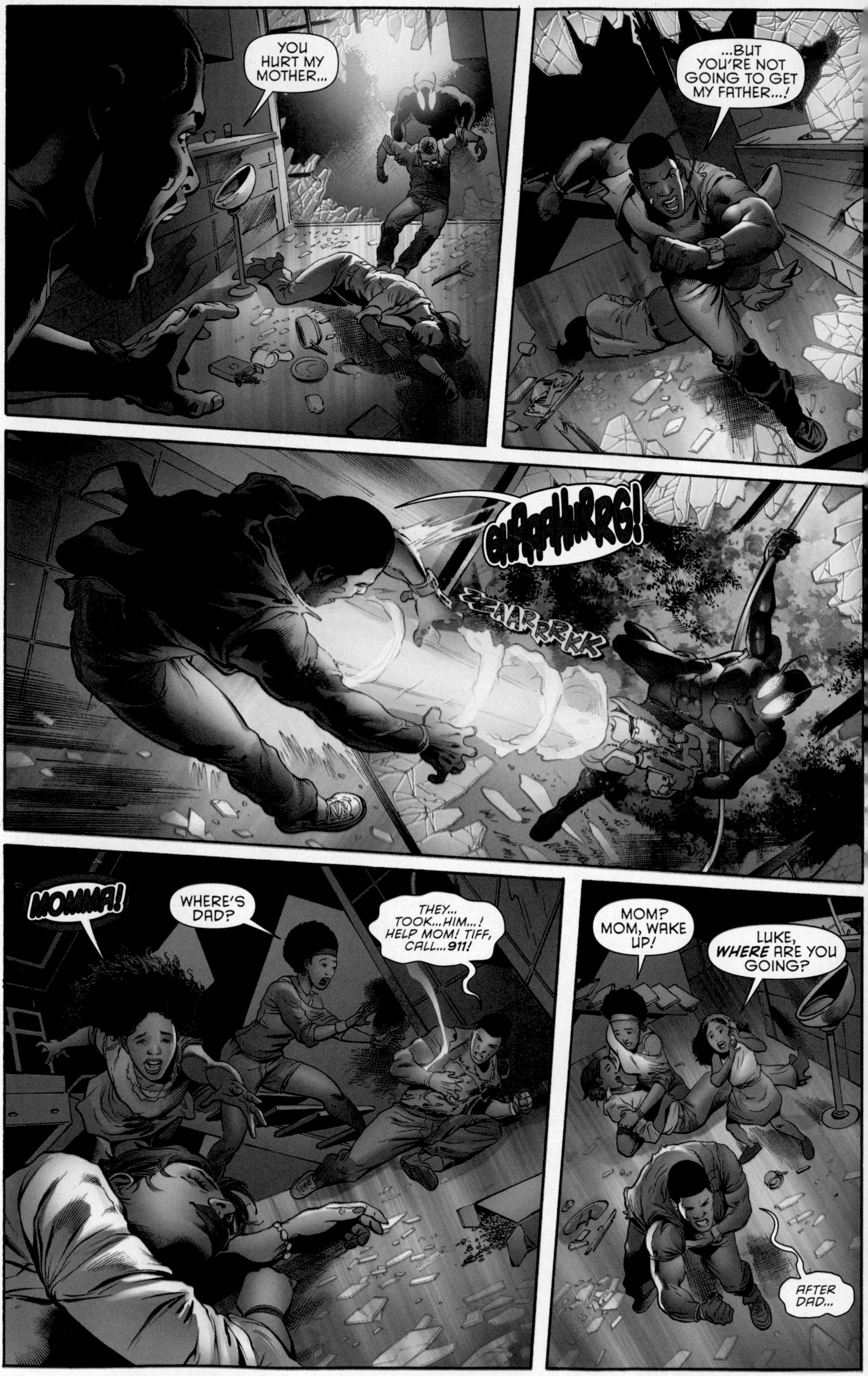
YOU HURT MY MOTHER...
...BUT YOU'RE NOT GOING TO GET MY FATHER...!
GHRAAHHRRG!
ZZAARRRKK
MOMMA!
WHERE'S DAD?
THEY... TOOK...HIM...! HELP MOM! TIFF, CALL...911!
MOM? MOM, WAKE UP!
LUKE, WHERE ARE YOU GOING?
AFTER DAD...

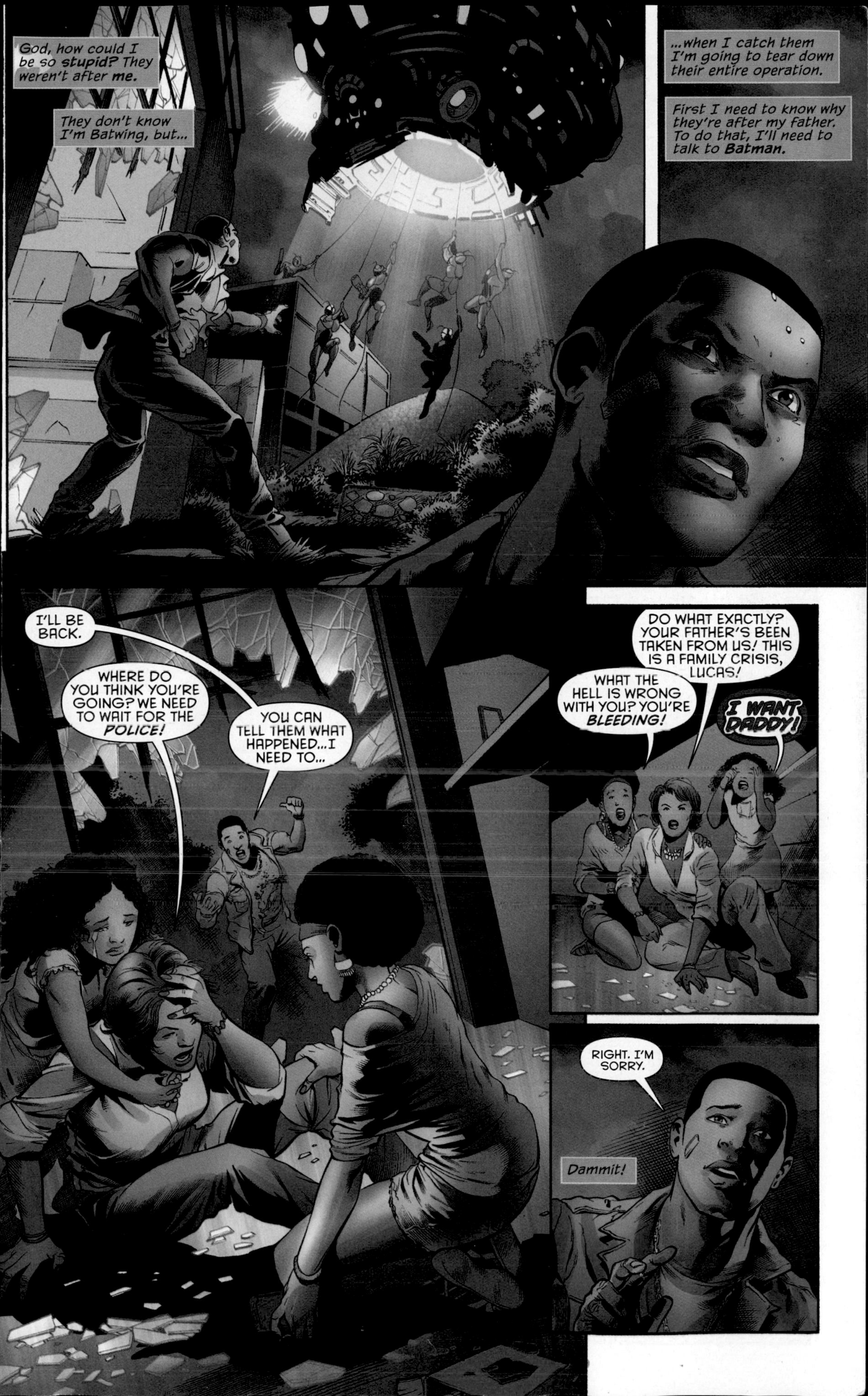
God, how could I be so stupid? They weren't after me.
They don't know I'm Batwing, but...
...when I catch them I'm going to tear down their entire operation.
First I need to know why they're after my father. To do that, I'll need to talk to Batman.
I'LL BE BACK.
WHERE DO YOU THINK YOU'RE GOING? WE NEED TO WAIT FOR THE POLICE!
YOU CAN TELL THEM WHAT HAPPENED...I NEED TO...
WHAT THE HELL IS WRONG WITH YOU? YOU'RE BLEEDING!
DO WHAT EXACTLY? YOUR FATHER'S BEEN TAKEN FROM US! THIS IS A FAMILY CRISIS, LUCAS!
I WANT DADDY!
RIGHT. I'M SORRY.
Dammit!

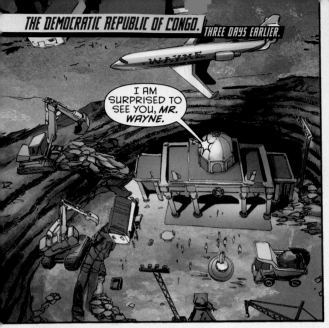

THE DEMOCRATIC REPUBLIC OF CONGO.
THREE DAYS EARLIER.
WAYNE
I AM SURPRISED TO SEE YOU, MR. WAYNE.
I WANTED THE OPPORTUNITY TO SURVEY THE SITE AND CHANGES WAYNE ENTERPRISES HAS IMPLEMENTED FOLLOWING THE MINE'S EXPOSURE, MR. MOBUTU.
MY GOVERNMENT HAS PUBLICLY APOLOGIZED FOR OUR FORMER BUSINESS PARTNER'S ACTIONS HERE.
GOOD. I'D LIKE TO SEE YOUR GOVERNMENT OFFER COMPENSATION TO THE WORKERS AND THEIR FAMILIES TO COINCIDE WITH THE FAIR WAGES I'M OFFERING AND THE NEW HOUSING DEVELOPMENT UNDER CONSTRUCTION ON THE SOUTH RIDGE.
I SEE YOU'VE DONE WONDERS WITH THE AREA, MR. WAYNE.
MY NAME IS ATTICUS FONTAINE. I REPRESENT THE GLOBAL INTERESTS OF SECLORUM, THE PARENT COMPANY OF THE IMPERIAL DIAMOND EXCHANGE.
THE I.D.E. WERE OPERATING THIS MINE ILLEGALLY, WHICH MEANS YOU TOO WERE...
ALAS, MR. WAYNE, WITH A CORPORATION AS LARGE AS SECLORUM, IT IS SOMETIMES IMPOSSIBLE TO KEEP TRACK OF EVERY ENTERPRISE.
AS YOU RECENTLY WITNESSED WITH THE FINANCIAL COLLAPSE, THERE ARE INSTANCES WHERE EMPLOYEES ARE NOT ACTING IN THE BEST INTERESTS OF THEIR PARENT COMPANY.
I'VE COME TO HELP SMOOTH THINGS OVER WITH MR. MOBUTU'S GOVERNMENT AND THE PEOPLE OF THE D.R.C.
I'M ALSO AUTHORIZED ON BEHALF OF SECLORUM TO OFFER YOU A SUBSTANTIAL SUM OF MONEY IN THE HOPE THAT WE COULD REPURCHASE THE MINE.
WHAT'S SO SPECIAL ABOUT THIS PARTICULAR MINE?
IT'S MORE OF A PUBLIC RELATIONS MOVE IN LIGHT OF WHAT HAPPENED HERE.

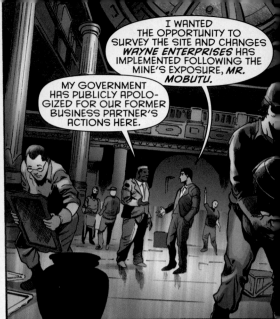

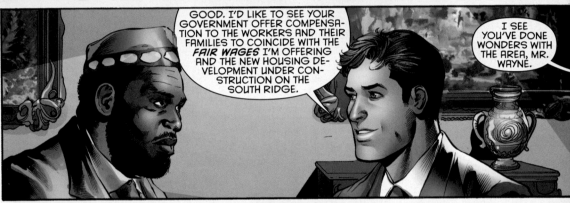

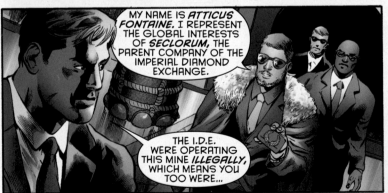

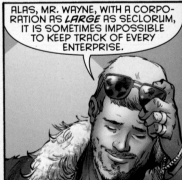

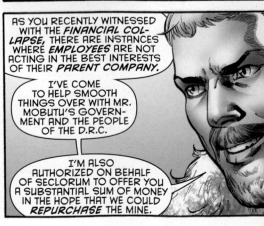

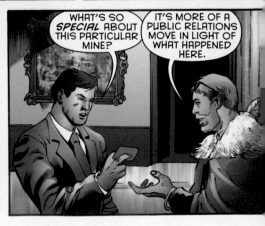

I DON'T BUY IT, MR. FONTAINE.

SECLORUM IS ONE OF THE LARGEST CORPORATIONS ON THE PLANET AND YET MOST PEOPLE, OUTSIDE OF A SELECT FEW, AREN'T *AWARE* OF ITS EXISTENCE.

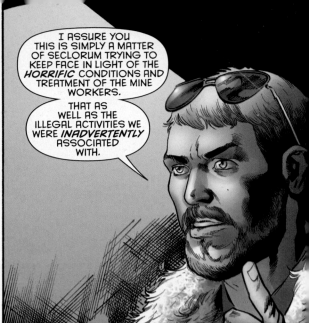

I ASSURE YOU THIS IS SIMPLY A MATTER OF SECLORUM TRYING TO KEEP FACE IN LIGHT OF THE *HORRIFIC* CONDITIONS AND TREATMENT OF THE MINE WORKERS.

THAT AS WELL AS THE ILLEGAL ACTIVITIES WE WERE *INADVERTENTLY* ASSOCIATED WITH.

I HAVE NO INTEREST IN SELLING THE MINE, MR. FONTAINE.

THERE'S A NUMBER ON THE BACK OF MY CARD. IT CONTAINS AN UNGODLY AMOUNT OF ZEROES.

I'M SORRY YOU FLEW ALL THIS WAY, BUT THANK YOU FOR THE OFFER.

YOU WOULD BE WISE TO *RECONSIDER.*

SECLORUM CAN BE A POWERFUL ALLY OR A DANGEROUS... *COMPETITOR.*

ARE YOU *THREATENING* ME, MR. FONTAINE?

JUST DON'T WANT YOU TO THINK WE DIDN'T WARN YOU, MR. WAYNE.

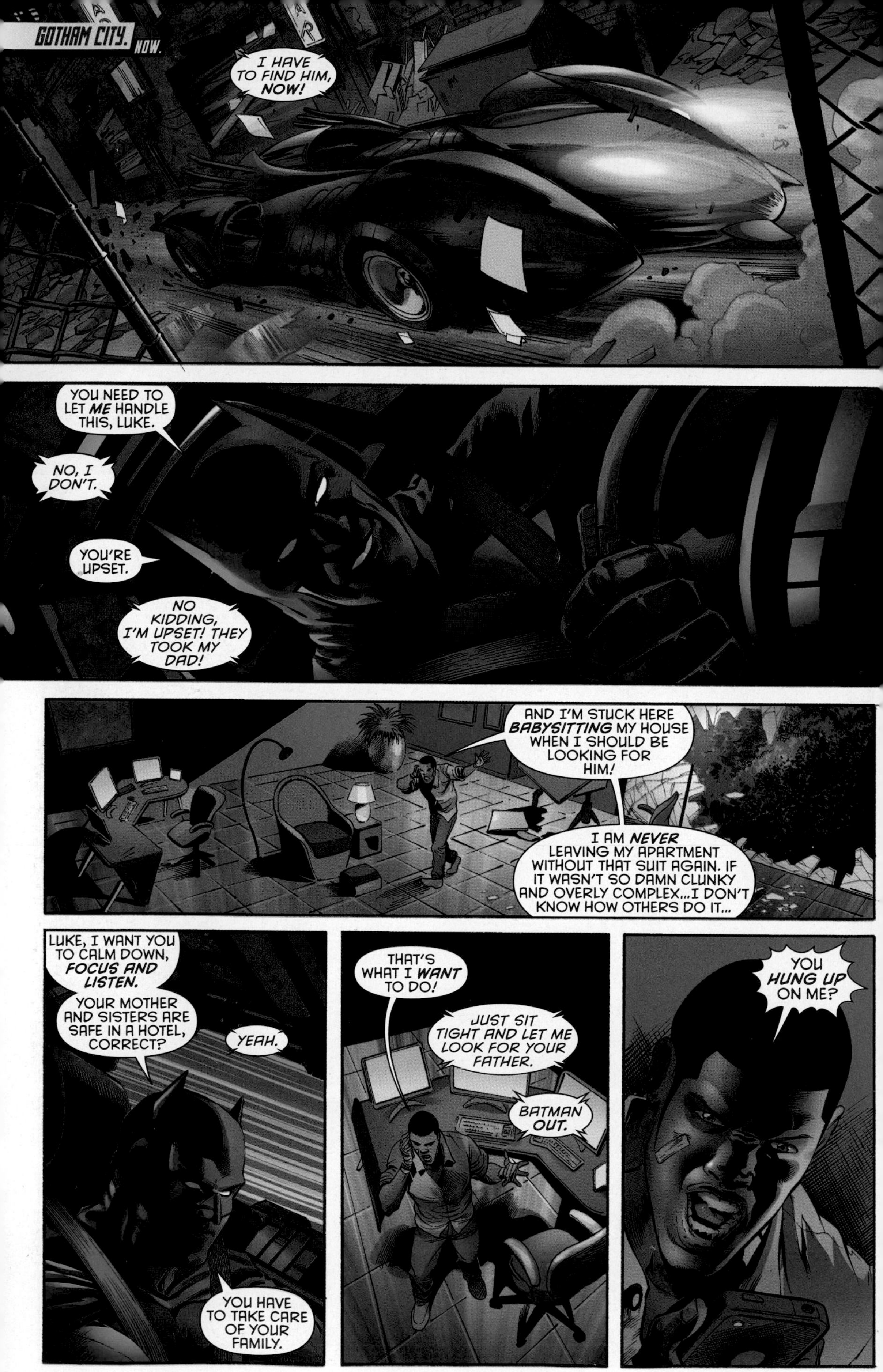
GOTHAM CITY. NOW.
I HAVE TO FIND HIM, NOW!
YOU NEED TO LET ME HANDLE THIS, LUKE.
NO, I DON'T.
YOU'RE UPSET.
NO KIDDING, I'M UPSET! THEY TOOK MY DAD!
AND I'M STUCK HERE BABYSITTING MY HOUSE WHEN I SHOULD BE LOOKING FOR HIM!
I AM NEVER LEAVING MY APARTMENT WITHOUT THAT SUIT AGAIN. IF IT WASN'T SO DAMN CLUNKY AND OVERLY COMPLEX...I DON'T KNOW HOW OTHERS DO IT...
LUKE, I WANT YOU TO CALM DOWN, FOCUS AND LISTEN.
YOUR MOTHER AND SISTERS ARE SAFE IN A HOTEL, CORRECT?
YEAH.
YOU HAVE TO TAKE CARE OF YOUR FAMILY.
THAT'S WHAT I WANT TO DO!
JUST SIT TIGHT AND LET ME LOOK FOR YOUR FATHER.
BATMAN OUT.
YOU HUNG UP ON ME?

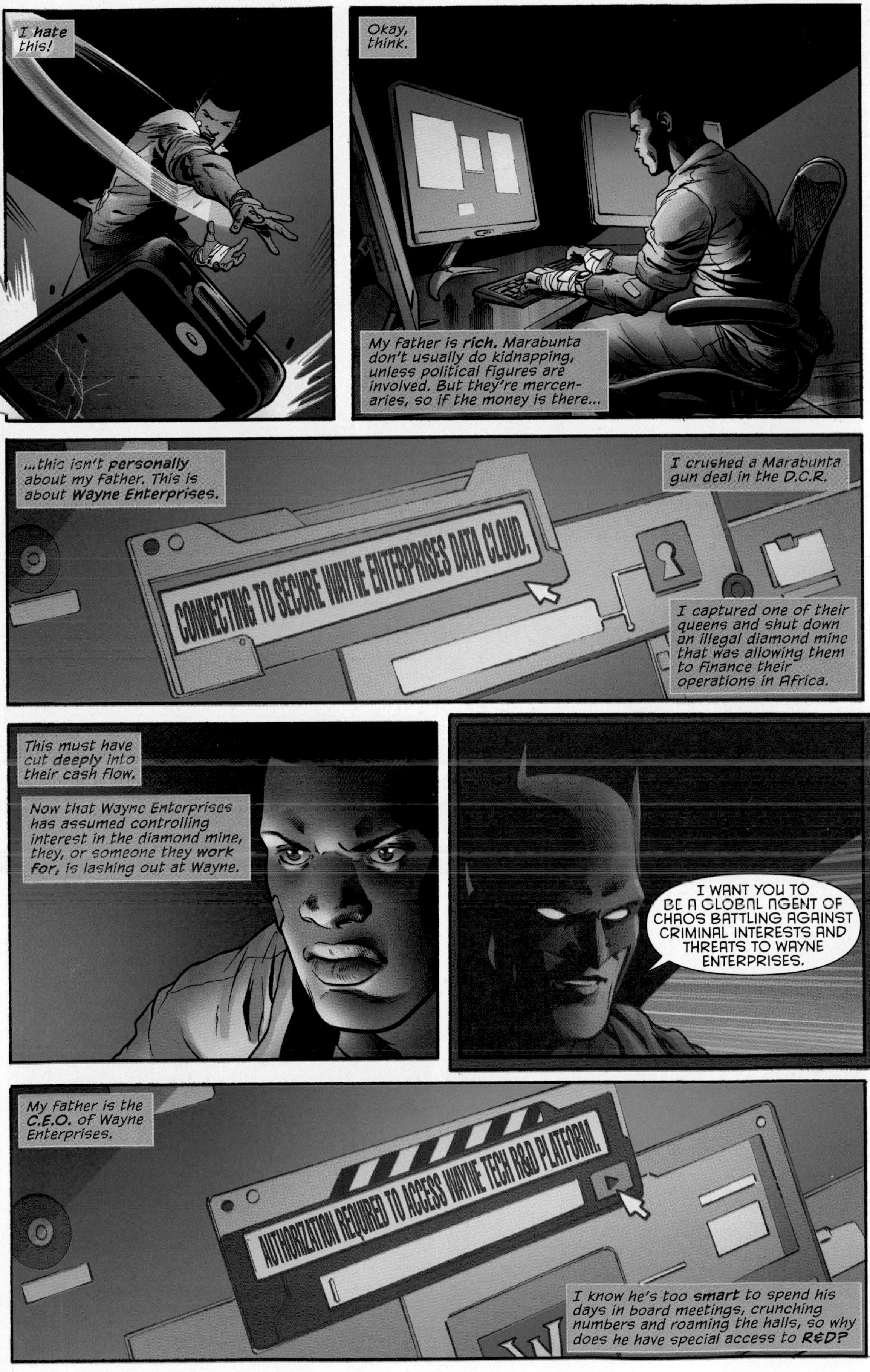
I hate this!
Okay, think.
My father is rich. Marabunta don't usually do kidnapping, unless political figures are involved. But they're mercenaries, so if the money is there...
...this isn't personally about my father. This is about Wayne Enterprises.
CONNECTING TO SECURE WAYNE ENTERPRISES DATA CLOUD.
I crushed a Marabunta gun deal in the D.C.R.
I captured one of their queens and shut down an illegal diamond mine that was allowing them to finance their operations in Africa.
This must have cut deeply into their cash flow.
Now that Wayne Enterprises has assumed controlling interest in the diamond mine, they, or someone they work for, is lashing out at Wayne.
I WANT YOU TO BE A GLOBAL AGENT OF CHAOS BATTLING AGAINST CRIMINAL INTERESTS AND THREATS TO WAYNE ENTERPRISES.
My father is the C.E.O. of Wayne Enterprises.
AUTHORIZATION REQUIRED TO ACCESS WAYNE TECH R&D PLATFORM.
I know he's too smart to spend his days in board meetings, crunching numbers and roaming the halls, so why does he have special access to R&D?

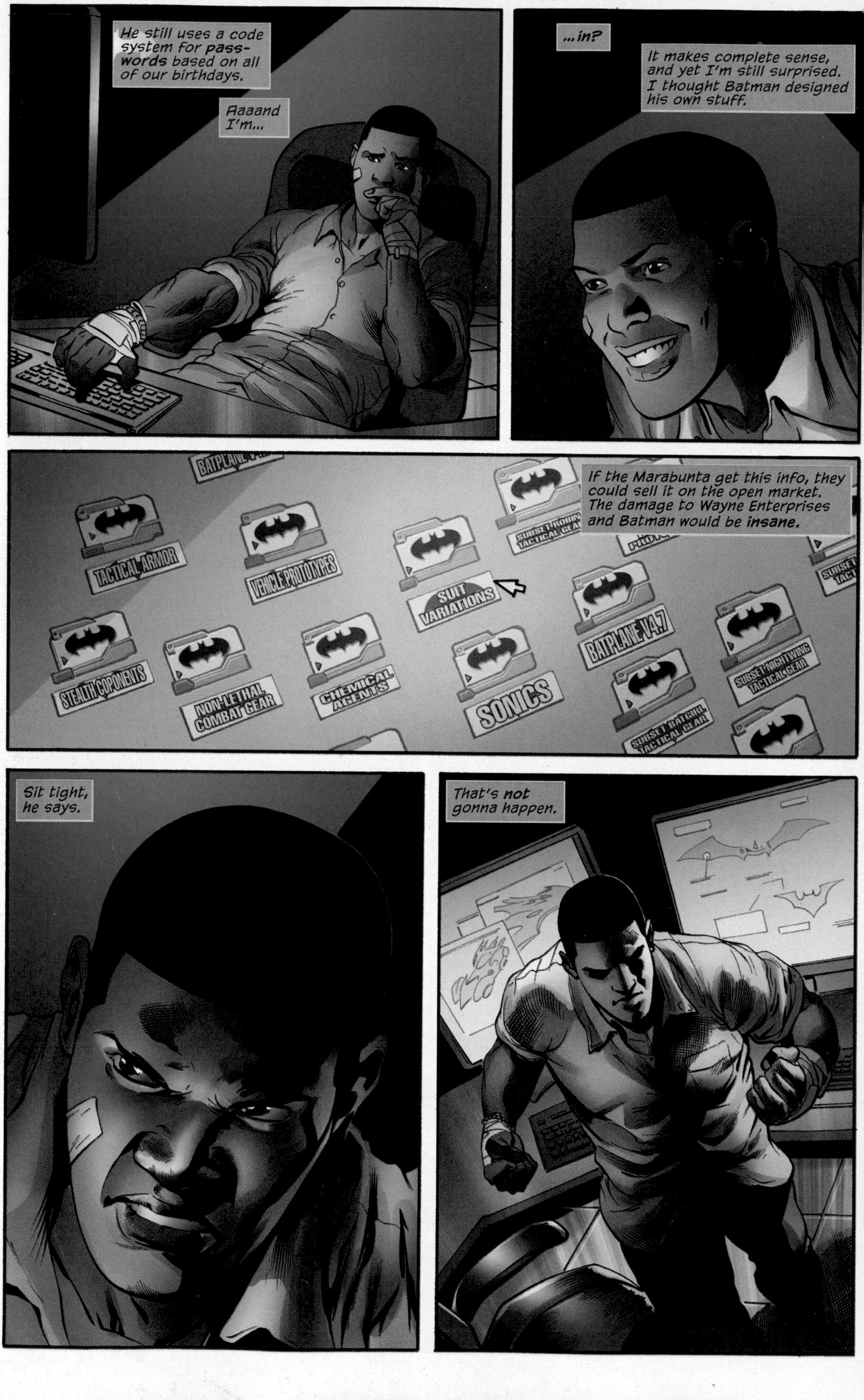
He still uses a code system for **pass-words** based on all of our birthdays.
Aaaand I'm...
...in?
It makes complete sense, and yet I'm still surprised. I thought Batman designed his own stuff.
If the Marabunta get this info, they could sell it on the open market. The damage to Wayne Enterprises and Batman would be **insane.**
TACTICAL ARMOR
VEHICLE PROTOTYPES
SUIT VARIATIONS
BATPLANE V4.7
SUBSET NIGHTWING TACTICAL GEAR
STEALTH COPONENTS
NON-LETHAL COMBAT GEAR
CHEMICAL AGENTS
SONICS
SUBSET BATGIRL TACTICAL GEAR
Sit tight, he says.
That's **not** gonna happen.

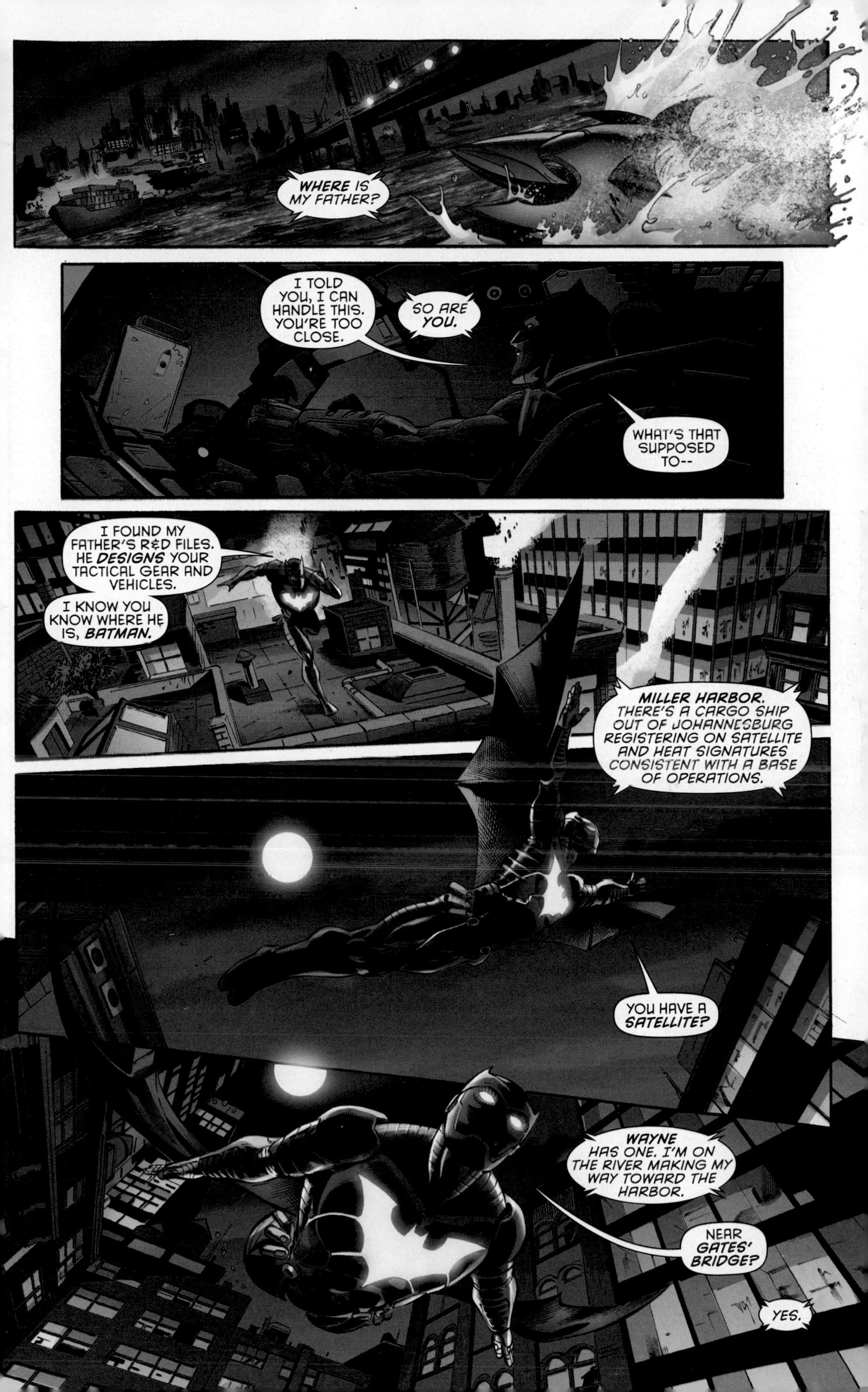
WHERE IS MY FATHER?
I TOLD YOU, I CAN HANDLE THIS. YOU'RE TOO CLOSE.
SO ARE YOU.
WHAT'S THAT SUPPOSED TO--
I FOUND MY FATHER'S R&D FILES. HE DESIGNS YOUR TACTICAL GEAR AND VEHICLES.
I KNOW YOU KNOW WHERE HE IS, BATMAN.
MILLER HARBOR. THERE'S A CARGO SHIP OUT OF JOHANNESBURG REGISTERING ON SATELLITE AND HEAT SIGNATURES CONSISTENT WITH A BASE OF OPERATIONS.
YOU HAVE A SATELLITE?
WAYNE HAS ONE. I'M ON THE RIVER MAKING MY WAY TOWARD THE HARBOR.
NEAR GATES' BRIDGE?
YES.

I'LL BE THERE IN A MINUTE. BATWING OUT.

WHAT THE... *BATMAN?!*

BATWING. I NEED A LIFT.

OFFICIAL SUPERHERO CRIME FIGHTING BUSINESS. ARE YOU IN?

HELLS YEAH. WHERE ARE WE HEADED, *BATWING?*

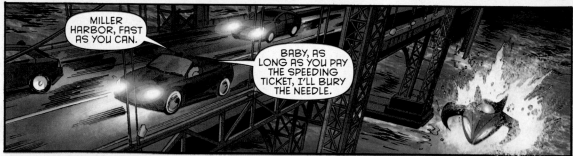

MILLER HARBOR, FAST AS YOU CAN.

BABY, AS LONG AS YOU PAY THE SPEEDING TICKET, I'LL BURY THE NEEDLE.

HANG ON. CHANGE OF PLAN. I SEE MY *RIDE.*

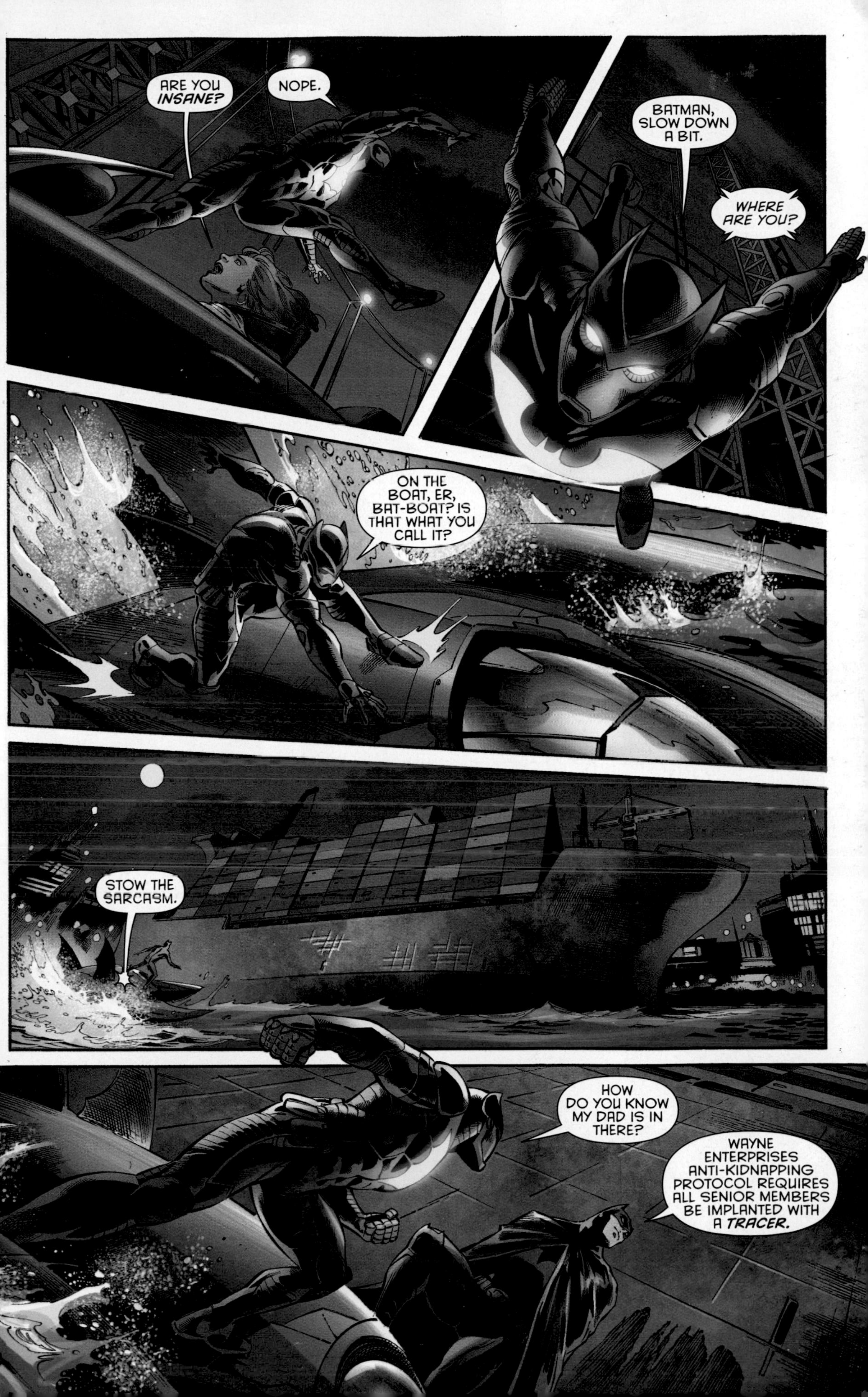
ARE YOU *INSANE?*
NOPE.
BATMAN, SLOW DOWN A BIT.
WHERE ARE YOU?
ON THE BOAT, ER, BAT-BOAT? IS THAT WHAT YOU CALL IT?
STOW THE SARCASM.
HOW DO YOU KNOW MY DAD IS IN THERE?
WAYNE ENTERPRISES ANTI-KIDNAPPING PROTOCOL REQUIRES ALL SENIOR MEMBERS BE IMPLANTED WITH A *TRACER.*

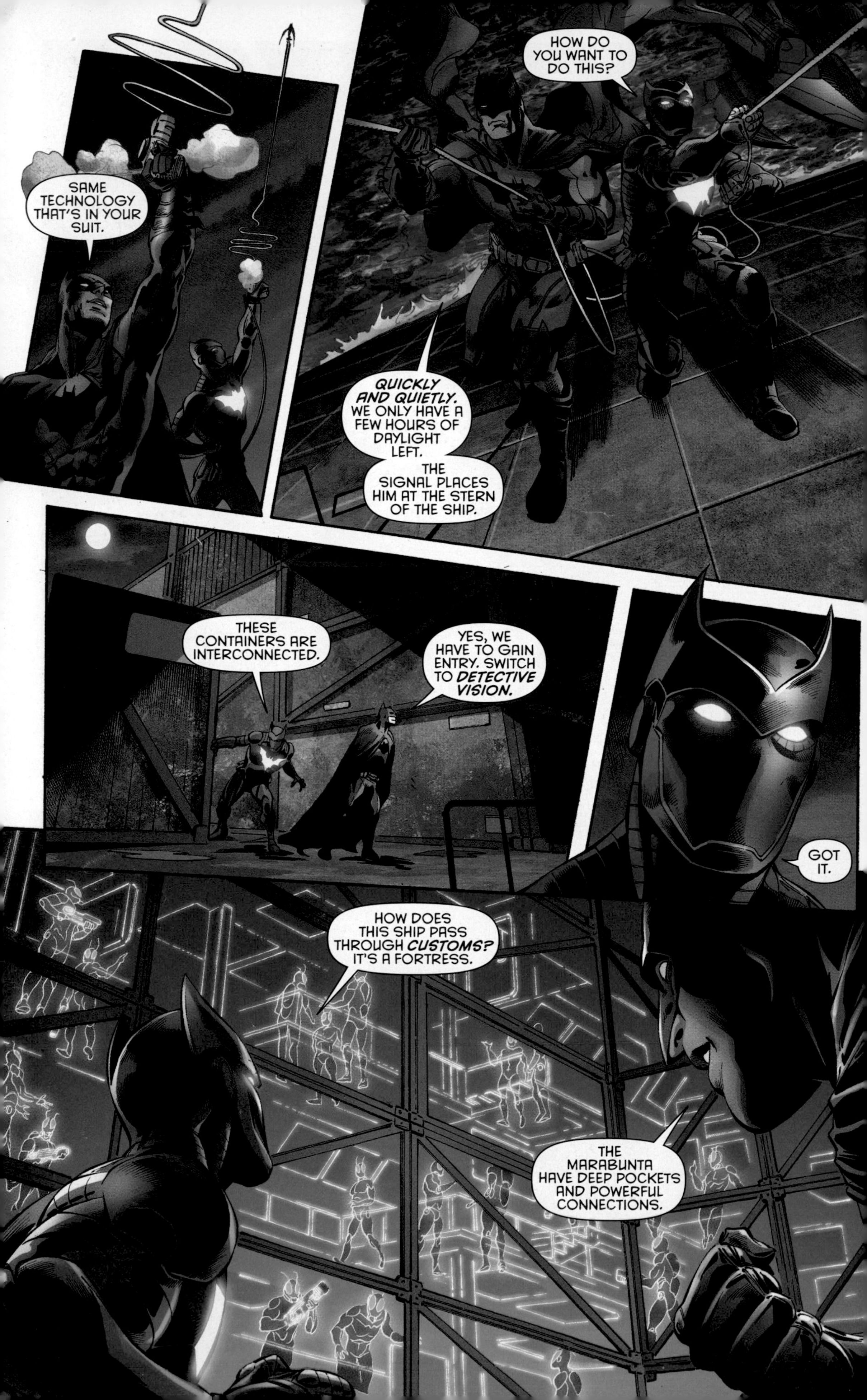
SAME TECHNOLOGY THAT'S IN YOUR SUIT.
HOW DO YOU WANT TO DO THIS?
QUICKLY AND QUIETLY. WE ONLY HAVE A FEW HOURS OF DAYLIGHT LEFT.
THE SIGNAL PLACES HIM AT THE STERN OF THE SHIP.
THESE CONTAINERS ARE INTERCONNECTED.
YES, WE HAVE TO GAIN ENTRY. SWITCH TO *DETECTIVE VISION.*
GOT IT.
HOW DOES THIS SHIP PASS THROUGH *CUSTOMS?* IT'S A FORTRESS.
THE MARABUNTA HAVE DEEP POCKETS AND POWERFUL CONNECTIONS.

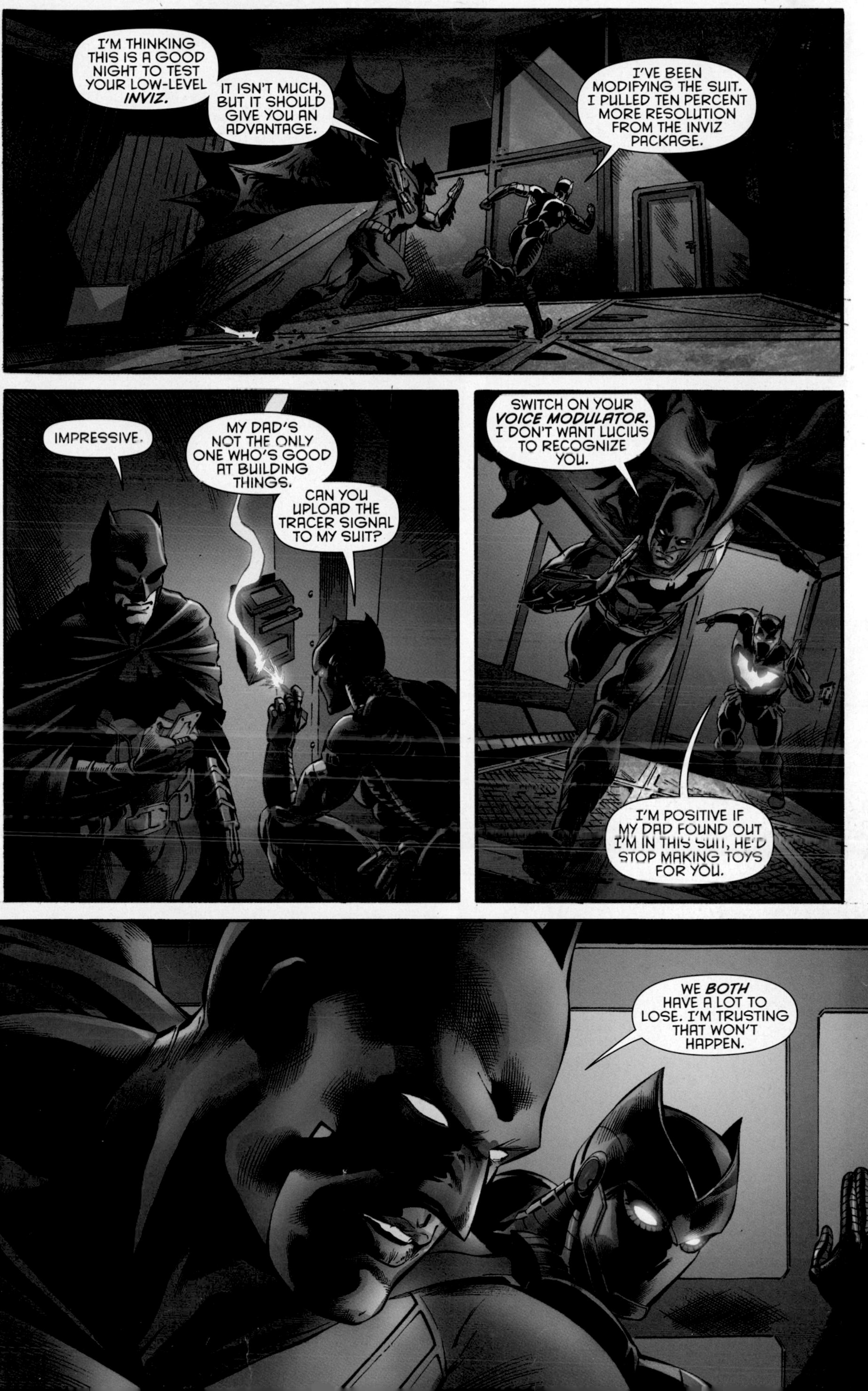
I'M THINKING THIS IS A GOOD NIGHT TO TEST YOUR LOW-LEVEL *INVIZ.*
IT ISN'T MUCH, BUT IT SHOULD GIVE YOU AN ADVANTAGE.
I'VE BEEN MODIFYING THE SUIT. I PULLED TEN PERCENT MORE RESOLUTION FROM THE INVIZ PACKAGE.
IMPRESSIVE.
MY DAD'S NOT THE ONLY ONE WHO'S GOOD AT BUILDING THINGS.
CAN YOU UPLOAD THE TRACER SIGNAL TO MY SUIT?
SWITCH ON YOUR *VOICE MODULATOR.* I DON'T WANT LUCIUS TO RECOGNIZE YOU.
I'M POSITIVE IF MY DAD FOUND OUT I'M IN THIS SUIT, HE'D STOP MAKING TOYS FOR YOU.
WE *BOTH* HAVE A LOT TO LOSE. I'M TRUSTING THAT WON'T HAPPEN.

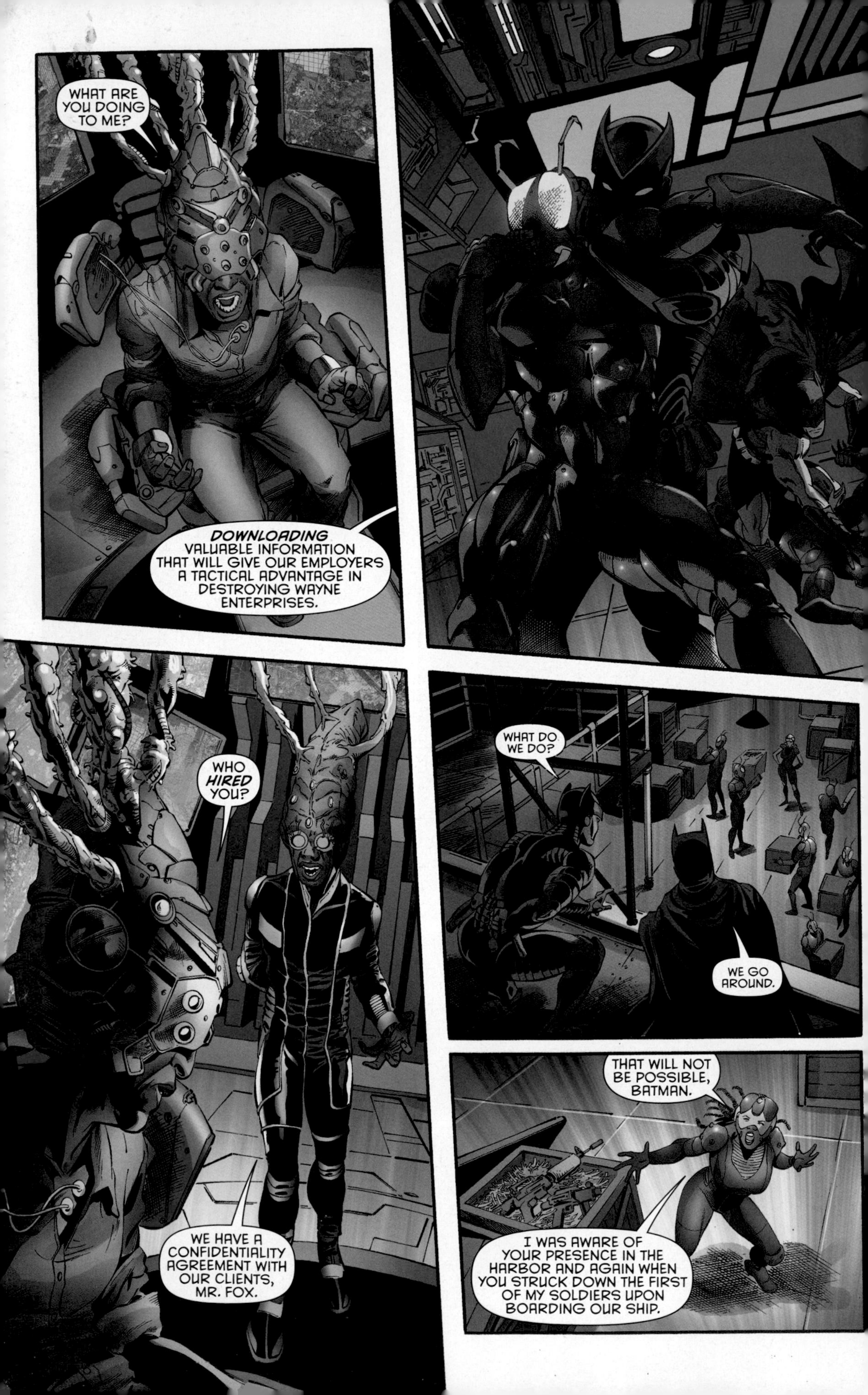
WHAT ARE YOU DOING TO ME?
DOWNLOADING VALUABLE INFORMATION THAT WILL GIVE OUR EMPLOYERS A TACTICAL ADVANTAGE IN DESTROYING WAYNE ENTERPRISES.
WHO HIRED YOU?
WE HAVE A CONFIDENTIALITY AGREEMENT WITH OUR CLIENTS, MR. FOX.
WHAT DO WE DO?
WE GO AROUND.
THAT WILL NOT BE POSSIBLE, BATMAN.
I WAS AWARE OF YOUR PRESENCE IN THE HARBOR AND AGAIN WHEN YOU STRUCK DOWN THE FIRST OF MY SOLDIERS UPON BOARDING OUR SHIP.

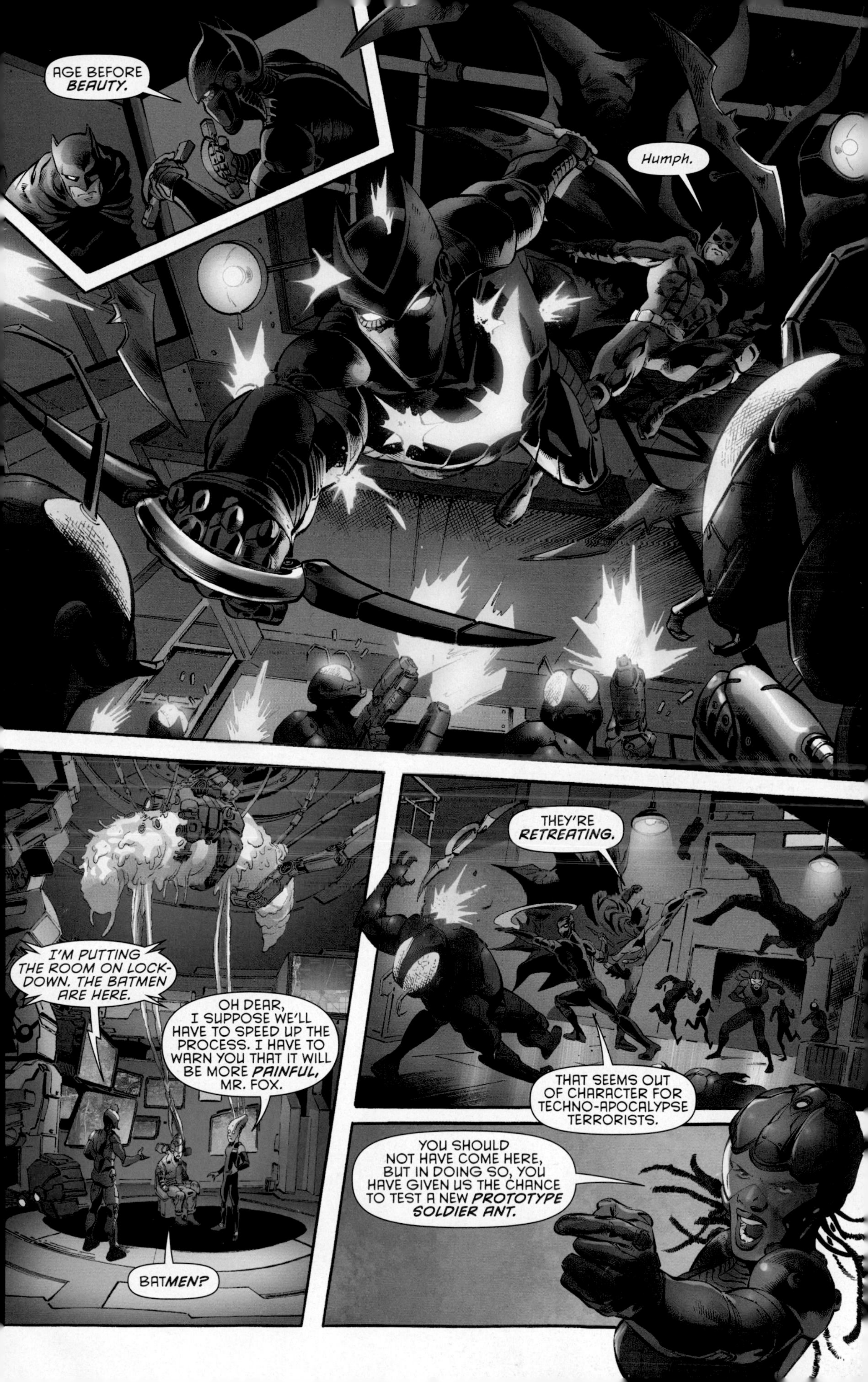
AGE BEFORE BEAUTY.
Humph.
I'M PUTTING THE ROOM ON LOCK-DOWN. THE BATMEN ARE HERE.
OH DEAR, I SUPPOSE WE'LL HAVE TO SPEED UP THE PROCESS. I HAVE TO WARN YOU THAT IT WILL BE MORE PAINFUL, MR. FOX.
BATMEN?
THEY'RE RETREATING.
THAT SEEMS OUT OF CHARACTER FOR TECHNO-APOCALYPSE TERRORISTS.
YOU SHOULD NOT HAVE COME HERE, BUT IN DOING SO, YOU HAVE GIVEN US THE CHANCE TO TEST A NEW PROTOTYPE SOLDIER ANT.

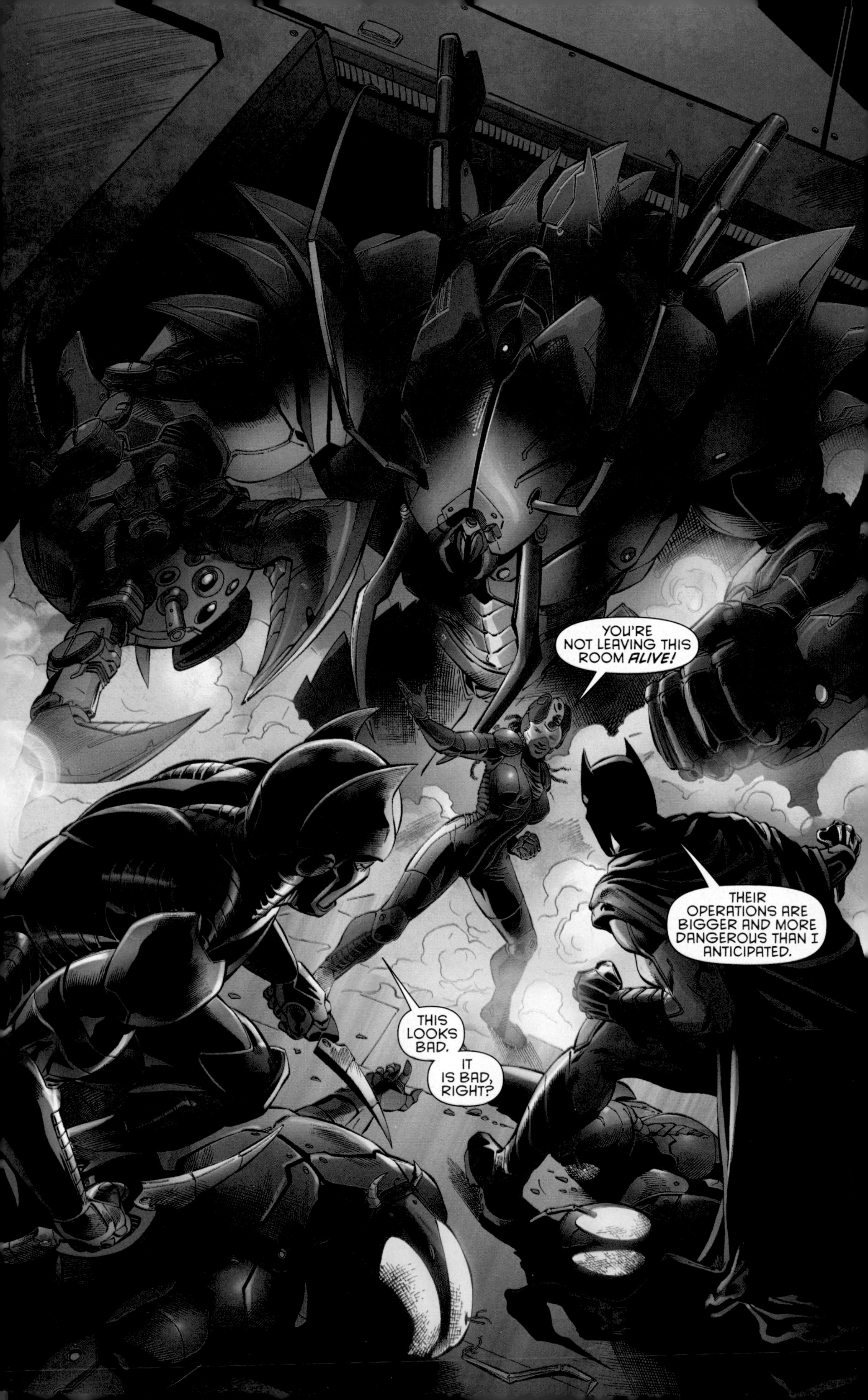
YOU'RE NOT LEAVING THIS ROOM ALIVE!
THEIR OPERATIONS ARE BIGGER AND MORE DANGEROUS THAN I ANTICIPATED.
THIS LOOKS BAD.
IT IS BAD, RIGHT?

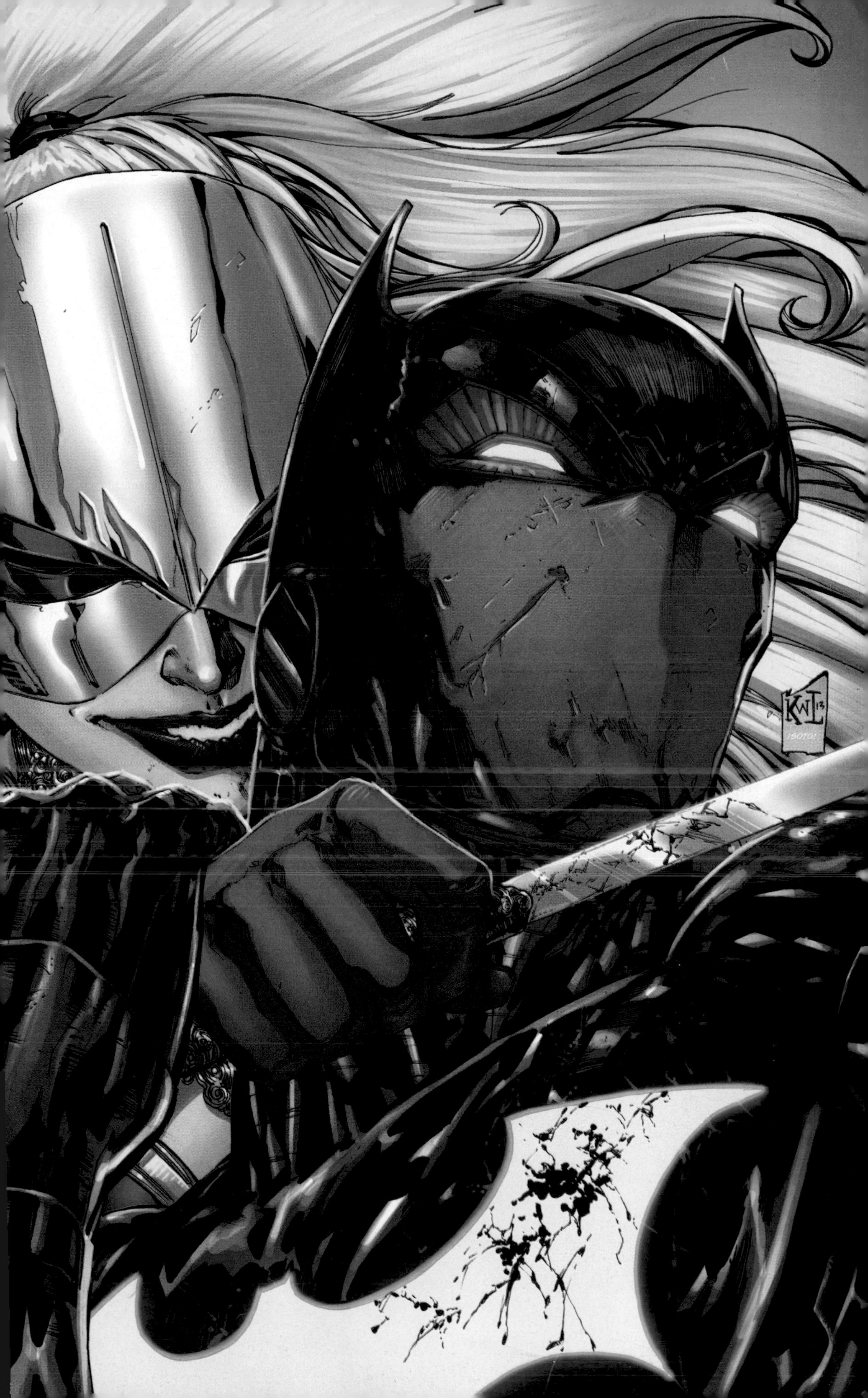

SMASH

cover art by **KEN LASHLEY & CHRIS SOTOMAYOR**

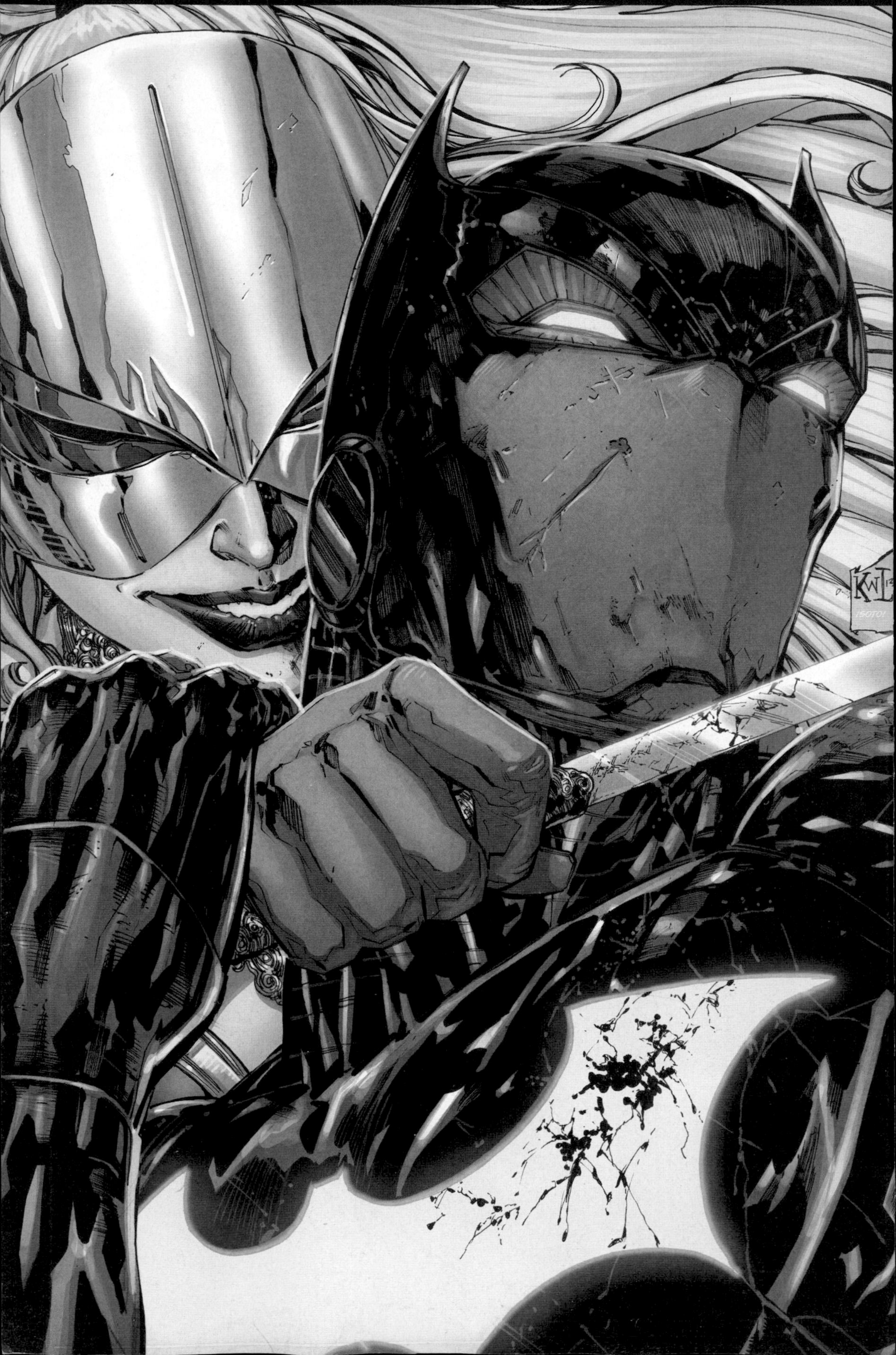

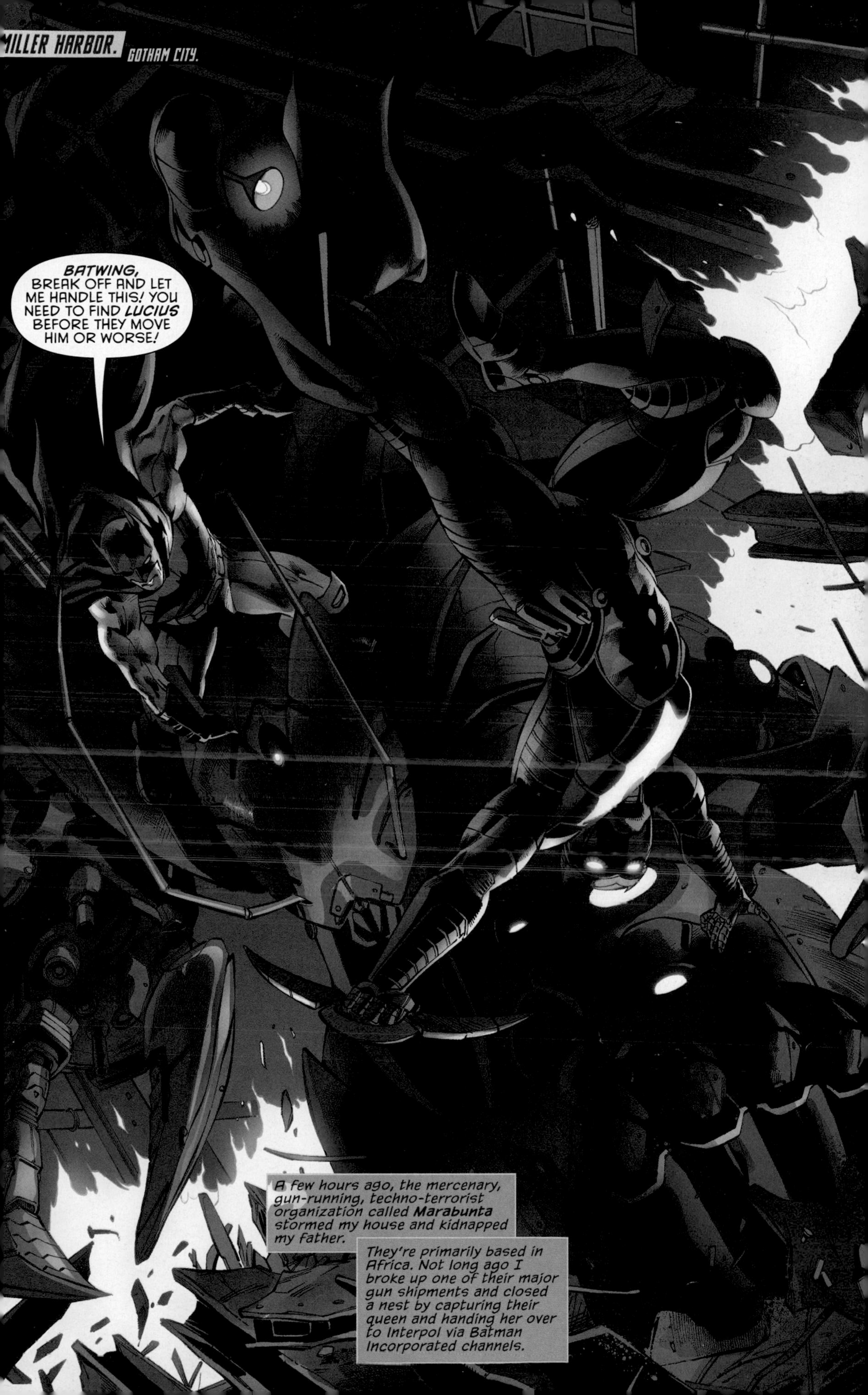
MILLER HARBOR. GOTHAM CITY.
BATWING, BREAK OFF AND LET ME HANDLE THIS! YOU NEED TO FIND LUCIUS BEFORE THEY MOVE HIM OR WORSE!
A few hours ago, the mercenary, gun-running, techno-terrorist organization called Marabunta stormed my house and kidnapped my father.
They're primarily based in Africa. Not long ago I broke up one of their major gun shipments and closed a nest by capturing their queen and handing her over to Interpol via Batman Incorporated channels.

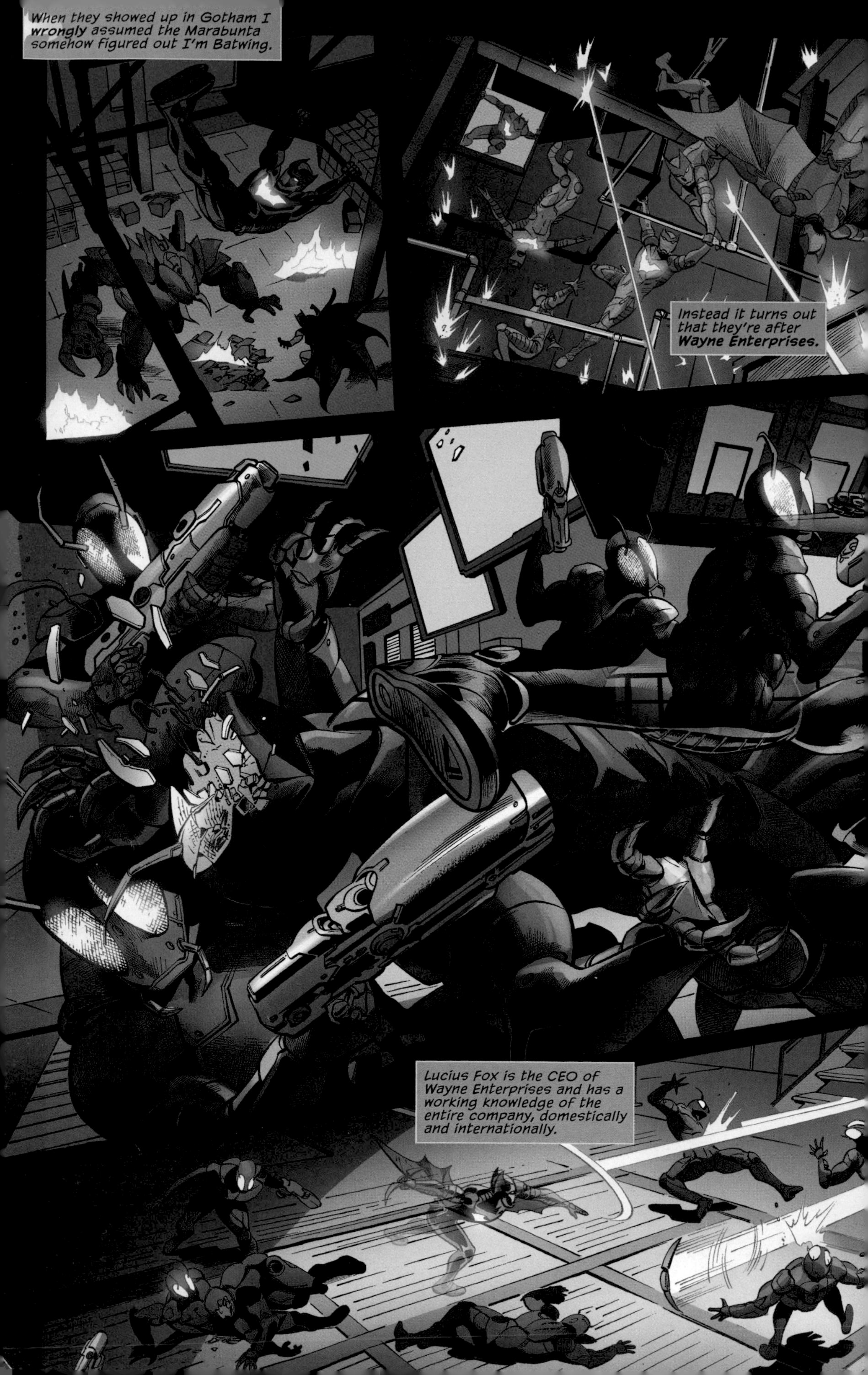
When they showed up in Gotham I wrongly assumed the Marabunta somehow figured out I'm Batwing.
Instead it turns out that they're after Wayne Enterprises.
Lucius Fox is the CEO of Wayne Enterprises and has a working knowledge of the entire company, domestically and internationally.

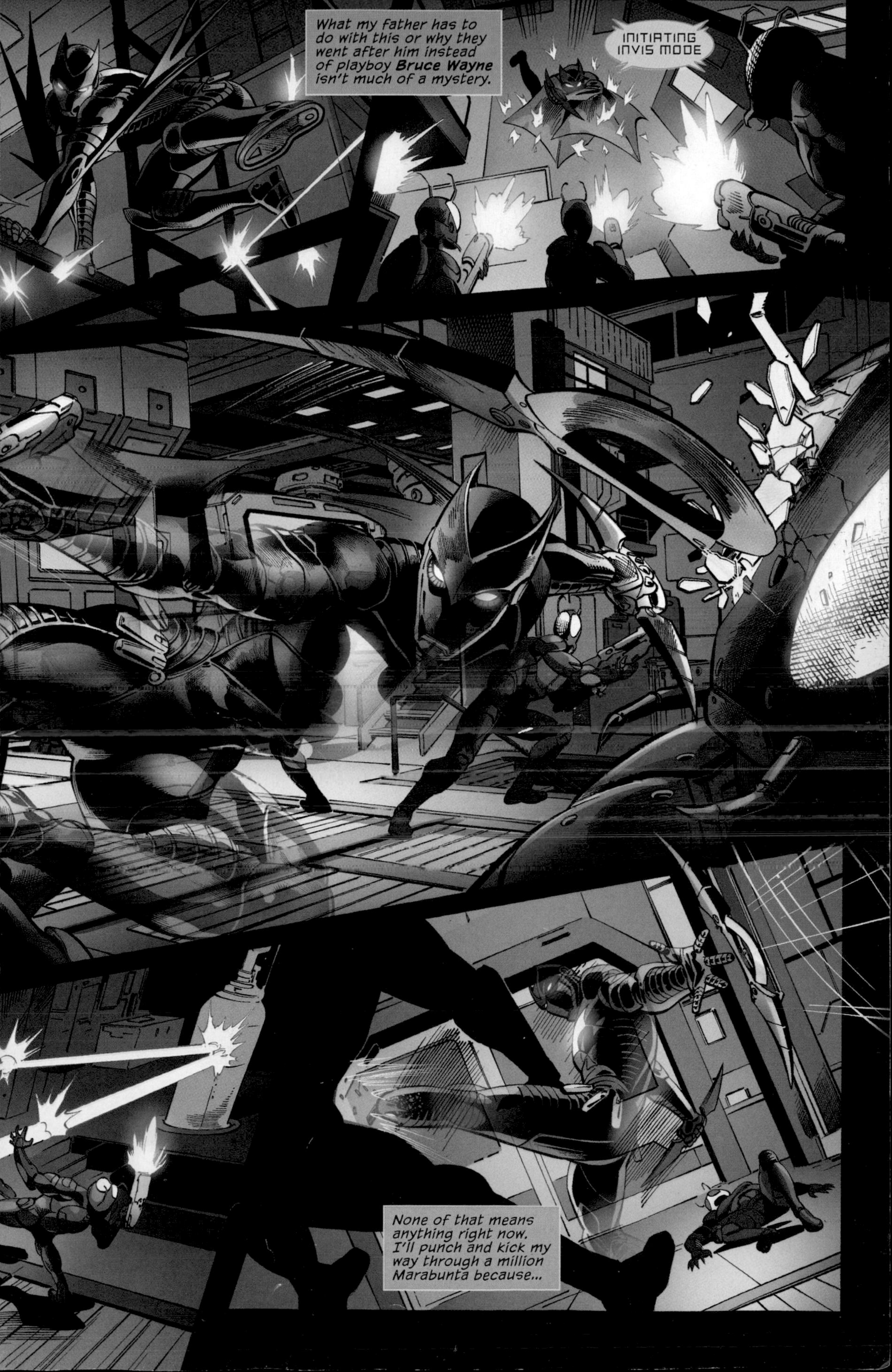
What my father has to do with this or why they went after him instead of playboy **Bruce Wayne** isn't much of a mystery.
INITIATING INVIS MODE
None of that means anything right now. I'll punch and kick my way through a million Marabunta because...

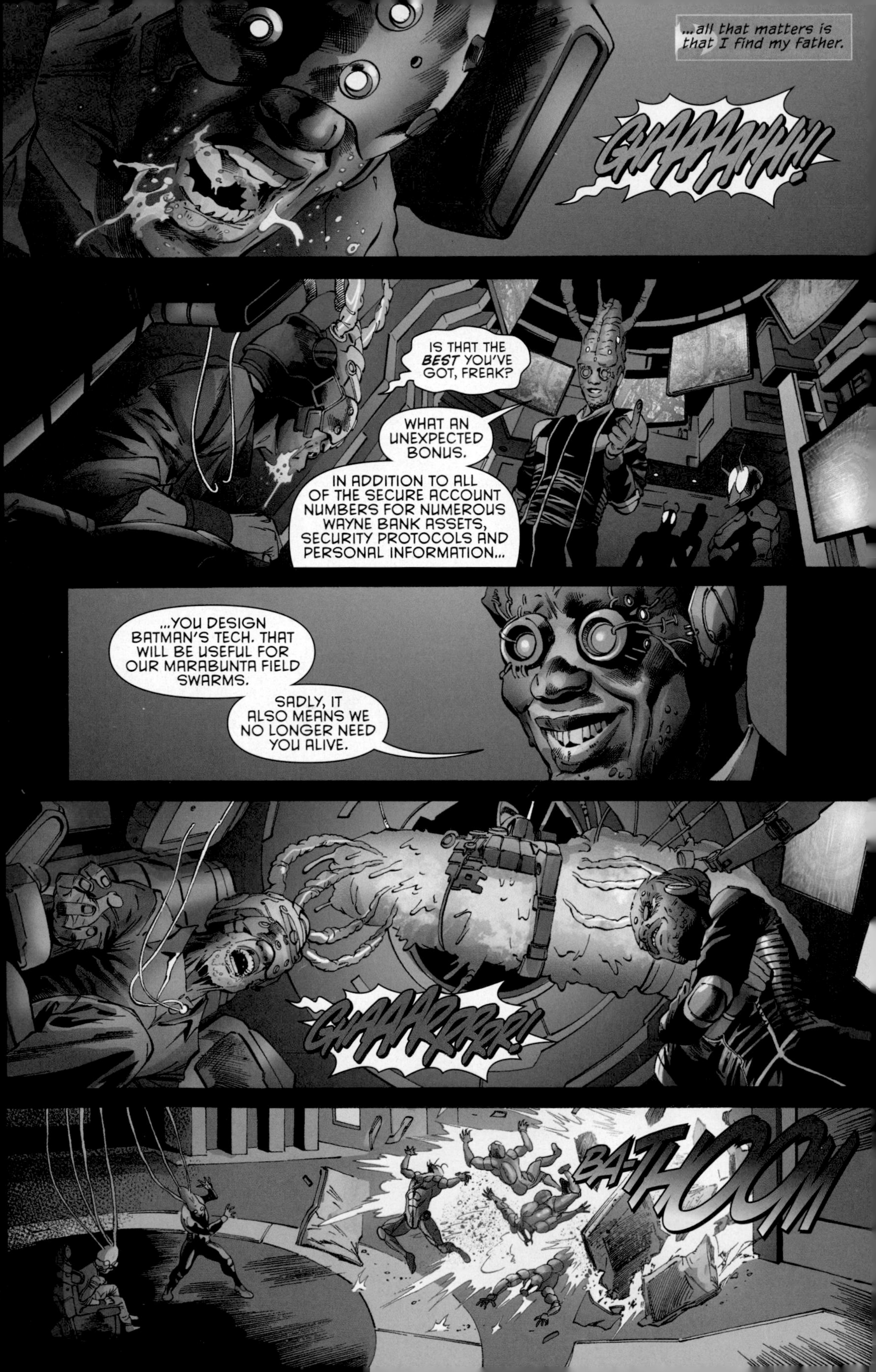

...all that matters is that I find my father.
GHAAAAHHH!
IS THAT THE BEST YOU'VE GOT, FREAK?
WHAT AN UNEXPECTED BONUS.
IN ADDITION TO ALL OF THE SECURE ACCOUNT NUMBERS FOR NUMEROUS WAYNE BANK ASSETS, SECURITY PROTOCOLS AND PERSONAL INFORMATION...
...YOU DESIGN BATMAN'S TECH. THAT WILL BE USEFUL FOR OUR MARABUNTA FIELD SWARMS.
SADLY, IT ALSO MEANS WE NO LONGER NEED YOU ALIVE.
GHAAARRRR!
BA-THOOM

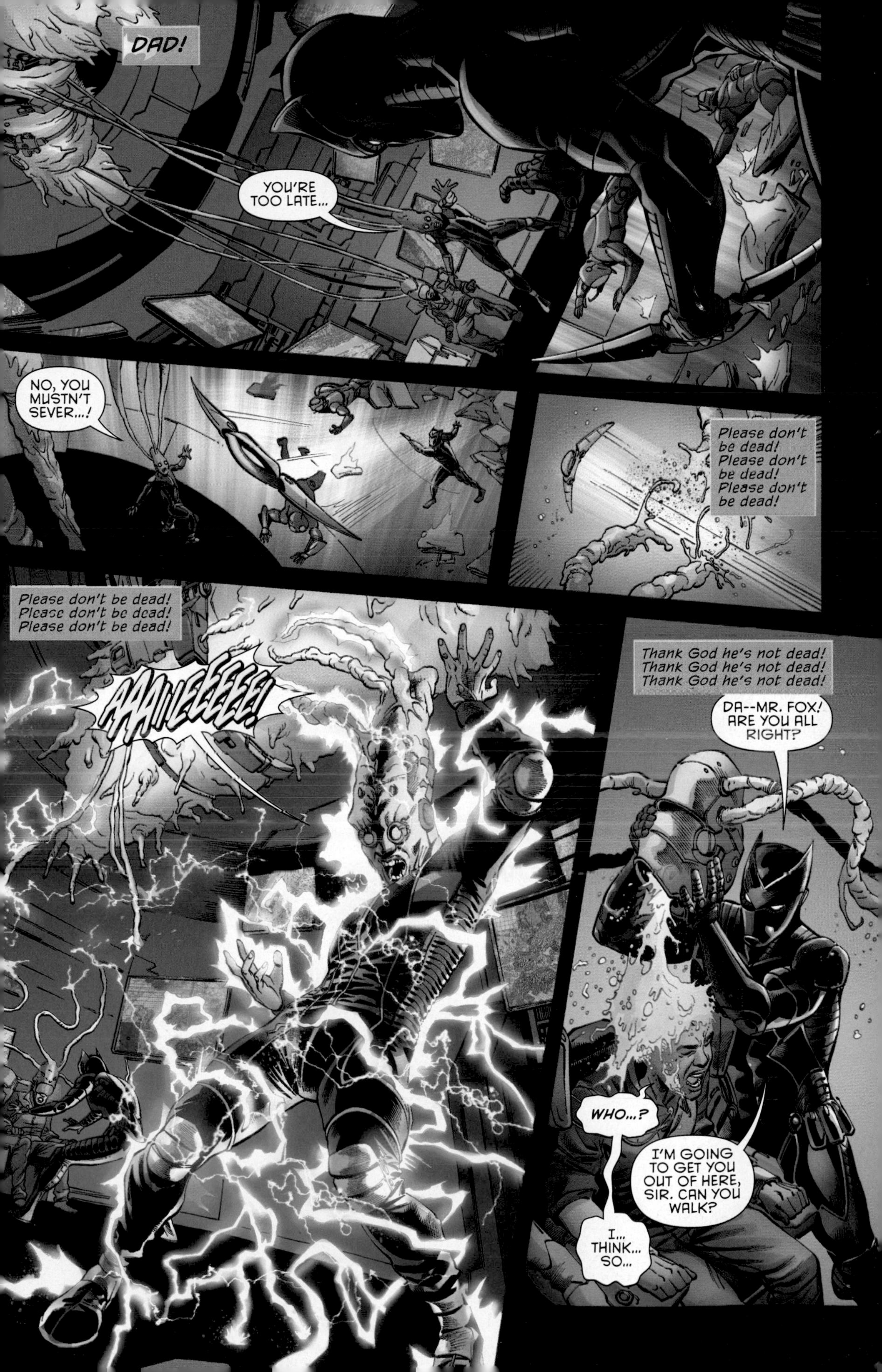
DAD!
YOU'RE TOO LATE...
NO, YOU MUSTN'T SEVER...!
Please don't be dead! Please don't be dead! Please don't be dead!
Please don't be dead! Please don't be dead! Please don't be dead!
AAAIEEEEE!
Thank God he's not dead! Thank God he's not dead! Thank God he's not dead!
DA--MR. FOX! ARE YOU ALL RIGHT?
WHO...?
I'M GOING TO GET YOU OUT OF HERE, SIR. CAN YOU WALK?
I... THINK... SO...

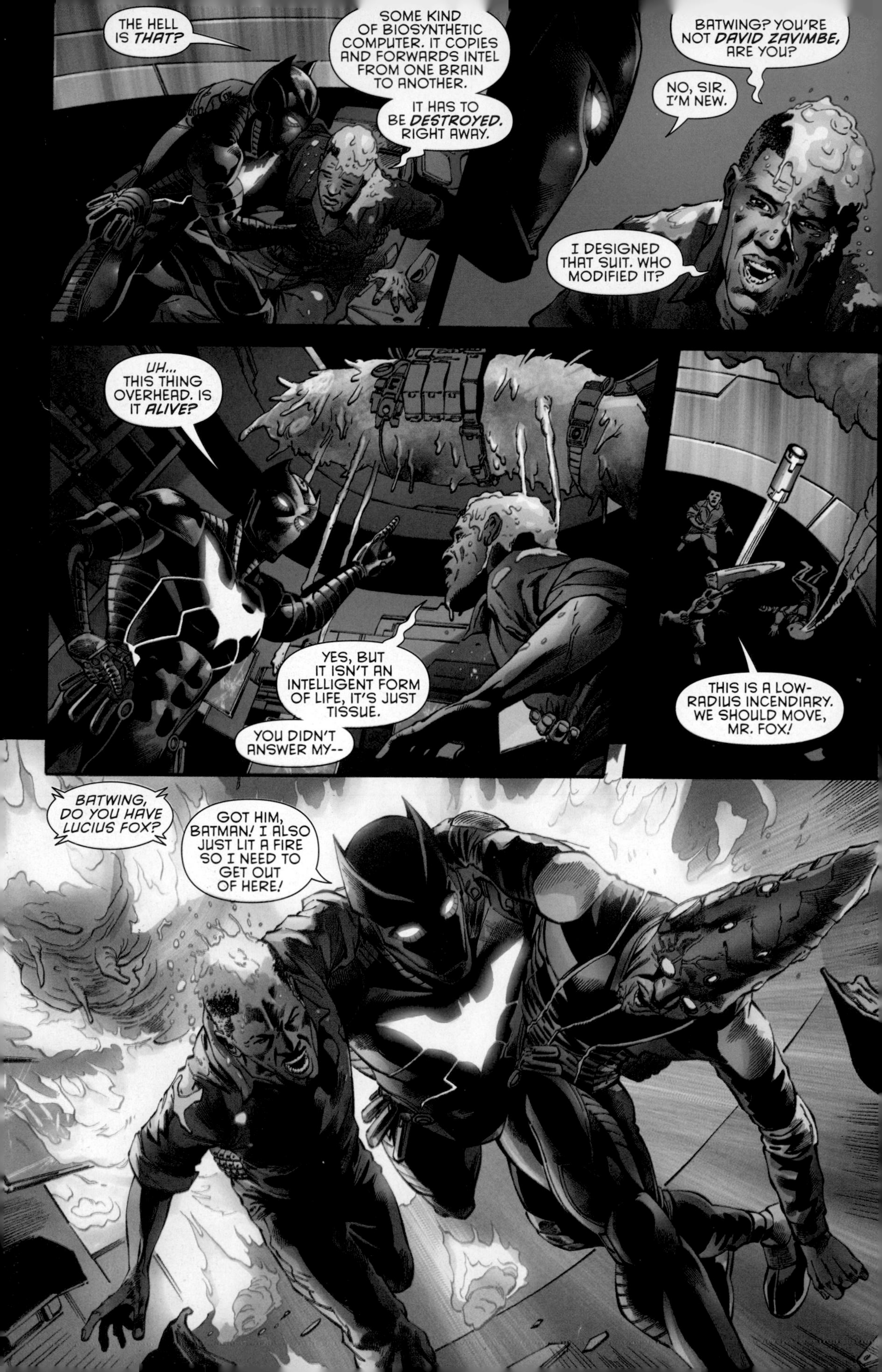
THE HELL IS *THAT?*
SOME KIND OF BIOSYNTHETIC COMPUTER. IT COPIES AND FORWARDS INTEL FROM ONE BRAIN TO ANOTHER.
IT HAS TO BE ***DESTROYED.*** RIGHT AWAY.
BATWING? YOU'RE NOT ***DAVID ZAVIMBE,*** ARE YOU?
NO, SIR. I'M NEW.
I DESIGNED THAT SUIT. WHO MODIFIED IT?
*UH... THIS THING OVERHEAD. IS IT **ALIVE?***
YES, BUT IT ISN'T AN INTELLIGENT FORM OF LIFE, IT'S JUST TISSUE.
YOU DIDN'T ANSWER MY--
THIS IS A LOW-RADIUS INCENDIARY. WE SHOULD MOVE, MR. FOX!
BATWING, DO YOU HAVE LUCIUS FOX?
GOT HIM, BATMAN! I ALSO JUST LIT A FIRE SO I NEED TO GET OUT OF HERE!

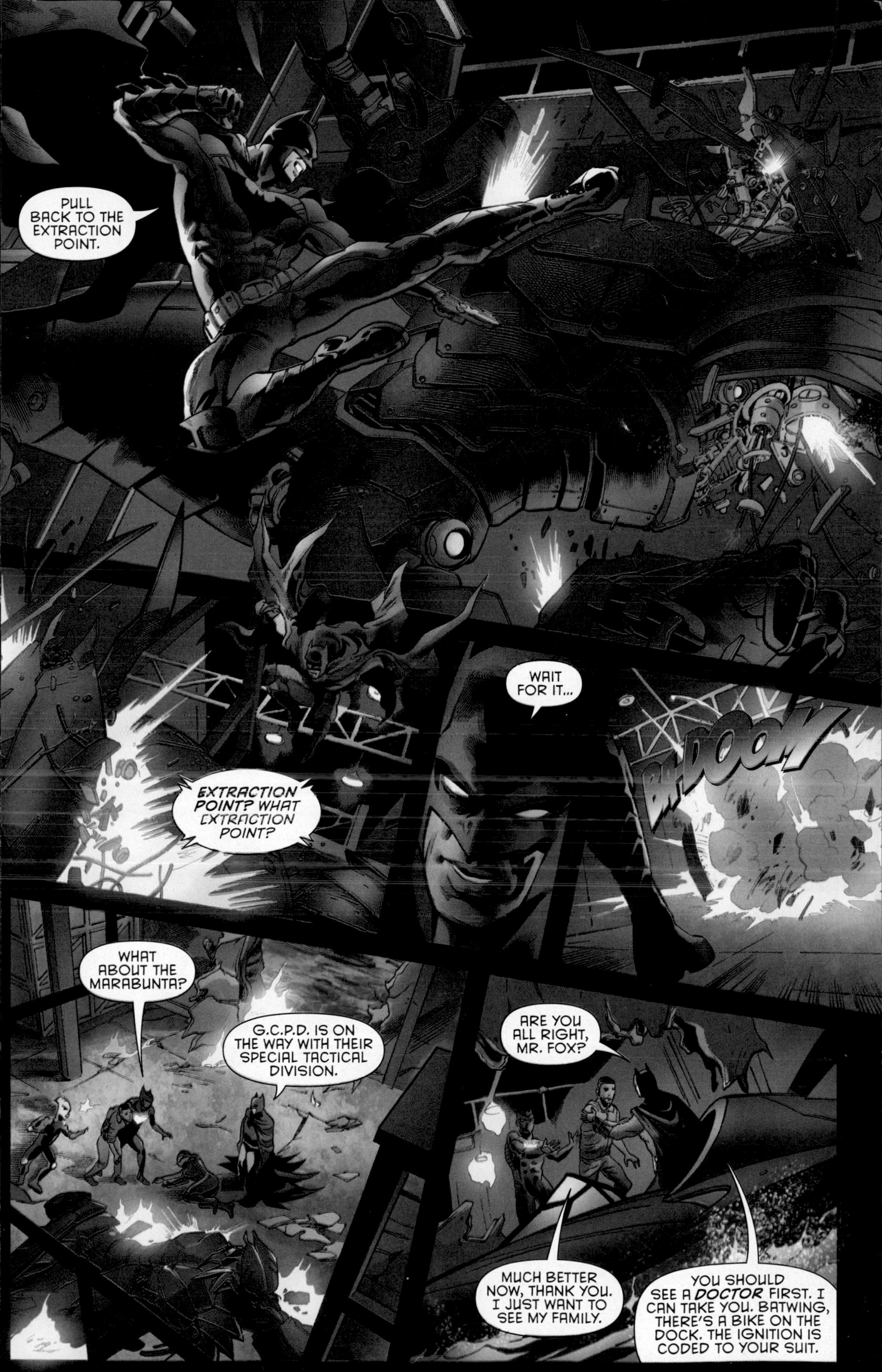
PULL BACK TO THE EXTRACTION POINT.
EXTRACTION POINT? WHAT EXTRACTION POINT?
WAIT FOR IT...
BADOOM
WHAT ABOUT THE MARABUNTA?
G.C.P.D. IS ON THE WAY WITH THEIR SPECIAL TACTICAL DIVISION.
ARE YOU ALL RIGHT, MR. FOX?
MUCH BETTER NOW, THANK YOU. I JUST WANT TO SEE MY FAMILY.
YOU SHOULD SEE A DOCTOR FIRST. I CAN TAKE YOU. BATWING, THERE'S A BIKE ON THE DOCK. THE IGNITION IS CODED TO YOUR SUIT.

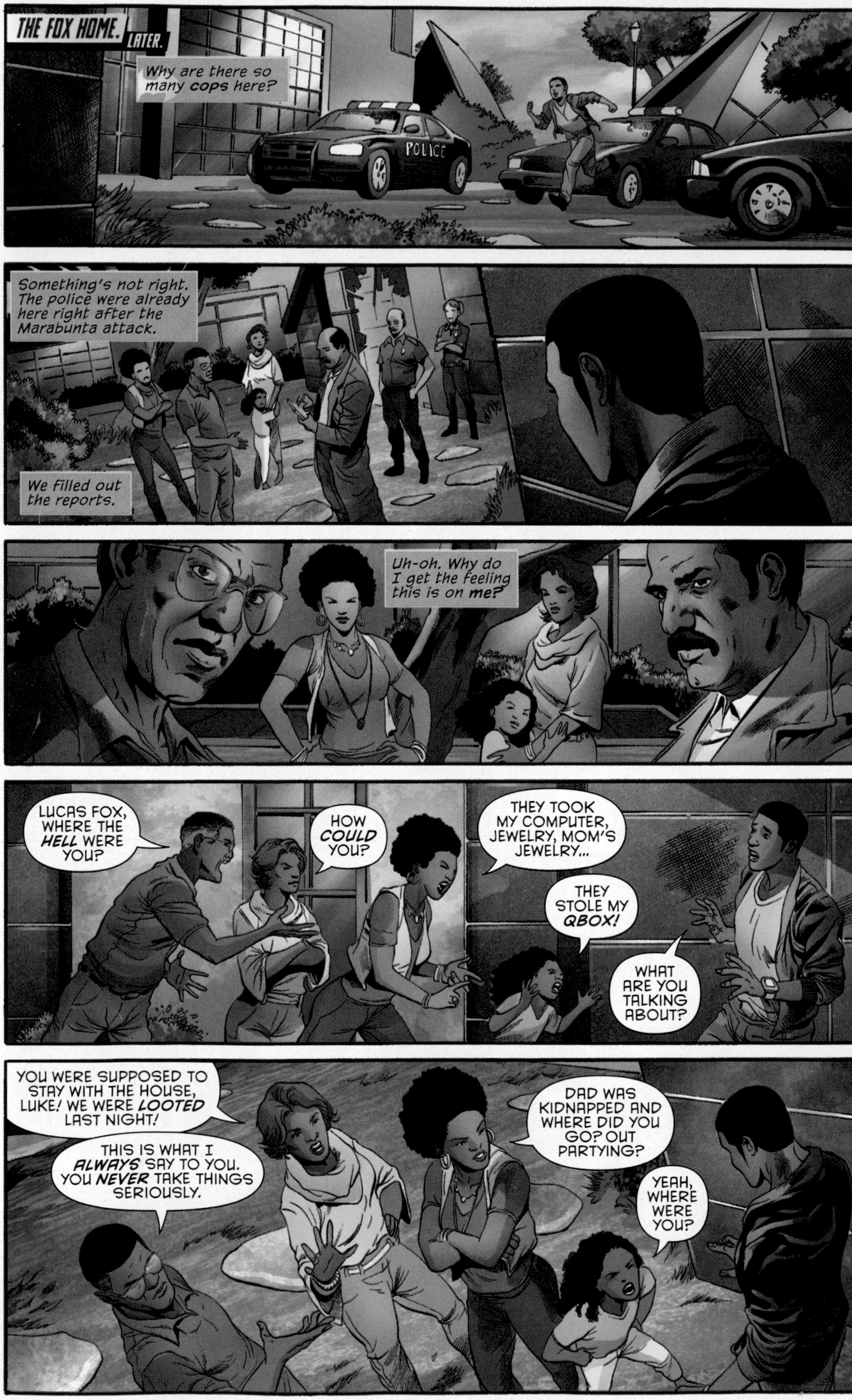
THE FOX HOME.
LATER.
Why are there so many cops here?
POLICE
Something's not right. The police were already here right after the Marabunta attack.
We filled out the reports.
Uh-oh. Why do I get the feeling this is on me?
LUCAS FOX, WHERE THE HELL WERE YOU?
HOW COULD YOU?
THEY TOOK MY COMPUTER, JEWELRY, MOM'S JEWELRY...
THEY STOLE MY QBOX!
WHAT ARE YOU TALKING ABOUT?
YOU WERE SUPPOSED TO STAY WITH THE HOUSE, LUKE! WE WERE LOOTED LAST NIGHT!
THIS IS WHAT I ALWAYS SAY TO YOU. YOU NEVER TAKE THINGS SERIOUSLY.
DAD WAS KIDNAPPED AND WHERE DID YOU GO? OUT PARTYING?
YEAH, WHERE WERE YOU?

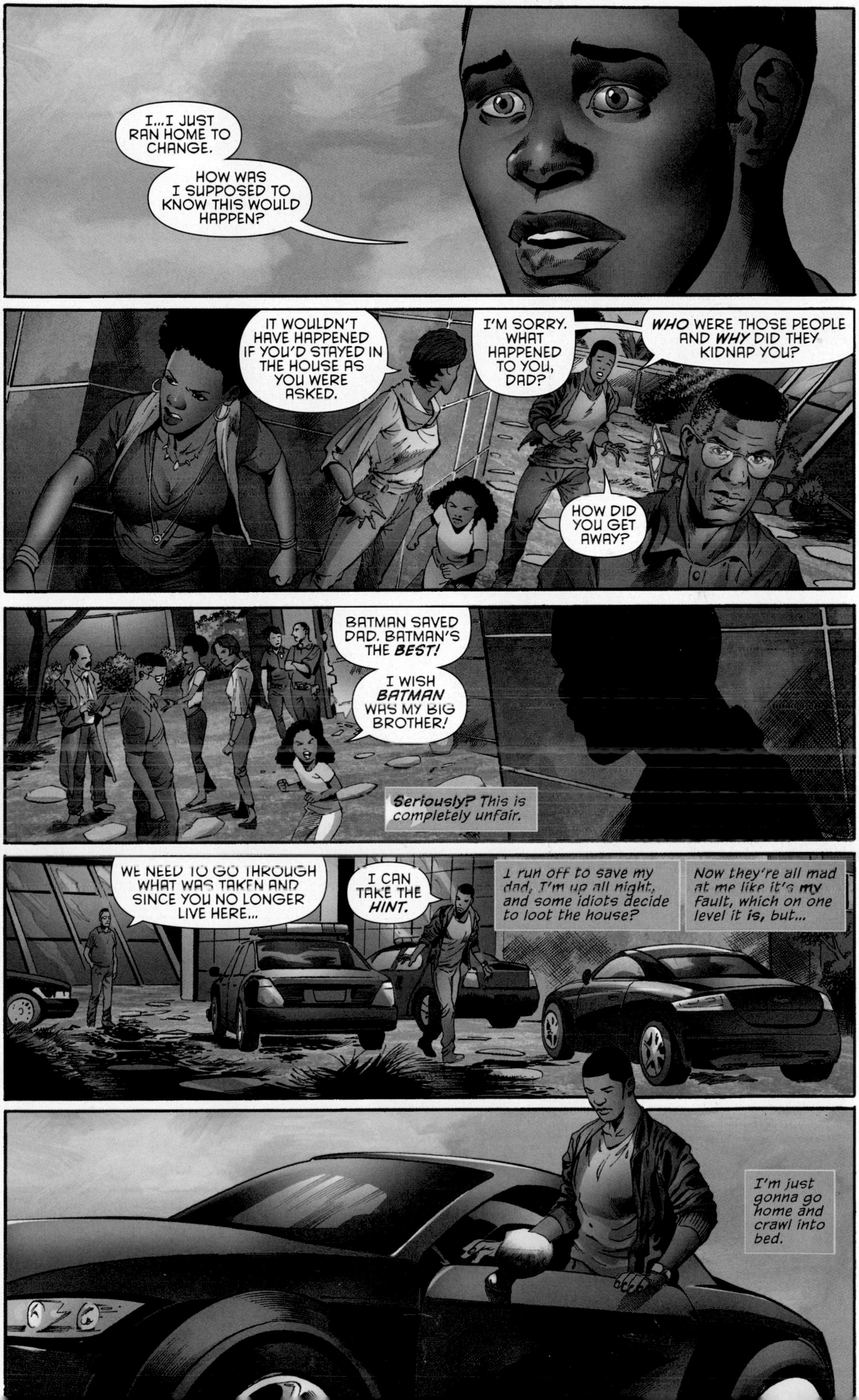

I...I JUST RAN HOME TO CHANGE.
HOW WAS I SUPPOSED TO KNOW THIS WOULD HAPPEN?
IT WOULDN'T HAVE HAPPENED IF YOU'D STAYED IN THE HOUSE AS YOU WERE ASKED.
I'M SORRY. WHAT HAPPENED TO YOU, DAD?
WHO WERE THOSE PEOPLE AND WHY DID THEY KIDNAP YOU?
HOW DID YOU GET AWAY?
BATMAN SAVED DAD. BATMAN'S THE BEST!
I WISH BATMAN WAS MY BIG BROTHER!
Seriously? This is completely unfair.
WE NEED TO GO THROUGH WHAT WAS TAKEN AND SINCE YOU NO LONGER LIVE HERE...
I CAN TAKE THE HINT.
I run off to save my dad, I'm up all night, and some idiots decide to loot the house?
Now they're all mad at me like it's my fault, which on one level it is, but...
I'm just gonna go home and crawl into bed.

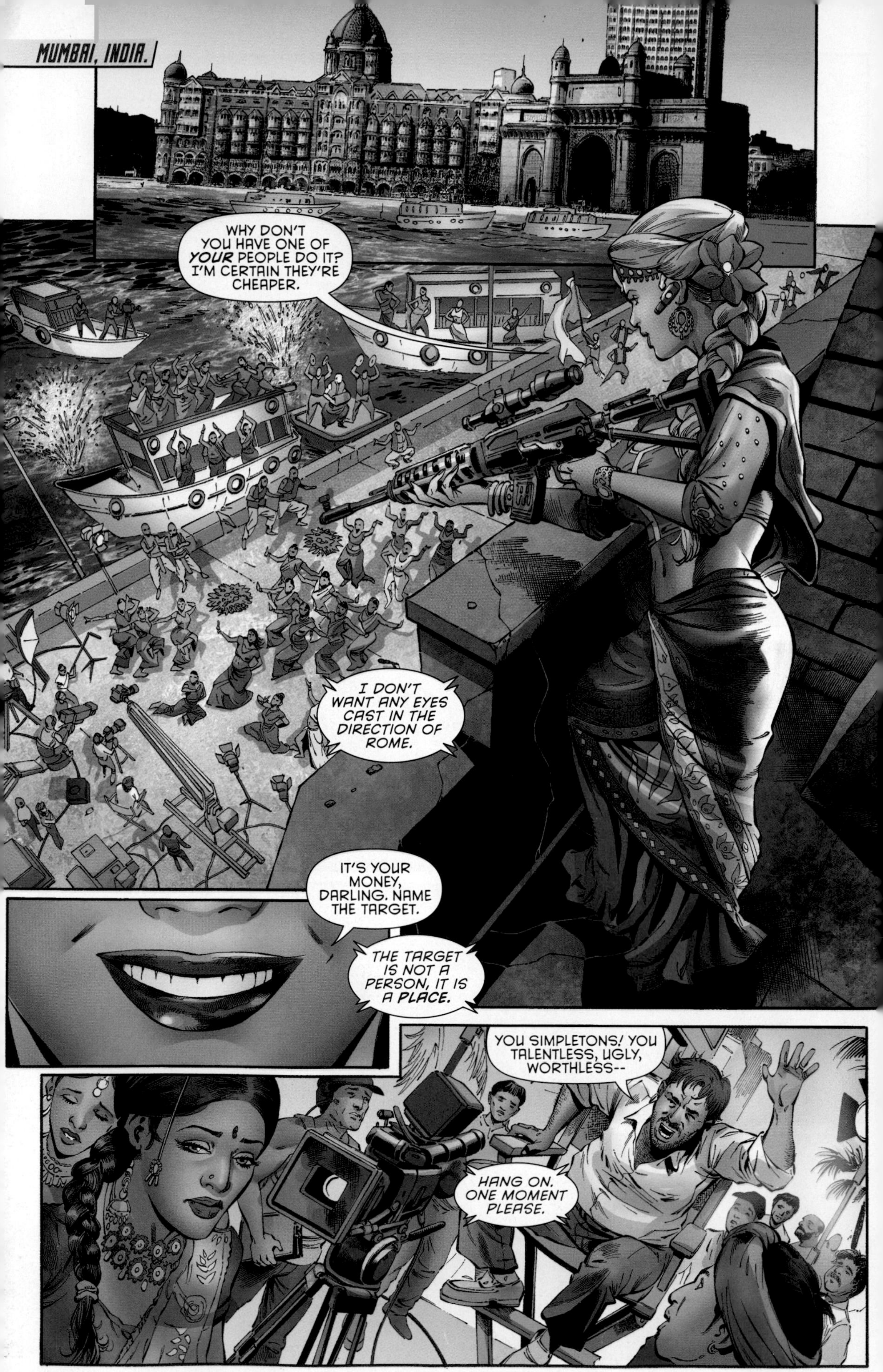
MUMBAI, INDIA.
WHY DON'T YOU HAVE ONE OF *YOUR* PEOPLE DO IT? I'M CERTAIN THEY'RE CHEAPER.
I DON'T WANT ANY EYES CAST IN THE DIRECTION OF ROME.
IT'S YOUR MONEY, DARLING. NAME THE TARGET.
THE TARGET IS NOT A PERSON, IT IS A *PLACE*.
YOU SIMPLETONS! YOU TALENTLESS, UGLY, WORTHLESS--
HANG ON. ONE MOMENT PLEASE.

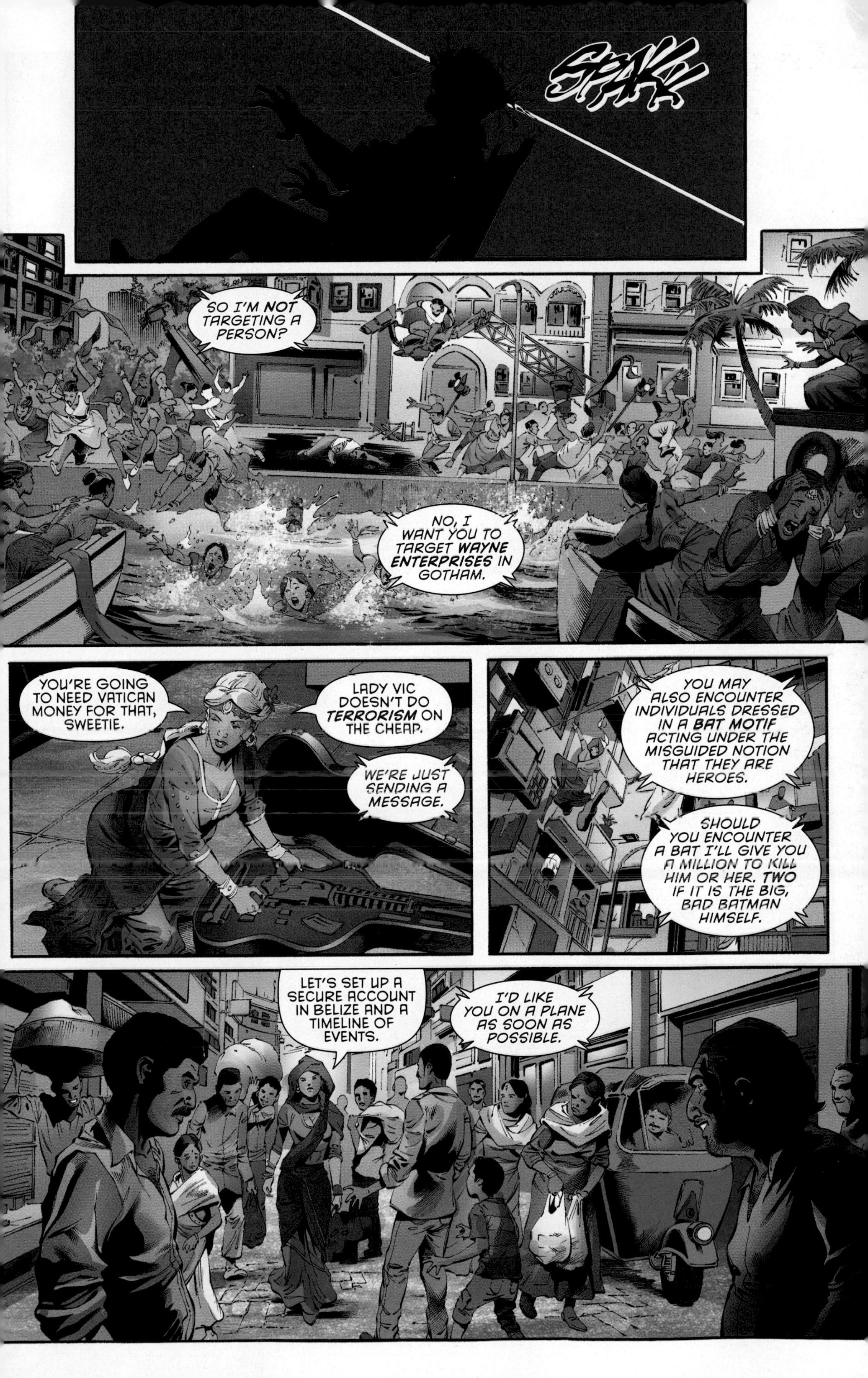
SPAK!!
SO I'M NOT TARGETING A PERSON?
NO, I WANT YOU TO TARGET WAYNE ENTERPRISES IN GOTHAM.
YOU'RE GOING TO NEED VATICAN MONEY FOR THAT, SWEETIE.
LADY VIC DOESN'T DO TERRORISM ON THE CHEAP.
WE'RE JUST SENDING A MESSAGE.
YOU MAY ALSO ENCOUNTER INDIVIDUALS DRESSED IN A BAT MOTIF ACTING UNDER THE MISGUIDED NOTION THAT THEY ARE HEROES.
SHOULD YOU ENCOUNTER A BAT I'LL GIVE YOU A MILLION TO KILL HIM OR HER. TWO IF IT IS THE BIG, BAD BATMAN HIMSELF.
LET'S SET UP A SECURE ACCOUNT IN BELIZE AND A TIMELINE OF EVENTS.
I'D LIKE YOU ON A PLANE AS SOON AS POSSIBLE.

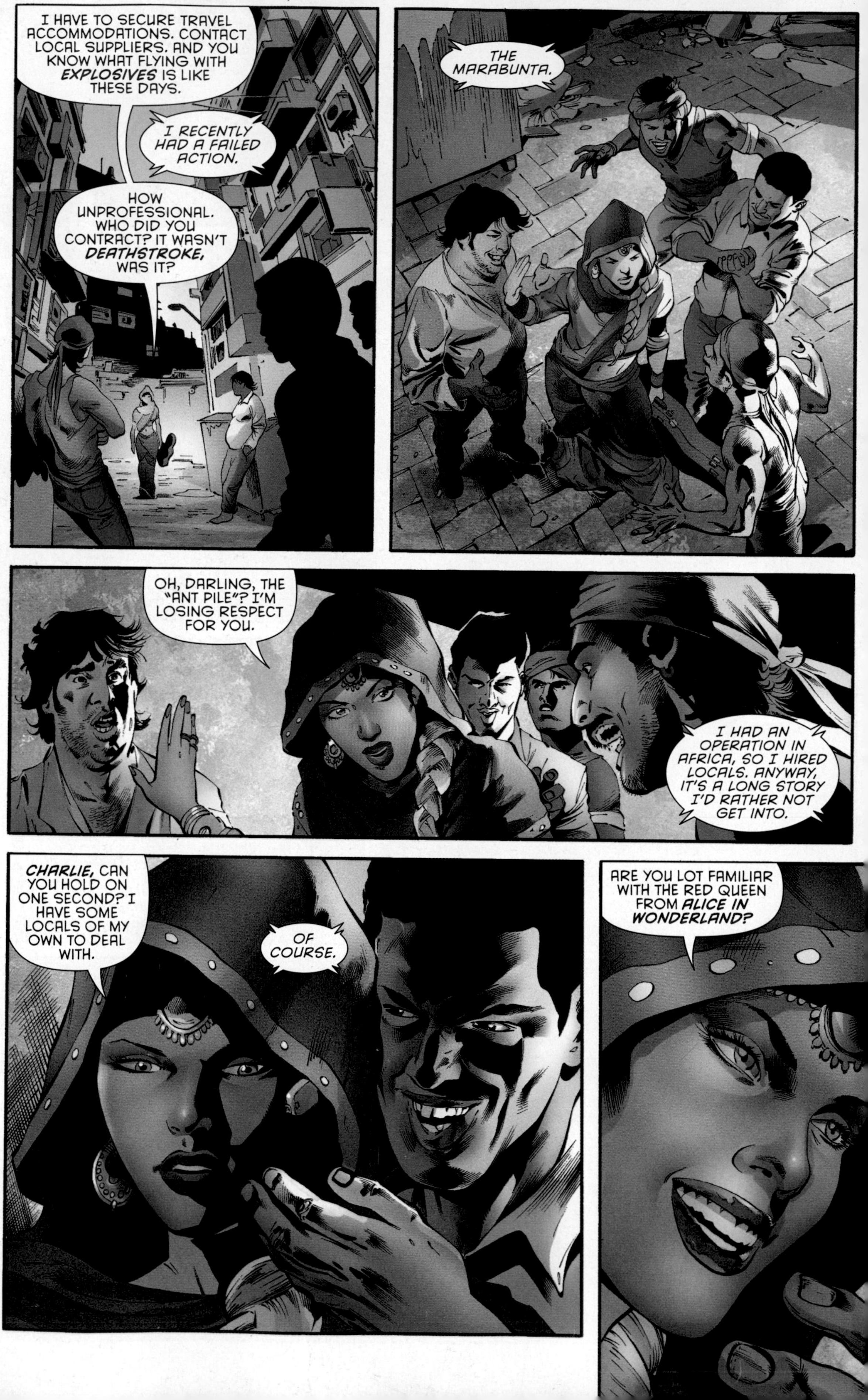

I HAVE TO SECURE TRAVEL ACCOMMODATIONS. CONTACT LOCAL SUPPLIERS. AND YOU KNOW WHAT FLYING WITH EXPLOSIVES IS LIKE THESE DAYS.
I RECENTLY HAD A FAILED ACTION.
HOW UNPROFESSIONAL. WHO DID YOU CONTRACT? IT WASN'T DEATHSTROKE, WAS IT?
THE MARABUNTA.
OH, DARLING, THE "ANT PILE"? I'M LOSING RESPECT FOR YOU.
I HAD AN OPERATION IN AFRICA, SO I HIRED LOCALS. ANYWAY, IT'S A LONG STORY I'D RATHER NOT GET INTO.
CHARLIE, CAN YOU HOLD ON ONE SECOND? I HAVE SOME LOCALS OF MY OWN TO DEAL WITH.
OF COURSE.
ARE YOU LOT FAMILIAR WITH THE RED QUEEN FROM ALICE IN WONDERLAND?

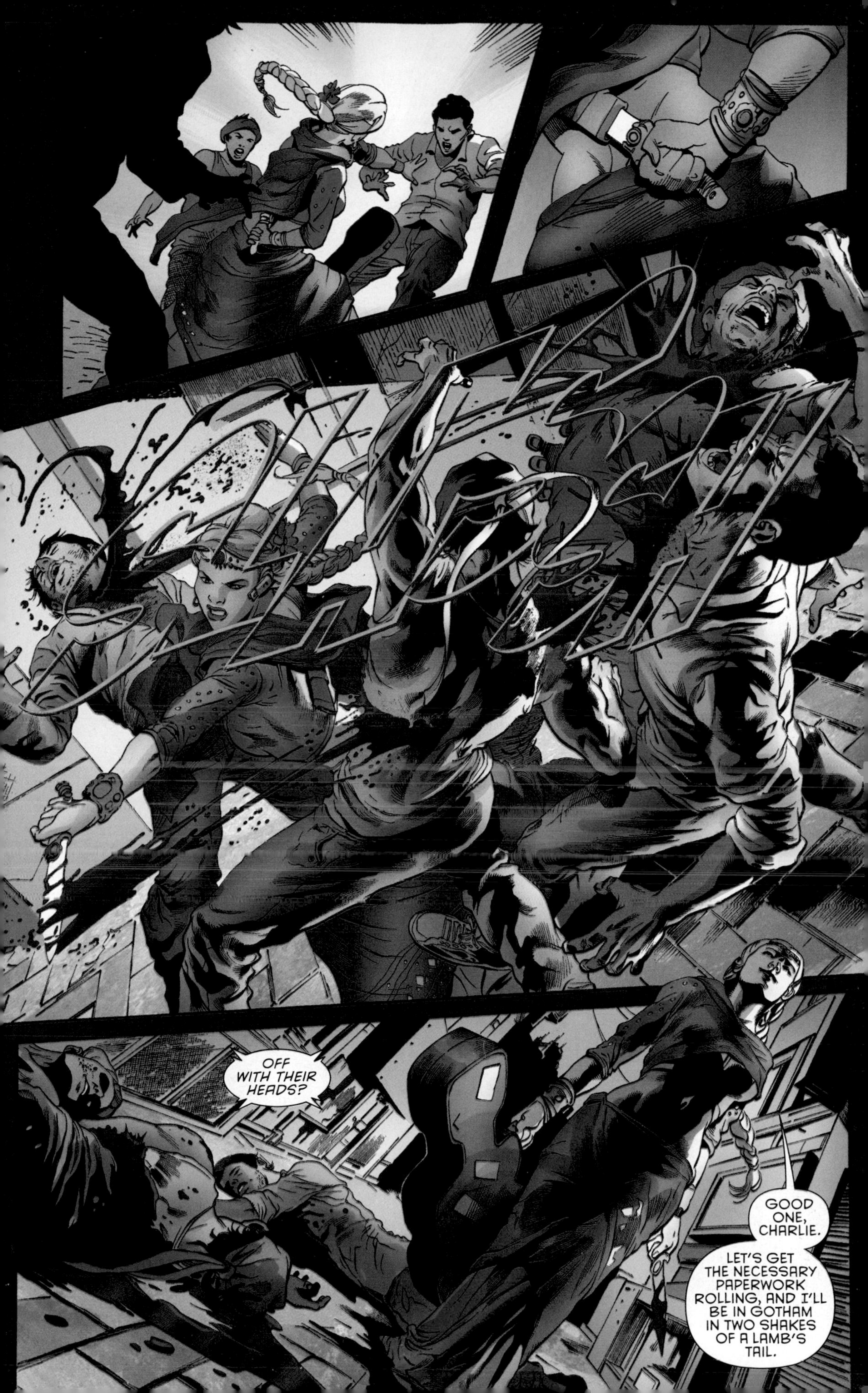
OFF WITH THEIR HEADS?
GOOD ONE, CHARLIE.
LET'S GET THE NECESSARY PAPERWORK ROLLING, AND I'LL BE IN GOTHAM IN TWO SHAKES OF A LAMB'S TAIL.

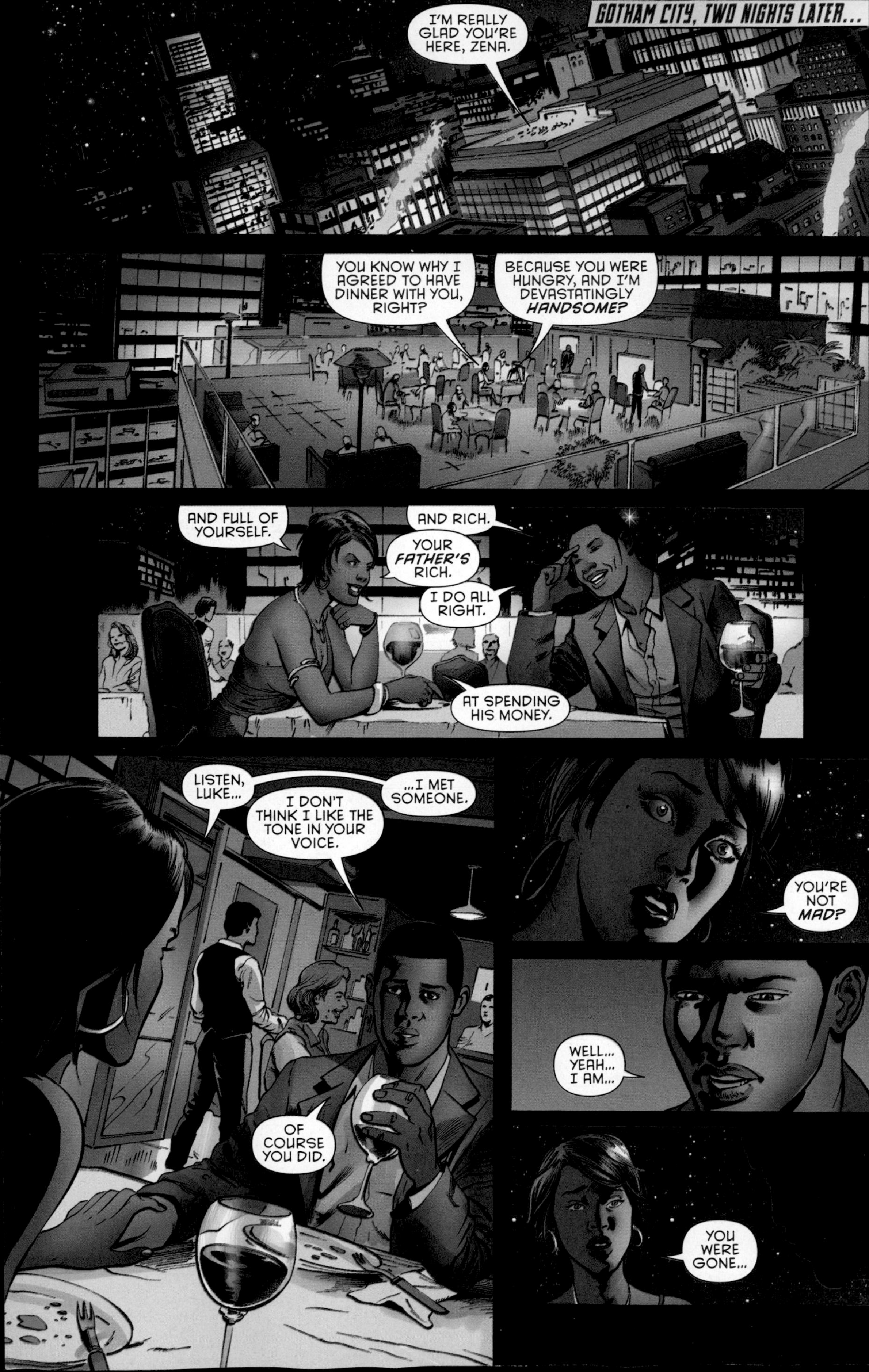
GOTHAM CITY, TWO NIGHTS LATER...
I'M REALLY GLAD YOU'RE HERE, ZENA.
YOU KNOW WHY I AGREED TO HAVE DINNER WITH YOU, RIGHT?
BECAUSE YOU WERE HUNGRY, AND I'M DEVASTATINGLY HANDSOME?
AND FULL OF YOURSELF.
AND RICH.
YOUR FATHER'S RICH.
I DO ALL RIGHT.
AT SPENDING HIS MONEY.
LISTEN, LUKE...
...I MET SOMEONE.
I DON'T THINK I LIKE THE TONE IN YOUR VOICE.
OF COURSE YOU DID.
YOU'RE NOT MAD?
WELL... YEAH... I AM...
YOU WERE GONE...

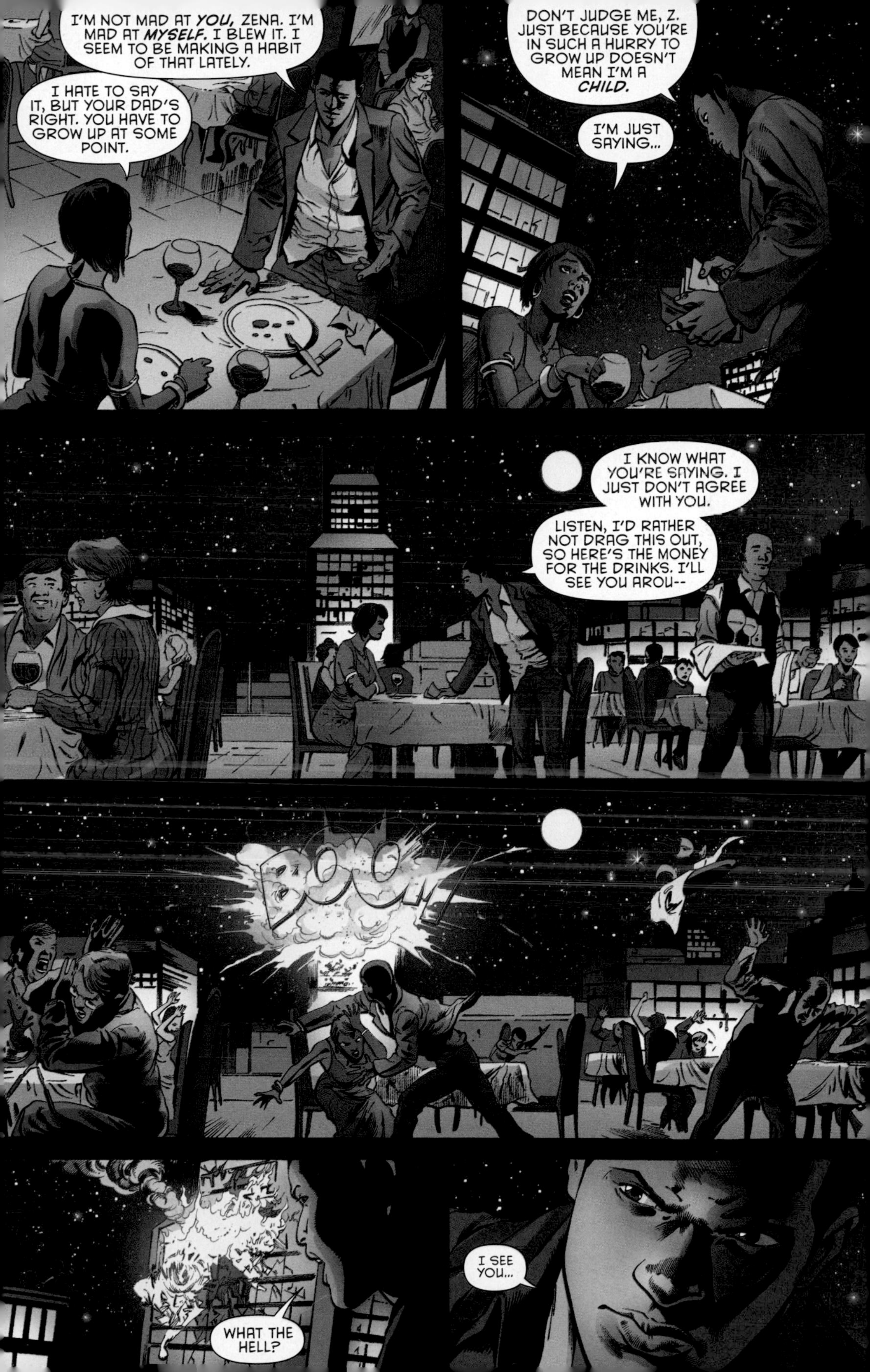
I'M NOT MAD AT YOU, ZENA. I'M MAD AT MYSELF. I BLEW IT. I SEEM TO BE MAKING A HABIT OF THAT LATELY.
I HATE TO SAY IT, BUT YOUR DAD'S RIGHT. YOU HAVE TO GROW UP AT SOME POINT.
DON'T JUDGE ME, Z. JUST BECAUSE YOU'RE IN SUCH A HURRY TO GROW UP DOESN'T MEAN I'M A CHILD.
I'M JUST SAYING...
I KNOW WHAT YOU'RE SAYING. I JUST DON'T AGREE WITH YOU.
LISTEN, I'D RATHER NOT DRAG THIS OUT, SO HERE'S THE MONEY FOR THE DRINKS. I'LL SEE YOU AROU--
BOOM
WHAT THE HELL?
I SEE YOU...

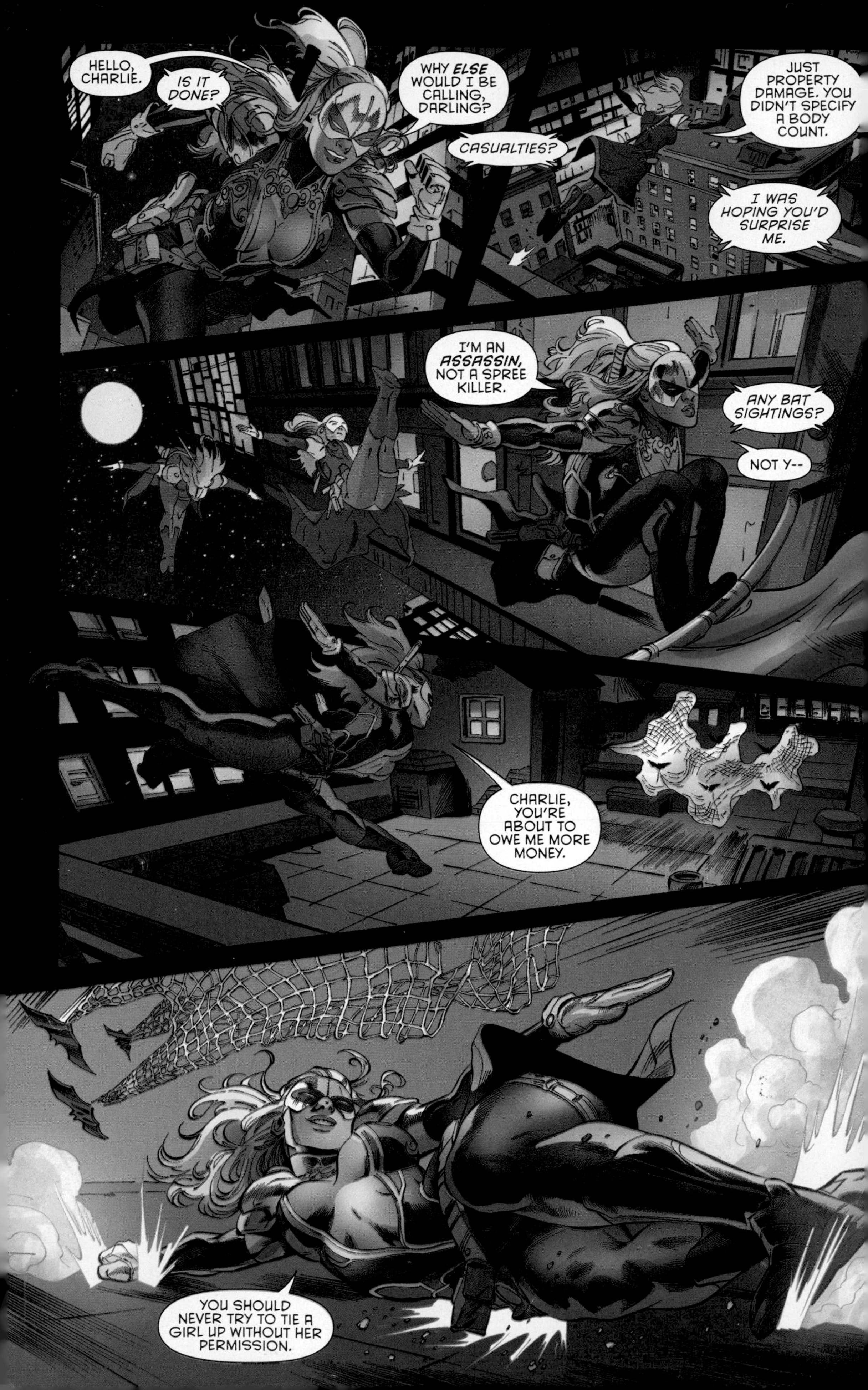
HELLO, CHARLIE.
IS IT DONE?
WHY ELSE WOULD I BE CALLING, DARLING?
CASUALTIES?
JUST PROPERTY DAMAGE. YOU DIDN'T SPECIFY A BODY COUNT.
I WAS HOPING YOU'D SURPRISE ME.
I'M AN ASSASSIN, NOT A SPREE KILLER.
ANY BAT SIGHTINGS?
NOT Y--
CHARLIE, YOU'RE ABOUT TO OWE ME MORE MONEY.
YOU SHOULD NEVER TRY TO TIE A GIRL UP WITHOUT HER PERMISSION.

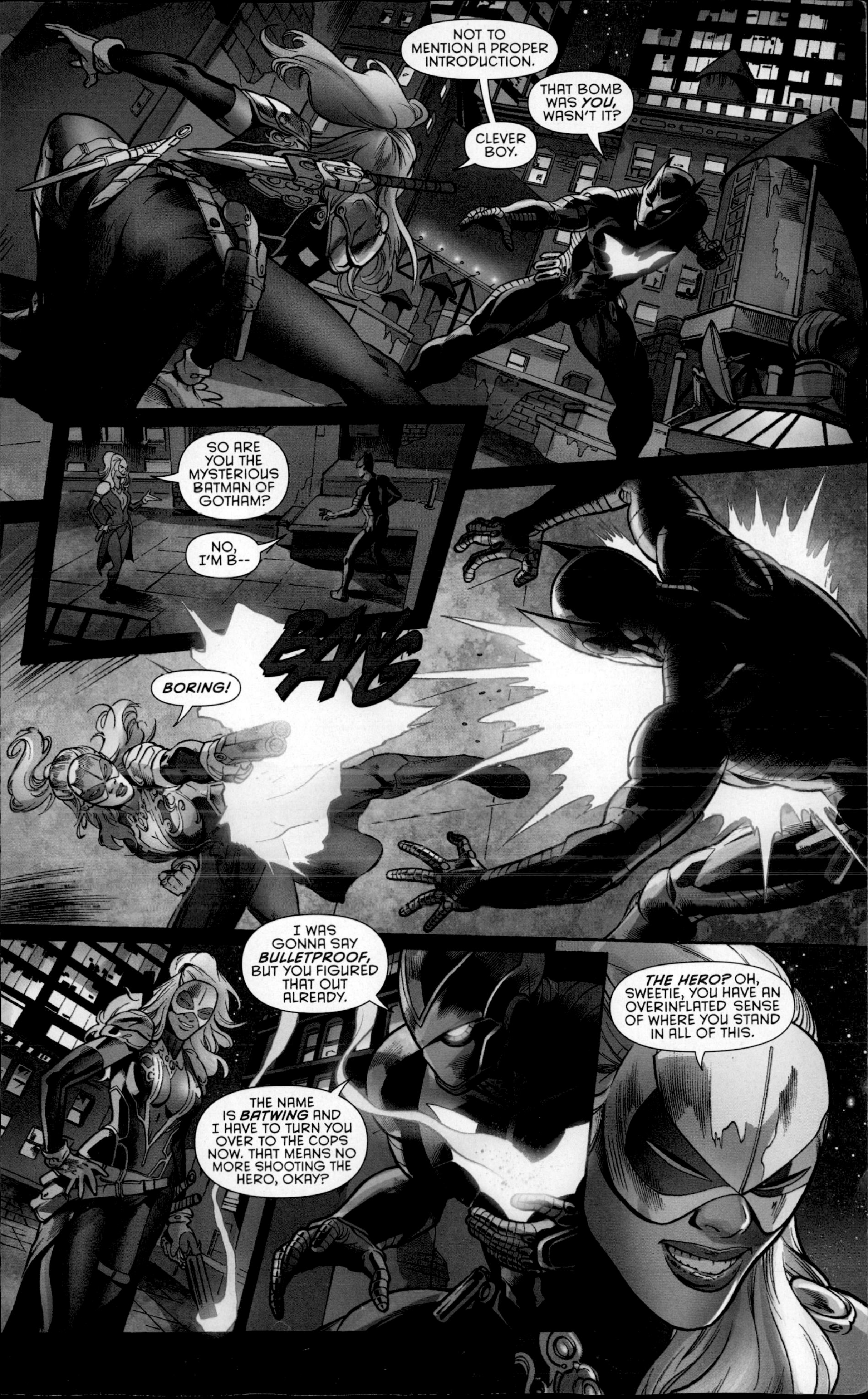
NOT TO MENTION A PROPER INTRODUCTION.
CLEVER BOY.
THAT BOMB WAS *YOU,* WASN'T IT?
SO ARE YOU THE MYSTERIOUS BATMAN OF GOTHAM?
NO, I'M B--
BANG
BORING!
I WAS GONNA SAY *BULLETPROOF,* BUT YOU FIGURED THAT OUT ALREADY.
THE NAME IS *BATWING* AND I HAVE TO TURN YOU OVER TO THE COPS NOW. THAT MEANS NO MORE SHOOTING THE HERO, OKAY?
THE HERO? OH, SWEETIE, YOU HAVE AN OVERINFLATED SENSE OF WHERE YOU STAND IN ALL OF THIS.

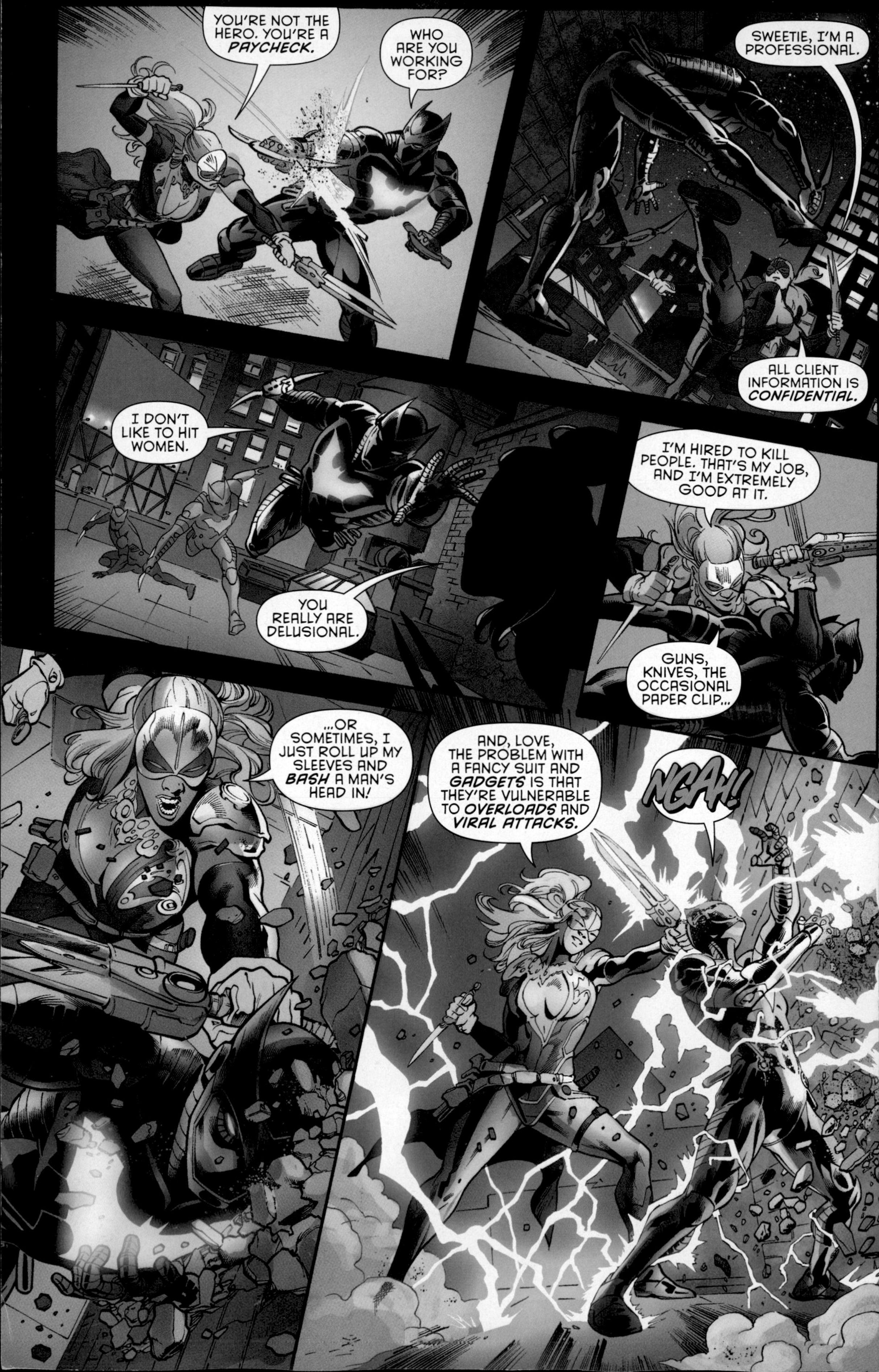
YOU'RE NOT THE HERO. YOU'RE A *PAYCHECK.*
WHO ARE YOU WORKING FOR?
SWEETIE, I'M A PROFESSIONAL.
ALL CLIENT INFORMATION IS *CONFIDENTIAL.*
I DON'T LIKE TO HIT WOMEN.
YOU REALLY ARE DELUSIONAL.
I'M HIRED TO KILL PEOPLE. THAT'S MY JOB, AND I'M EXTREMELY GOOD AT IT.
GUNS, KNIVES, THE OCCASIONAL PAPER CLIP...
...OR SOMETIMES, I JUST ROLL UP MY SLEEVES AND *BASH* A MAN'S HEAD IN!
AND, LOVE, THE PROBLEM WITH A FANCY SUIT AND *GADGETS* IS THAT THEY'RE VULNERABLE TO *OVERLOADS* AND *VIRAL ATTACKS.*
NGAH!

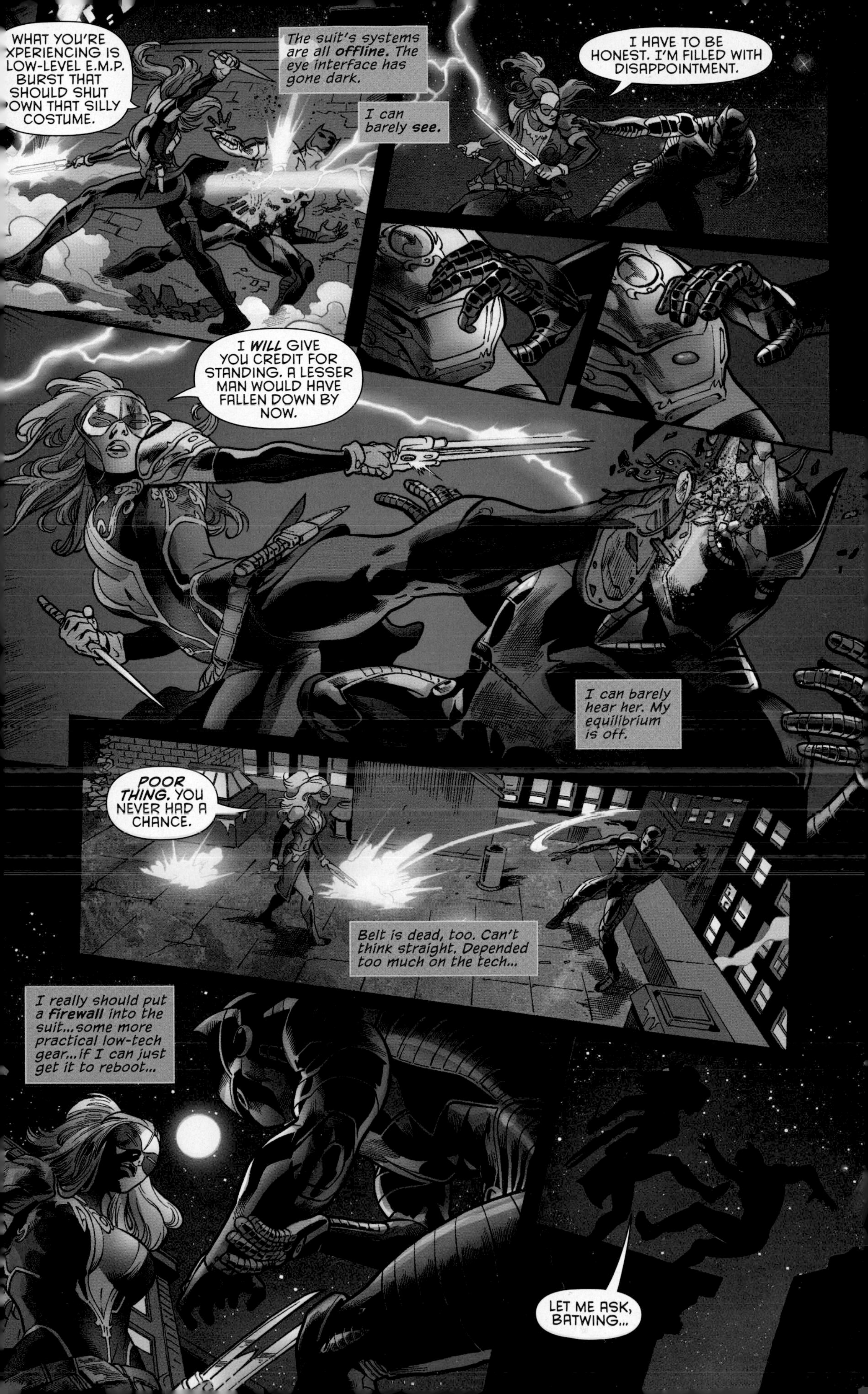
WHAT YOU'RE XPERIENCING IS LOW-LEVEL E.M.P. BURST THAT SHOULD SHUT OWN THAT SILLY COSTUME.
The suit's systems are all offline. The eye interface has gone dark.
I can barely see.
I HAVE TO BE HONEST. I'M FILLED WITH DISAPPOINTMENT.
I WILL GIVE YOU CREDIT FOR STANDING. A LESSER MAN WOULD HAVE FALLEN DOWN BY NOW.
I can barely hear her. My equilibrium is off.
POOR THING. YOU NEVER HAD A CHANCE.
Belt is dead, too. Can't think straight. Depended too much on the tech...
I really should put a firewall into the suit...some more practical low-tech gear...if I can just get it to reboot...
LET ME ASK, BATWING...

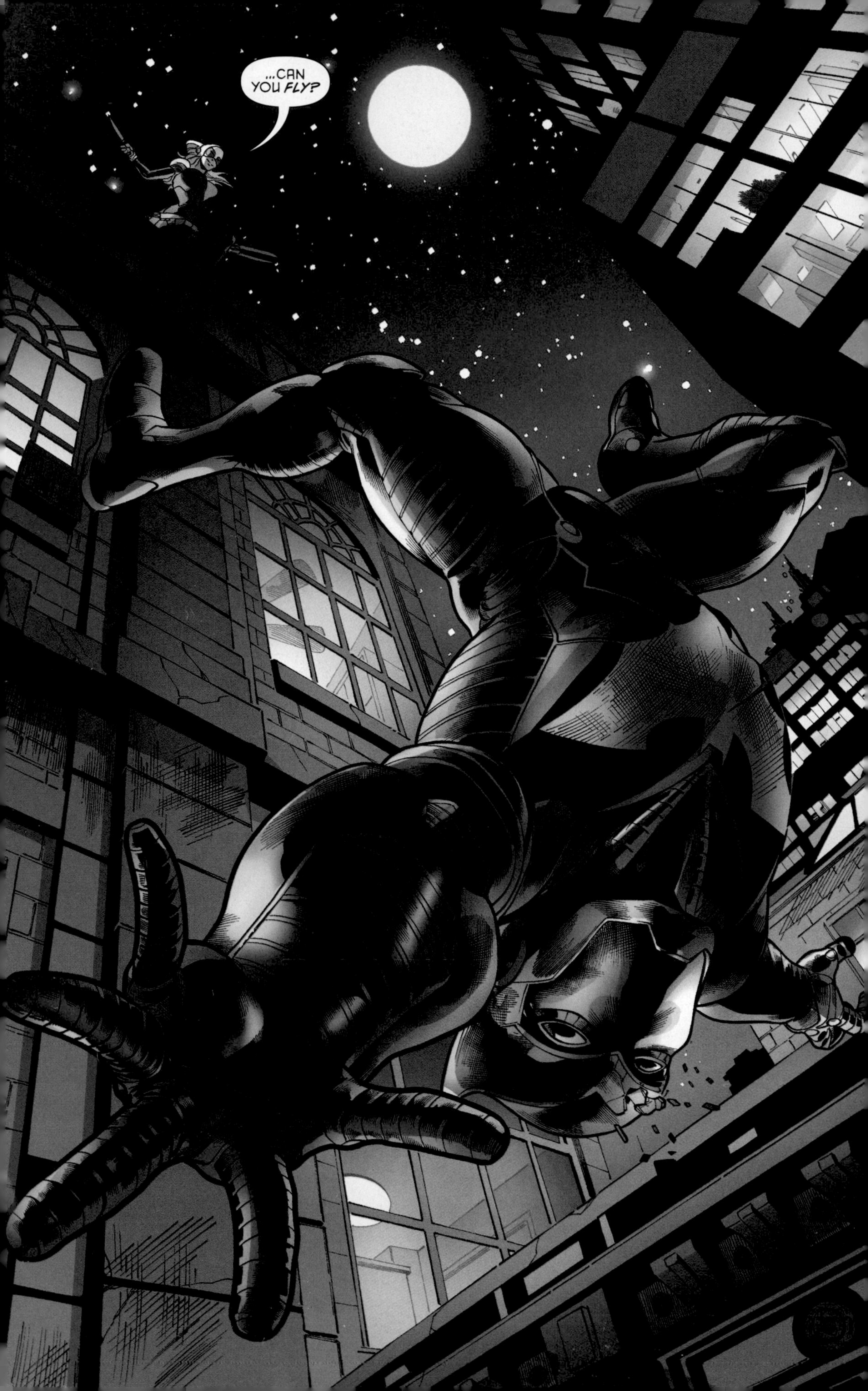
...CAN YOU FLY?

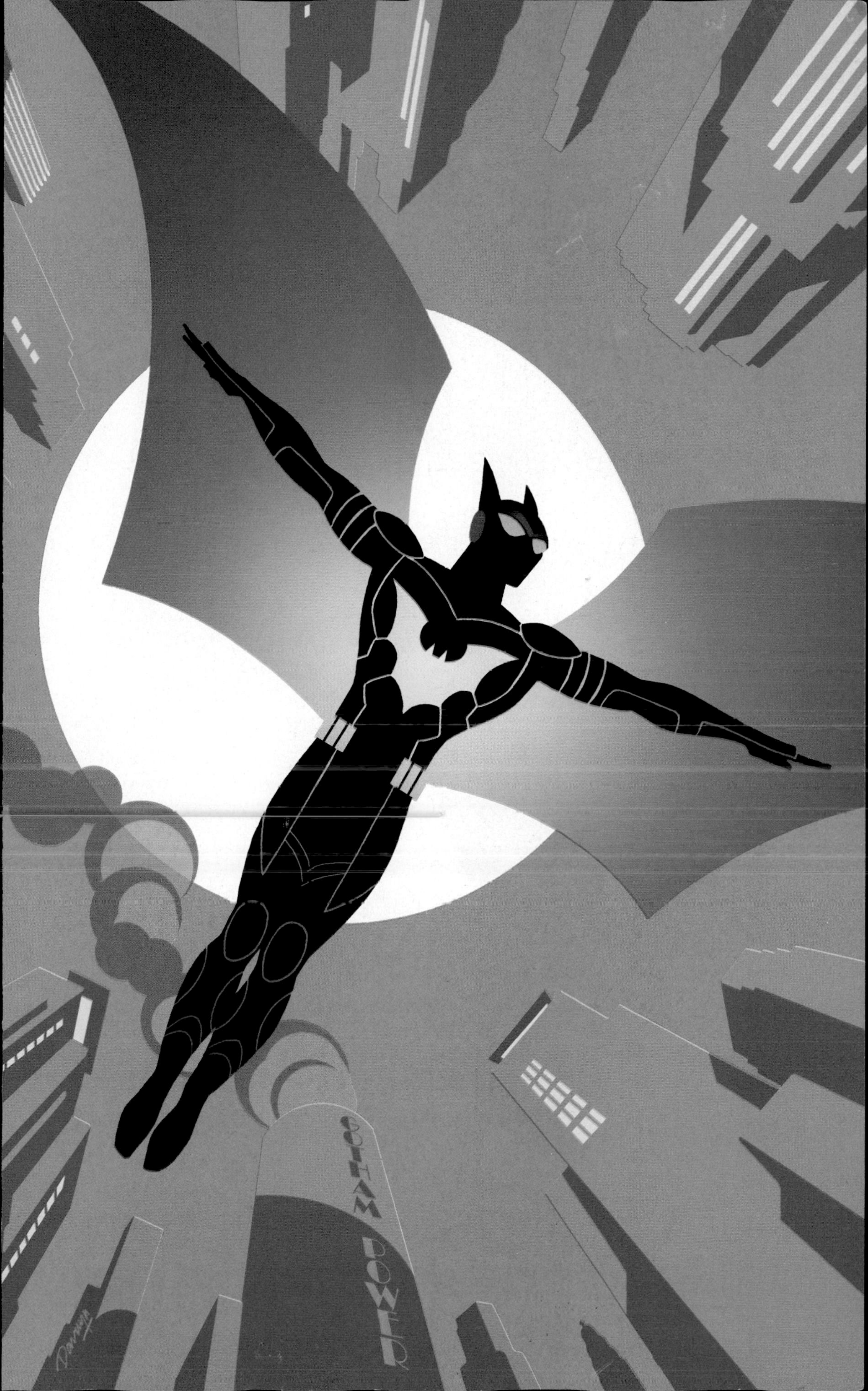
GOTHAM
POWER

I CAN'T CATCH A BREAK

cover art by DARWYN COOKE

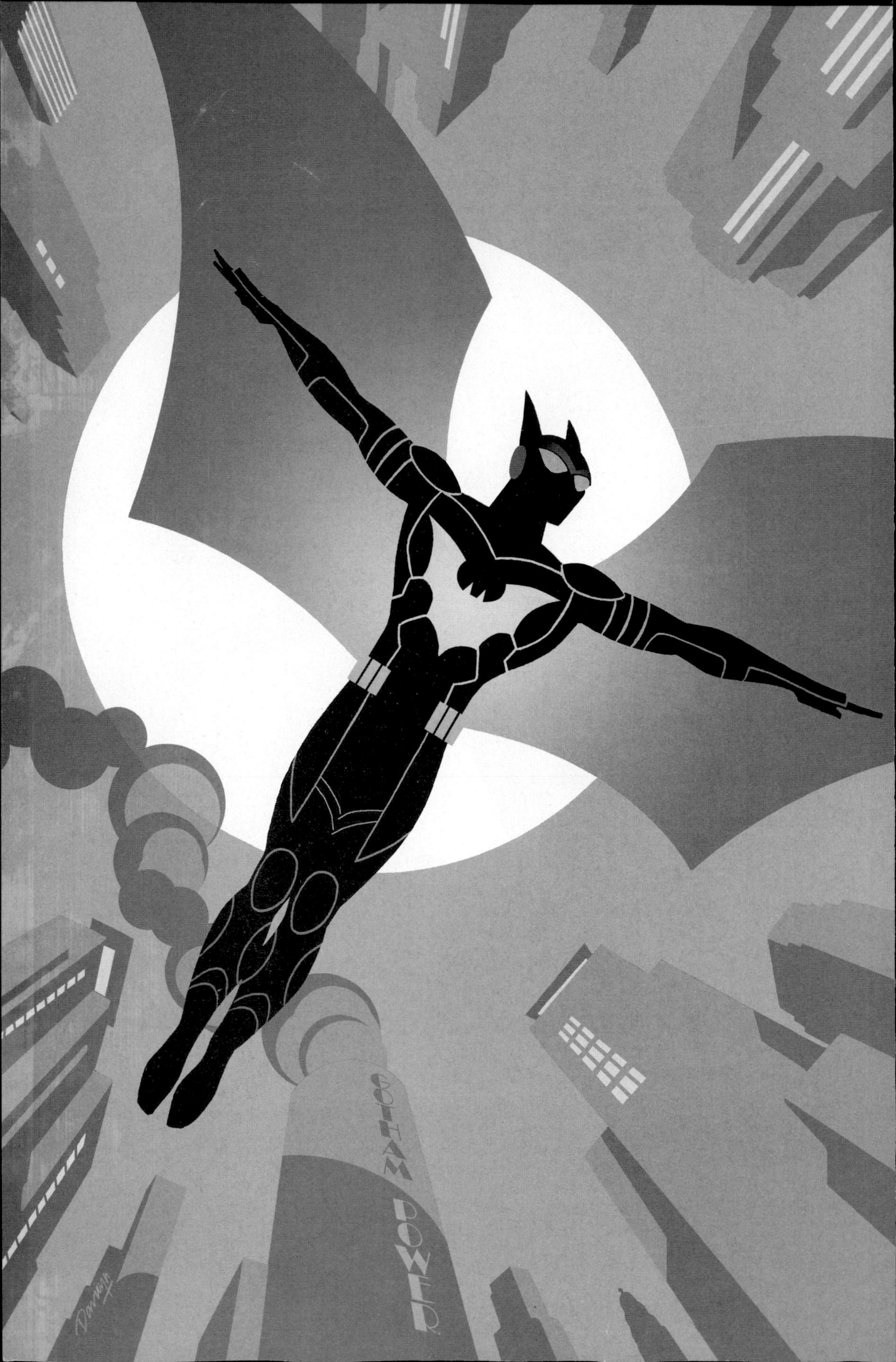
GOTHAM TOWER
Darwyn

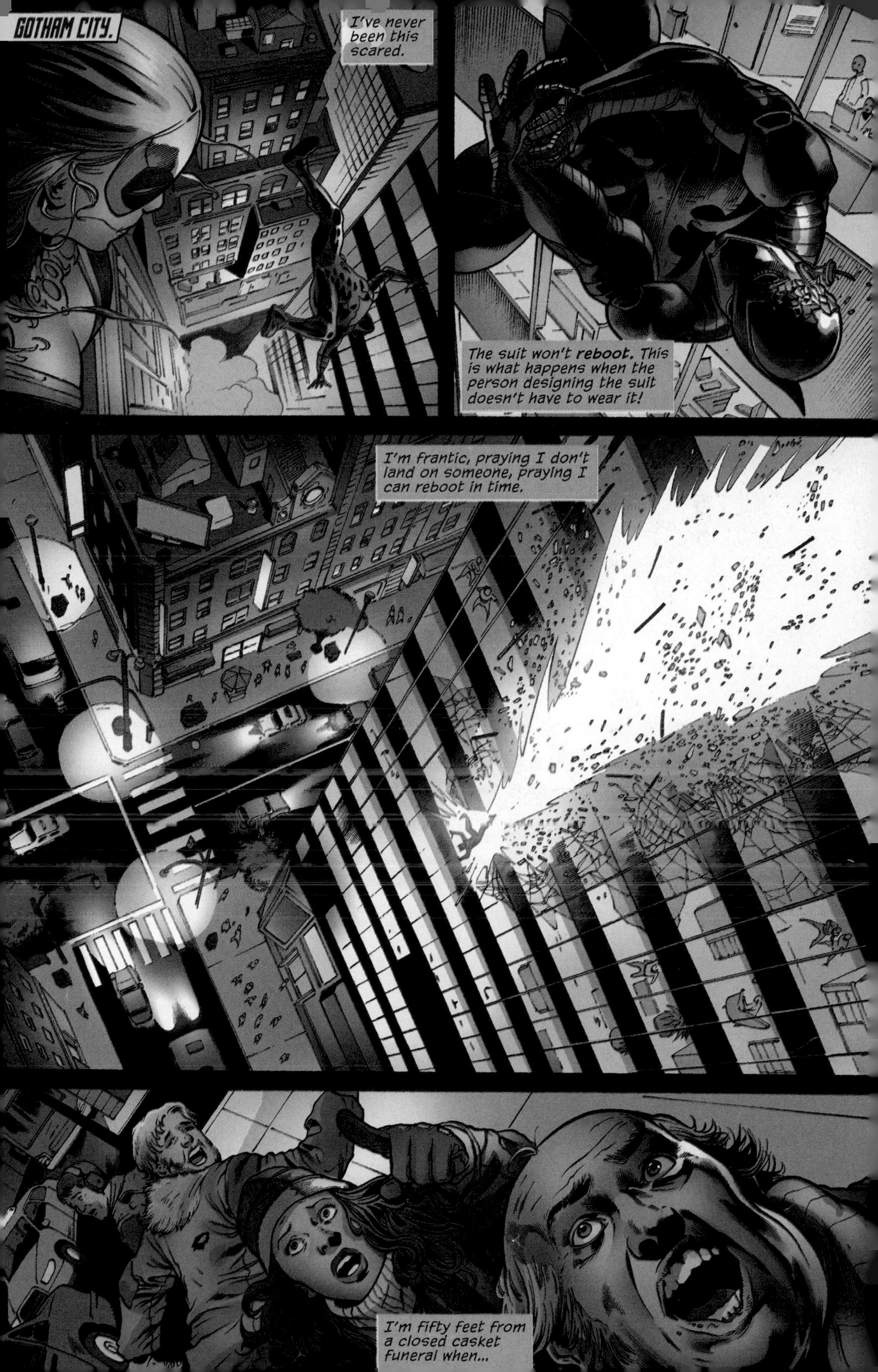

GOTHAM CITY.
I've never been this scared.
The suit won't reboot. This is what happens when the person designing the suit doesn't have to wear it!
I'm frantic, praying I don't land on someone, praying I can reboot in time.
I'm fifty feet from a closed casket funeral when...

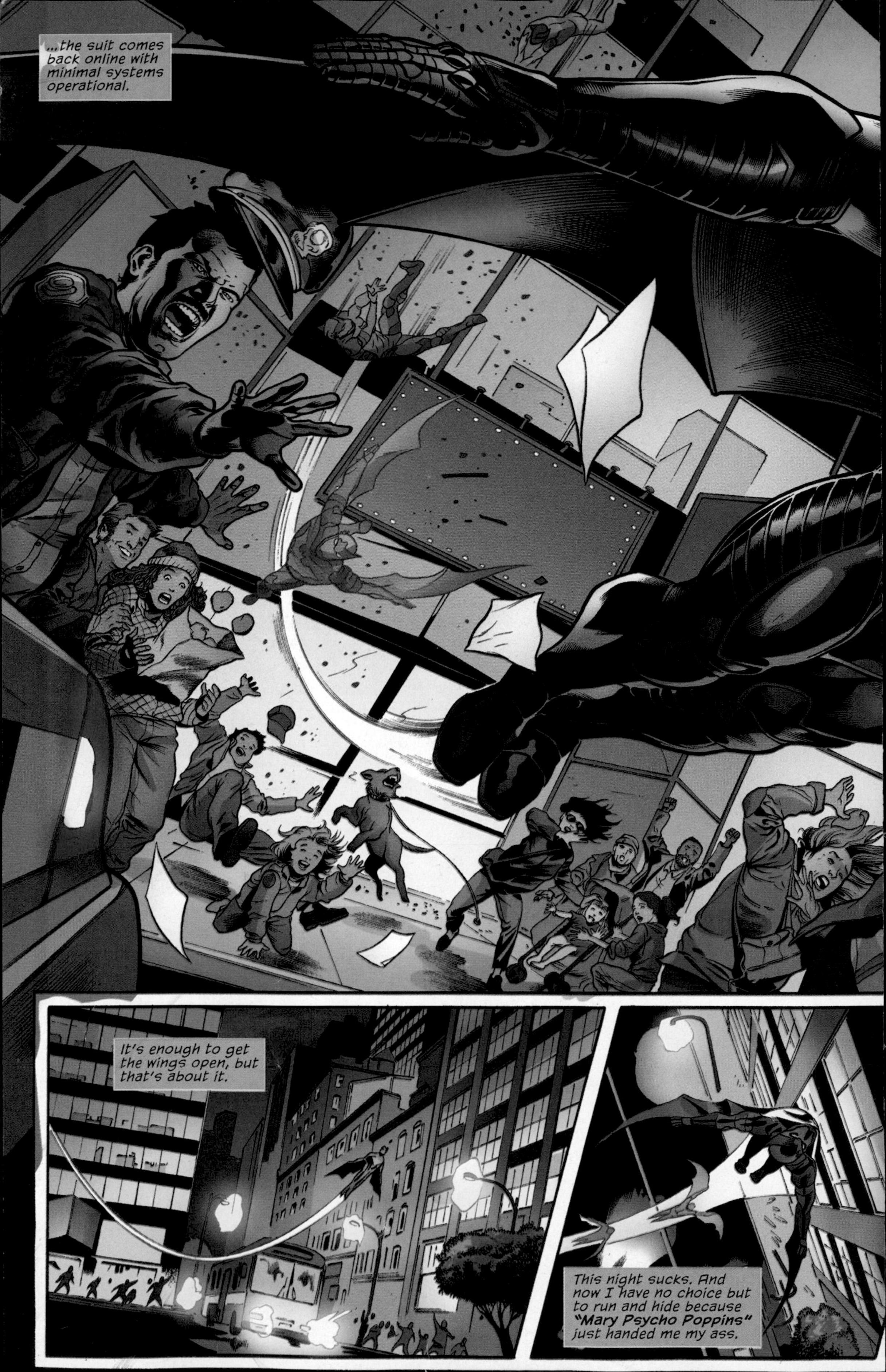
...the suit comes back online with minimal systems operational.
It's enough to get the wings open, but that's about it.
This night sucks. And now I have no choice but to run and hide because "Mary Psycho Poppins" just handed me my ass.

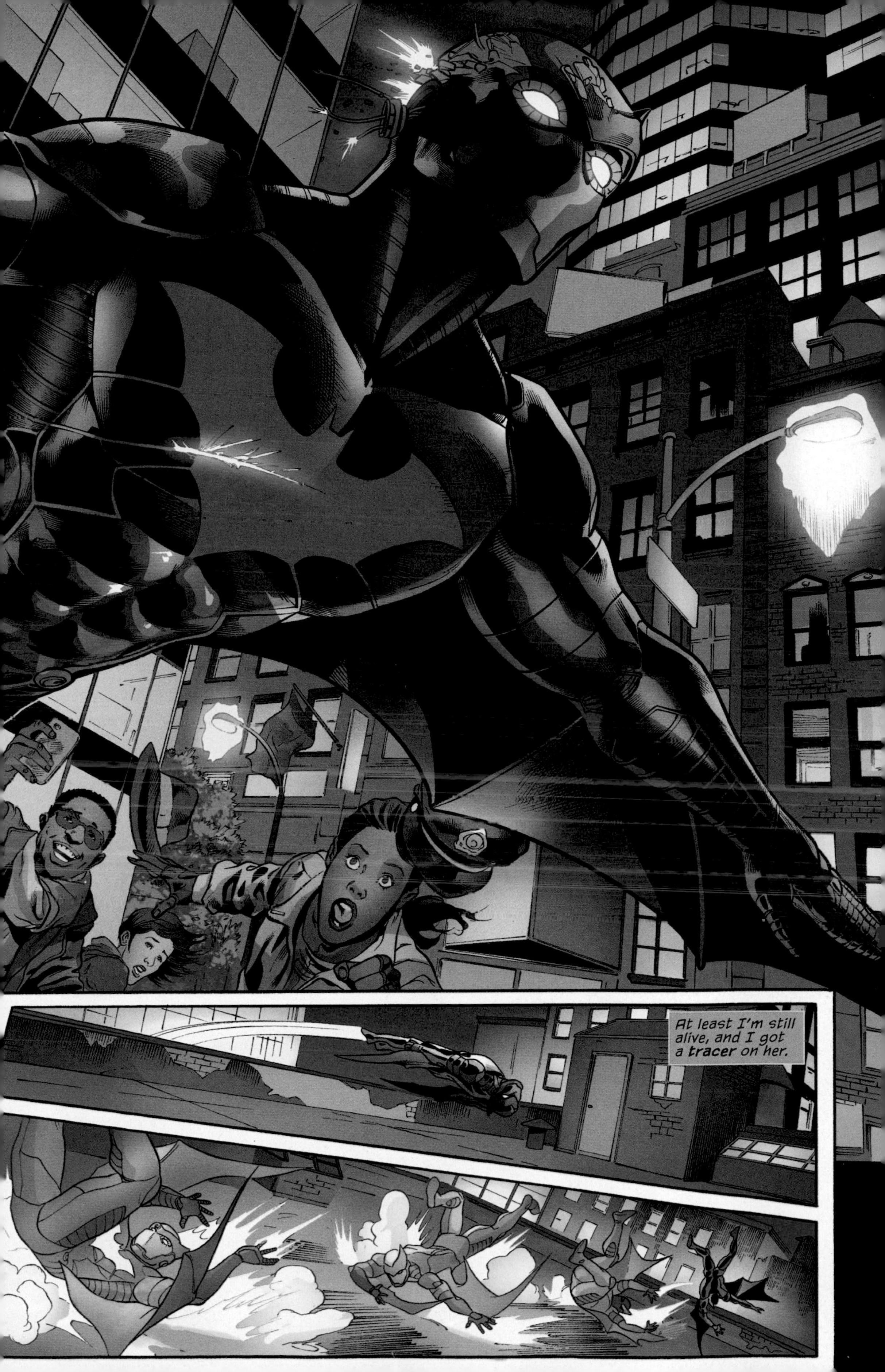
At least I'm still alive, and I got a tracer on her.

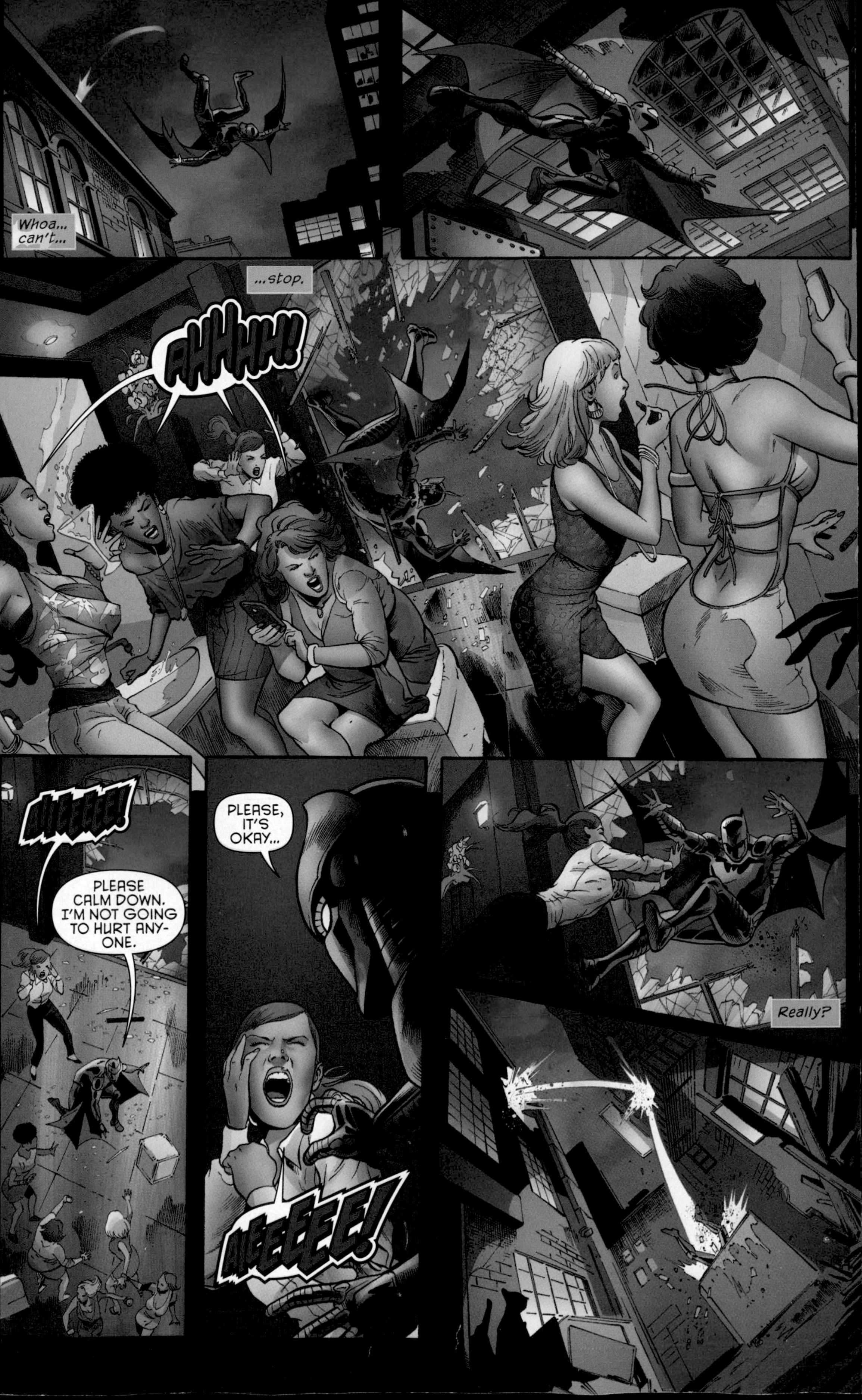
Whoa... can't...
...stop.
AHHHHH!
PLEASE CALM DOWN. I'M NOT GOING TO HURT ANY-ONE.
PLEASE, IT'S OKAY...
Really?

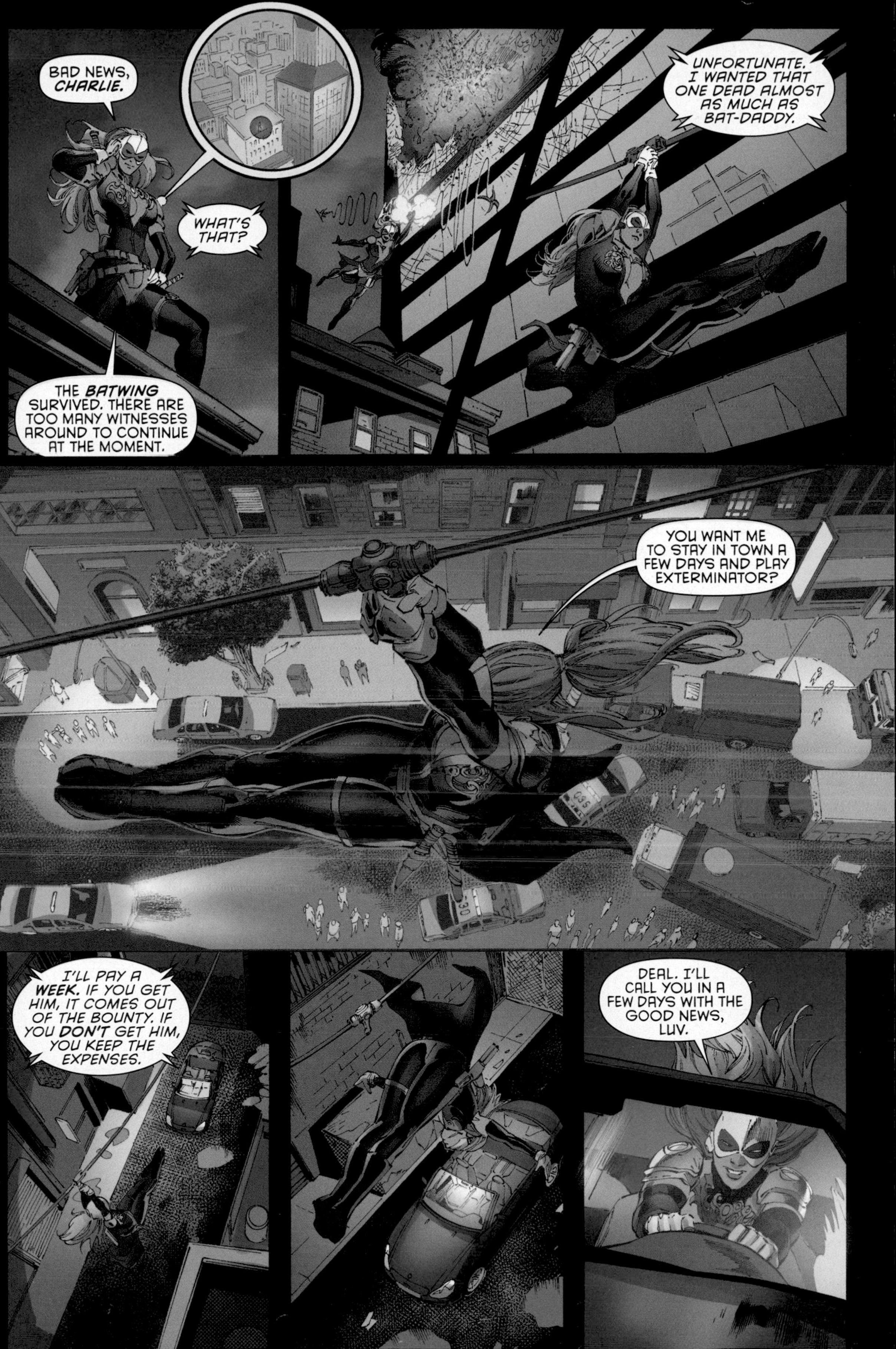
BAD NEWS, CHARLIE.
THE BATWING SURVIVED. THERE ARE TOO MANY WITNESSES AROUND TO CONTINUE AT THE MOMENT.
WHAT'S THAT?
UNFORTUNATE. I WANTED THAT ONE DEAD ALMOST AS MUCH AS BAT-DADDY.
YOU WANT ME TO STAY IN TOWN A FEW DAYS AND PLAY EXTERMINATOR?
I'LL PAY A WEEK. IF YOU GET HIM, IT COMES OUT OF THE BOUNTY. IF YOU DON'T GET HIM, YOU KEEP THE EXPENSES.
DEAL. I'LL CALL YOU IN A FEW DAYS WITH THE GOOD NEWS, LUV.

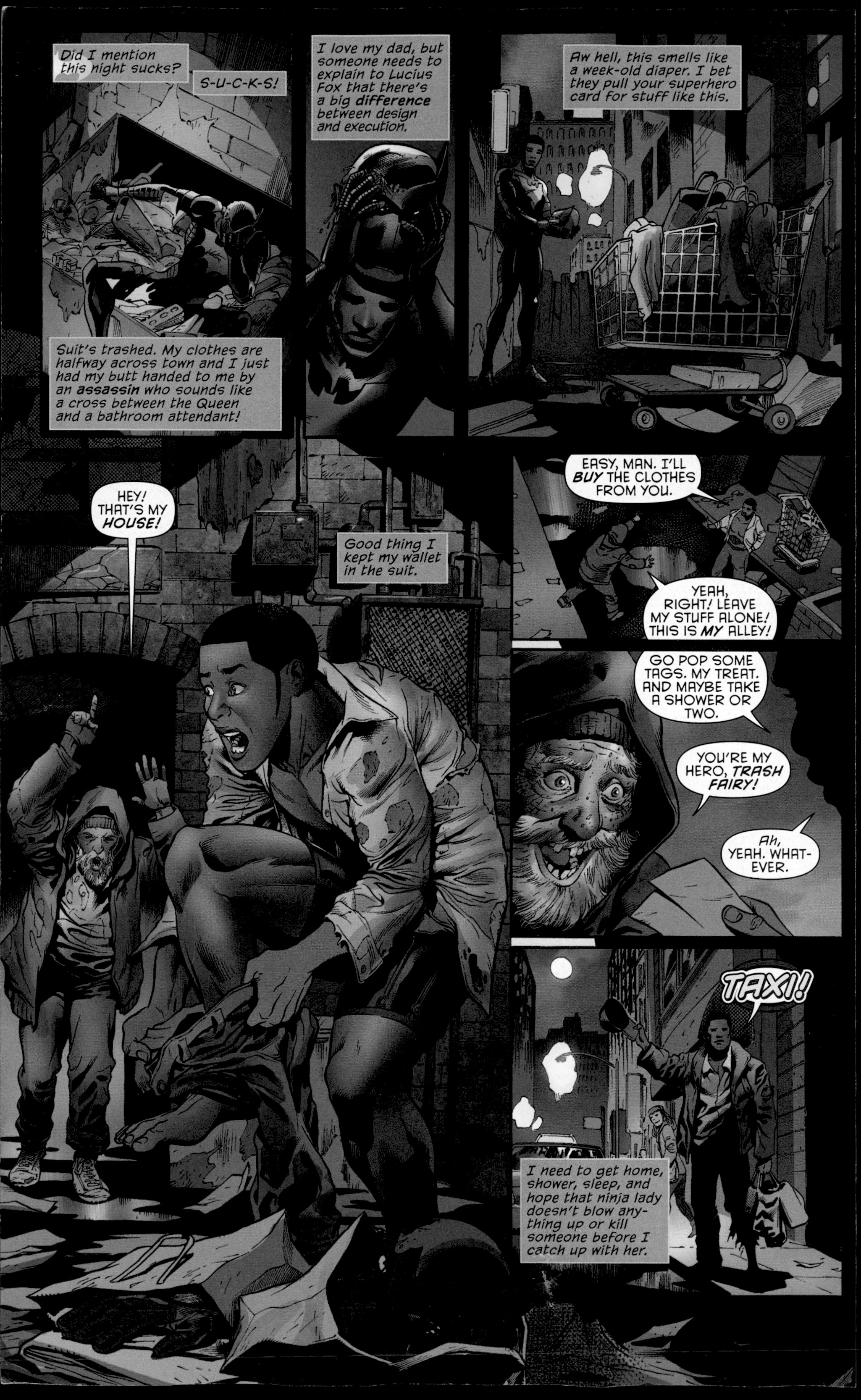
Did I mention this night sucks?
S-U-C-K-S!
Suit's trashed. My clothes are halfway across town and I just had my butt handed to me by an **assassin** who sounds like a cross between the Queen and a bathroom attendant!
I love my dad, but someone needs to explain to Lucius Fox that there's a big **difference** between design and execution.
Aw hell, this smells like a week-old diaper. I bet they pull your superhero card for stuff like this.
HEY! THAT'S MY *HOUSE!*
Good thing I kept my wallet in the suit.
EASY, MAN. I'LL *BUY* THE CLOTHES FROM YOU.
YEAH, RIGHT! LEAVE MY STUFF ALONE! THIS IS *MY* ALLEY!
GO POP SOME TAGS. MY TREAT. AND MAYBE TAKE A SHOWER OR TWO.
YOU'RE MY HERO, *TRASH FAIRY!*
Ah, YEAH. WHAT-EVER.
TAXI!
I need to get home, shower, sleep, and hope that ninja lady doesn't blow anything up or kill someone before I catch up with her.

TAKE A *BATH,* FREAK!

LOVE YOU, TOO.

What is Zena doing here?

I CALLED AND LEFT MESSAGES ALL NIGHT.

WAIT, YOU JUST *BROKE UP* WITH ME. NOW YOU'RE HERE WAITING FOR ME? WHAT THE HELL, Z?

IT'S MY... HE'S...MY DAD IS *DEAD,* LUKE. A MASSIVE HEART ATTACK.

I FOUND HIM WHEN I GOT HOME AND I CAN'T GO BACK AND SLEEP IN THE HOUSE.

I DIDN'T KNOW WHERE ELSE TO GO BECAUSE BECCA IS OUT OF TOWN.

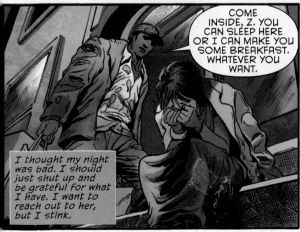

COME INSIDE, Z. YOU CAN SLEEP HERE OR I CAN MAKE YOU SOME BREAKFAST. WHATEVER YOU WANT.

I thought my night was bad. I should just shut up and be grateful for what I have. I want to reach out to her, but I stink.

THANKS...

COME ON.

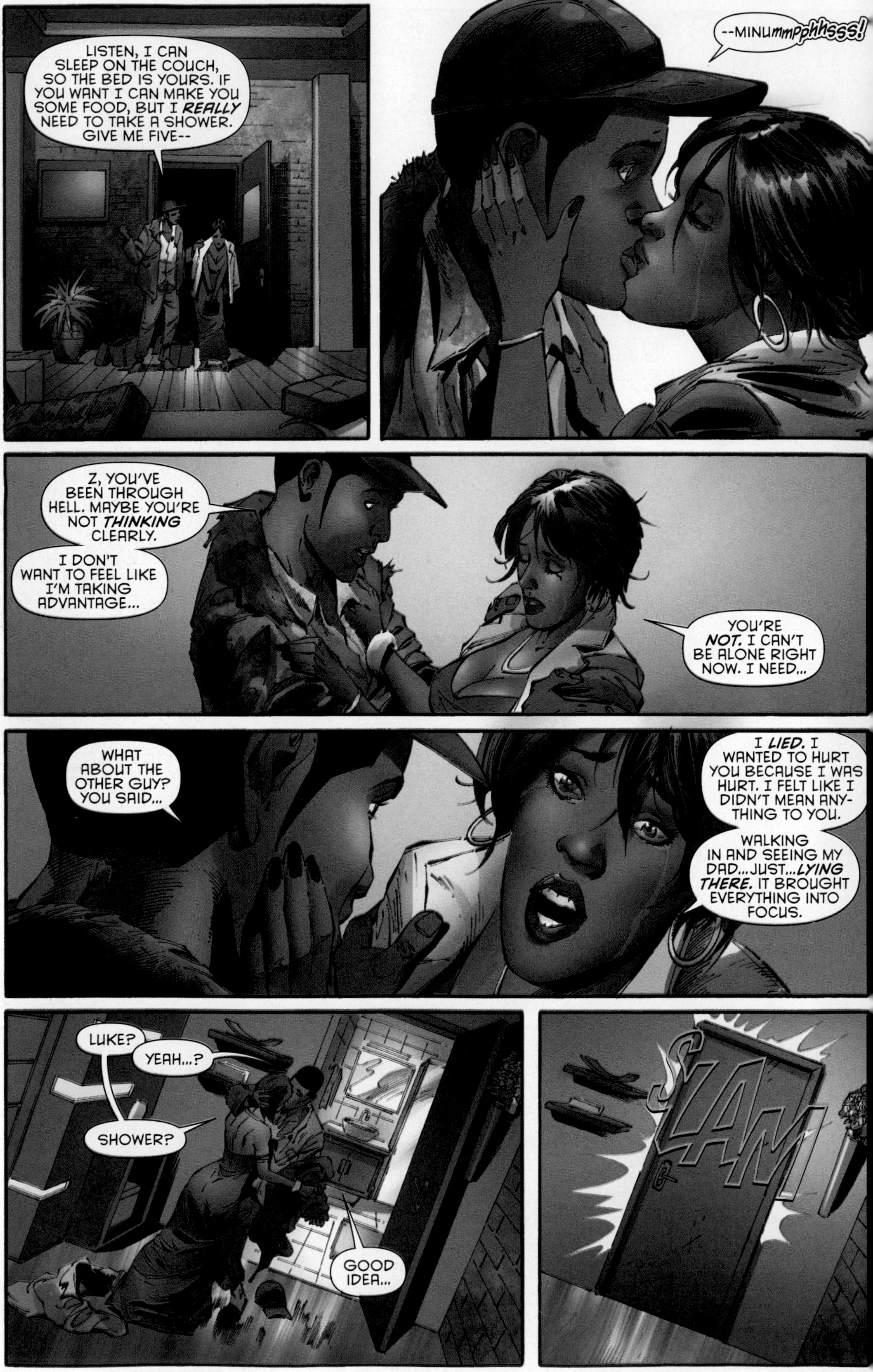
LISTEN, I CAN SLEEP ON THE COUCH, SO THE BED IS YOURS. IF YOU WANT I CAN MAKE YOU SOME FOOD, BUT I REALLY NEED TO TAKE A SHOWER. GIVE ME FIVE--
--MINUmmpphhsss!
Z, YOU'VE BEEN THROUGH HELL. MAYBE YOU'RE NOT THINKING CLEARLY.
I DON'T WANT TO FEEL LIKE I'M TAKING ADVANTAGE...
YOU'RE NOT. I CAN'T BE ALONE RIGHT NOW. I NEED...
WHAT ABOUT THE OTHER GUY? YOU SAID...
I LIED. I WANTED TO HURT YOU BECAUSE I WAS HURT. I FELT LIKE I DIDN'T MEAN ANY-THING TO YOU.
WALKING IN AND SEEING MY DAD...JUST...LYING THERE. IT BROUGHT EVERYTHING INTO FOCUS.
LUKE?
YEAH...?
SHOWER?
GOOD IDEA...
SLAM

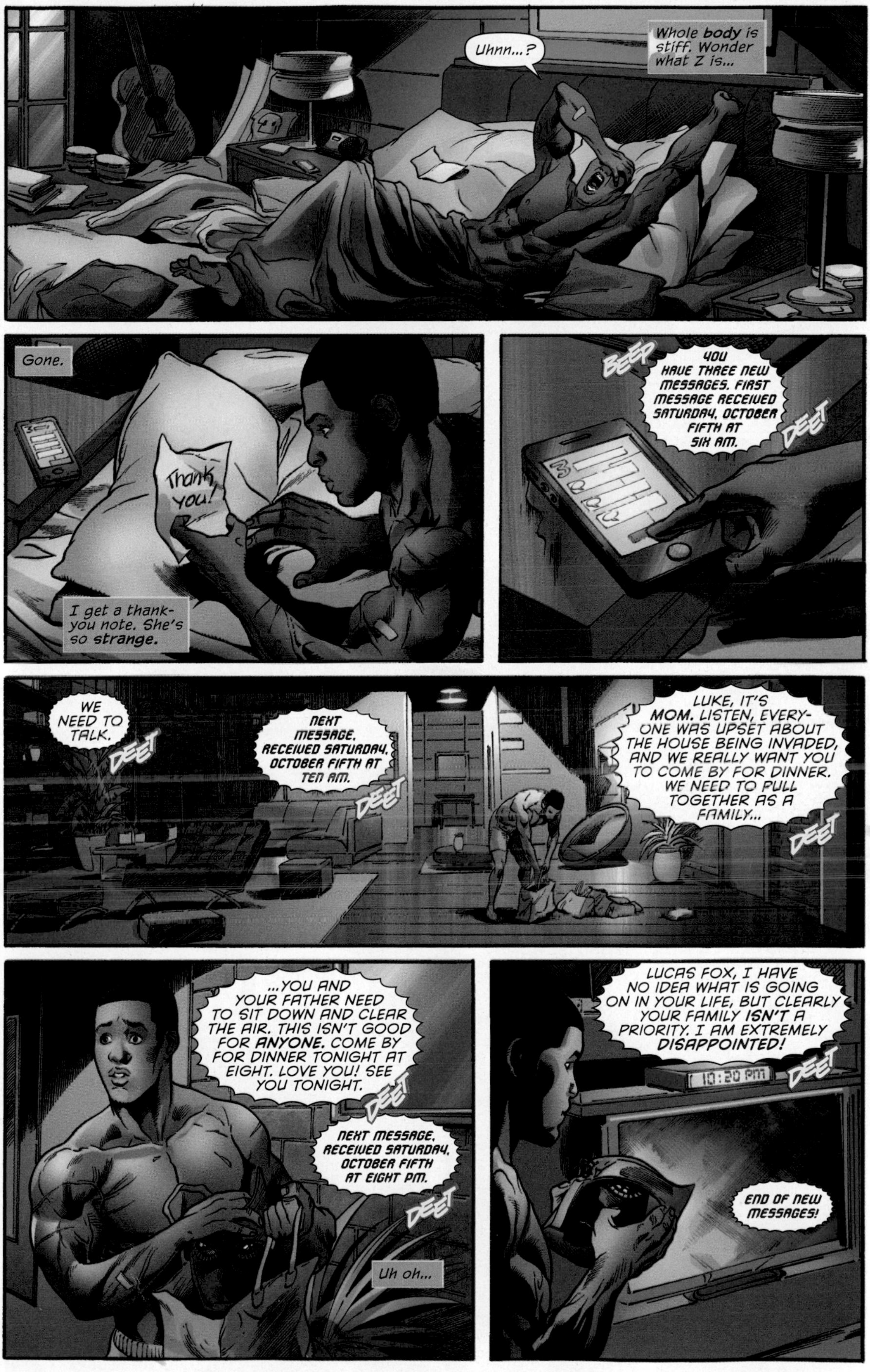
Uhnn...?
Whole body is stiff. Wonder what Z is...
Gone.
I get a thank-you note. She's so strange.
Thank you!
BEEP
YOU HAVE THREE NEW MESSAGES. FIRST MESSAGE RECEIVED SATURDAY, OCTOBER FIFTH AT SIX AM.
DEET
WE NEED TO TALK.
DEET
NEXT MESSAGE, RECEIVED SATURDAY, OCTOBER FIFTH AT TEN AM.
DEET
LUKE, IT'S MOM. LISTEN, EVERYONE WAS UPSET ABOUT THE HOUSE BEING INVADED, AND WE REALLY WANT YOU TO COME BY FOR DINNER. WE NEED TO PULL TOGETHER AS A FAMILY...
DEET
...YOU AND YOUR FATHER NEED TO SIT DOWN AND CLEAR THE AIR. THIS ISN'T GOOD FOR ANYONE. COME BY FOR DINNER TONIGHT AT EIGHT. LOVE YOU! SEE YOU TONIGHT.
DEET
NEXT MESSAGE, RECEIVED SATURDAY, OCTOBER FIFTH AT EIGHT PM.
DEET
Uh oh...
LUCAS FOX, I HAVE NO IDEA WHAT IS GOING ON IN YOUR LIFE, BUT CLEARLY YOUR FAMILY ISN'T A PRIORITY. I AM EXTREMELY DISAPPOINTED!
10:20 PM
DEET
END OF NEW MESSAGES!

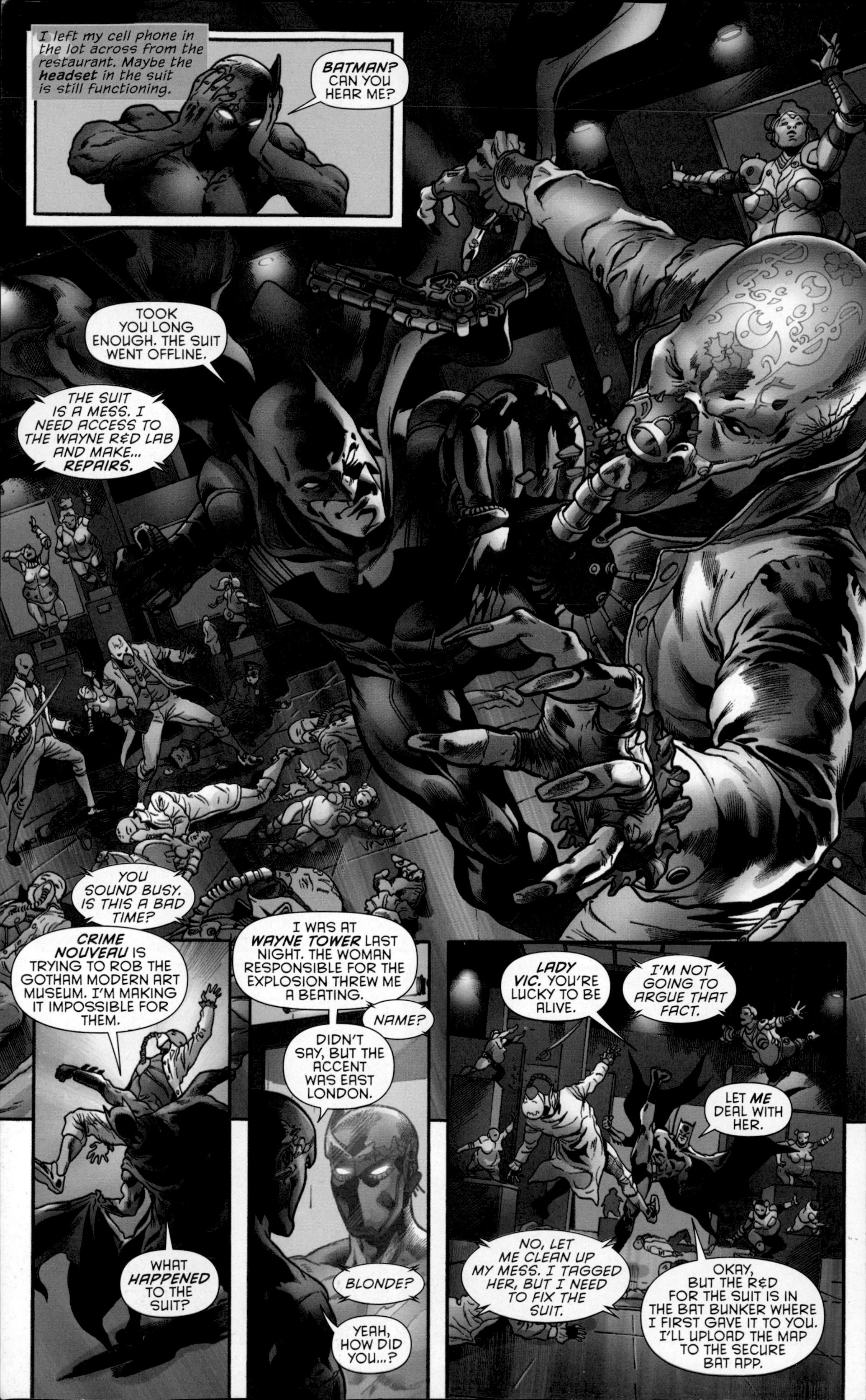
I left my cell phone in the lot across from the restaurant. Maybe the *headset* in the suit is still functioning.
BATMAN? CAN YOU HEAR ME?
TOOK YOU LONG ENOUGH. THE SUIT WENT OFFLINE.
THE SUIT IS A MESS. I NEED ACCESS TO THE WAYNE R&D LAB AND MAKE... *REPAIRS.*
YOU SOUND BUSY. IS THIS A BAD TIME?
CRIME NOUVEAU IS TRYING TO ROB THE GOTHAM MODERN ART MUSEUM. I'M MAKING IT IMPOSSIBLE FOR THEM.
WHAT *HAPPENED* TO THE SUIT?
I WAS AT *WAYNE TOWER* LAST NIGHT. THE WOMAN RESPONSIBLE FOR THE EXPLOSION THREW ME A BEATING.
NAME?
DIDN'T SAY, BUT THE ACCENT WAS EAST LONDON.
BLONDE?
YEAH, HOW DID YOU...?
LADY VIC. YOU'RE LUCKY TO BE ALIVE.
I'M NOT GOING TO ARGUE THAT FACT.
LET *ME* DEAL WITH HER.
NO, LET ME CLEAN UP MY MESS. I TAGGED HER, BUT I NEED TO FIX THE SUIT.
OKAY, BUT THE R&D FOR THE SUIT IS IN THE BAT BUNKER WHERE I FIRST GAVE IT TO YOU. I'LL UPLOAD THE MAP TO THE SECURE BAT APP.

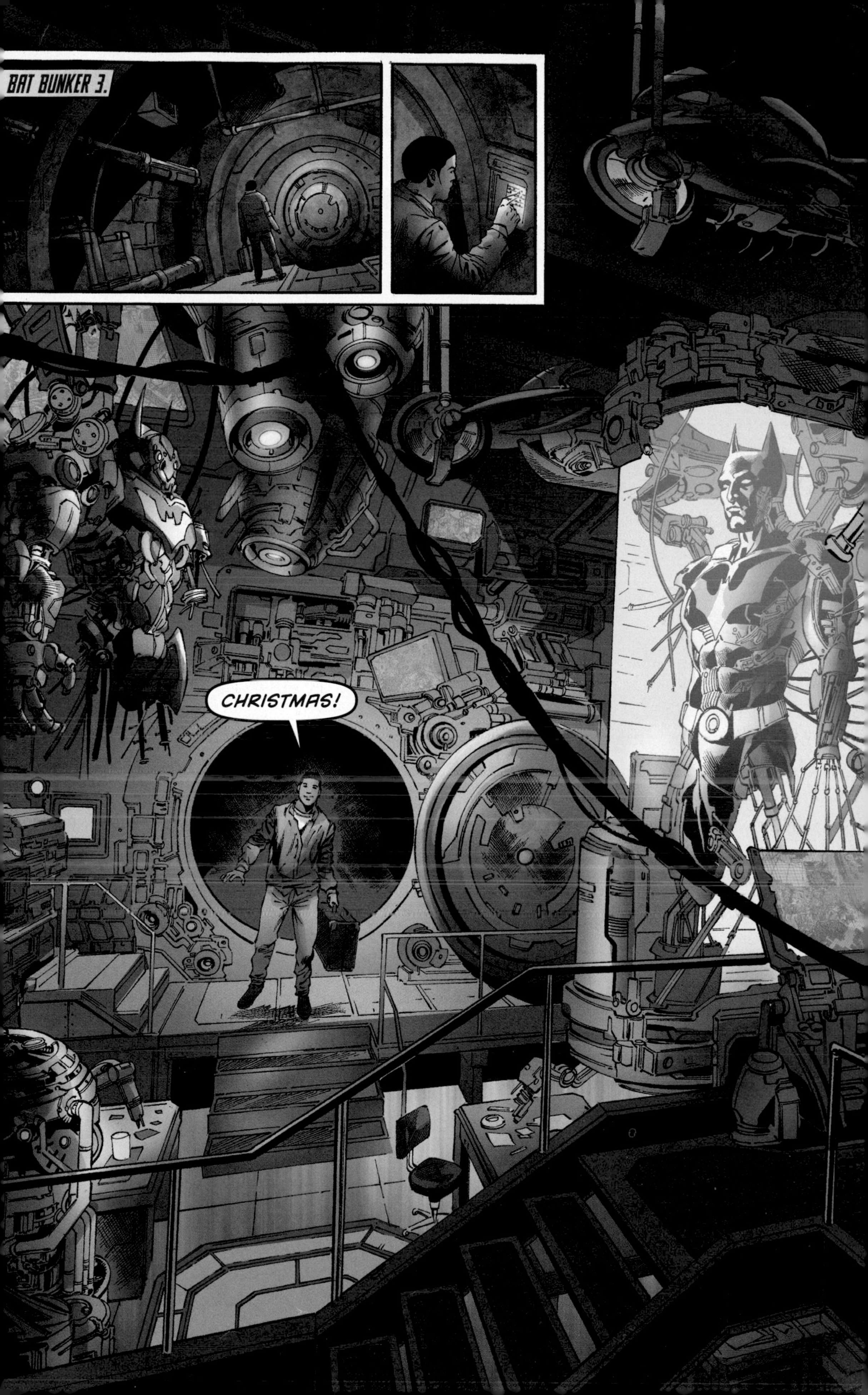
BAT BUNKER 3.
CHRISTMAS!

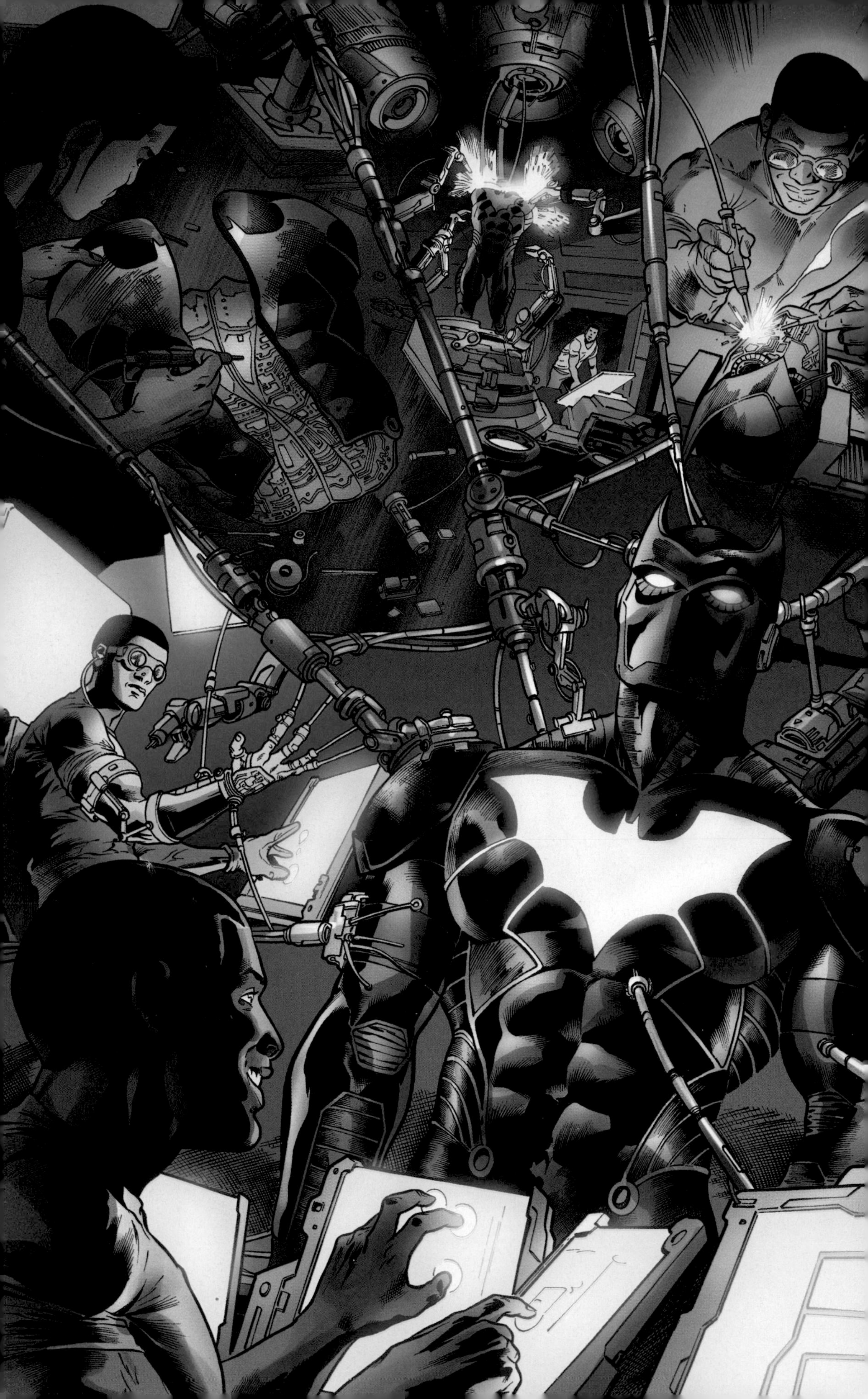

LATER. FOX MANSION.

EXCUSE ME.

LOOK WHO DECIDED TO SHOW UP.

MOM, I'M *SORRY*.

YOU SHOULD BE. I HAD YOUR FATHER CALM, REASONABLE AND READY TO TALK, AND YOU DON'T EVEN HAVE THE DECENCY TO CALL?

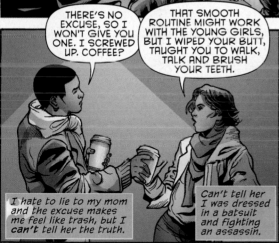

THERE'S NO EXCUSE, SO I WON'T GIVE YOU ONE. I SCREWED UP. COFFEE?

THAT SMOOTH ROUTINE MIGHT WORK WITH THE YOUNG GIRLS, BUT I WIPED YOUR BUTT, TAUGHT YOU TO WALK, TALK AND BRUSH YOUR TEETH.

I hate to lie to my mom and the excuse makes me feel like trash, but I can't tell her the truth.

Can't tell her I was dressed in a batsuit and fighting an assassin.

ZENA'S DAD DIED THE NIGHT BEFORE YOU CALLED. WE WERE UP ALL NIGHT AND BY THE TIME I WOKE UP I WAS ALREADY MORE THAN AN HOUR LATE FOR DINNER.

I NEVER EVEN SAW YOUR MESSAGES.

OH. THAT POOR GIRL.

I'M HERE NOW, SO ANYTHING YOU NEED, JUST ASK.

EVERYTHING IS UNDER CONTROL. YOU SHOULD BE WITH ZENA. I *LIKE* HER.

WE'LL SET UP ANOTHER DINNER. I PROMISE.

SURE, AND LET ME KNOW WHEN THE WAKE IS AND WHERE WE CAN SEND FLOWERS.

THANKS, MOM. LOVE YOU.

LOVE YOU TOO, SON.

I feel like such a jerk right now.

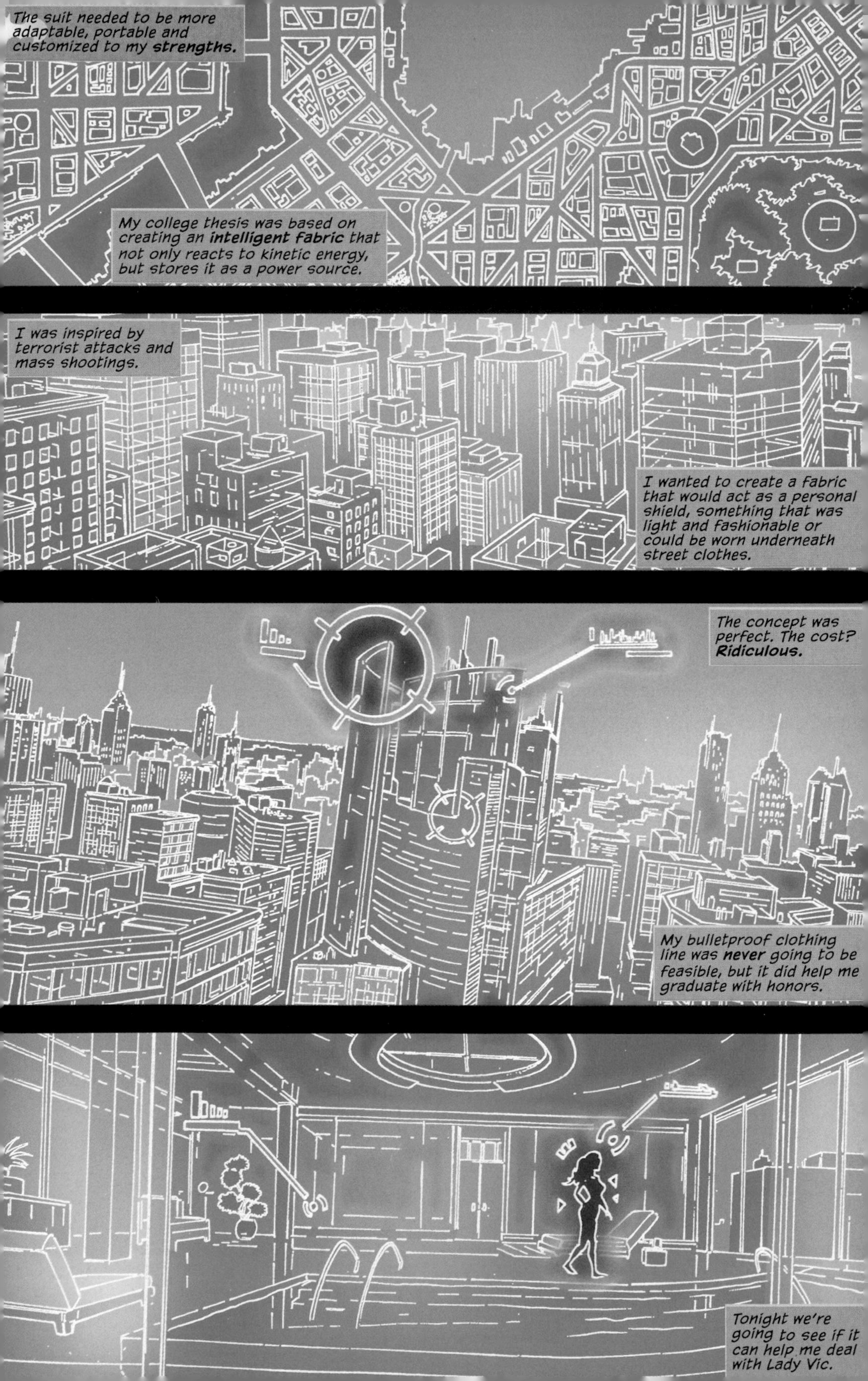

The suit needed to be more adaptable, portable and customized to my **strengths.**
My college thesis was based on creating an **intelligent fabric** that not only reacts to kinetic energy, but stores it as a power source.
I was inspired by terrorist attacks and mass shootings.
I wanted to create a fabric that would act as a personal shield, something that was light and fashionable or could be worn underneath street clothes.
The concept was perfect. The cost? **Ridiculous.**
My bulletproof clothing line was **never** going to be feasible, but it did help me graduate with honors.
Tonight we're going to see if it can help me deal with Lady Vic.

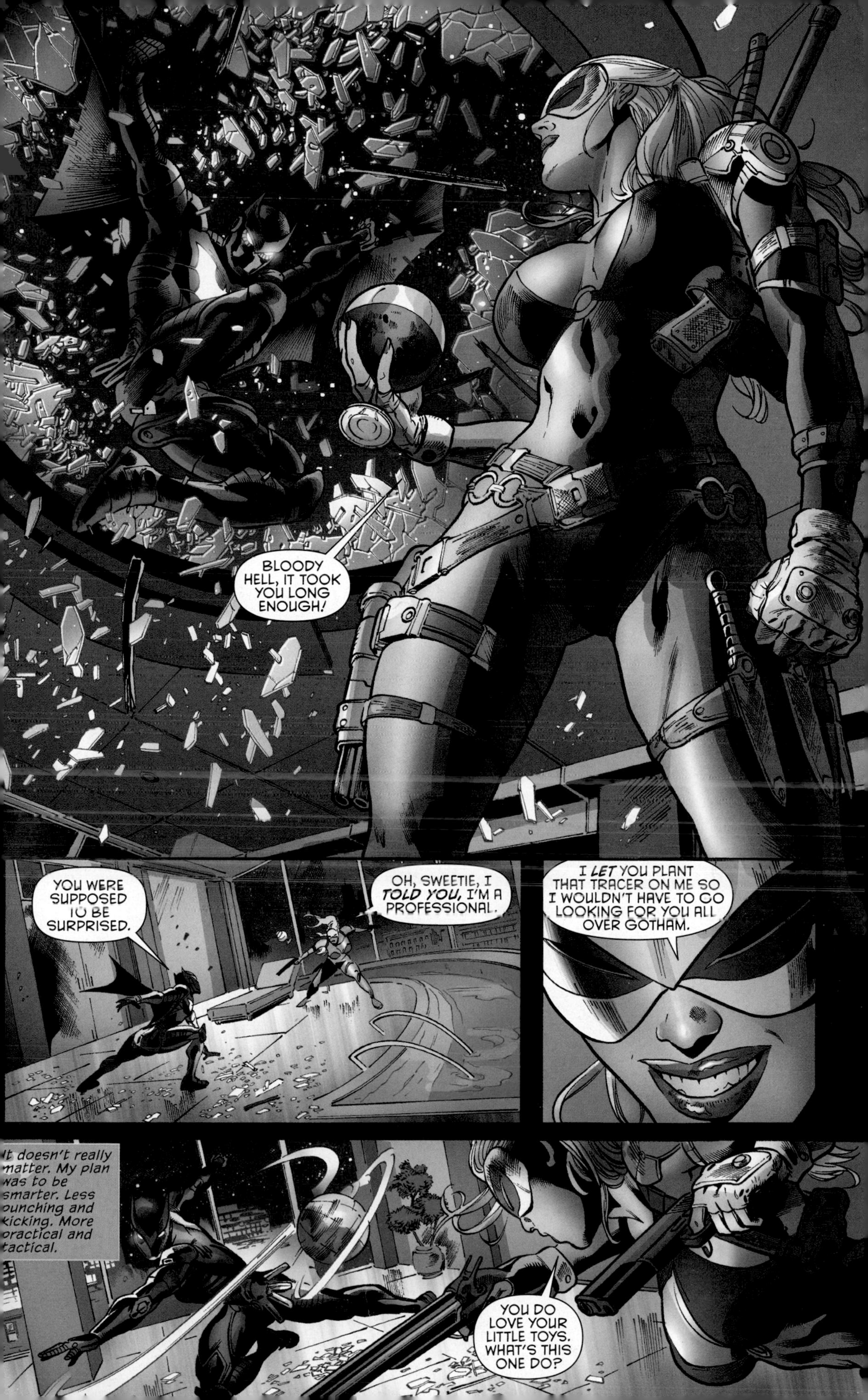
BLOODY HELL, IT TOOK YOU LONG ENOUGH!
YOU WERE SUPPOSED TO BE SURPRISED.
OH, SWEETIE, I TOLD YOU, I'M A PROFESSIONAL.
I LET YOU PLANT THAT TRACER ON ME SO I WOULDN'T HAVE TO GO LOOKING FOR YOU ALL OVER GOTHAM.
It doesn't really matter. My plan was to be smarter. Less punching and kicking. More practical and tactical.
YOU DO LOVE YOUR LITTLE TOYS. WHAT'S THIS ONE DO?

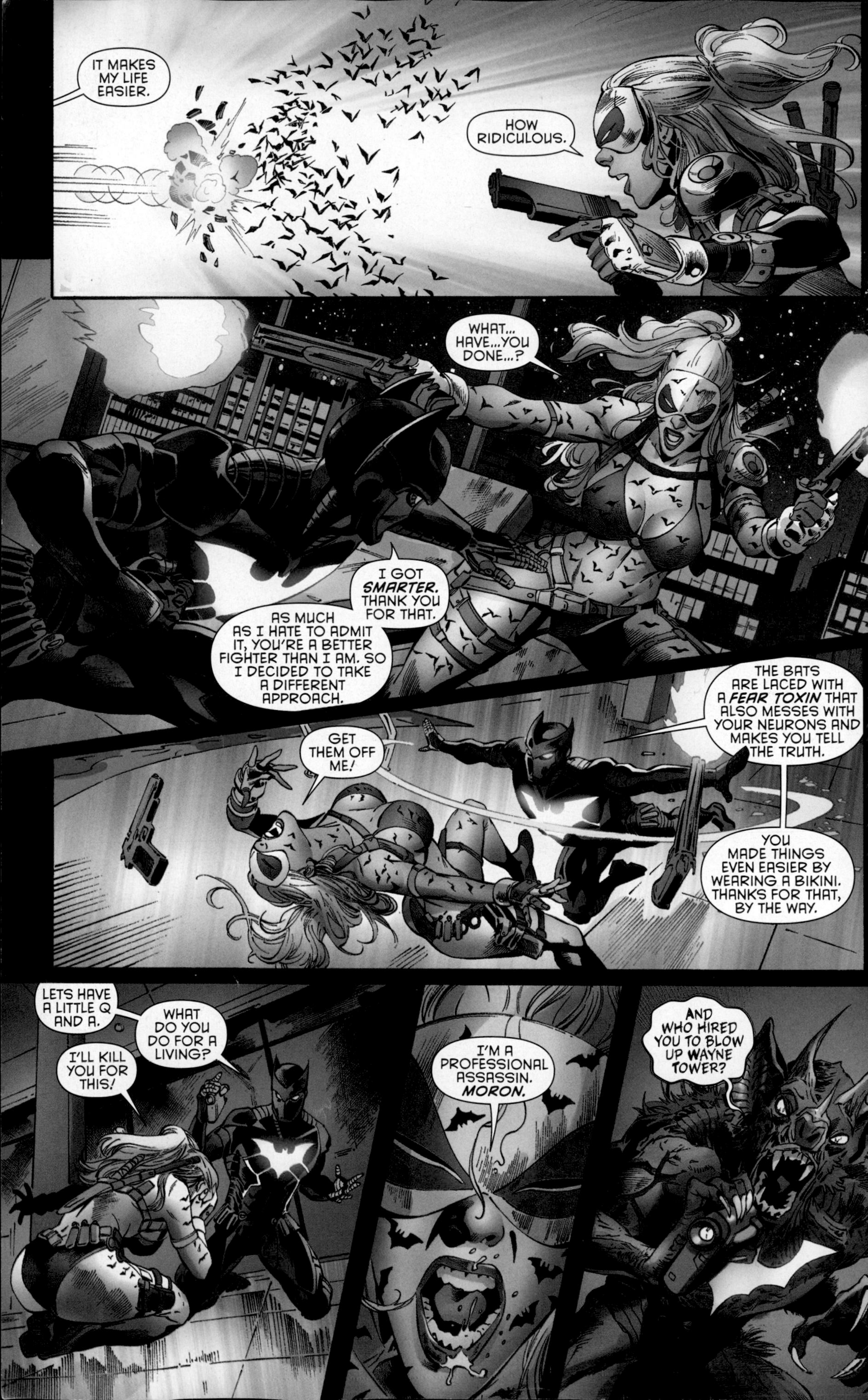
IT MAKES MY LIFE EASIER.
HOW RIDICULOUS.
WHAT... HAVE...YOU DONE...?
I GOT SMARTER. THANK YOU FOR THAT.
AS MUCH AS I HATE TO ADMIT IT, YOU'RE A BETTER FIGHTER THAN I AM. SO I DECIDED TO TAKE A DIFFERENT APPROACH.
THE BATS ARE LACED WITH A FEAR TOXIN THAT ALSO MESSES WITH YOUR NEURONS AND MAKES YOU TELL THE TRUTH.
GET THEM OFF ME!
YOU MADE THINGS EVEN EASIER BY WEARING A BIKINI. THANKS FOR THAT, BY THE WAY.
LETS HAVE A LITTLE Q AND A.
WHAT DO YOU DO FOR A LIVING?
I'LL KILL YOU FOR THIS!
I'M A PROFESSIONAL ASSASSIN. MORON.
AND WHO HIRED YOU TO BLOW UP WAYNE TOWER?

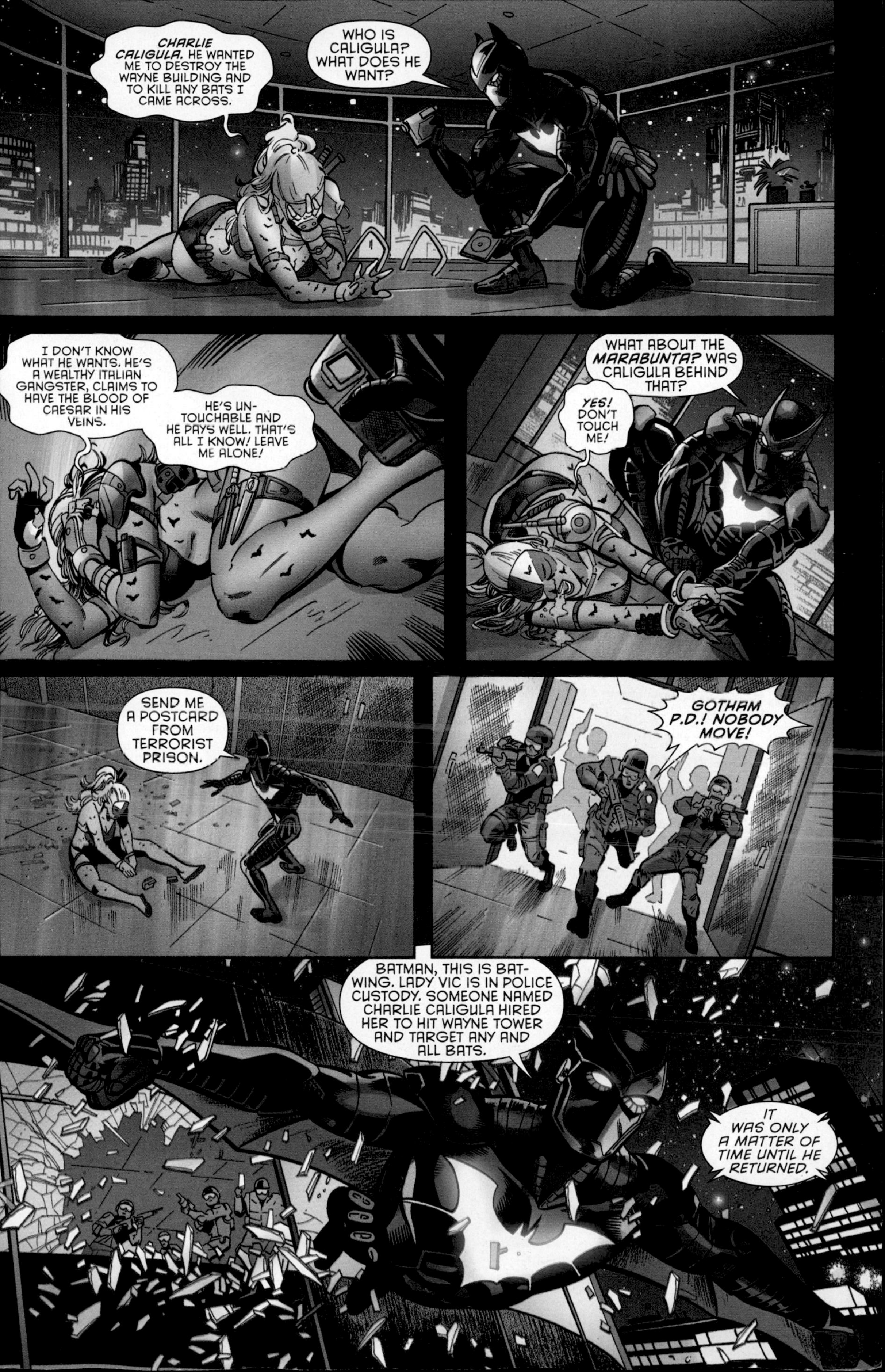
CHARLIE CALIGULA. HE WANTED ME TO DESTROY THE WAYNE BUILDING AND TO KILL ANY BATS I CAME ACROSS.
WHO IS CALIGULA? WHAT DOES HE WANT?
I DON'T KNOW WHAT HE WANTS. HE'S A WEALTHY ITALIAN GANGSTER, CLAIMS TO HAVE THE BLOOD OF CAESAR IN HIS VEINS.
HE'S UN-TOUCHABLE AND HE PAYS WELL. THAT'S ALL I KNOW! LEAVE ME ALONE!
WHAT ABOUT THE MARABUNTA? WAS CALIGULA BEHIND THAT?
YES! DON'T TOUCH ME!
SEND ME A POSTCARD FROM TERRORIST PRISON.
GOTHAM P.D.! NOBODY MOVE!
BATMAN, THIS IS BAT-WING. LADY VIC IS IN POLICE CUSTODY. SOMEONE NAMED CHARLIE CALIGULA HIRED HER TO HIT WAYNE TOWER AND TARGET ANY AND ALL BATS.
IT WAS ONLY A MATTER OF TIME UNTIL HE RETURNED.

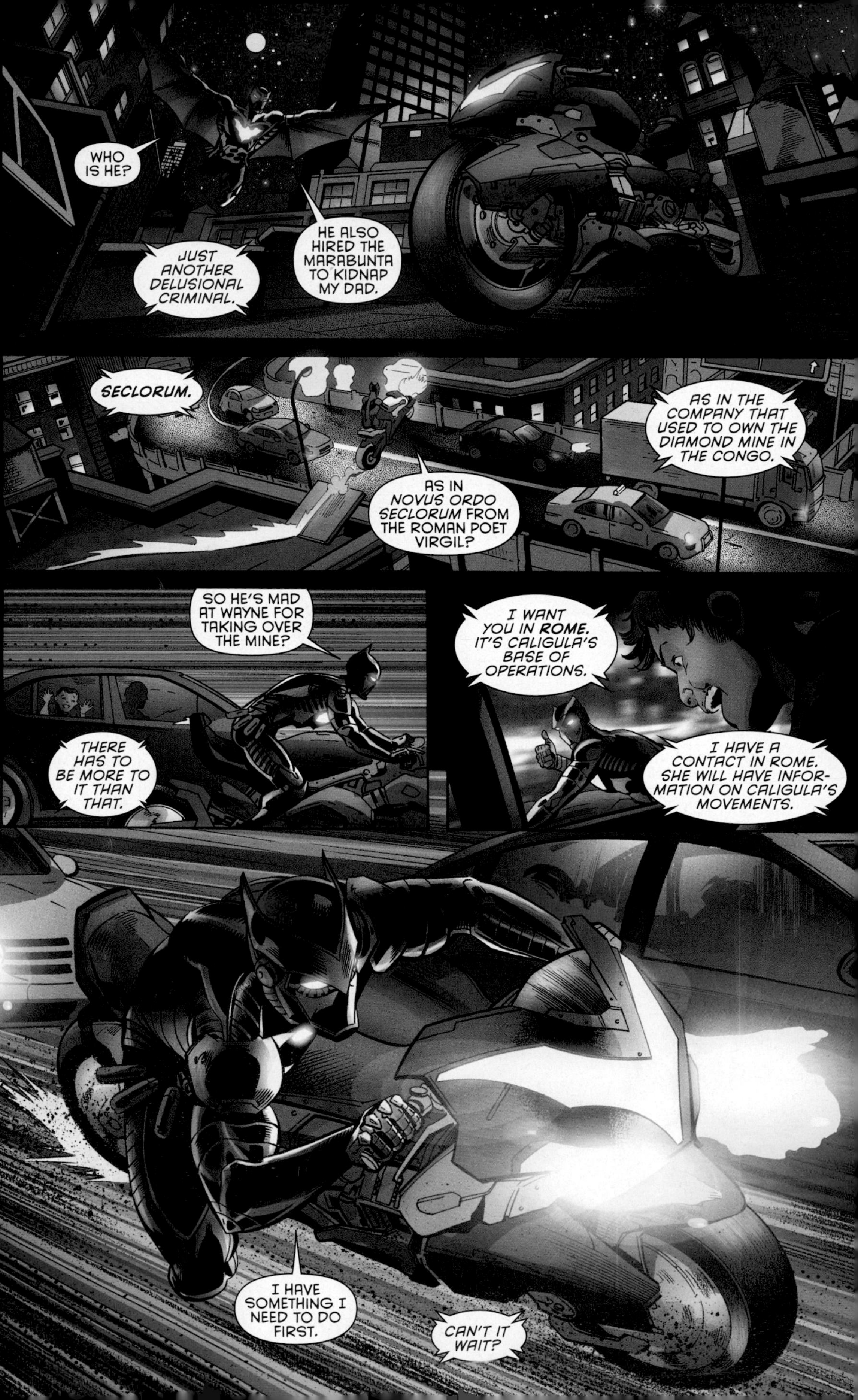
WHO IS HE?
JUST ANOTHER DELUSIONAL CRIMINAL.
HE ALSO HIRED THE MARABUNTA TO KIDNAP MY DAD.
SECLORUM.
AS IN NOVUS ORDO SECLORUM FROM THE ROMAN POET VIRGIL?
AS IN THE COMPANY THAT USED TO OWN THE DIAMOND MINE IN THE CONGO.
SO HE'S MAD AT WAYNE FOR TAKING OVER THE MINE?
THERE HAS TO BE MORE TO IT THAN THAT.
I WANT YOU IN ROME. IT'S CALIGULA'S BASE OF OPERATIONS.
I HAVE A CONTACT IN ROME. SHE WILL HAVE INFORMATION ON CALIGULA'S MOVEMENTS.
I HAVE SOMETHING I NEED TO DO FIRST.
CAN'T IT WAIT?

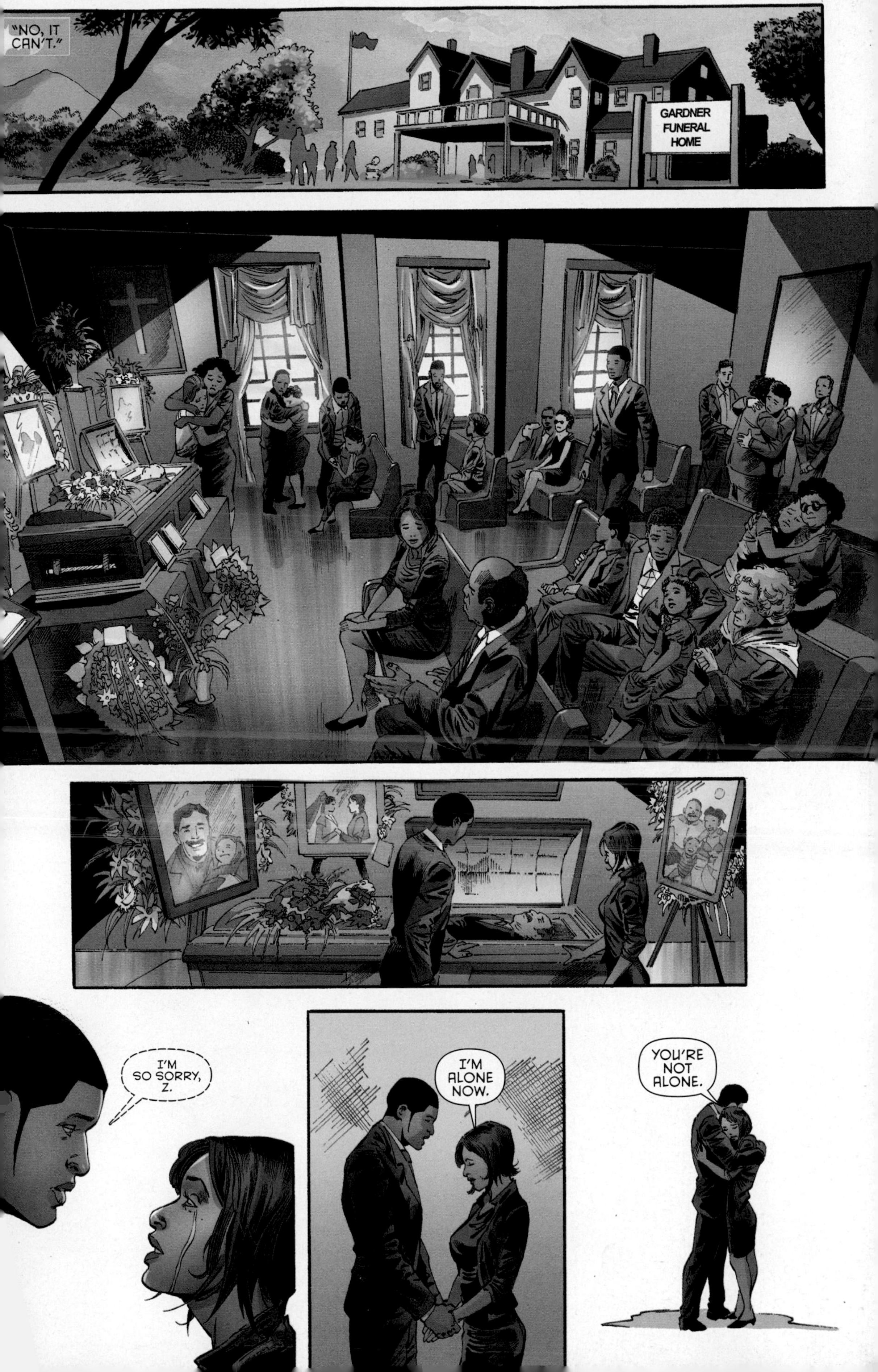
"NO, IT CAN'T."
GARDNER FUNERAL HOME
I'M SO SORRY, Z.
I'M ALONE NOW.
YOU'RE NOT ALONE.

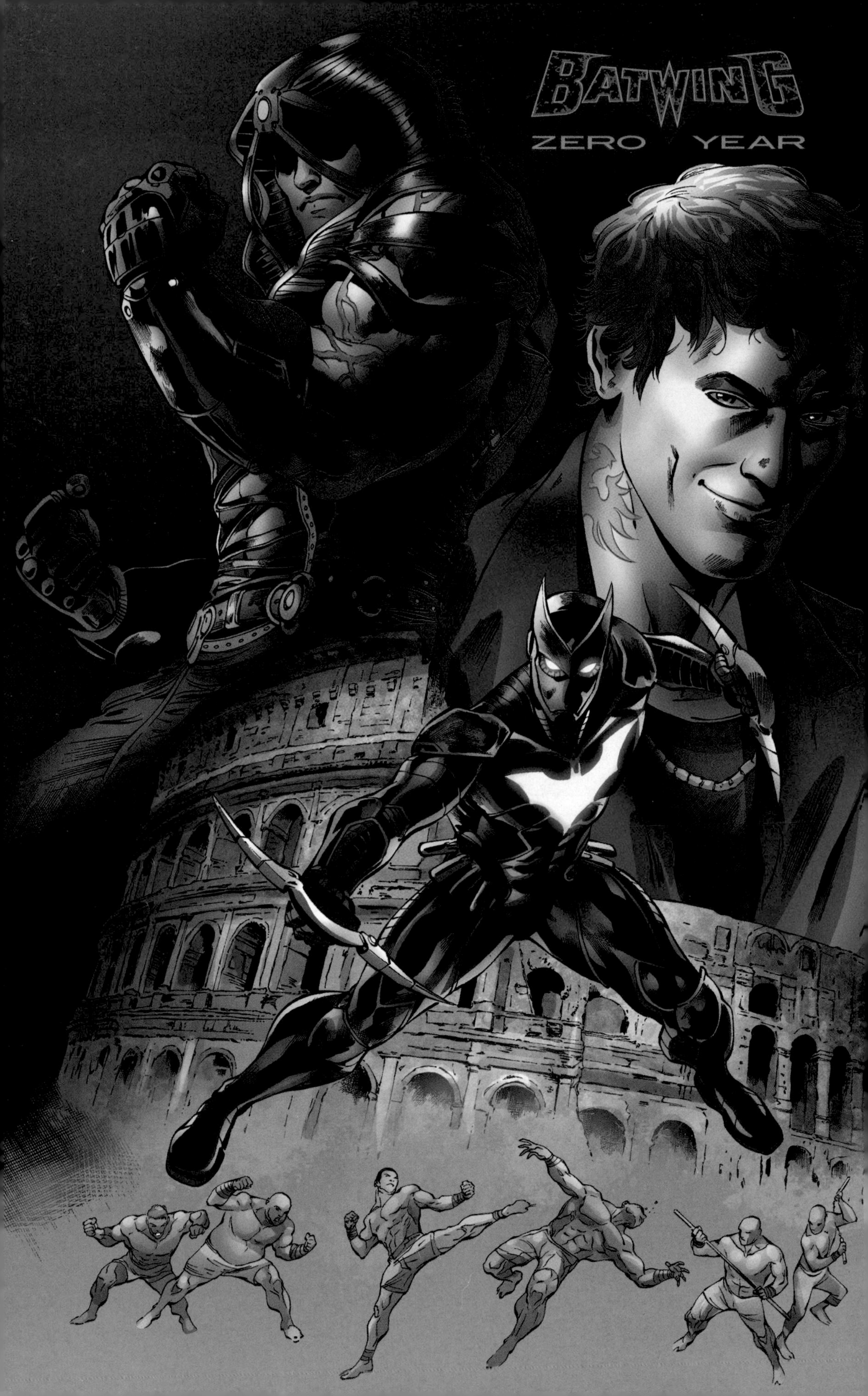
BATWING
ZERO YEAR

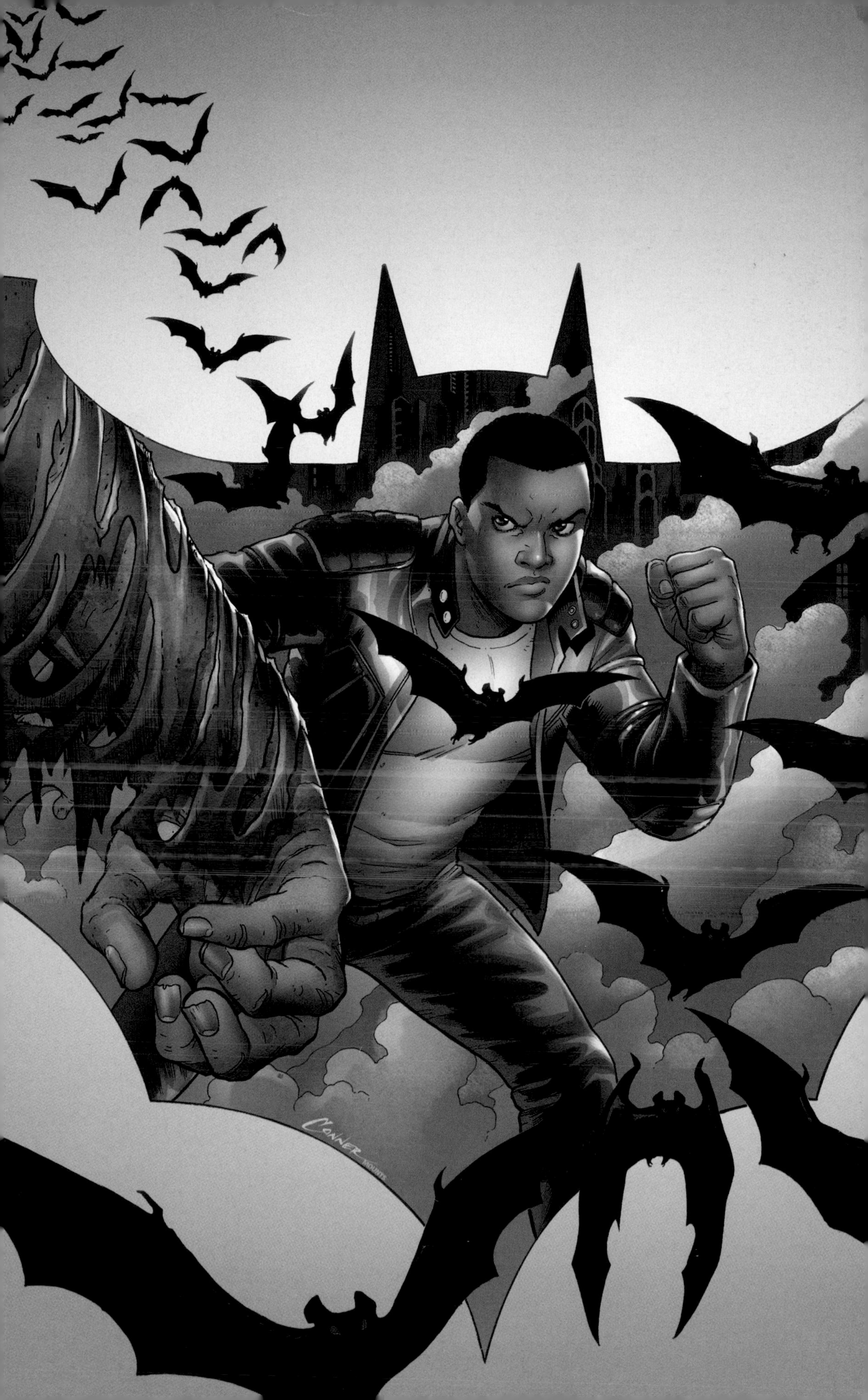

KEEP YOUR ENEMIES CLOSER
cover art by **AMANDA CONNER & PAUL MOUNTS**

Most of us are taught at a very young age that life is fair.

We're taught to share, to take turns and to treat everyone fairly and equally.

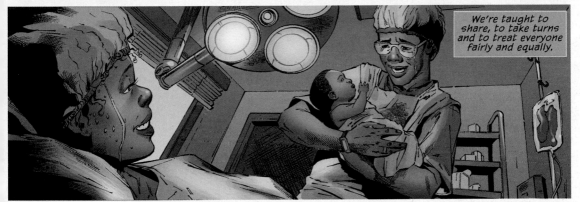

They say there are no winners or losers.

They say all that matters is that you tried your best.

None of this is useful in the real world.

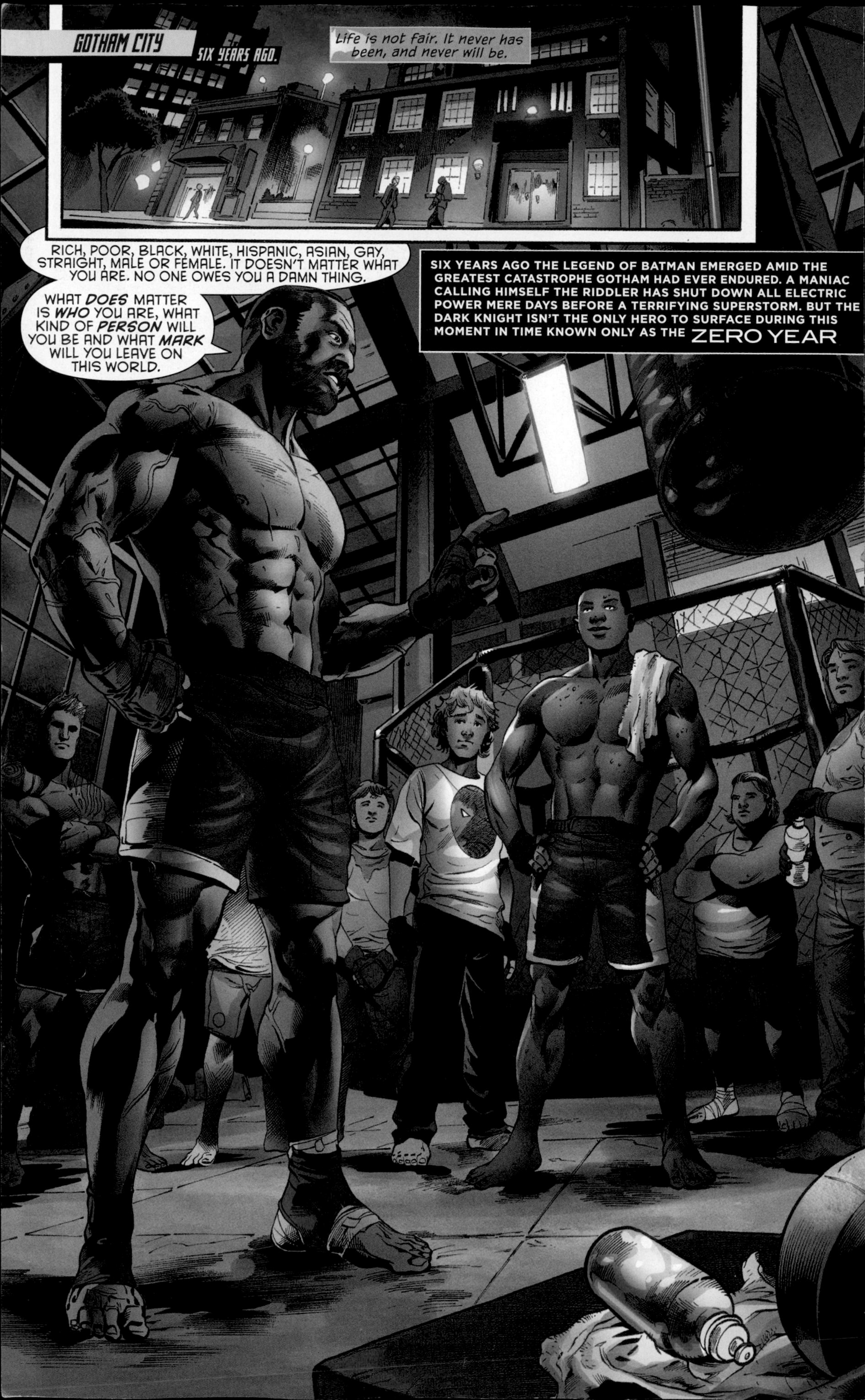
GOTHAM CITY
SIX YEARS AGO.
Life is not fair. It never has been, and never will be.
RICH, POOR, BLACK, WHITE, HISPANIC, ASIAN, GAY, STRAIGHT, MALE OR FEMALE. IT DOESN'T MATTER WHAT YOU ARE. NO ONE OWES YOU A DAMN THING.
WHAT DOES MATTER IS WHO YOU ARE, WHAT KIND OF PERSON WILL YOU BE AND WHAT MARK WILL YOU LEAVE ON THIS WORLD.
SIX YEARS AGO THE LEGEND OF BATMAN EMERGED AMID THE GREATEST CATASTROPHE GOTHAM HAD EVER ENDURED. A MANIAC CALLING HIMSELF THE RIDDLER HAS SHUT DOWN ALL ELECTRIC POWER MERE DAYS BEFORE A TERRIFYING SUPERSTORM. BUT THE DARK KNIGHT ISN'T THE ONLY HERO TO SURFACE DURING THIS MOMENT IN TIME KNOWN ONLY AS THE ZERO YEAR

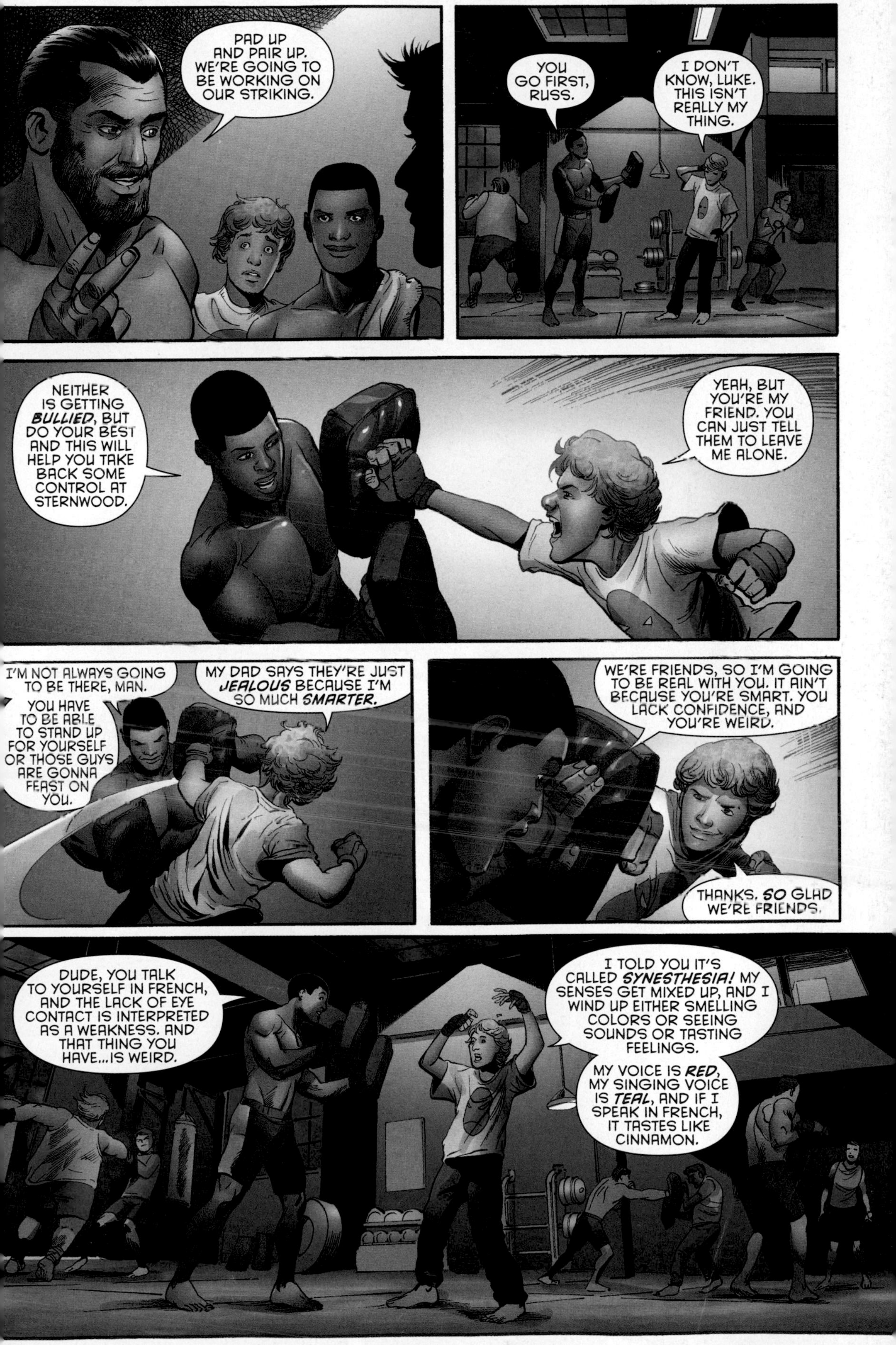
PAD UP AND PAIR UP. WE'RE GOING TO BE WORKING ON OUR STRIKING.
YOU GO FIRST, RUSS.
I DON'T KNOW, LUKE. THIS ISN'T REALLY MY THING.
NEITHER IS GETTING BULLIED, BUT DO YOUR BEST AND THIS WILL HELP YOU TAKE BACK SOME CONTROL AT STERNWOOD.
YEAH, BUT YOU'RE MY FRIEND. YOU CAN JUST TELL THEM TO LEAVE ME ALONE.
I'M NOT ALWAYS GOING TO BE THERE, MAN.
YOU HAVE TO BE ABLE TO STAND UP FOR YOURSELF OR THOSE GUYS ARE GONNA FEAST ON YOU.
MY DAD SAYS THEY'RE JUST JEALOUS BECAUSE I'M SO MUCH SMARTER.
WE'RE FRIENDS, SO I'M GOING TO BE REAL WITH YOU. IT AIN'T BECAUSE YOU'RE SMART. YOU LACK CONFIDENCE, AND YOU'RE WEIRD.
THANKS. SO GLAD WE'RE FRIENDS.
DUDE, YOU TALK TO YOURSELF IN FRENCH, AND THE LACK OF EYE CONTACT IS INTERPRETED AS A WEAKNESS. AND THAT THING YOU HAVE...IS WEIRD.
I TOLD YOU IT'S CALLED SYNESTHESIA! MY SENSES GET MIXED UP, AND I WIND UP EITHER SMELLING COLORS OR SEEING SOUNDS OR TASTING FEELINGS.
MY VOICE IS RED, MY SINGING VOICE IS TEAL, AND IF I SPEAK IN FRENCH, IT TASTES LIKE CINNAMON.

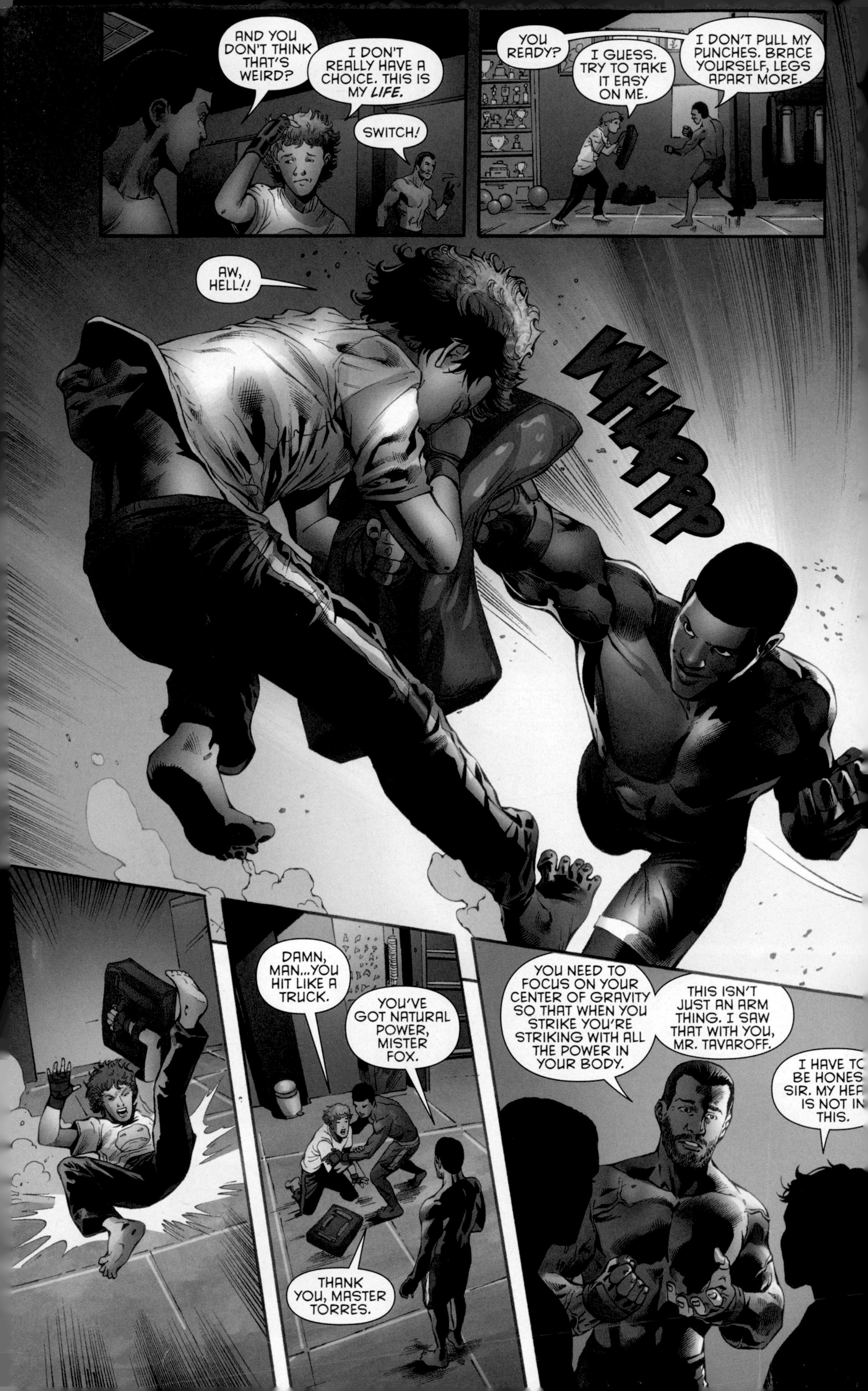
AND YOU DON'T THINK THAT'S WEIRD?
I DON'T REALLY HAVE A CHOICE. THIS IS MY LIFE.
SWITCH!
YOU READY?
I GUESS. TRY TO TAKE IT EASY ON ME.
I DON'T PULL MY PUNCHES. BRACE YOURSELF, LEGS APART MORE.
AW, HELL!!
WHAPPP
DAMN, MAN...YOU HIT LIKE A TRUCK.
YOU'VE GOT NATURAL POWER, MISTER FOX.
THANK YOU, MASTER TORRES.
YOU NEED TO FOCUS ON YOUR CENTER OF GRAVITY SO THAT WHEN YOU STRIKE YOU'RE STRIKING WITH ALL THE POWER IN YOUR BODY.
THIS ISN'T JUST AN ARM THING. I SAW THAT WITH YOU, MR. TAVAROFF.
I HAVE TO BE HONES SIR. MY HEA IS NOT IN THIS.

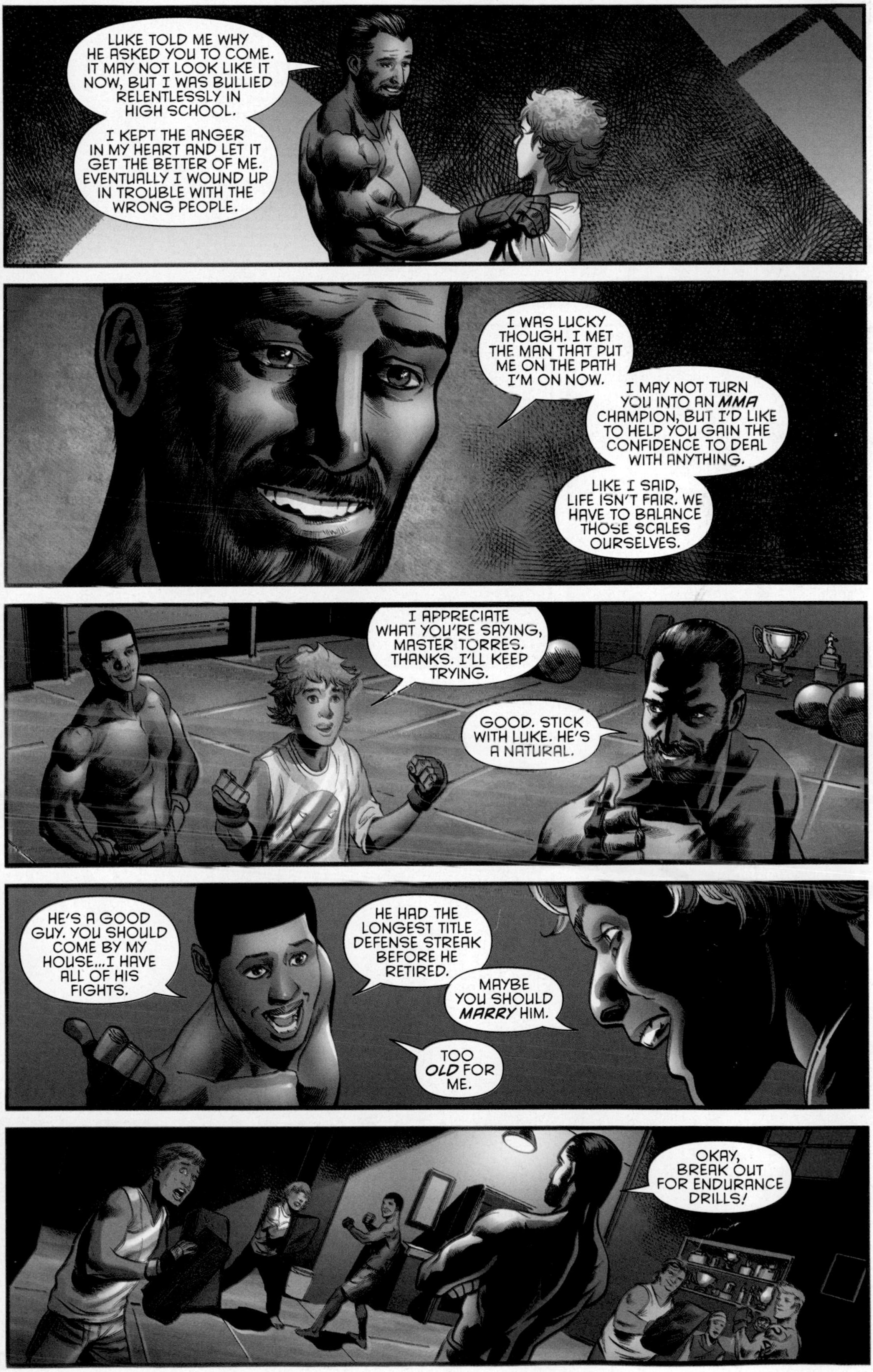
LUKE TOLD ME WHY HE ASKED YOU TO COME. IT MAY NOT LOOK LIKE IT NOW, BUT I WAS BULLIED RELENTLESSLY IN HIGH SCHOOL.
I KEPT THE ANGER IN MY HEART AND LET IT GET THE BETTER OF ME. EVENTUALLY I WOUND UP IN TROUBLE WITH THE WRONG PEOPLE.
I WAS LUCKY THOUGH. I MET THE MAN THAT PUT ME ON THE PATH I'M ON NOW.
I MAY NOT TURN YOU INTO AN *MMA* CHAMPION, BUT I'D LIKE TO HELP YOU GAIN THE CONFIDENCE TO DEAL WITH ANYTHING.
LIKE I SAID, LIFE ISN'T FAIR. WE HAVE TO BALANCE THOSE SCALES OURSELVES.
I APPRECIATE WHAT YOU'RE SAYING, MASTER TORRES. THANKS. I'LL KEEP TRYING.
GOOD. STICK WITH LUKE. HE'S A NATURAL.
HE'S A GOOD GUY. YOU SHOULD COME BY MY HOUSE...I HAVE ALL OF HIS FIGHTS.
HE HAD THE LONGEST TITLE DEFENSE STREAK BEFORE HE RETIRED.
MAYBE YOU SHOULD *MARRY* HIM.
TOO *OLD* FOR ME.
OKAY, BREAK OUT FOR ENDURANCE DRILLS!

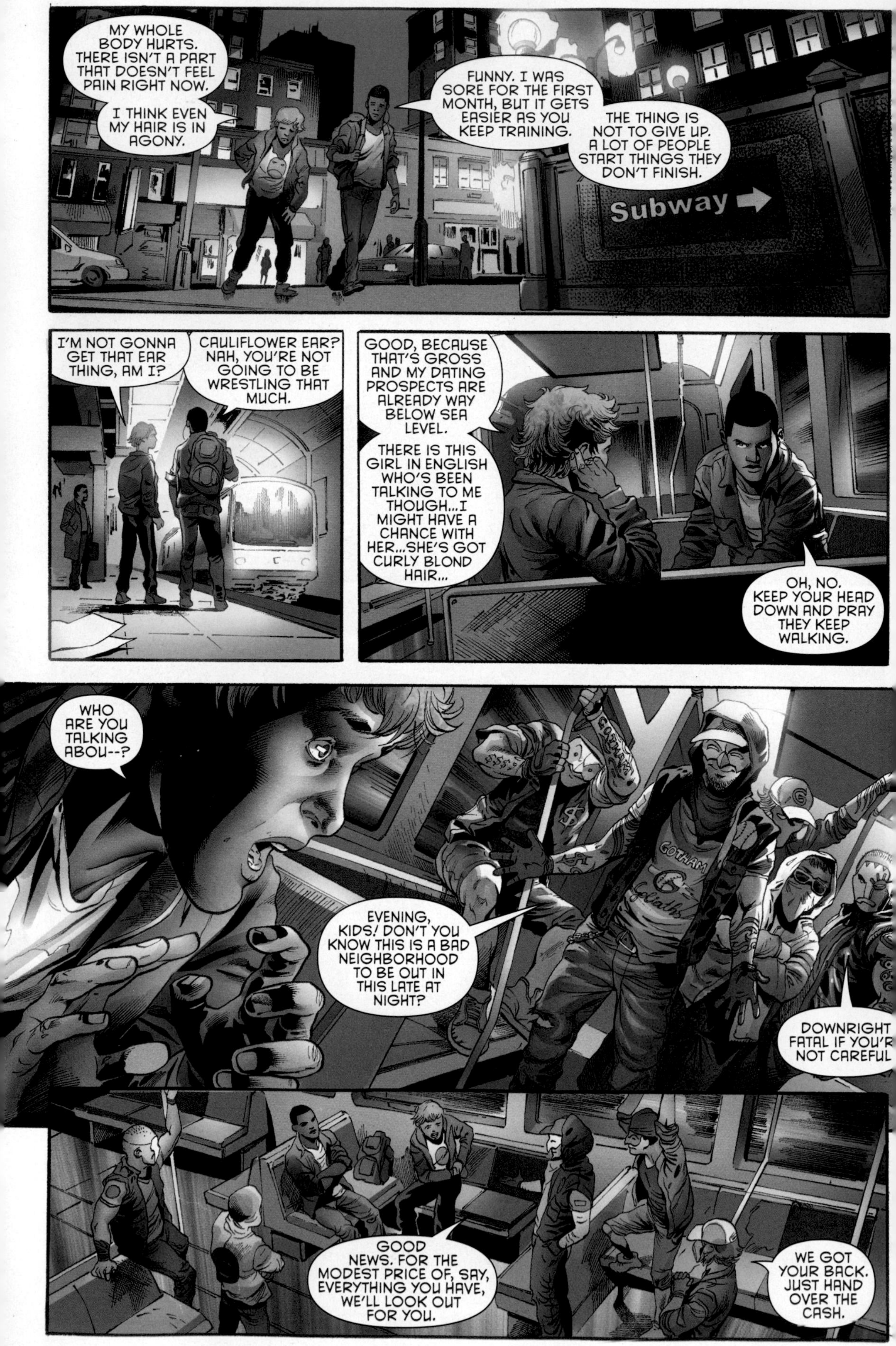
MY WHOLE BODY HURTS. THERE ISN'T A PART THAT DOESN'T FEEL PAIN RIGHT NOW.
I THINK EVEN MY HAIR IS IN AGONY.
FUNNY. I WAS SORE FOR THE FIRST MONTH, BUT IT GETS EASIER AS YOU KEEP TRAINING.
THE THING IS NOT TO GIVE UP. A LOT OF PEOPLE START THINGS THEY DON'T FINISH.
Subway
I'M NOT GONNA GET THAT EAR THING, AM I?
CAULIFLOWER EAR? NAH, YOU'RE NOT GOING TO BE WRESTLING THAT MUCH.
GOOD, BECAUSE THAT'S GROSS AND MY DATING PROSPECTS ARE ALREADY WAY BELOW SEA LEVEL.
THERE IS THIS GIRL IN ENGLISH WHO'S BEEN TALKING TO ME THOUGH...I MIGHT HAVE A CHANCE WITH HER...SHE'S GOT CURLY BLOND HAIR...
OH, NO. KEEP YOUR HEAD DOWN AND PRAY THEY KEEP WALKING.
WHO ARE YOU TALKING ABOU--?
EVENING, KIDS! DON'T YOU KNOW THIS IS A BAD NEIGHBORHOOD TO BE OUT IN THIS LATE AT NIGHT?
DOWNRIGHT FATAL IF YOU'R NOT CAREFUL
GOOD NEWS. FOR THE MODEST PRICE OF, SAY, EVERYTHING YOU HAVE, WE'LL LOOK OUT FOR YOU.
WE GOT YOUR BACK. JUST HAND OVER THE CASH.

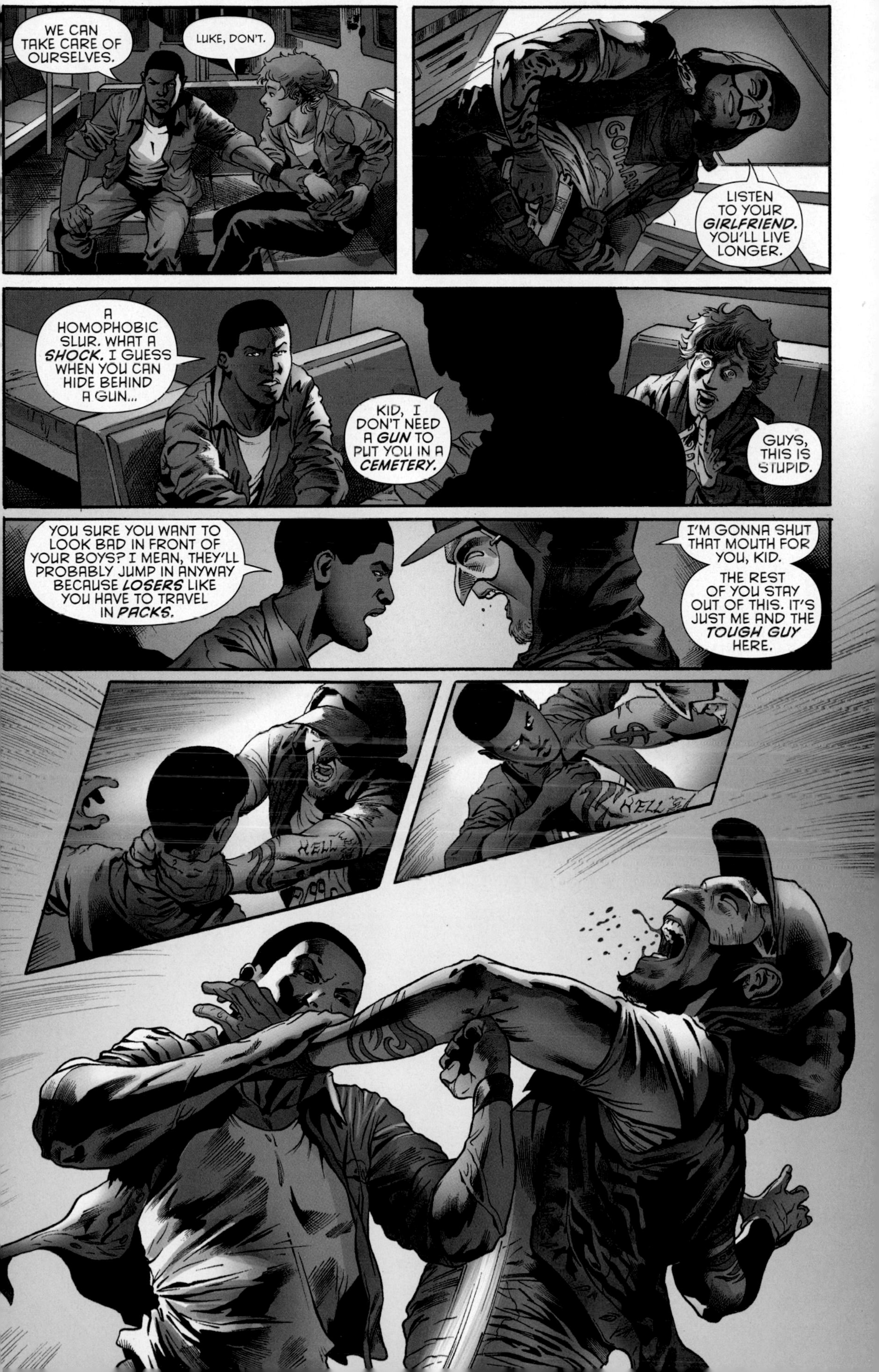
WE CAN TAKE CARE OF OURSELVES.
LUKE, DON'T.
LISTEN TO YOUR GIRLFRIEND. YOU'LL LIVE LONGER.
A HOMOPHOBIC SLUR. WHAT A SHOCK. I GUESS WHEN YOU CAN HIDE BEHIND A GUN...
KID, I DON'T NEED A GUN TO PUT YOU IN A CEMETERY.
GUYS, THIS IS STUPID.
YOU SURE YOU WANT TO LOOK BAD IN FRONT OF YOUR BOYS? I MEAN, THEY'LL PROBABLY JUMP IN ANYWAY BECAUSE LOSERS LIKE YOU HAVE TO TRAVEL IN PACKS.
I'M GONNA SHUT THAT MOUTH FOR YOU, KID.
THE REST OF YOU STAY OUT OF THIS. IT'S JUST ME AND THE TOUGH GUY HERE.

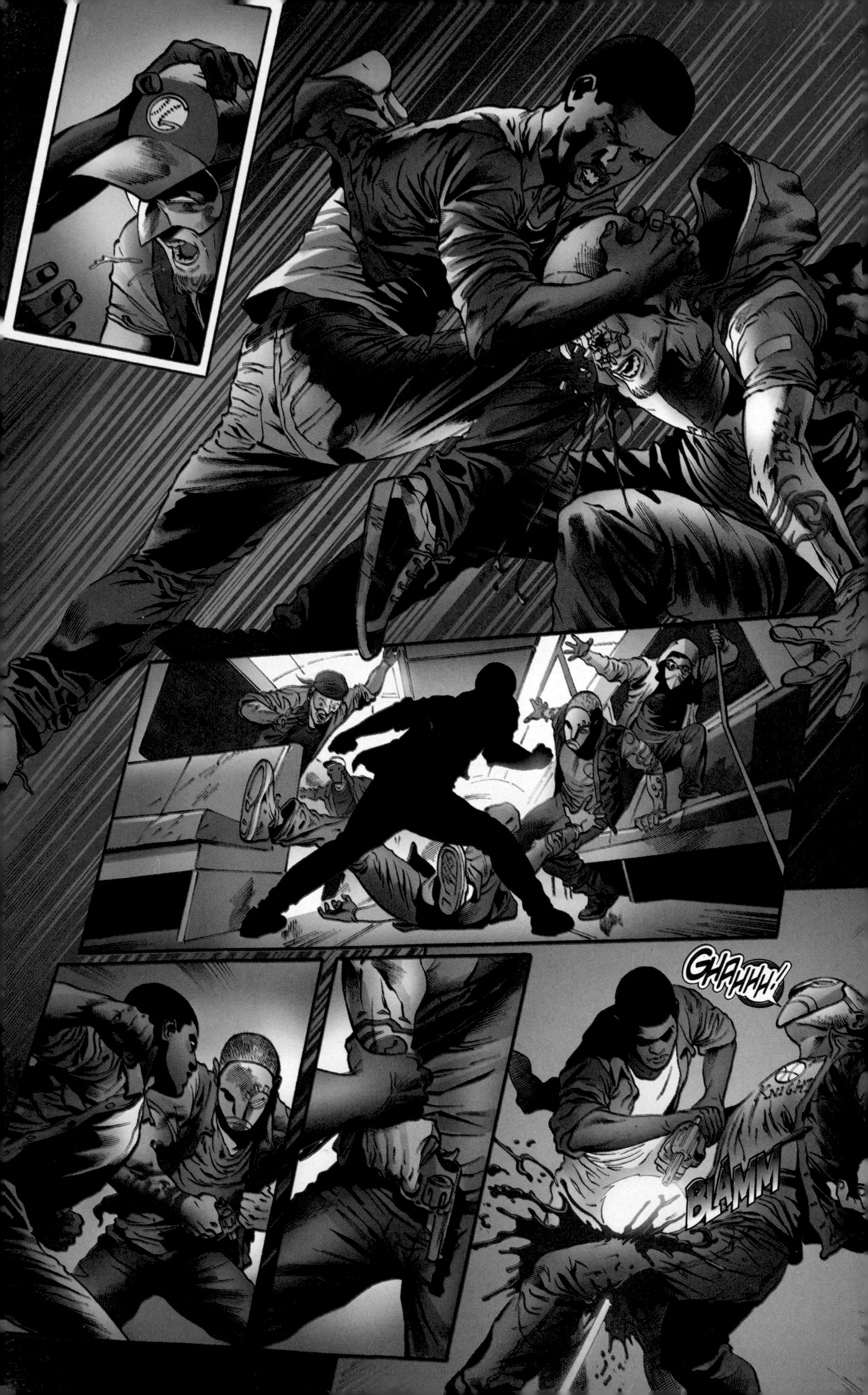
GHAHHH!
BLAMM

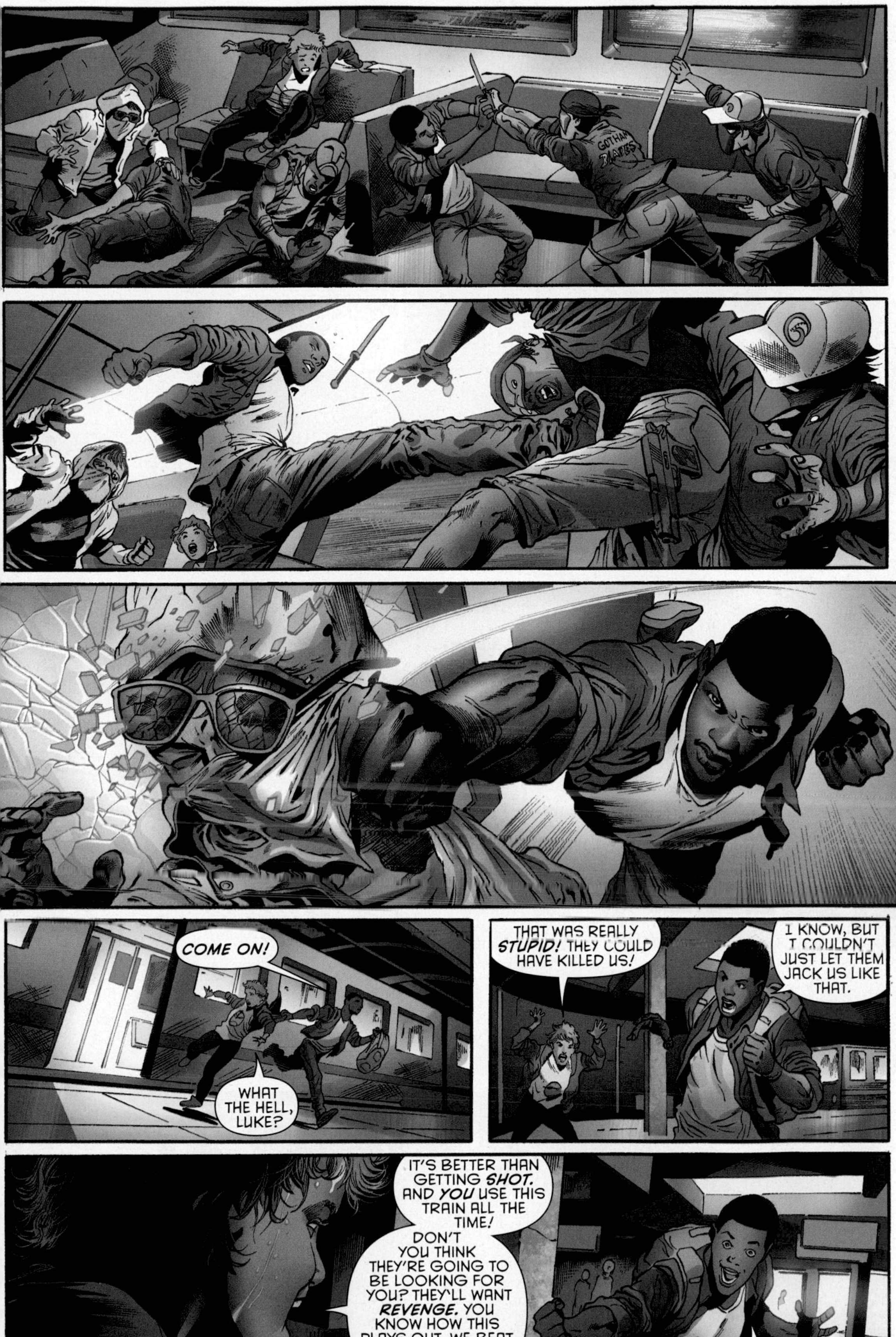
GOTHAM BLADES
COME ON!
WHAT THE HELL, LUKE?
THAT WAS REALLY STUPID! THEY COULD HAVE KILLED US!
I KNOW, BUT I COULDN'T JUST LET THEM JACK US LIKE THAT.
IT'S BETTER THAN GETTING SHOT. AND YOU USE THIS TRAIN ALL THE TIME!
DON'T YOU THINK THEY'RE GOING TO BE LOOKING FOR YOU? THEY'LL WANT REVENGE. YOU KNOW HOW THIS PLAYS OUT. WE BEAT THEM TODAY, AND TOMORROW WE ARE DEAD.
I JUST REACTED. MY ADRENALINE STARTED PUMPING MY HEART IS STILL POUNDING!

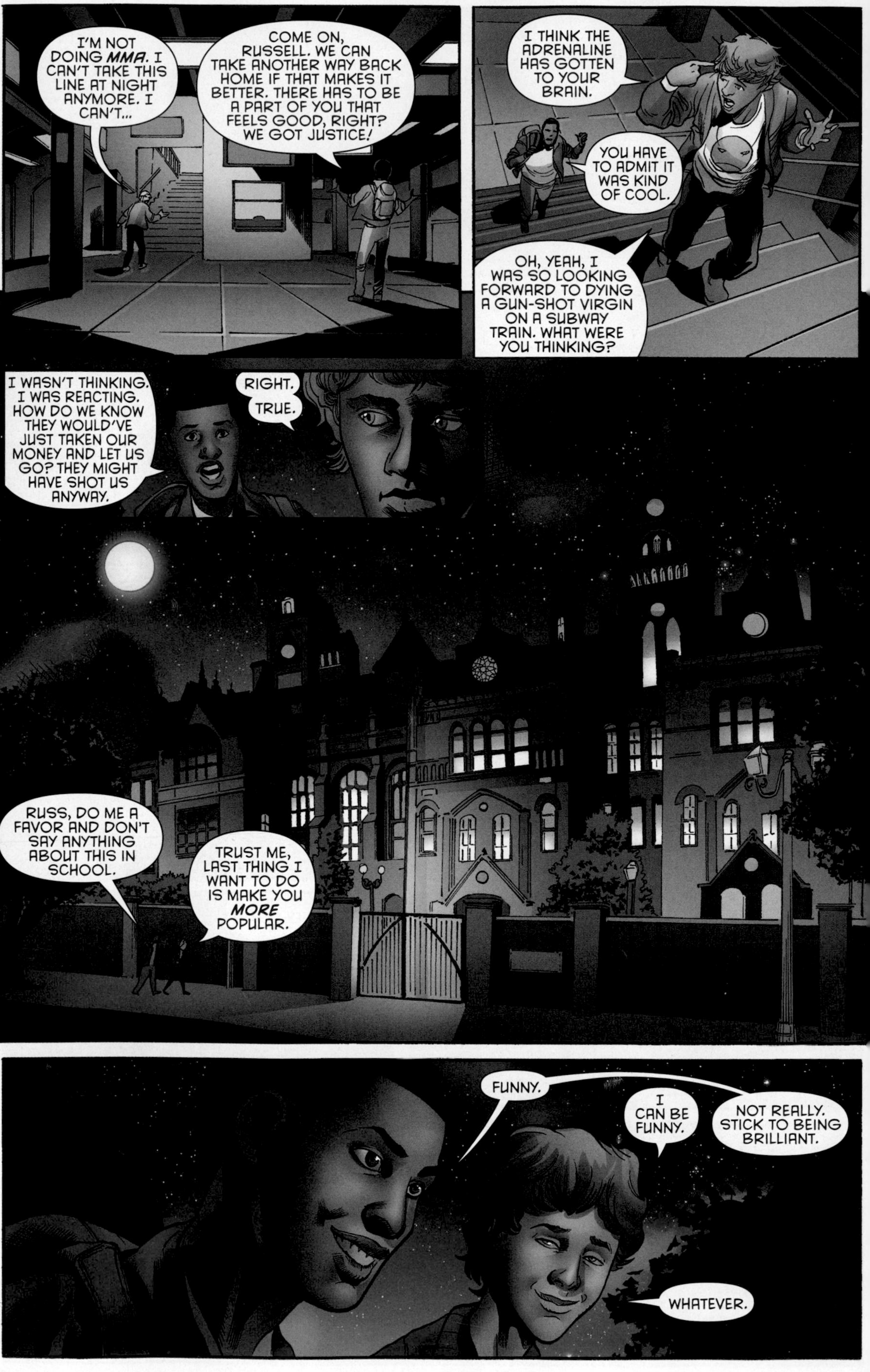
I'M NOT DOING MMA. I CAN'T TAKE THIS LINE AT NIGHT ANYMORE. I CAN'T...
COME ON, RUSSELL. WE CAN TAKE ANOTHER WAY BACK HOME IF THAT MAKES IT BETTER. THERE HAS TO BE A PART OF YOU THAT FEELS GOOD, RIGHT? WE GOT JUSTICE!
I THINK THE ADRENALINE HAS GOTTEN TO YOUR BRAIN.
YOU HAVE TO ADMIT IT WAS KIND OF COOL.
OH, YEAH, I WAS SO LOOKING FORWARD TO DYING A GUN-SHOT VIRGIN ON A SUBWAY TRAIN. WHAT WERE YOU THINKING?
I WASN'T THINKING. I WAS REACTING. HOW DO WE KNOW THEY WOULD'VE JUST TAKEN OUR MONEY AND LET US GO? THEY MIGHT HAVE SHOT US ANYWAY.
RIGHT. TRUE.
RUSS, DO ME A FAVOR AND DON'T SAY ANYTHING ABOUT THIS IN SCHOOL.
TRUST ME, LAST THING I WANT TO DO IS MAKE YOU MORE POPULAR.
FUNNY.
I CAN BE FUNNY.
NOT REALLY. STICK TO BEING BRILLIANT.
WHATEVER.

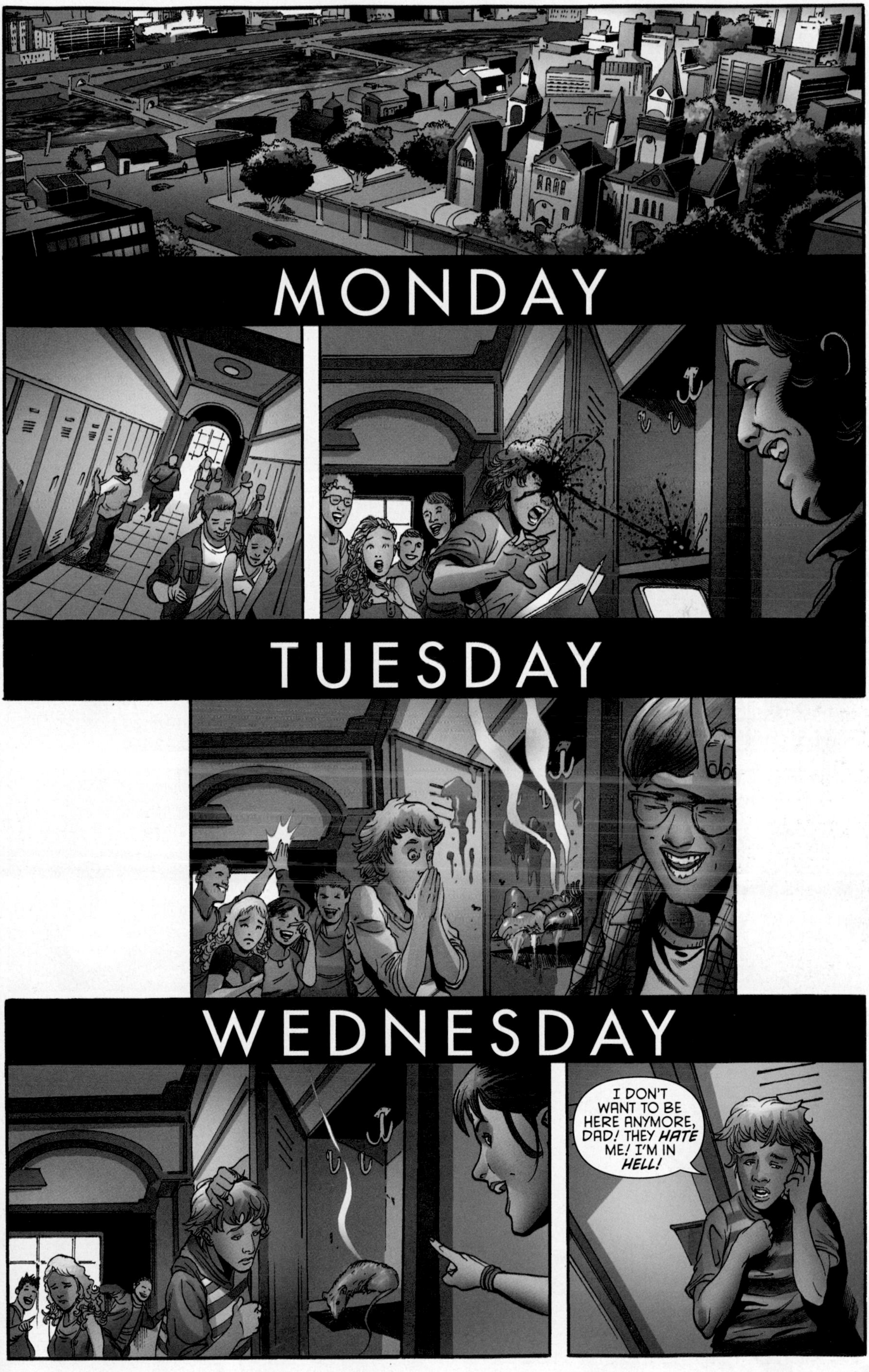
MONDAY
TUESDAY
WEDNESDAY
I DON'T WANT TO BE HERE ANYMORE, DAD! THEY HATE ME! I'M IN HELL!

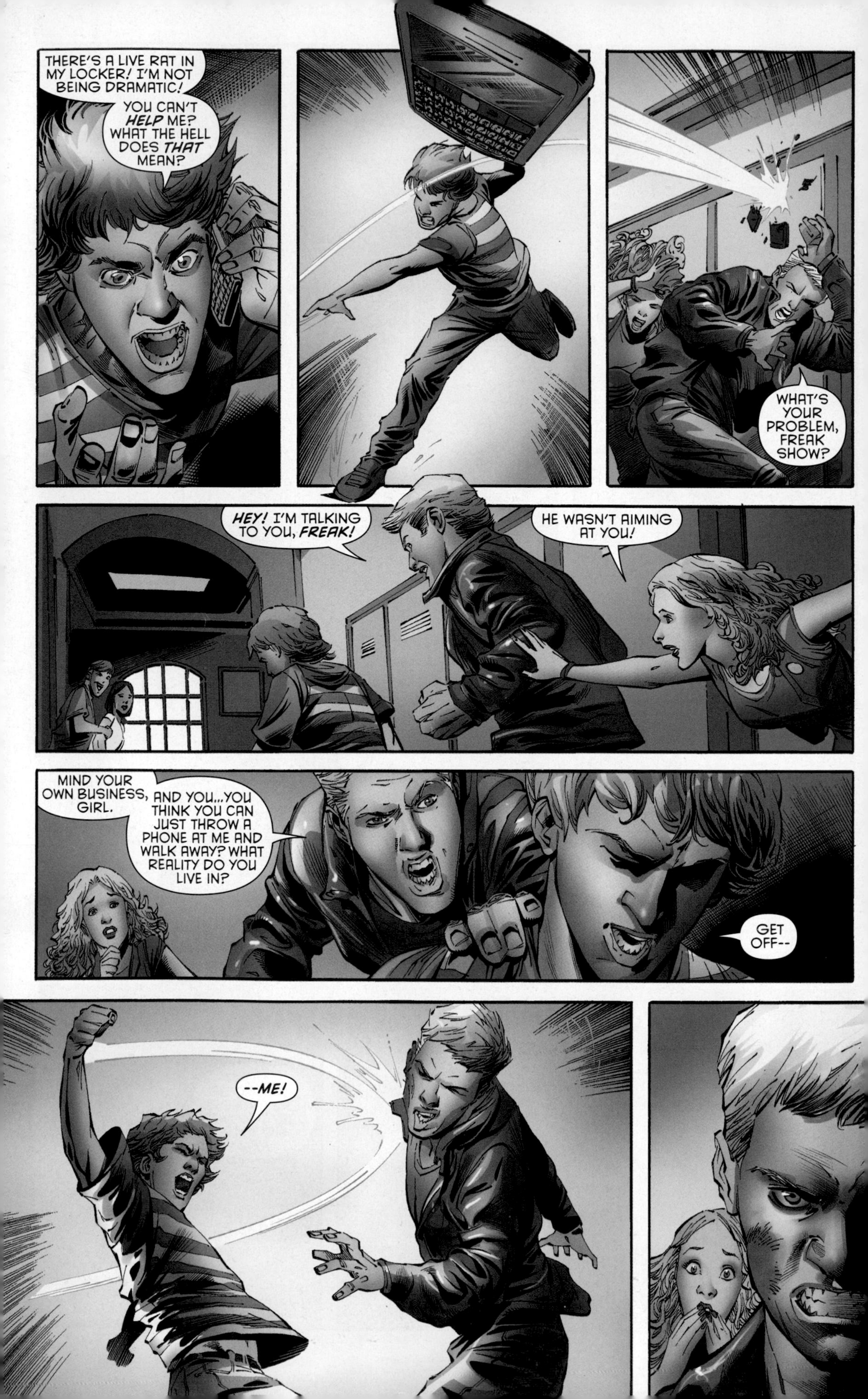
THERE'S A LIVE RAT IN MY LOCKER! I'M NOT BEING DRAMATIC!
YOU CAN'T HELP ME? WHAT THE HELL DOES THAT MEAN?
WHAT'S YOUR PROBLEM, FREAK SHOW?
HEY! I'M TALKING TO YOU, FREAK!
HE WASN'T AIMING AT YOU!
MIND YOUR OWN BUSINESS, GIRL.
AND YOU...YOU THINK YOU CAN JUST THROW A PHONE AT ME AND WALK AWAY? WHAT REALITY DO YOU LIVE IN?
GET OFF--
--ME!

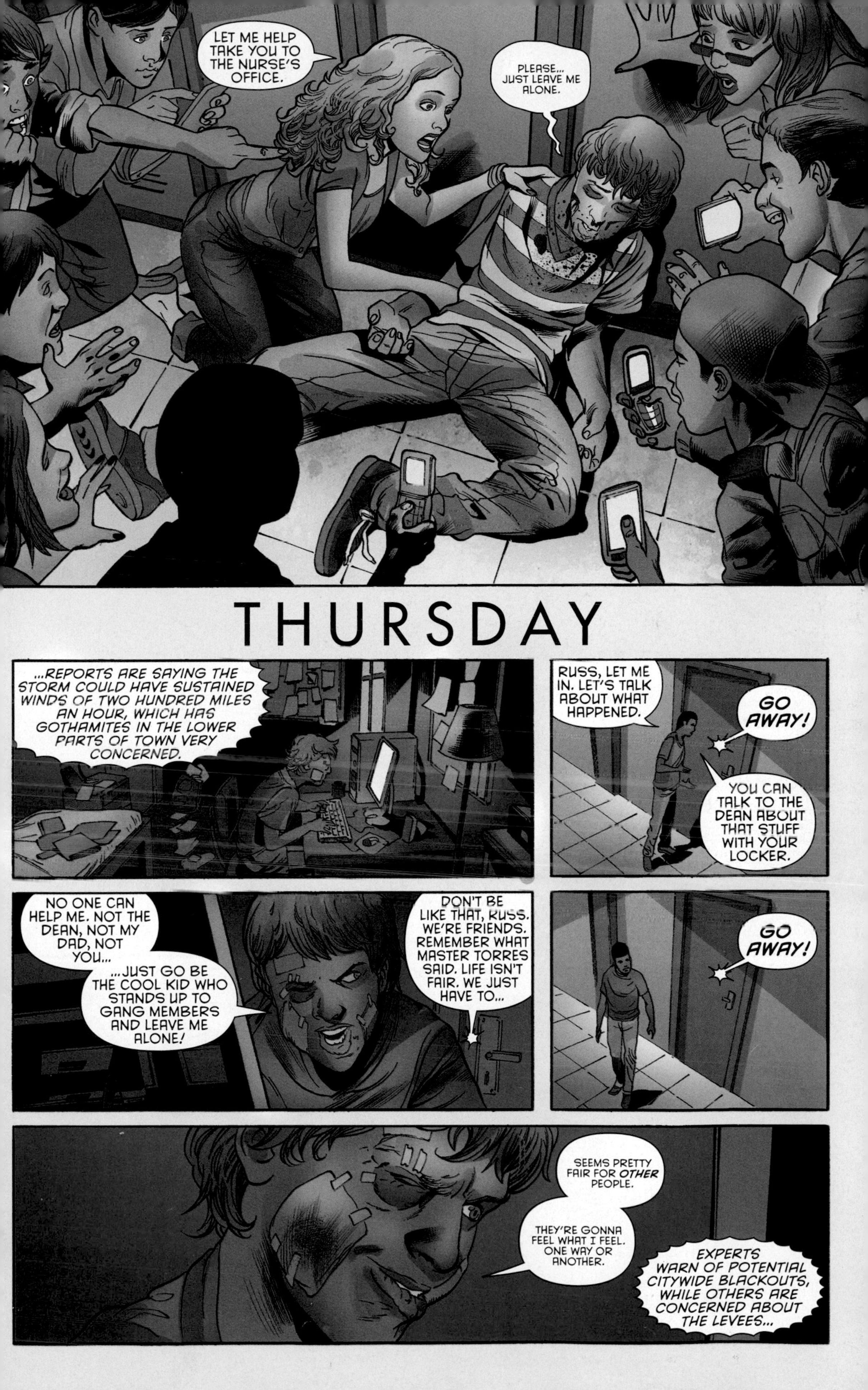
LET ME HELP TAKE YOU TO THE NURSE'S OFFICE.
PLEASE... JUST LEAVE ME ALONE.
THURSDAY
...REPORTS ARE SAYING THE STORM COULD HAVE SUSTAINED WINDS OF TWO HUNDRED MILES AN HOUR, WHICH HAS GOTHAMITES IN THE LOWER PARTS OF TOWN VERY CONCERNED.
RUSS, LET ME IN. LET'S TALK ABOUT WHAT HAPPENED.
GO AWAY!
YOU CAN TALK TO THE DEAN ABOUT THAT STUFF WITH YOUR LOCKER.
NO ONE CAN HELP ME. NOT THE DEAN, NOT MY DAD, NOT YOU...
...JUST GO BE THE COOL KID WHO STANDS UP TO GANG MEMBERS AND LEAVE ME ALONE!
DON'T BE LIKE THAT, RUSS. WE'RE FRIENDS. REMEMBER WHAT MASTER TORRES SAID. LIFE ISN'T FAIR. WE JUST HAVE TO...
GO AWAY!
SEEMS PRETTY FAIR FOR OTHER PEOPLE.
THEY'RE GONNA FEEL WHAT I FEEL. ONE WAY OR ANOTHER.
EXPERTS WARN OF POTENTIAL CITYWIDE BLACKOUTS, WHILE OTHERS ARE CONCERNED ABOUT THE LEVEES...

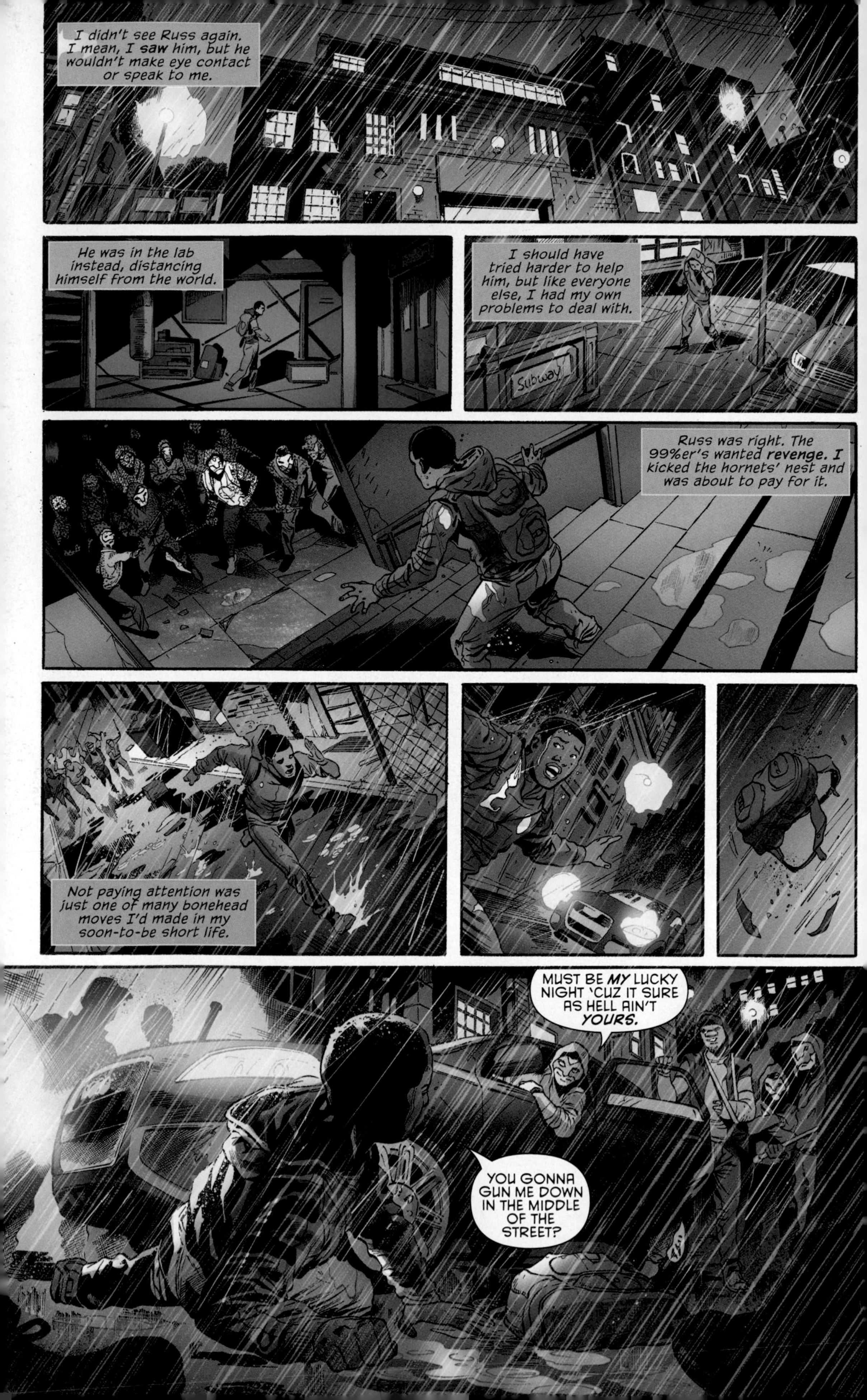
I didn't see Russ again. I mean, I saw him, but he wouldn't make eye contact or speak to me.
He was in the lab instead, distancing himself from the world.
I should have tried harder to help him, but like everyone else, I had my own problems to deal with.
Subway
Russ was right. The 99%er's wanted revenge. I kicked the hornets' nest and was about to pay for it.
Not paying attention was just one of many bonehead moves I'd made in my soon-to-be short life.
MUST BE MY LUCKY NIGHT 'CUZ IT SURE AS HELL AIN'T YOURS.
YOU GONNA GUN ME DOWN IN THE MIDDLE OF THE STREET?

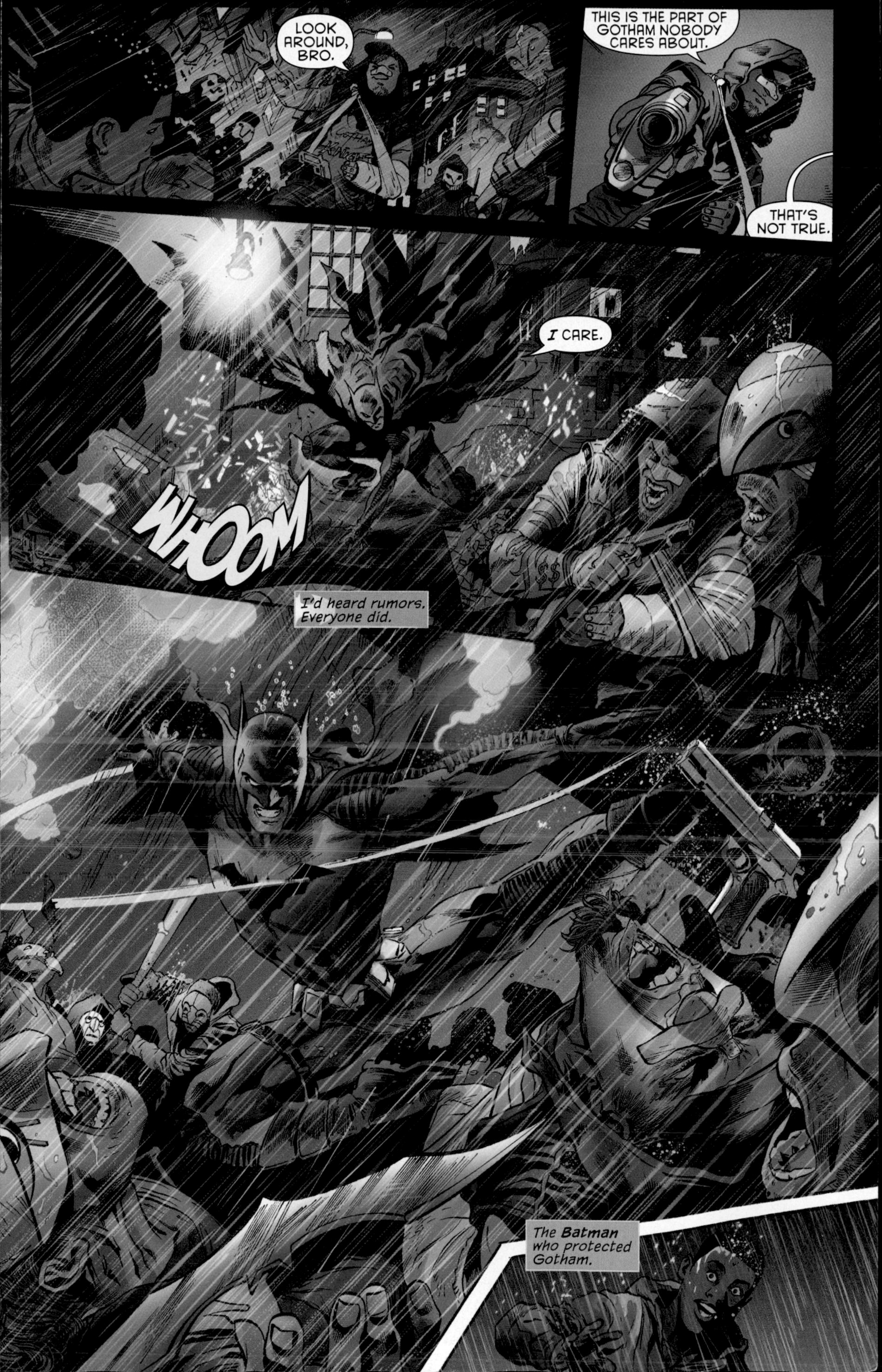
LOOK AROUND, BRO.
THIS IS THE PART OF GOTHAM NOBODY CARES ABOUT.
THAT'S NOT TRUE.
I CARE.
WHOOM
I'd heard rumors. Everyone did.
The Batman who protected Gotham.

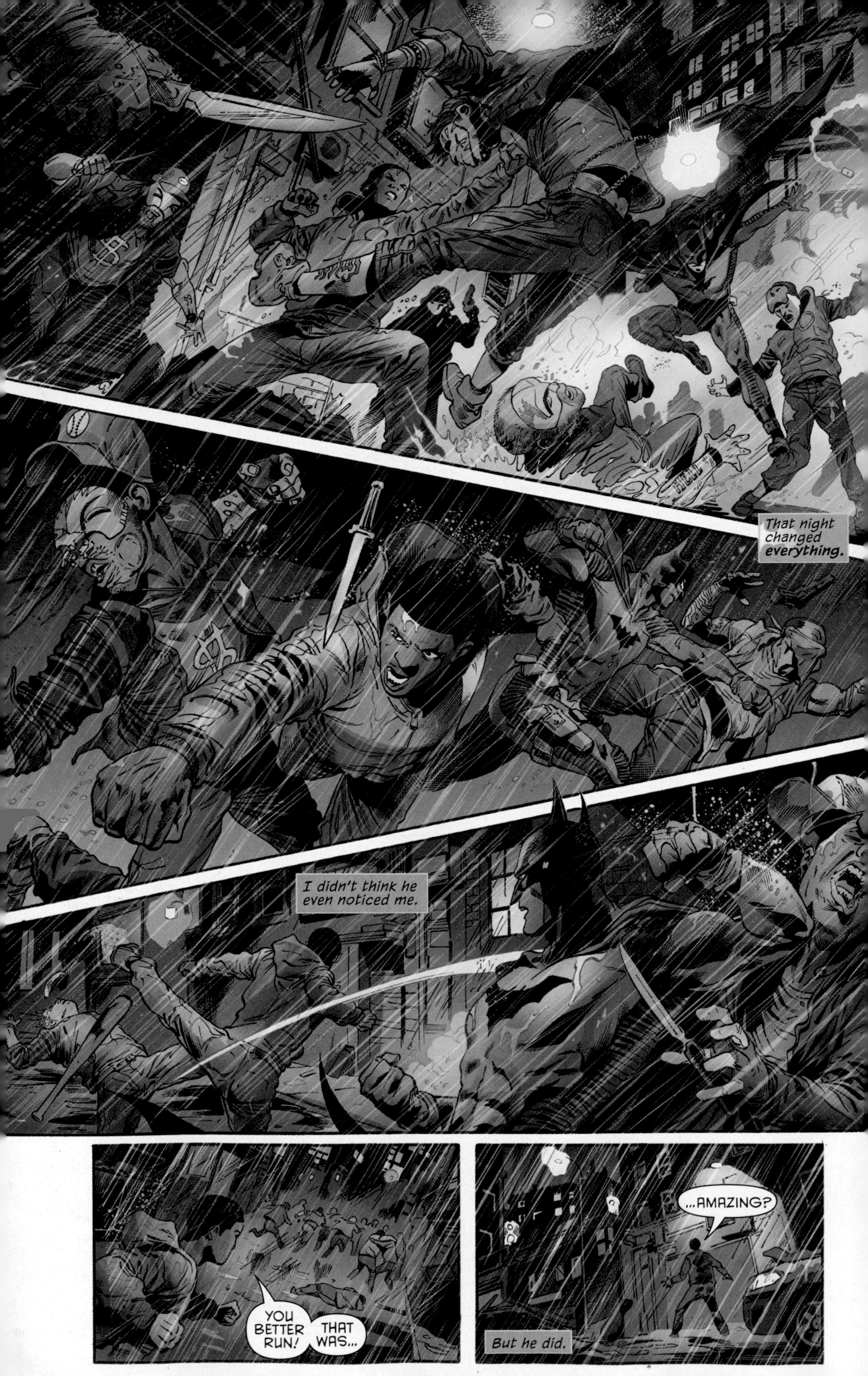
That night changed everything.
I didn't think he even noticed me.
YOU BETTER RUN!
THAT WAS...
...AMAZING?
But he did.

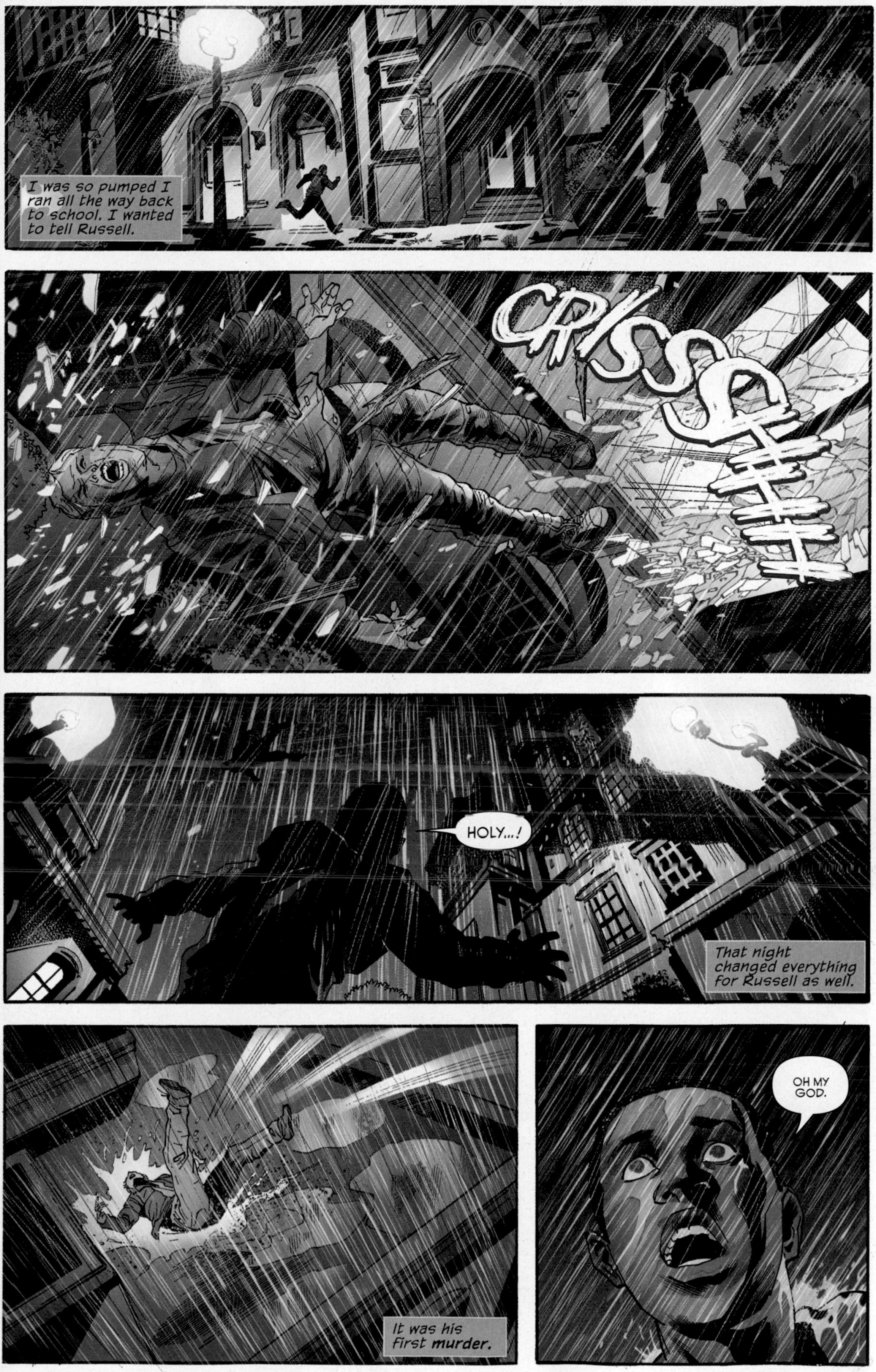
I was so pumped I ran all the way back to school. I wanted to tell Russell.
CRISSSHHH
HOLY...!
That night changed everything for Russell as well.
It was his first murder.
OH MY GOD.

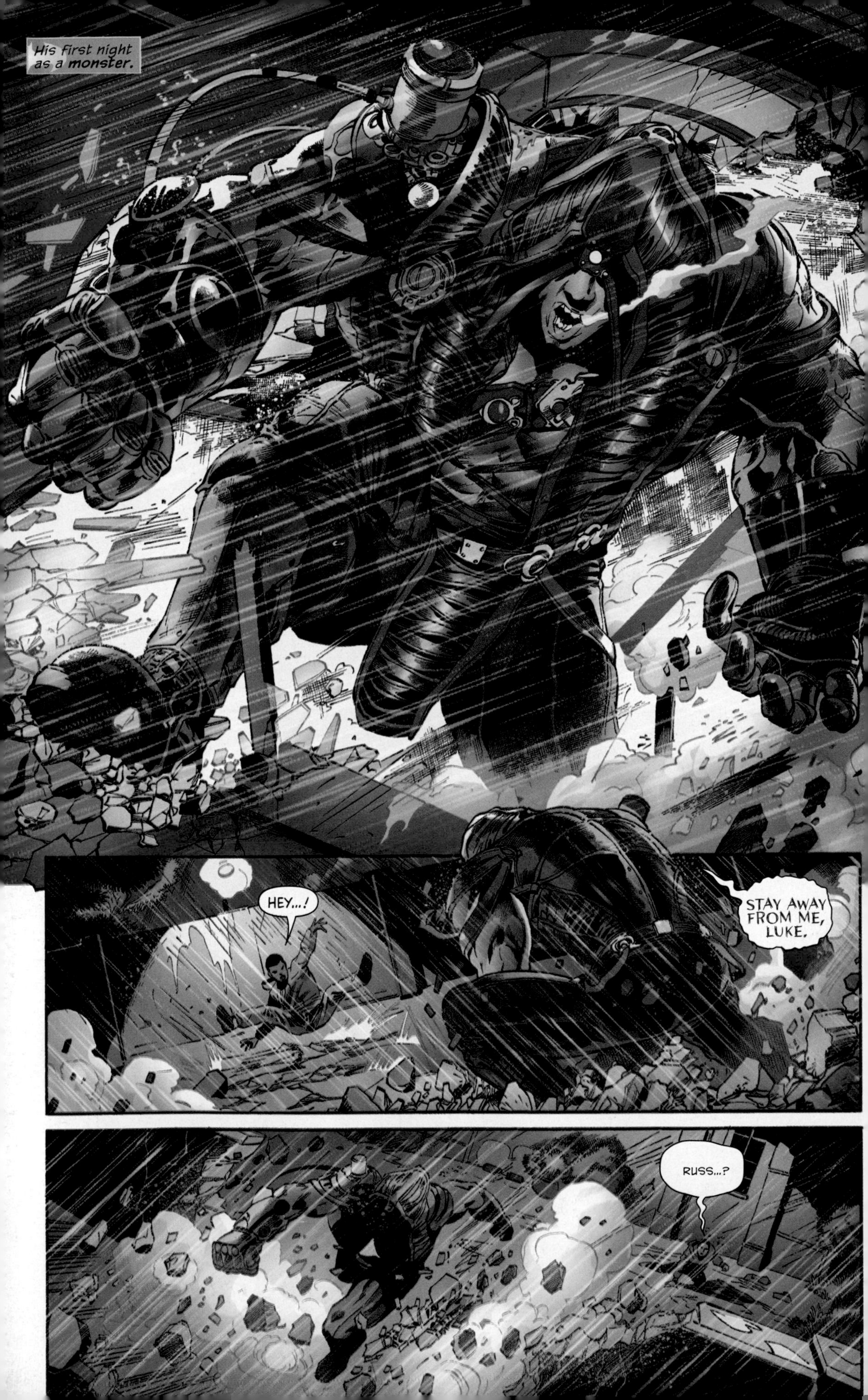
His first night as a monster.
HEY...!
STAY AWAY FROM ME, LUKE.
RUSS...?

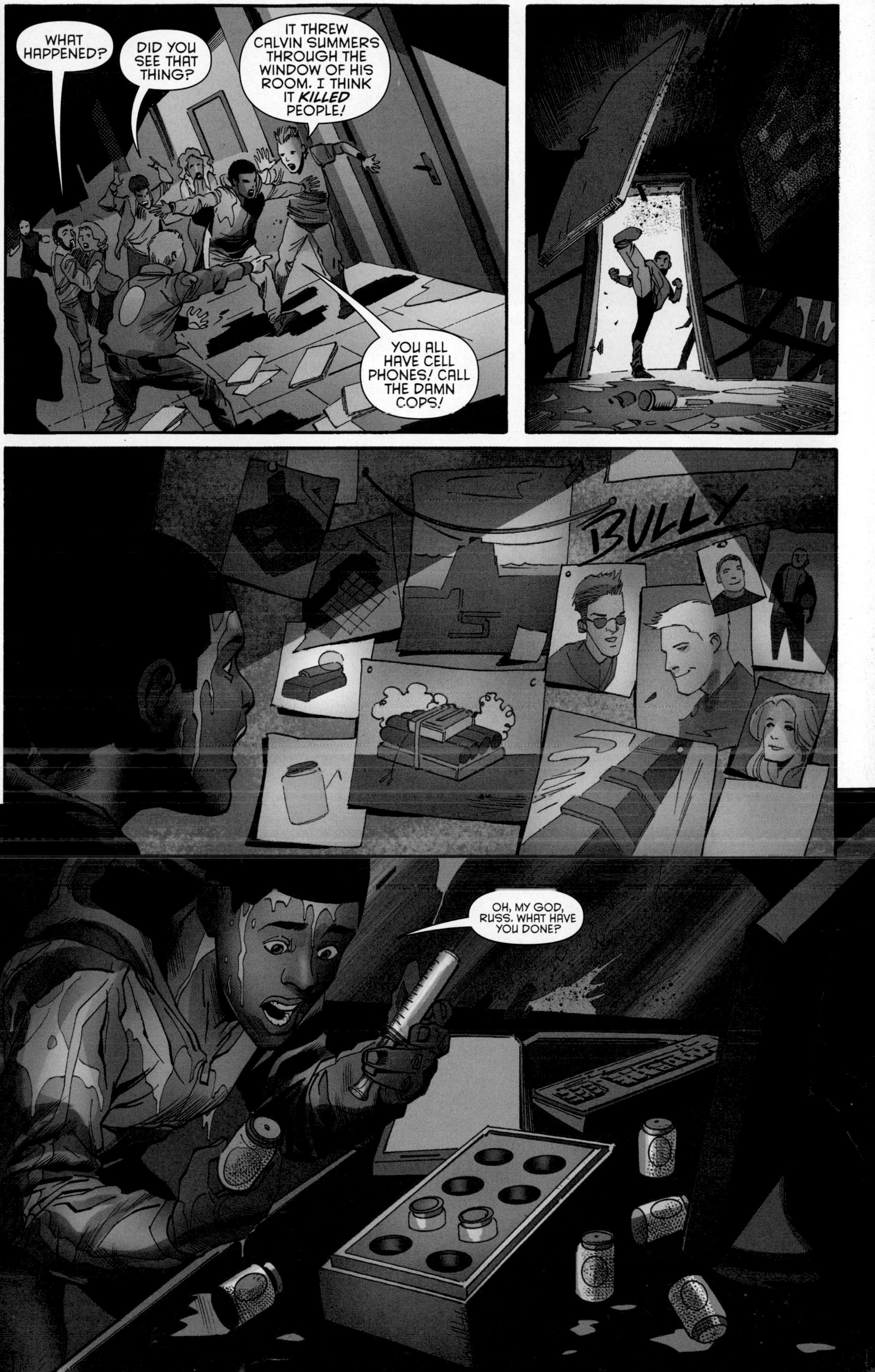
WHAT HAPPENED?
DID YOU SEE THAT THING?
IT THREW CALVIN SUMMERS THROUGH THE WINDOW OF HIS ROOM. I THINK IT *KILLED* PEOPLE!
YOU ALL HAVE CELL PHONES! CALL THE DAMN COPS!
BULLY
OH, MY GOD, RUSS. WHAT HAVE YOU DONE?

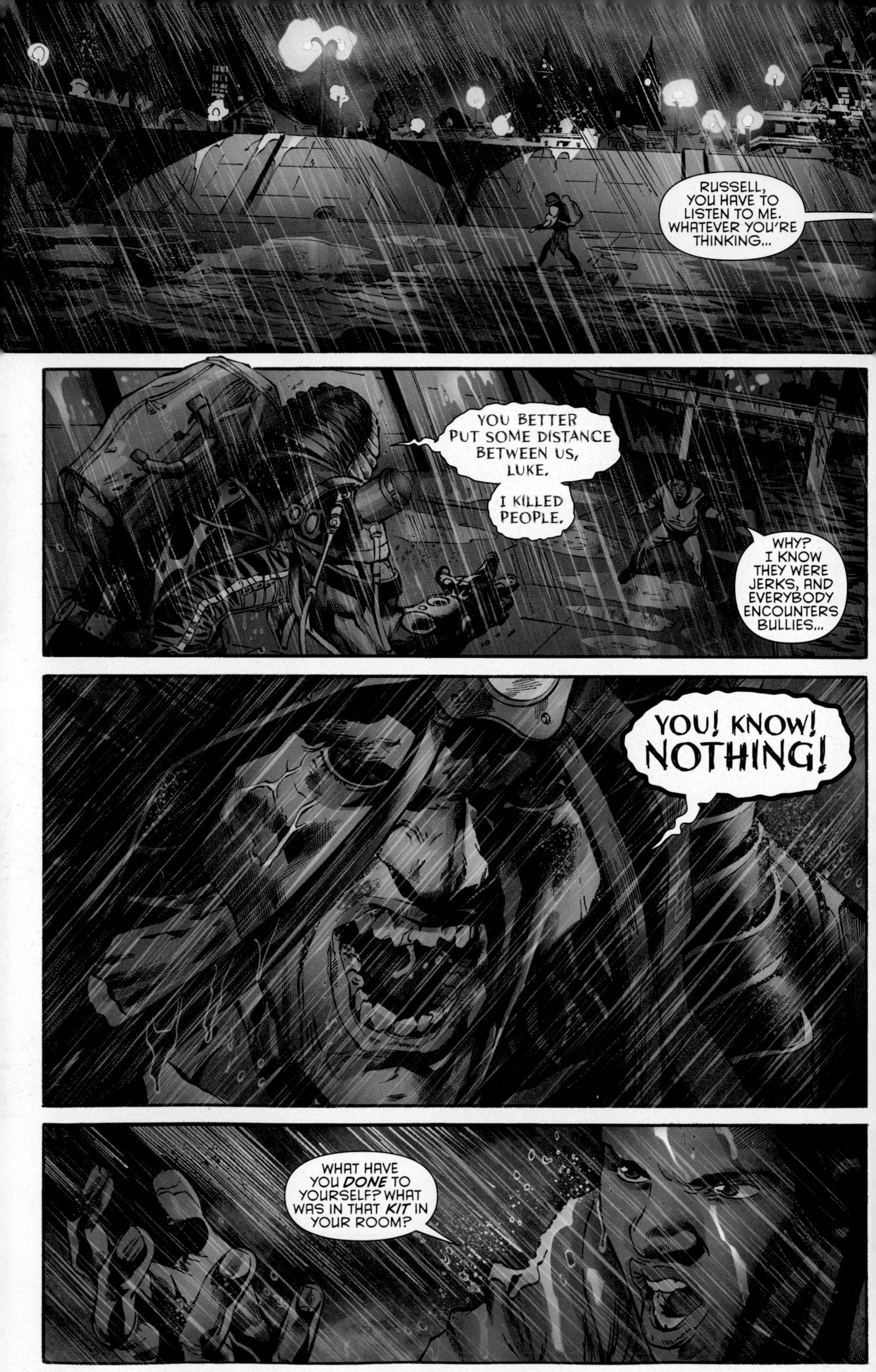
RUSSELL, YOU HAVE TO LISTEN TO ME. WHATEVER YOU'RE THINKING...
YOU BETTER PUT SOME DISTANCE BETWEEN US, LUKE.
I KILLED PEOPLE.
WHY? I KNOW THEY WERE JERKS, AND EVERYBODY ENCOUNTERS BULLIES...
YOU! KNOW! NOTHING!
WHAT HAVE YOU DONE TO YOURSELF? WHAT WAS IN THAT KIT IN YOUR ROOM?

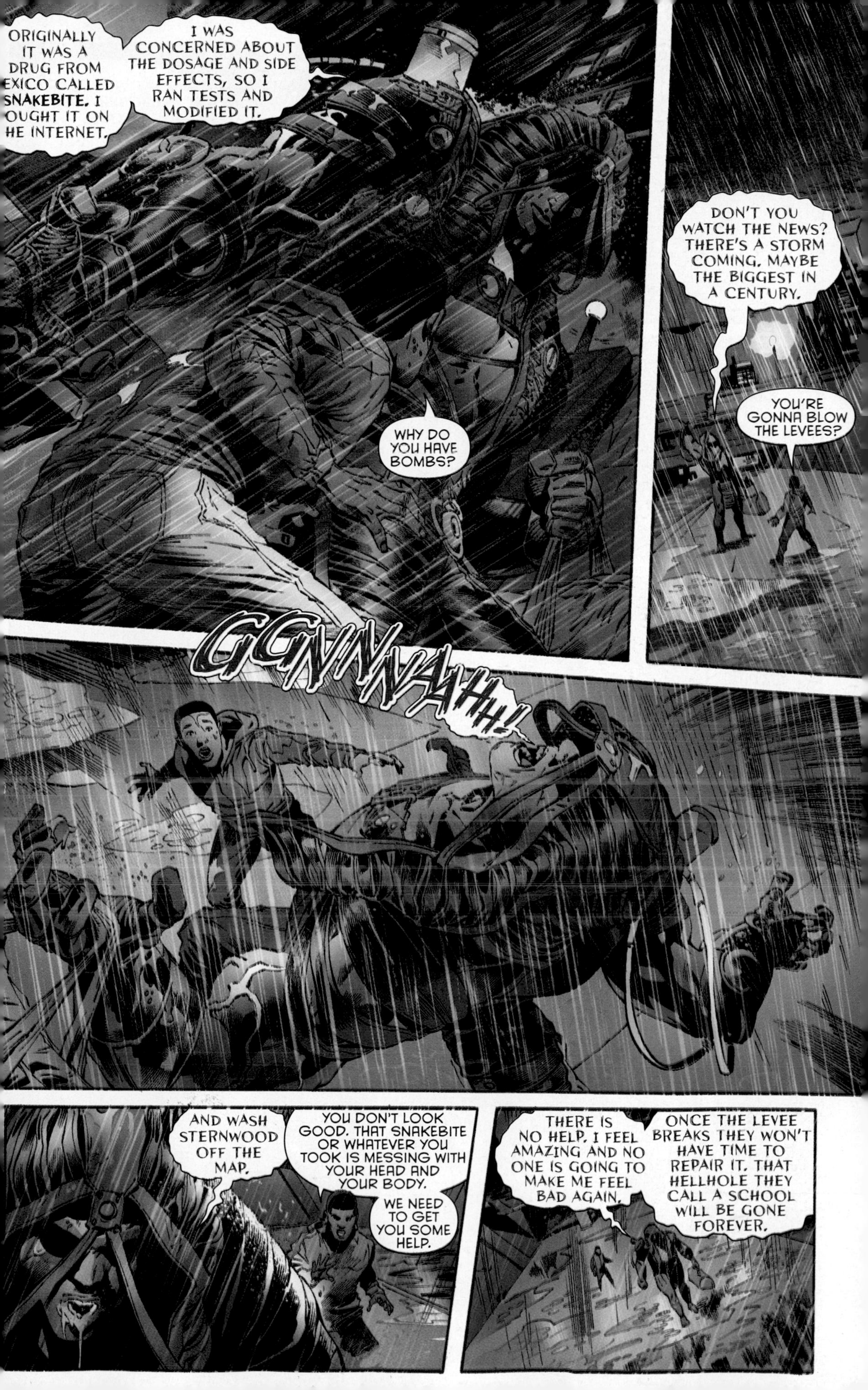
ORIGINALLY IT WAS A DRUG FROM EXICO CALLED SNAKEBITE. I OUGHT IT ON HE INTERNET.
I WAS CONCERNED ABOUT THE DOSAGE AND SIDE EFFECTS, SO I RAN TESTS AND MODIFIED IT.
WHY DO YOU HAVE BOMBS?
DON'T YOU WATCH THE NEWS? THERE'S A STORM COMING. MAYBE THE BIGGEST IN A CENTURY.
YOU'RE GONNA BLOW THE LEVEES?
GGNNNAHH!
AND WASH STERNWOOD OFF THE MAP.
YOU DON'T LOOK GOOD. THAT SNAKEBITE OR WHATEVER YOU TOOK IS MESSING WITH YOUR HEAD AND YOUR BODY.
WE NEED TO GET YOU SOME HELP.
THERE IS NO HELP. I FEEL AMAZING AND NO ONE IS GOING TO MAKE ME FEEL BAD AGAIN.
ONCE THE LEVEE BREAKS THEY WON'T HAVE TIME TO REPAIR IT. THAT HELLHOLE THEY CALL A SCHOOL WILL BE GONE FOREVER.

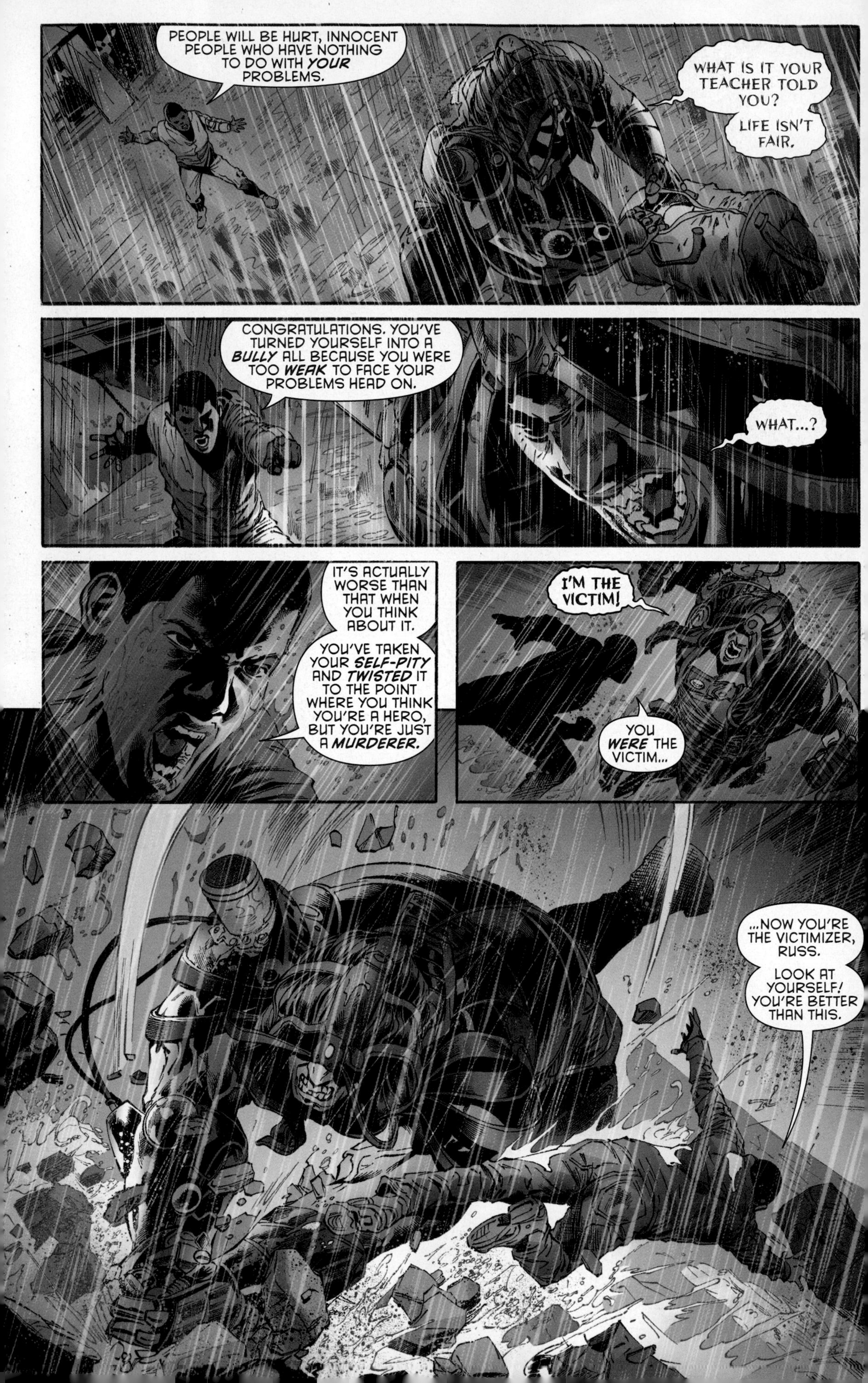
PEOPLE WILL BE HURT, INNOCENT PEOPLE WHO HAVE NOTHING TO DO WITH *YOUR* PROBLEMS.
WHAT IS IT YOUR TEACHER TOLD YOU?
LIFE ISN'T FAIR.
CONGRATULATIONS. YOU'VE TURNED YOURSELF INTO A *BULLY* ALL BECAUSE YOU WERE TOO *WEAK* TO FACE YOUR PROBLEMS HEAD ON.
WHAT...?
IT'S ACTUALLY WORSE THAN THAT WHEN YOU THINK ABOUT IT.
YOU'VE TAKEN YOUR *SELF-PITY* AND *TWISTED* IT TO THE POINT WHERE YOU THINK YOU'RE A HERO, BUT YOU'RE JUST A *MURDERER.*
I'M THE VICTIM!
YOU *WERE* THE VICTIM...
...NOW YOU'RE THE VICTIMIZER, RUSS.
LOOK AT YOURSELF! YOU'RE BETTER THAN THIS.

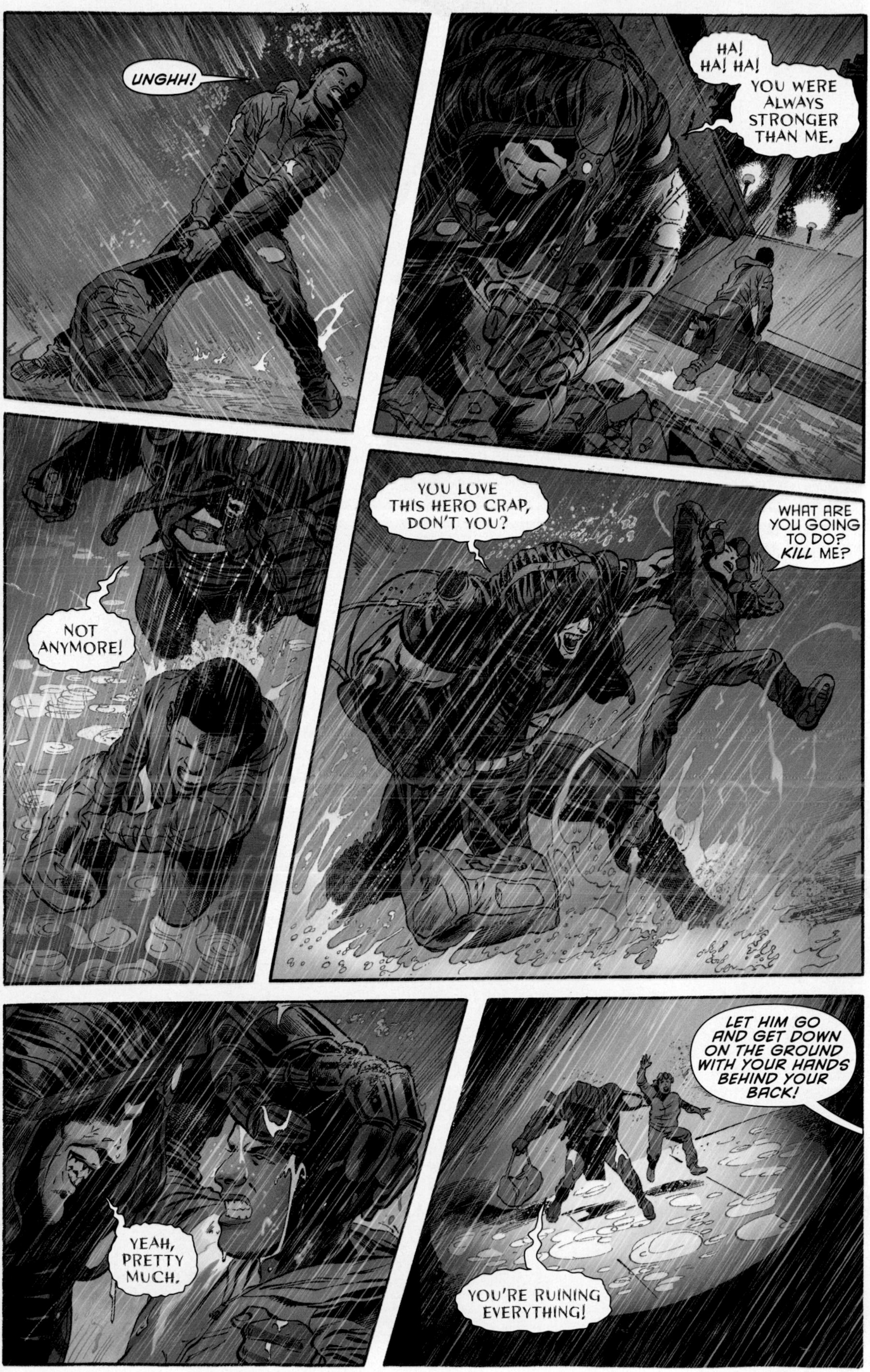
UNGHH!
HA! HA! HA!
YOU WERE ALWAYS STRONGER THAN ME.
NOT ANYMORE!
YOU LOVE THIS HERO CRAP, DON'T YOU?
WHAT ARE YOU GOING TO DO? KILL ME?
YEAH, PRETTY MUCH.
LET HIM GO AND GET DOWN ON THE GROUND WITH YOUR HANDS BEHIND YOUR BACK!
YOU'RE RUINING EVERYTHING!

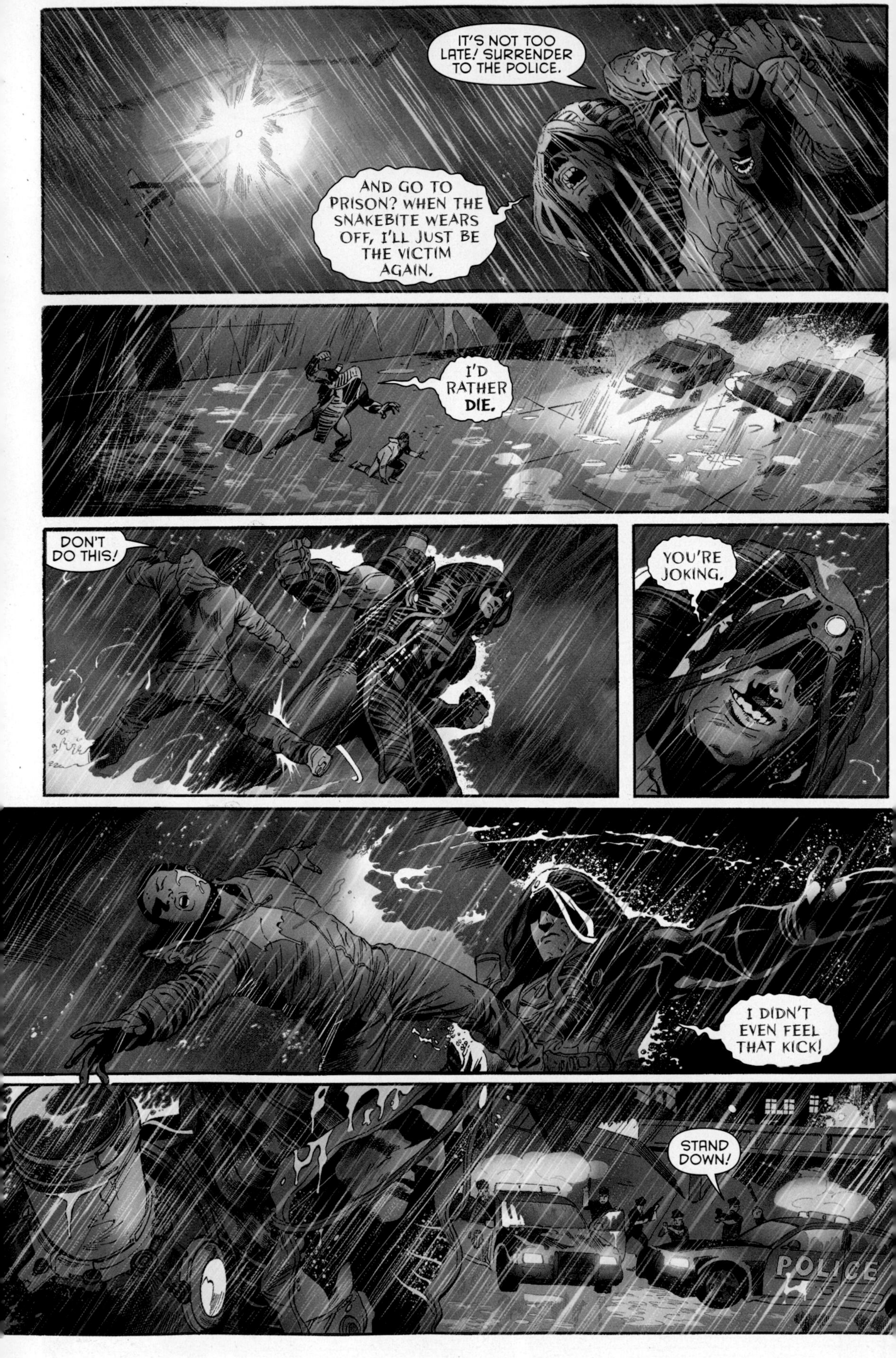
IT'S NOT TOO LATE! SURRENDER TO THE POLICE.
AND GO TO PRISON? WHEN THE SNAKEBITE WEARS OFF, I'LL JUST BE THE VICTIM AGAIN.
I'D RATHER **DIE.**
DON'T DO THIS!
YOU'RE JOKING.
I DIDN'T EVEN FEEL THAT KICK!
STAND DOWN!
POLICE

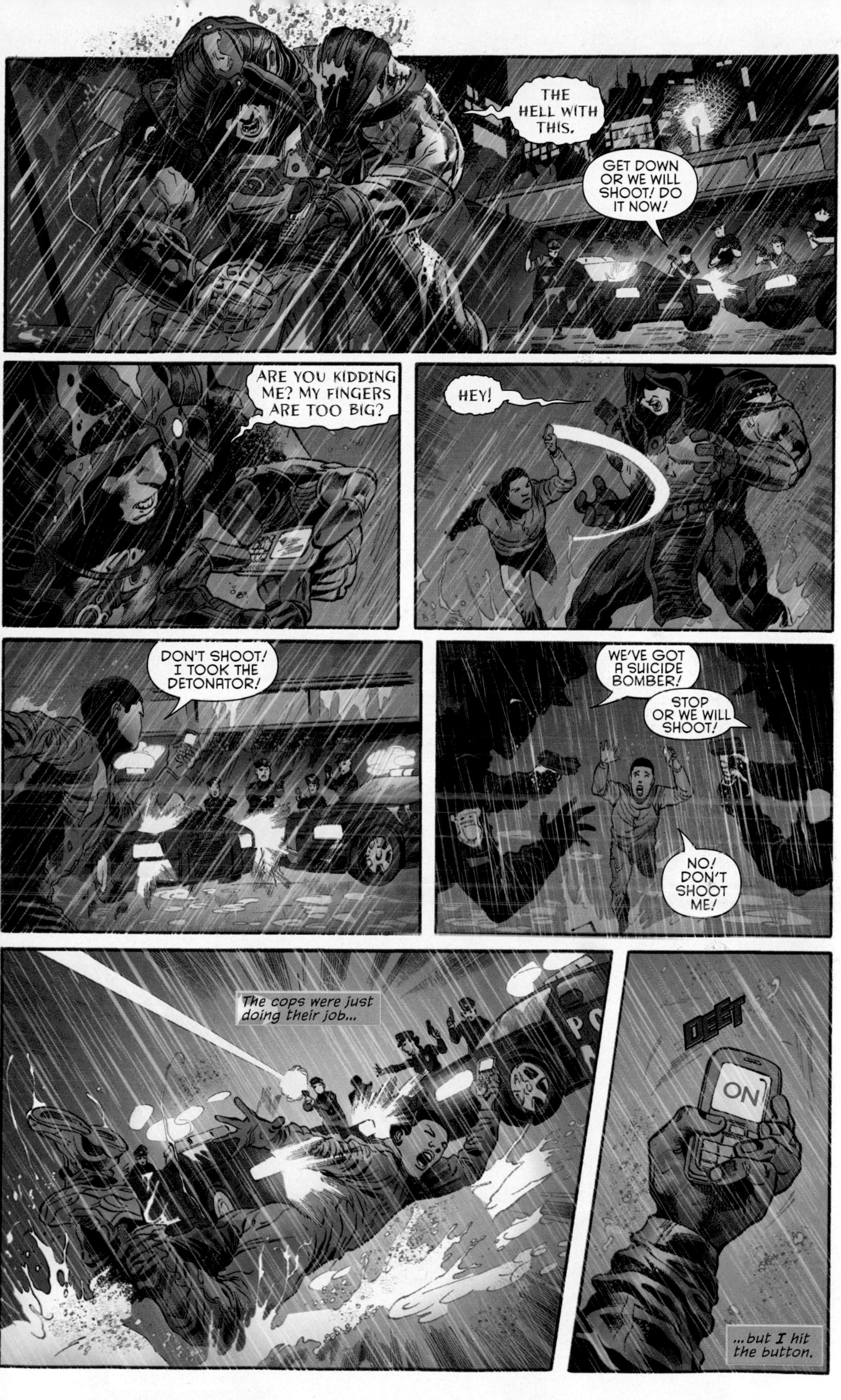
THE HELL WITH THIS.
GET DOWN OR WE WILL SHOOT! DO IT NOW!
ARE YOU KIDDING ME? MY FINGERS ARE TOO BIG?
HEY!
DON'T SHOOT! I TOOK THE DETONATOR!
WE'VE GOT A SUICIDE BOMBER!
STOP OR WE WILL SHOOT!
NO! DON'T SHOOT ME!
The cops were just doing their job...
DEET
ON
...but I hit the button.

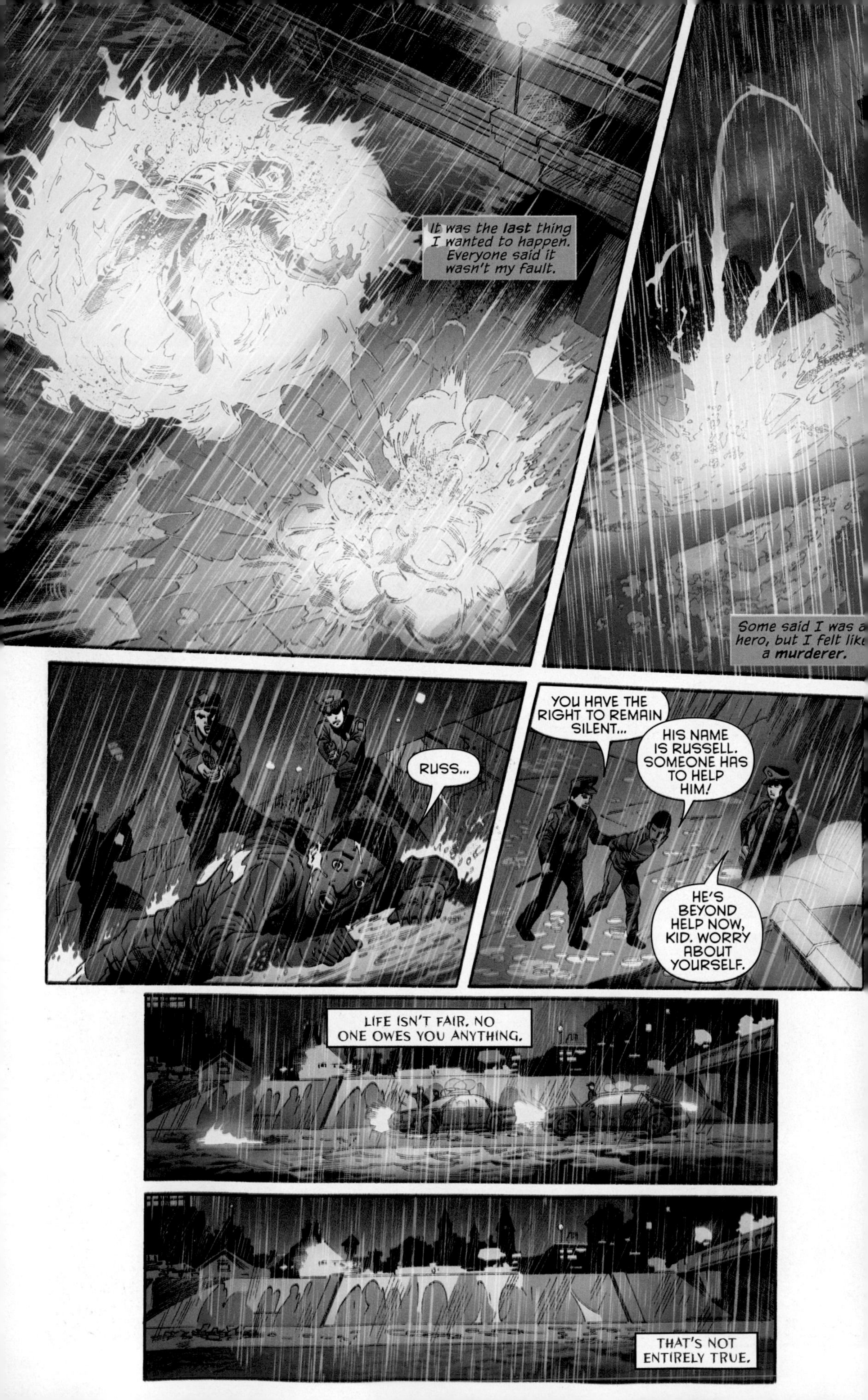
It was the last thing I wanted to happen. Everyone said it wasn't my fault.
Some said I was a hero, but I felt like a murderer.
RUSS...
YOU HAVE THE RIGHT TO REMAIN SILENT...
HIS NAME IS RUSSELL. SOMEONE HAS TO HELP HIM!
HE'S BEYOND HELP NOW, KID. WORRY ABOUT YOURSELF.
LIFE ISN'T FAIR. NO ONE OWES YOU ANYTHING.
THAT'S NOT ENTIRELY TRUE.

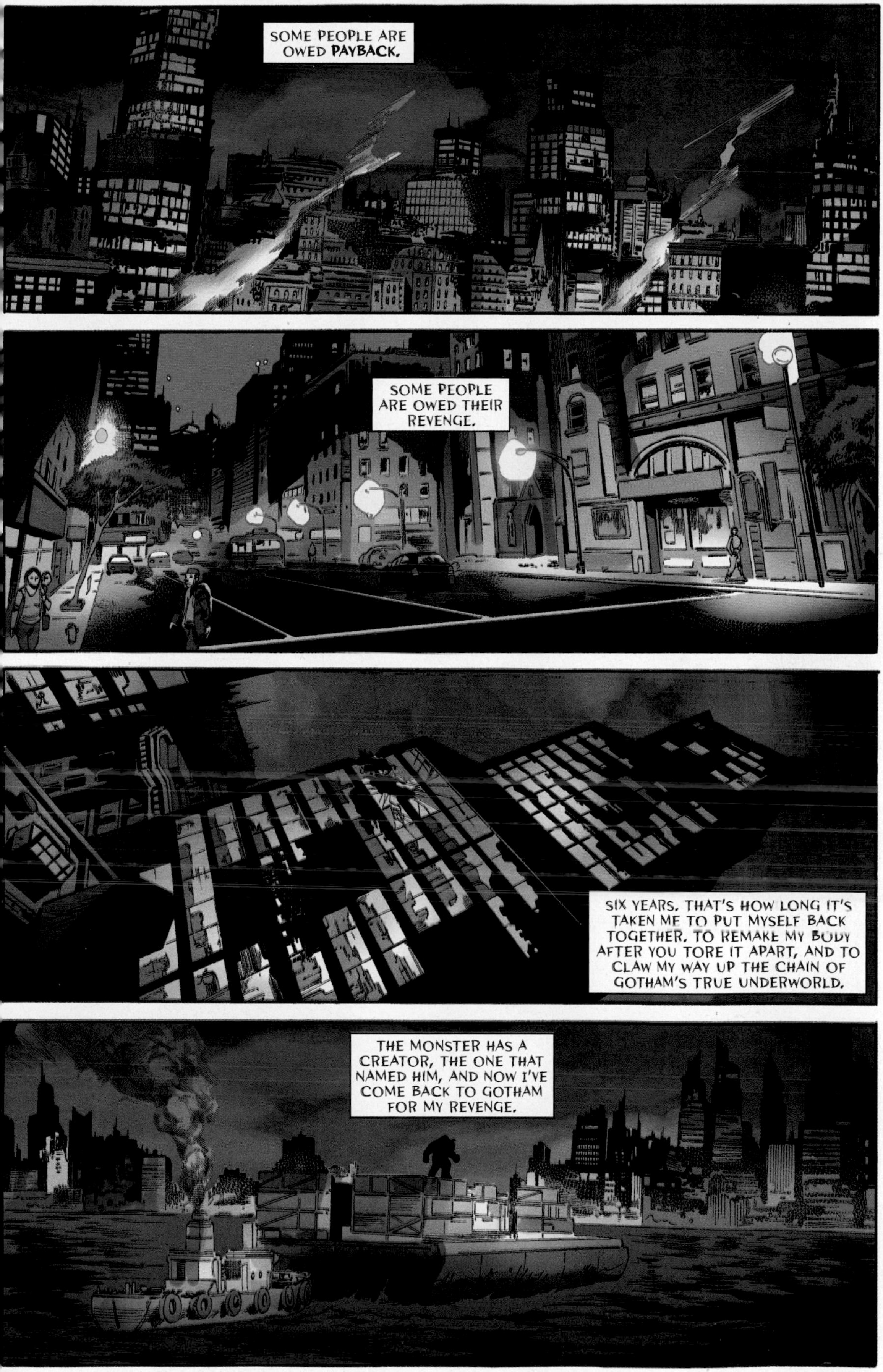
SOME PEOPLE ARE OWED PAYBACK.
SOME PEOPLE ARE OWED THEIR REVENGE.
SIX YEARS. THAT'S HOW LONG IT'S TAKEN ME TO PUT MYSELF BACK TOGETHER. TO REMAKE MY BODY AFTER YOU TORE IT APART, AND TO CLAW MY WAY UP THE CHAIN OF GOTHAM'S TRUE UNDERWORLD.
THE MONSTER HAS A CREATOR, THE ONE THAT NAMED HIM, AND NOW I'VE COME BACK TO GOTHAM FOR MY REVENGE.

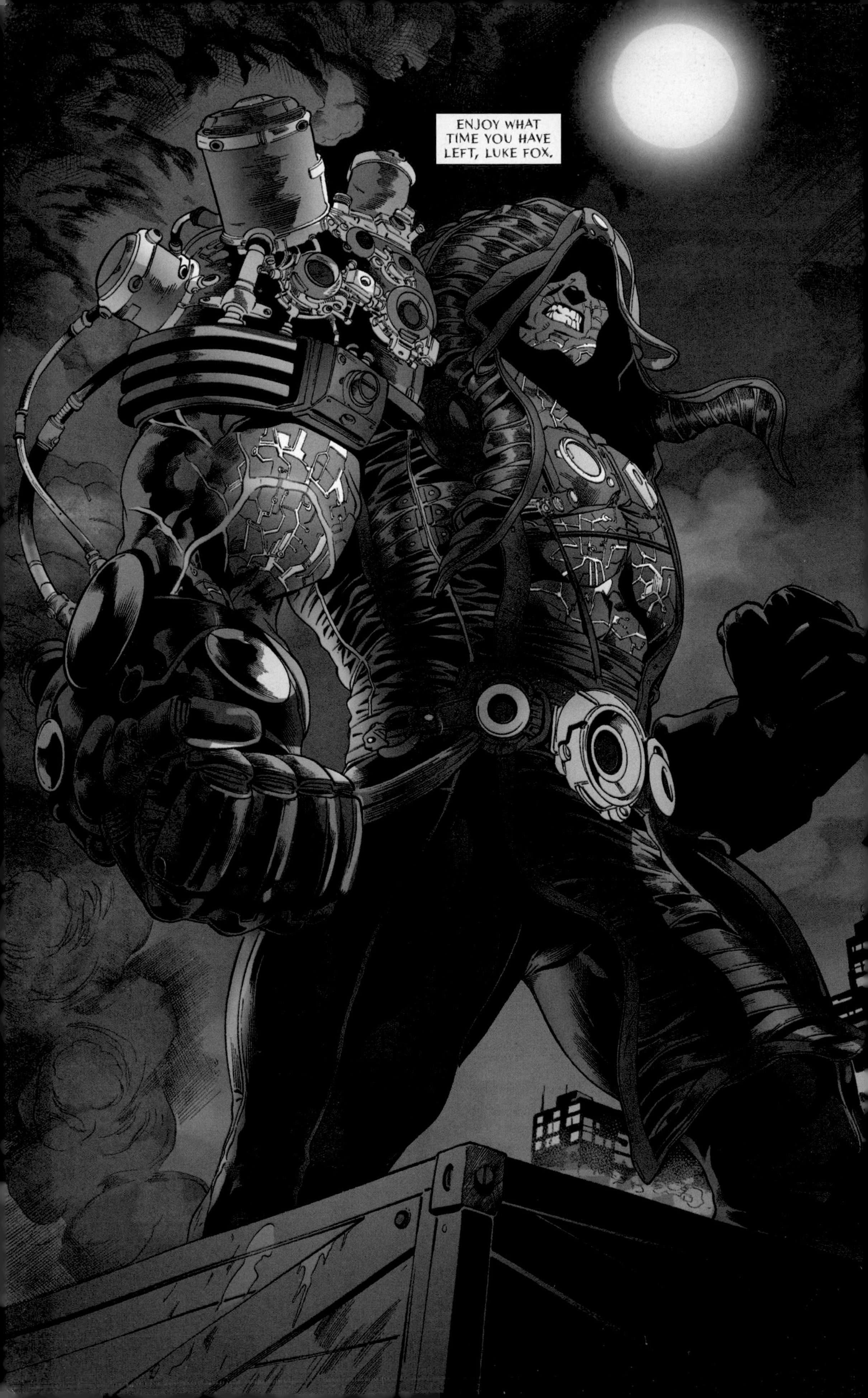
ENJOY WHAT TIME YOU HAVE LEFT, LUKE FOX.

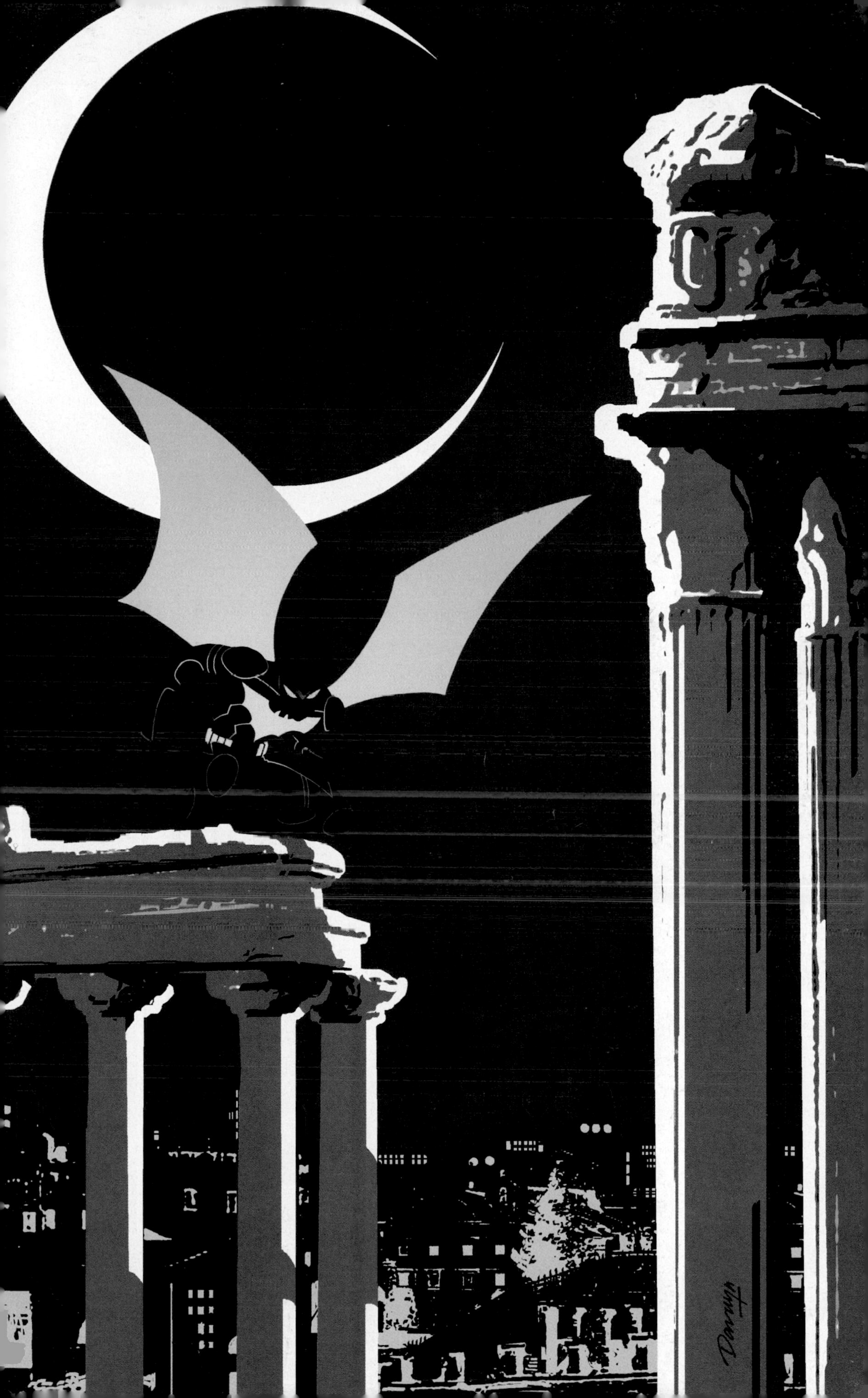

WHEN IN ROME (SORT OF)
cover art by **DARWYN COOKE**

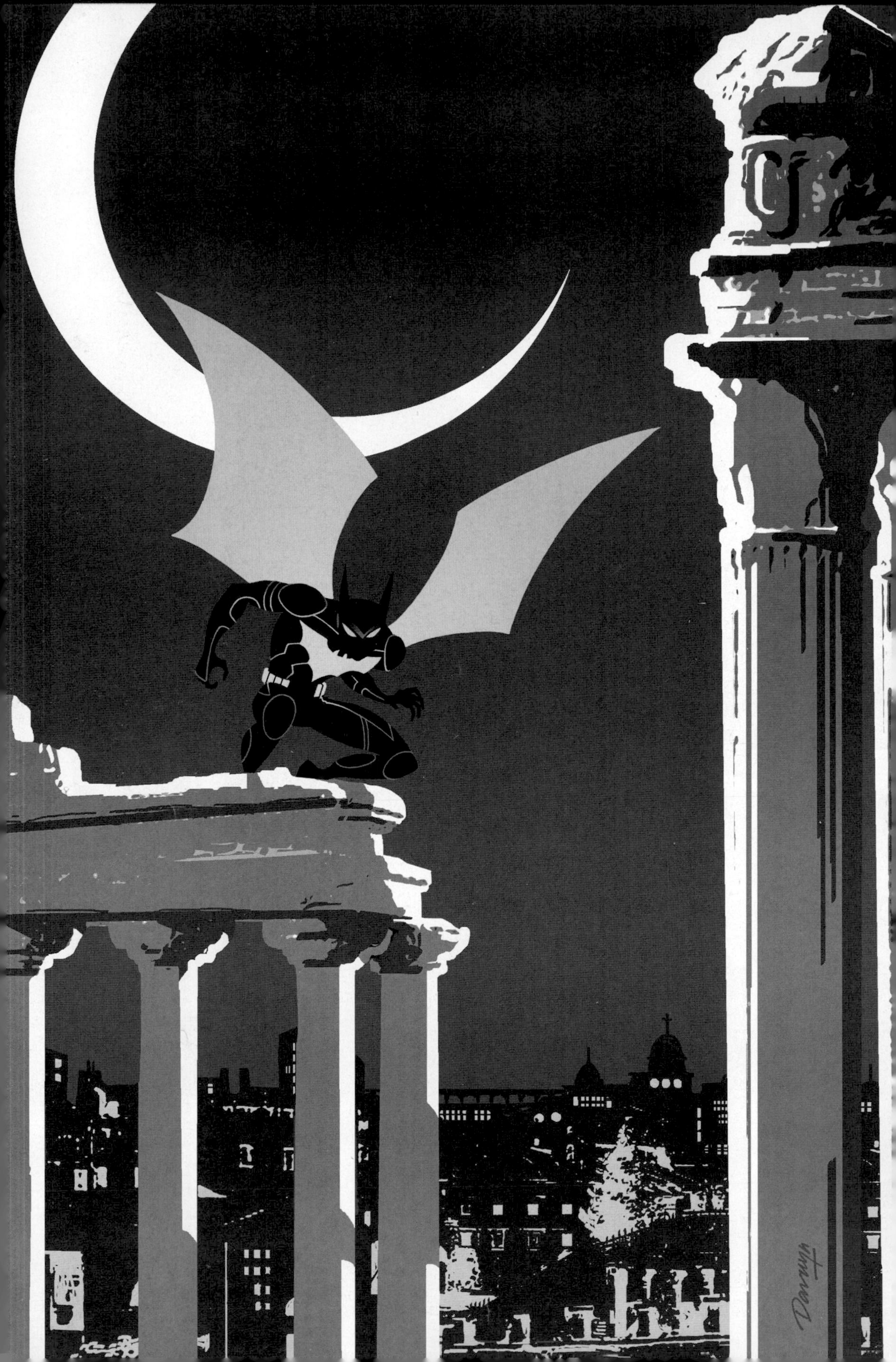

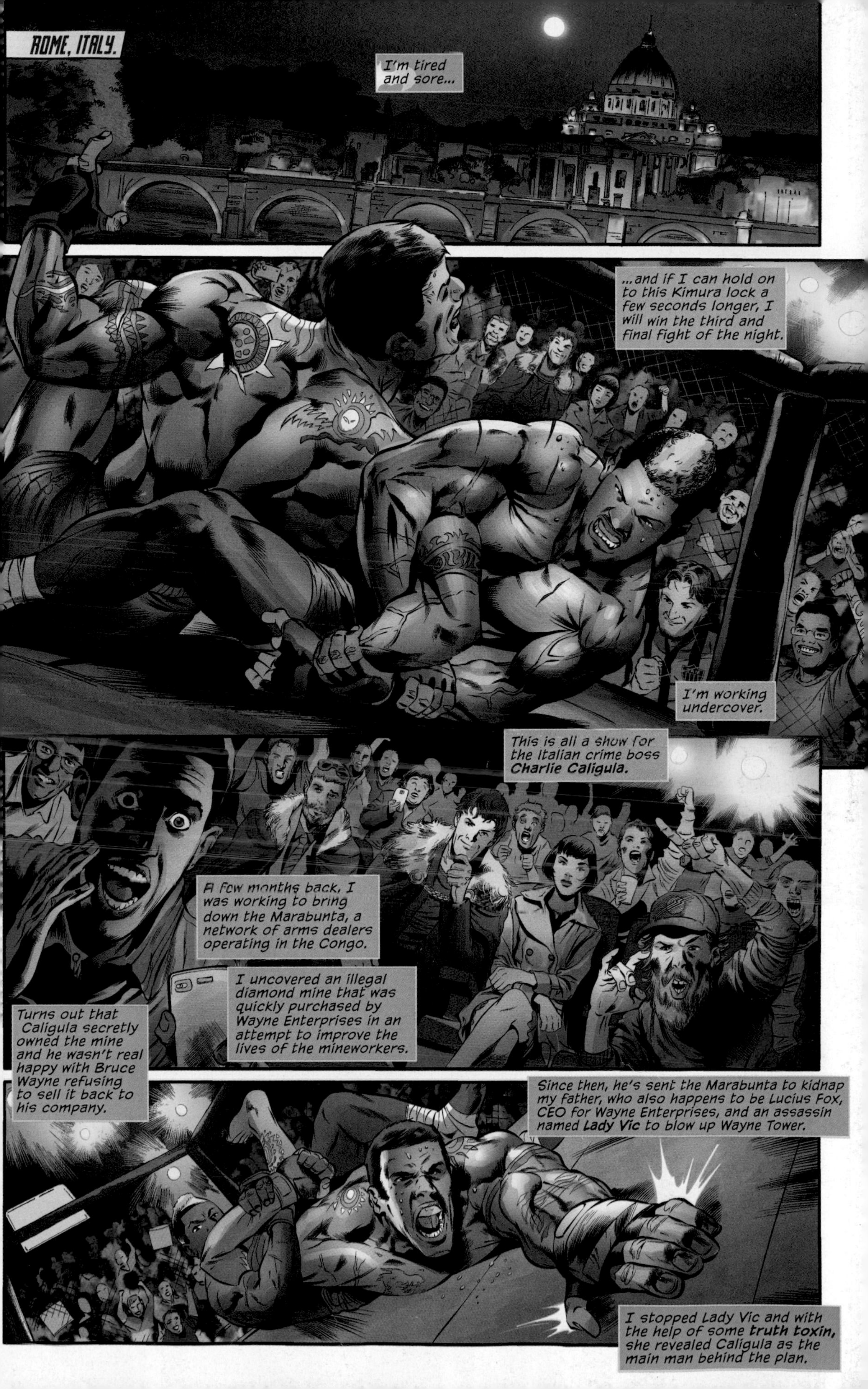
ROME, ITALY.
I'm tired and sore...
...and if I can hold on to this Kimura lock a few seconds longer, I will win the third and final fight of the night.
I'm working undercover.
This is all a show for the Italian crime boss Charlie Caligula.
A few months back, I was working to bring down the Marabunta, a network of arms dealers operating in the Congo.
I uncovered an illegal diamond mine that was quickly purchased by Wayne Enterprises in an attempt to improve the lives of the mineworkers.
Turns out that Caligula secretly owned the mine and he wasn't real happy with Bruce Wayne refusing to sell it back to his company.
Since then, he's sent the Marabunta to kidnap my father, who also happens to be Lucius Fox, CEO for Wayne Enterprises, and an assassin named Lady Vic to blow up Wayne Tower.
I stopped Lady Vic and with the help of some truth toxin, she revealed Caligula as the main man behind the plan.

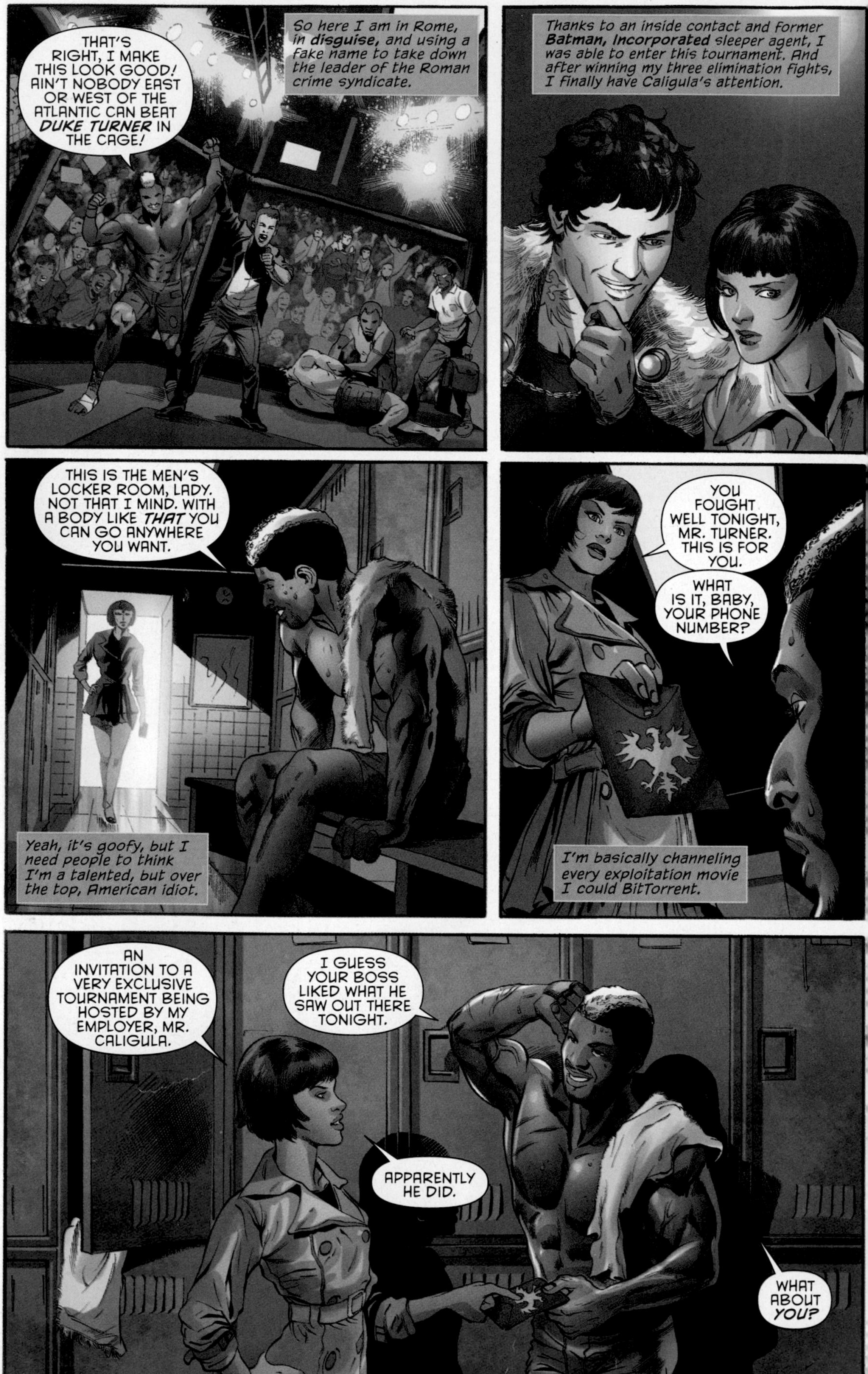
THAT'S RIGHT, I MAKE THIS LOOK GOOD! AIN'T NOBODY EAST OR WEST OF THE ATLANTIC CAN BEAT DUKE TURNER IN THE CAGE!
So here I am in Rome, in disguise, and using a fake name to take down the leader of the Roman crime syndicate.
Thanks to an inside contact and former Batman, Incorporated sleeper agent, I was able to enter this tournament. And after winning my three elimination fights, I finally have Caligula's attention.
THIS IS THE MEN'S LOCKER ROOM, LADY. NOT THAT I MIND. WITH A BODY LIKE THAT YOU CAN GO ANYWHERE YOU WANT.
Yeah, it's goofy, but I need people to think I'm a talented, but over the top, American idiot.
YOU FOUGHT WELL TONIGHT, MR. TURNER. THIS IS FOR YOU.
WHAT IS IT, BABY, YOUR PHONE NUMBER?
I'm basically channeling every exploitation movie I could BitTorrent.
AN INVITATION TO A VERY EXCLUSIVE TOURNAMENT BEING HOSTED BY MY EMPLOYER, MR. CALIGULA.
I GUESS YOUR BOSS LIKED WHAT HE SAW OUT THERE TONIGHT.
APPARENTLY HE DID.
WHAT ABOUT YOU?

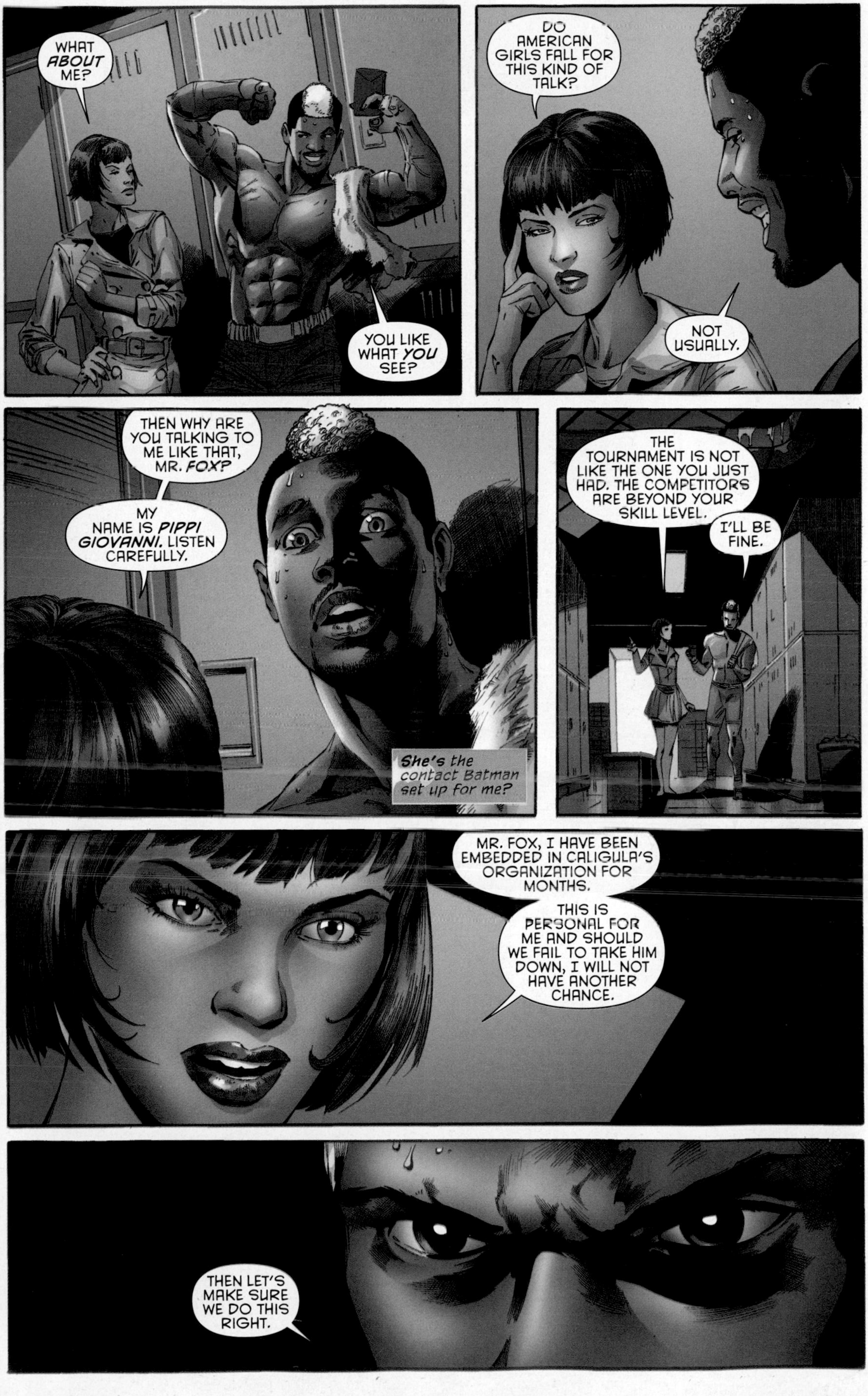
WHAT *ABOUT* ME?
YOU LIKE WHAT *YOU* SEE?
DO AMERICAN GIRLS FALL FOR THIS KIND OF TALK?
NOT USUALLY.
THEN WHY ARE YOU TALKING TO ME LIKE THAT, MR. *FOX*?
MY NAME IS *PIPPI GIOVANNI.* LISTEN CAREFULLY.
She's the contact Batman set up for me?
THE TOURNAMENT IS NOT LIKE THE ONE YOU JUST HAD. THE COMPETITORS ARE BEYOND YOUR SKILL LEVEL.
I'LL BE FINE.
MR. FOX, I HAVE BEEN EMBEDDED IN CALIGULA'S ORGANIZATION FOR MONTHS.
THIS IS PERSONAL FOR ME AND SHOULD WE FAIL TO TAKE HIM DOWN, I WILL NOT HAVE ANOTHER CHANCE.
THEN LET'S MAKE SURE WE DO THIS RIGHT.

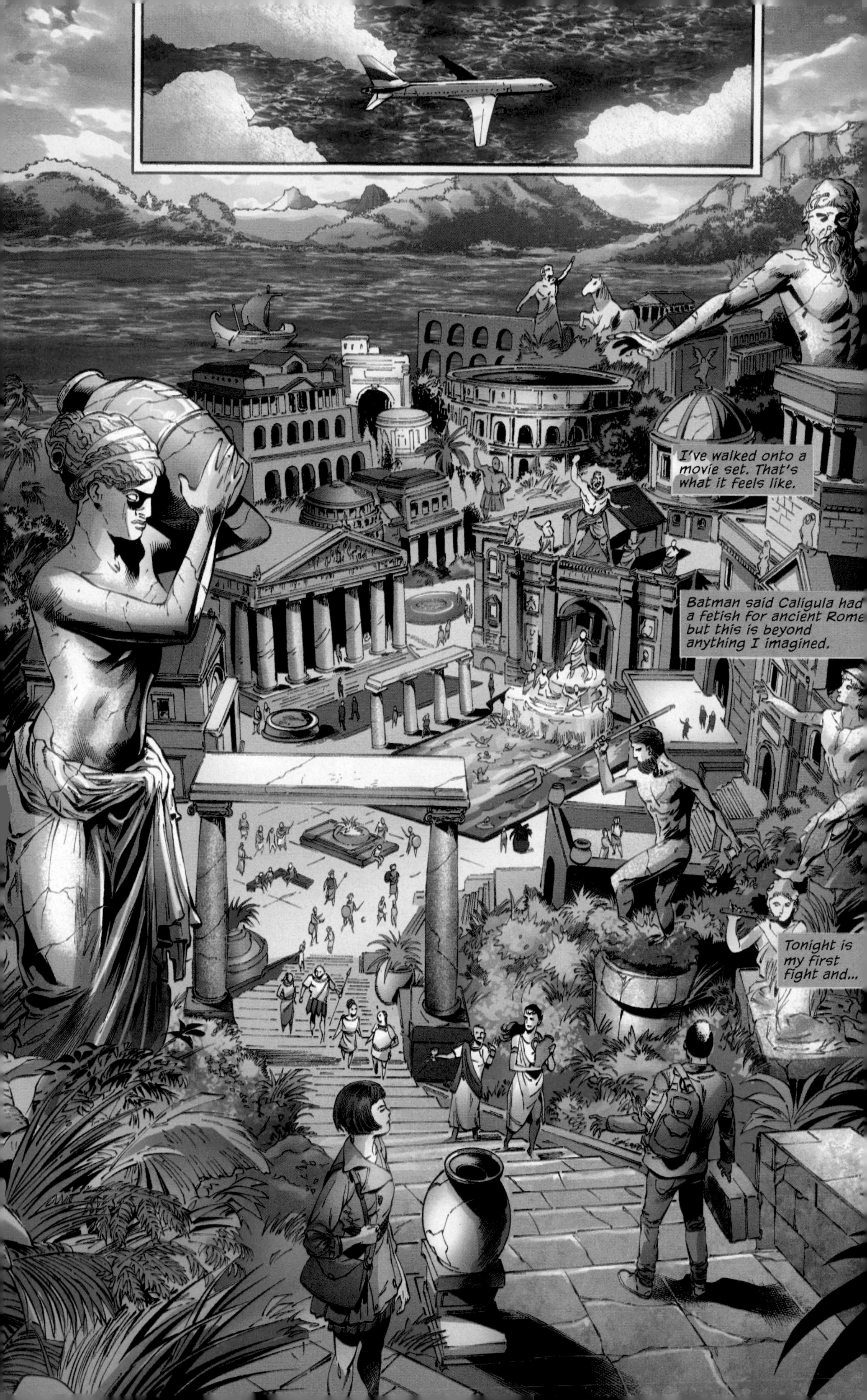
I've walked onto a movie set. That's what it feels like.
Batman said Caligula had a fetish for ancient Rome but this is beyond anything I imagined.
Tonight is my first fight and...

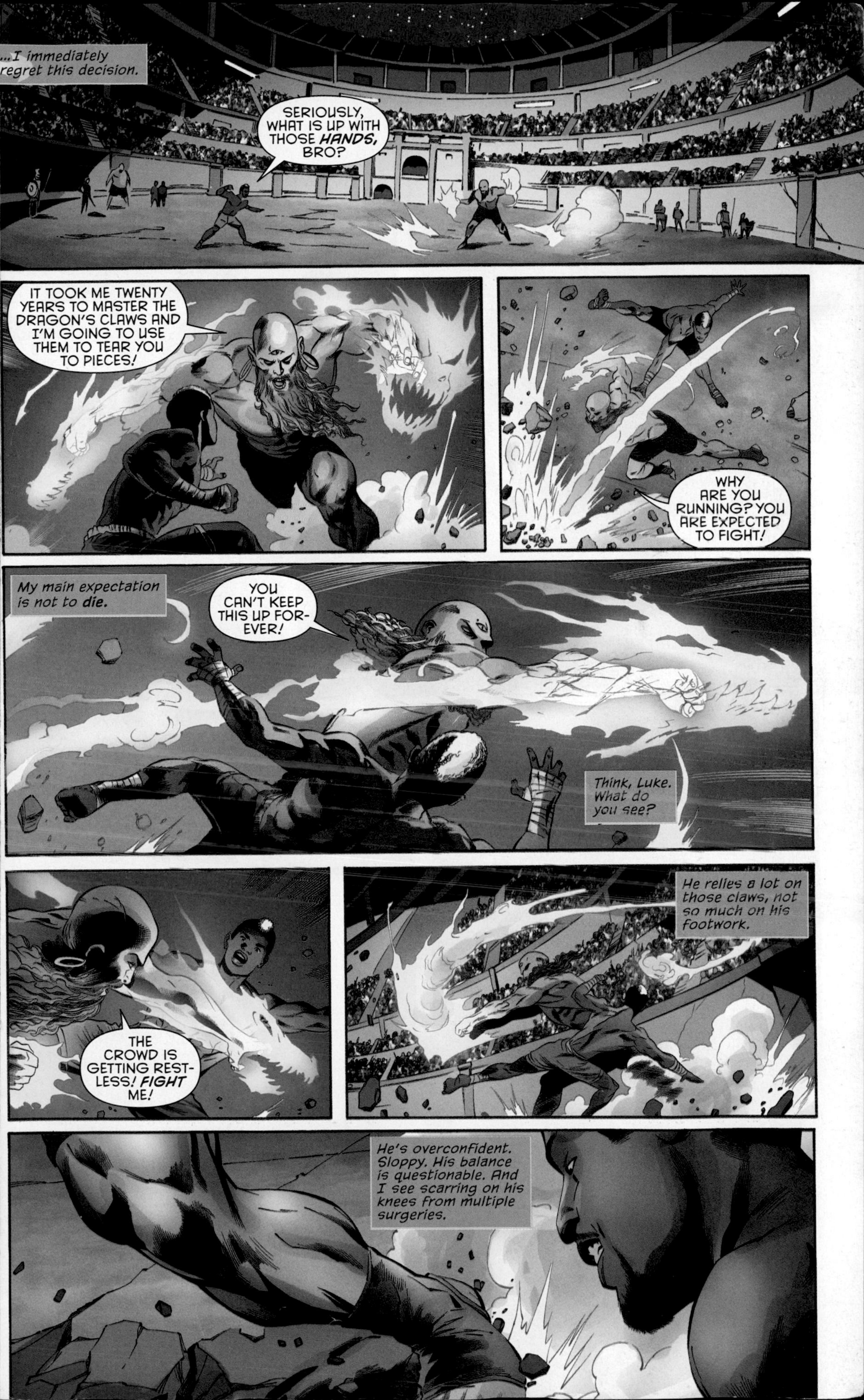
...I immediately regret this decision.
SERIOUSLY, WHAT IS UP WITH THOSE *HANDS,* BRO?
IT TOOK ME TWENTY YEARS TO MASTER THE DRAGON'S CLAWS AND I'M GOING TO USE THEM TO TEAR YOU TO PIECES!
WHY ARE YOU RUNNING? YOU ARE EXPECTED TO FIGHT!
My main expectation is not to **die.**
YOU CAN'T KEEP THIS UP FOREVER!
Think, Luke. What do you see?
THE CROWD IS GETTING RESTLESS! *FIGHT* ME!
He relies a lot on those claws, not so much on his footwork.
He's overconfident. Sloppy. His balance is questionable. And I see scarring on his knees from multiple surgeries.

I probably have one shot at this, so it has to count.

GHHAARR!

I can cripple his knee. Turn his thinking from attack to defense.

CHEAP SHOT!

GHHAA!

YOU'RE THE ONE WITH *SUPER POWERS*, BRO! I'M JUST TRYING TO SURVIVE IN HERE.

THAT'S NOT GOING TO HAPPEN. I INTEND TO WIN THIS...

That was too close.

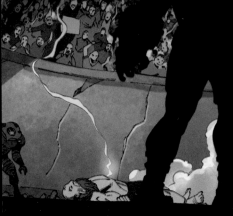

Look at these monsters.

I'm gonna get killed if I try to stay in the tourney.

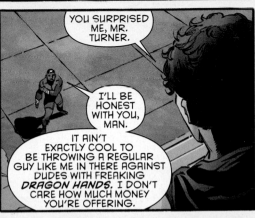

YOU SURPRISED ME, MR. TURNER.

I'LL BE HONEST WITH YOU, MAN.

IT AIN'T EXACTLY COOL TO BE THROWING A REGULAR GUY LIKE ME IN THERE AGAINST DUDES WITH FREAKING *DRAGON HANDS*. I DON'T CARE HOW MUCH MONEY YOU'RE OFFERING.

I AM YOUR *HOST*, MR. TURNER. YOU WILL ADDRESS ME AS *MR. CALIGULA*, OR I WILL HAVE YOU GUTTED AND THROWN IN THE OCEAN.

YOU WERE INVITED FOR ONE REASON AND ONE REASON ONLY. I NEEDED A LAMB FOR THE SLAUGHTER.

SORRY TO DISAPPOINT YOU.

I'M SURE YOU WON'T DISAPPOINT ME TOMORROW.

NEVER LET IT BE SAID I AM NOT A GENEROUS MAN. YOU MAY CHOOSE ANYONE SEATED WITH ME AS YOUR NIGHT'S ENTERTAINMENT.

YOU'RE SERIOUS? THEY'RE *PEOPLE*.

THEY'RE *MY* PEOPLE. THEY DO WHAT I SAY.

BOY OR GIRL, IT'S YOUR CHOICE, DUKE TURNER.

I WANT *HER*.

I'LL HAVE HER SENT TO YOUR ROOM.

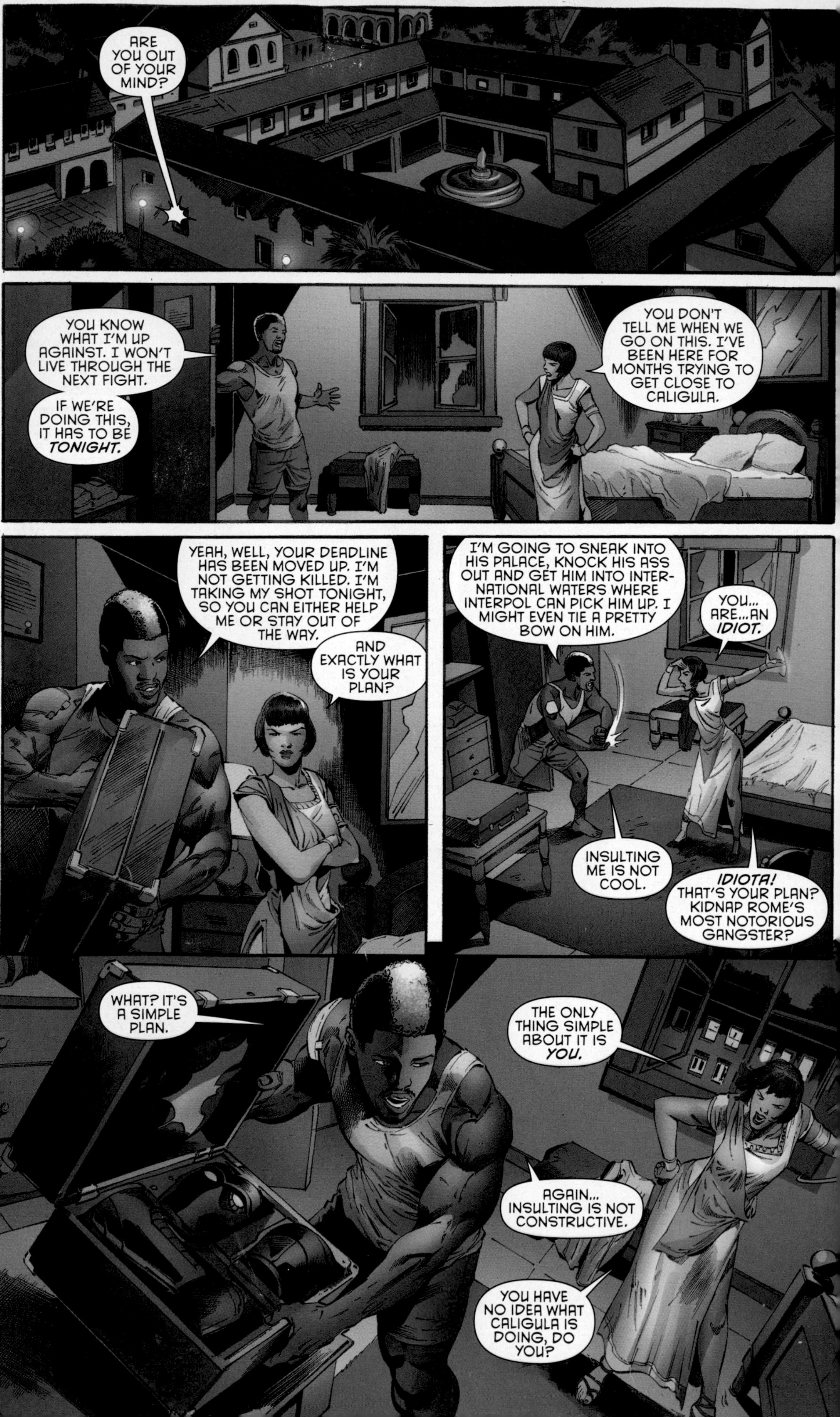
ARE YOU OUT OF YOUR MIND?
YOU KNOW WHAT I'M UP AGAINST. I WON'T LIVE THROUGH THE NEXT FIGHT.
IF WE'RE DOING THIS, IT HAS TO BE *TONIGHT.*
YOU DON'T TELL ME WHEN WE GO ON THIS. I'VE BEEN HERE FOR MONTHS TRYING TO GET CLOSE TO CALIGULA.
YEAH, WELL, YOUR DEADLINE HAS BEEN MOVED UP. I'M NOT GETTING KILLED. I'M TAKING MY SHOT TONIGHT, SO YOU CAN EITHER HELP ME OR STAY OUT OF THE WAY.
AND EXACTLY WHAT IS YOUR PLAN?
I'M GOING TO SNEAK INTO HIS PALACE, KNOCK HIS ASS OUT AND GET HIM INTO INTERNATIONAL WATERS WHERE INTERPOL CAN PICK HIM UP. I MIGHT EVEN TIE A PRETTY BOW ON HIM.
YOU... ARE...AN *IDIOT.*
INSULTING ME IS NOT COOL.
IDIOTA! THAT'S YOUR PLAN? KIDNAP ROME'S MOST NOTORIOUS GANGSTER?
WHAT? IT'S A SIMPLE PLAN.
THE ONLY THING SIMPLE ABOUT IT IS *YOU.*
AGAIN... INSULTING IS NOT CONSTRUCTIVE.
YOU HAVE NO IDEA WHAT CALIGULA IS DOING, DO YOU?

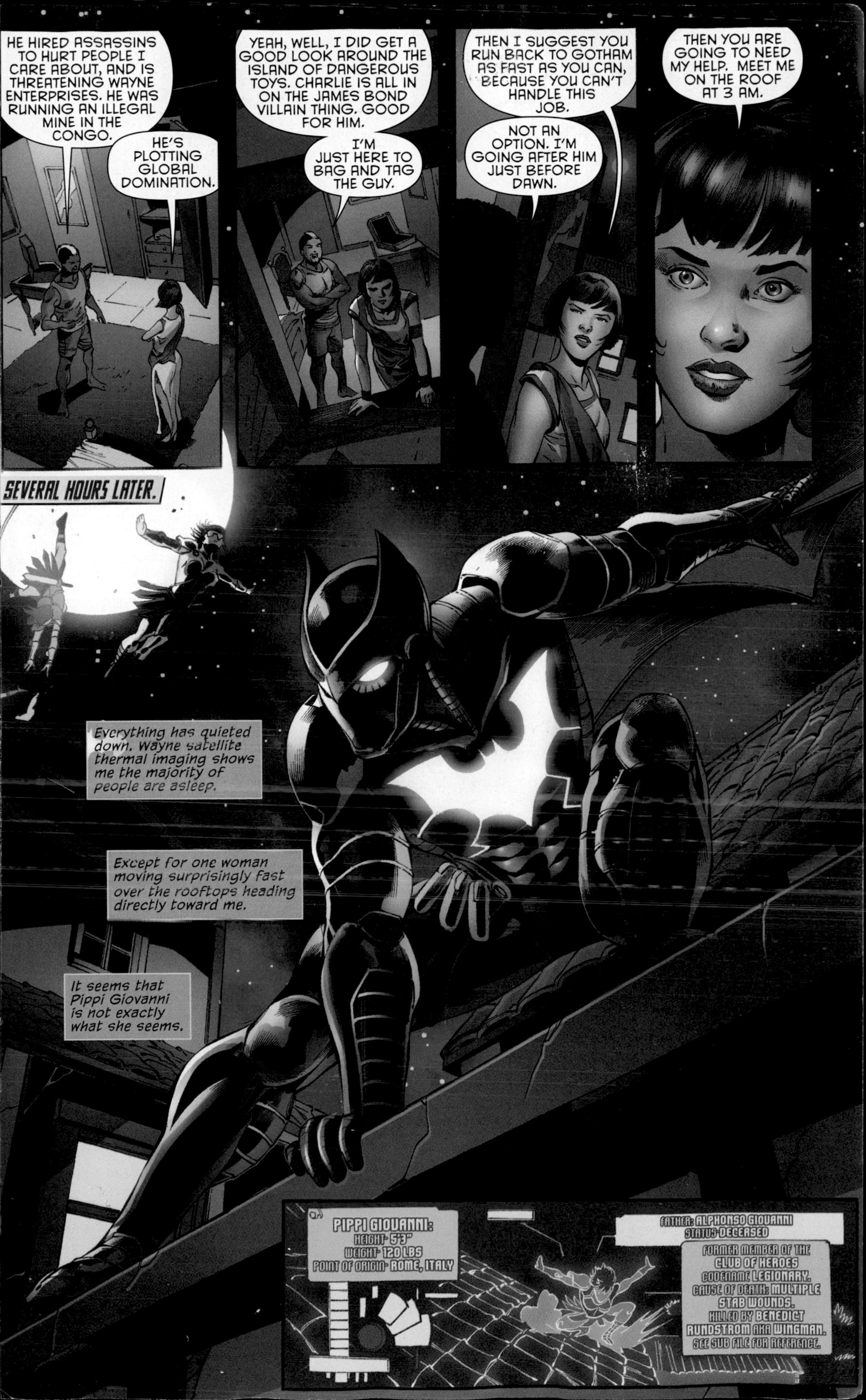

HE HIRED ASSASSINS TO HURT PEOPLE I CARE ABOUT, AND IS THREATENING WAYNE ENTERPRISES. HE WAS RUNNING AN ILLEGAL MINE IN THE CONGO.
HE'S PLOTTING GLOBAL DOMINATION.
YEAH, WELL, I DID GET A GOOD LOOK AROUND THE ISLAND OF DANGEROUS TOYS. CHARLIE IS ALL IN ON THE JAMES BOND VILLAIN THING. GOOD FOR HIM.
I'M JUST HERE TO BAG AND TAG THE GUY.
THEN I SUGGEST YOU RUN BACK TO GOTHAM AS FAST AS YOU CAN, BECAUSE YOU CAN'T HANDLE THIS JOB.
NOT AN OPTION. I'M GOING AFTER HIM JUST BEFORE DAWN.
THEN YOU ARE GOING TO NEED MY HELP. MEET ME ON THE ROOF AT 3 AM.
SEVERAL HOURS LATER.
Everything has quieted down. Wayne satellite thermal imaging shows me the majority of people are asleep.
Except for one woman moving surprisingly fast over the rooftops heading directly toward me.
It seems that Pippi Giovanni is not exactly what she seems.
PIPPI GIOVANNI:
HEIGHT- 5'3"
WEIGHT- 120 LBS
POINT OF ORIGIN- ROME, ITALY
FATHER: ALPHONSO GIOVANNI
STATUS-DECEASED
FORMER MEMBER OF THE CLUB OF HEROES CODENAME LEGIONARY. CAUSE OF DEATH: MULTIPLE STAB WOUNDS. KILLED BY BENEDICT RUNDSTROM AKA WINGMAN. SEE SUB FILE FOR REFERENCE.

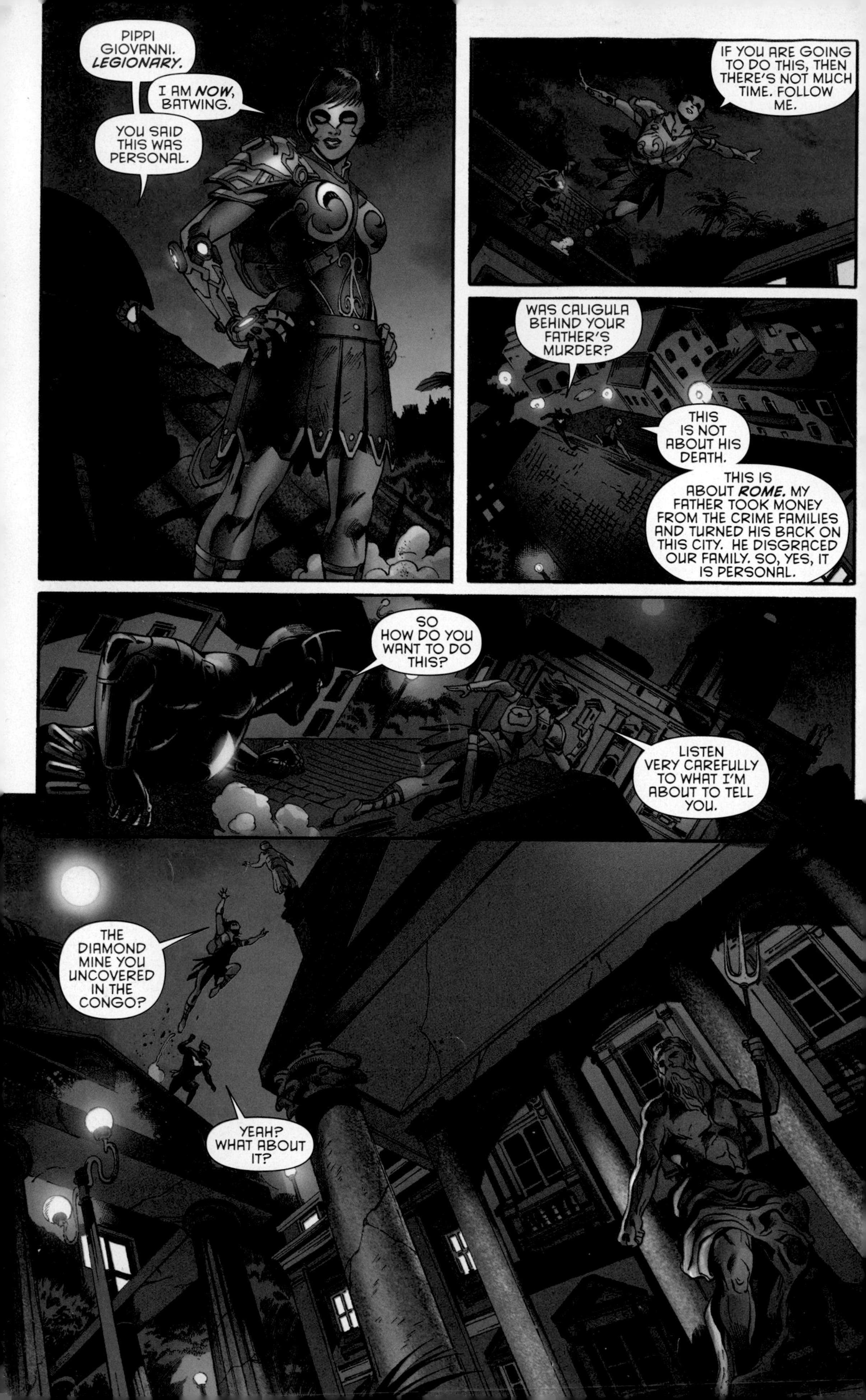
PIPPI GIOVANNI. LEGIONARY.
I AM NOW, BATWING.
YOU SAID THIS WAS PERSONAL.
IF YOU ARE GOING TO DO THIS, THEN THERE'S NOT MUCH TIME. FOLLOW ME.
WAS CALIGULA BEHIND YOUR FATHER'S MURDER?
THIS IS NOT ABOUT HIS DEATH.
THIS IS ABOUT ROME. MY FATHER TOOK MONEY FROM THE CRIME FAMILIES AND TURNED HIS BACK ON THIS CITY. HE DISGRACED OUR FAMILY. SO, YES, IT IS PERSONAL.
SO HOW DO YOU WANT TO DO THIS?
LISTEN VERY CAREFULLY TO WHAT I'M ABOUT TO TELL YOU.
THE DIAMOND MINE YOU UNCOVERED IN THE CONGO?
YEAH? WHAT ABOUT IT?

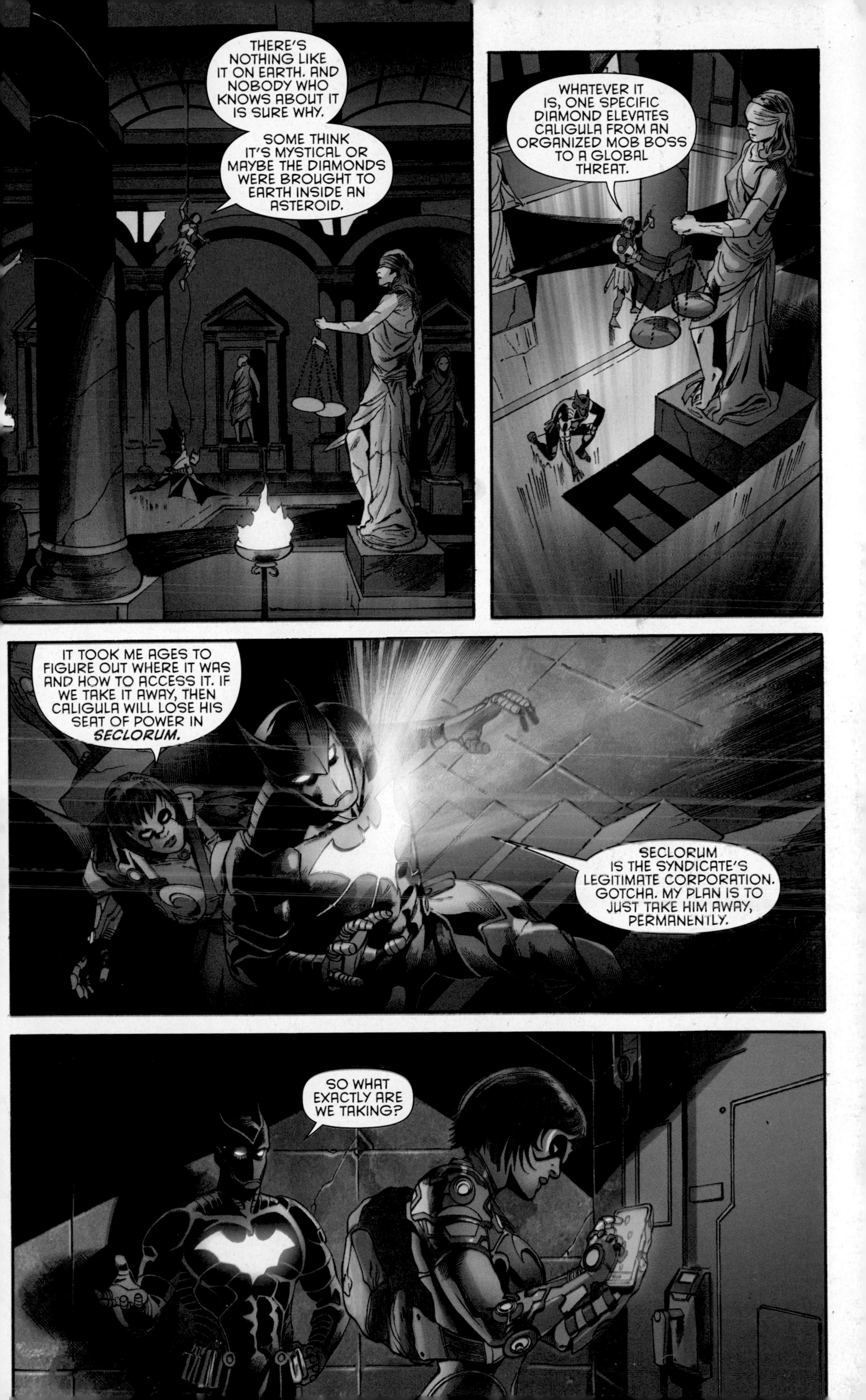
THERE'S NOTHING LIKE IT ON EARTH. AND NOBODY WHO KNOWS ABOUT IT IS SURE WHY.
SOME THINK IT'S MYSTICAL OR MAYBE THE DIAMONDS WERE BROUGHT TO EARTH INSIDE AN ASTEROID.
WHATEVER IT IS, ONE SPECIFIC DIAMOND ELEVATES CALIGULA FROM AN ORGANIZED MOB BOSS TO A GLOBAL THREAT.
IT TOOK ME AGES TO FIGURE OUT WHERE IT WAS AND HOW TO ACCESS IT. IF WE TAKE IT AWAY, THEN CALIGULA WILL LOSE HIS SEAT OF POWER IN SECLORUM.
SECLORUM IS THE SYNDICATE'S LEGITIMATE CORPORATION. GOTCHA. MY PLAN IS TO JUST TAKE HIM AWAY, PERMANENTLY.
SO WHAT EXACTLY ARE WE TAKING?

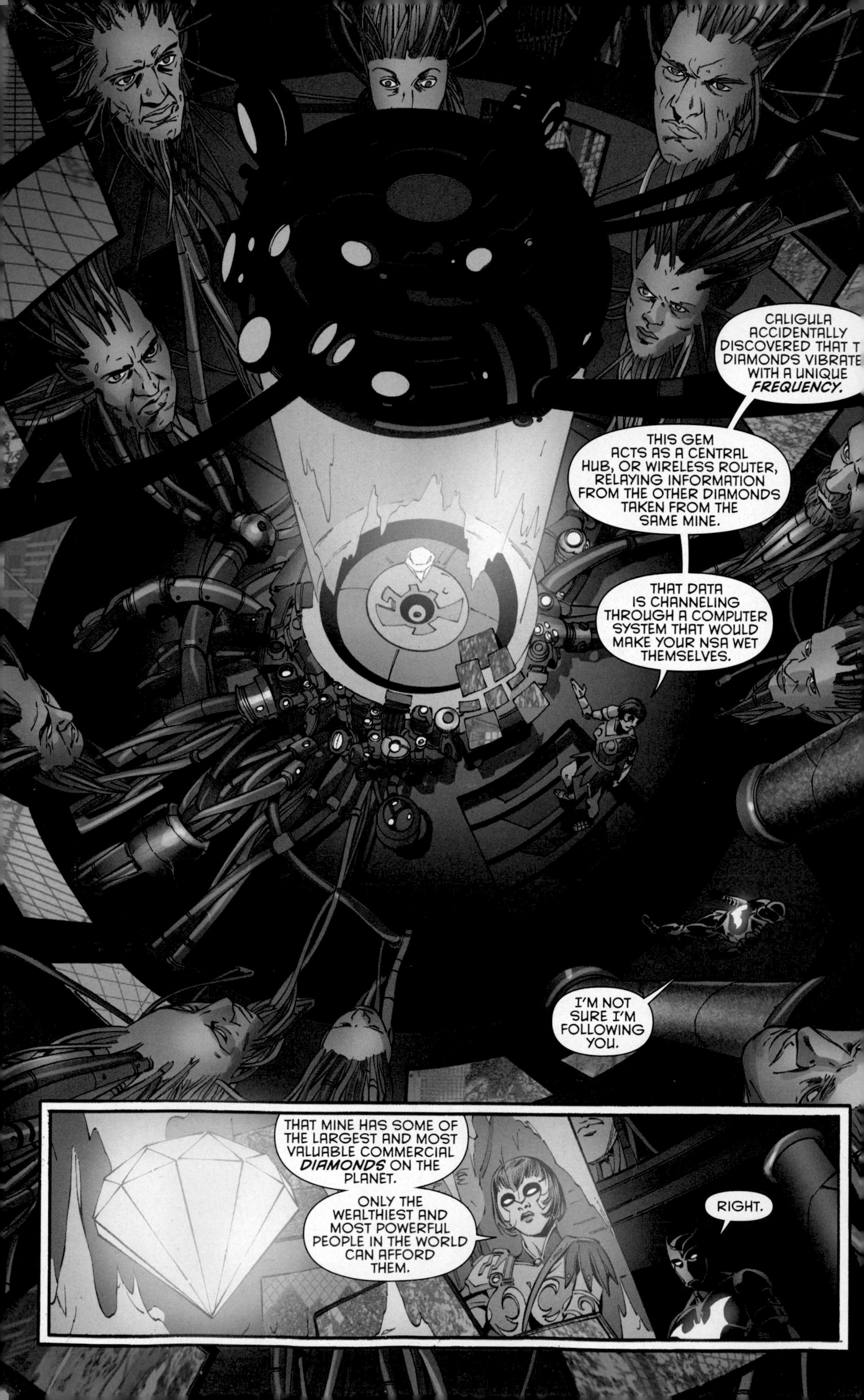
CALIGULA ACCIDENTALLY DISCOVERED THAT T DIAMONDS VIBRATE WITH A UNIQUE FREQUENCY.
THIS GEM ACTS AS A CENTRAL HUB, OR WIRELESS ROUTER, RELAYING INFORMATION FROM THE OTHER DIAMONDS TAKEN FROM THE SAME MINE.
THAT DATA IS CHANNELING THROUGH A COMPUTER SYSTEM THAT WOULD MAKE YOUR NSA WET THEMSELVES.
I'M NOT SURE I'M FOLLOWING YOU.
THAT MINE HAS SOME OF THE LARGEST AND MOST VALUABLE COMMERCIAL DIAMONDS ON THE PLANET.
ONLY THE WEALTHIEST AND MOST POWERFUL PEOPLE IN THE WORLD CAN AFFORD THEM.
RIGHT.

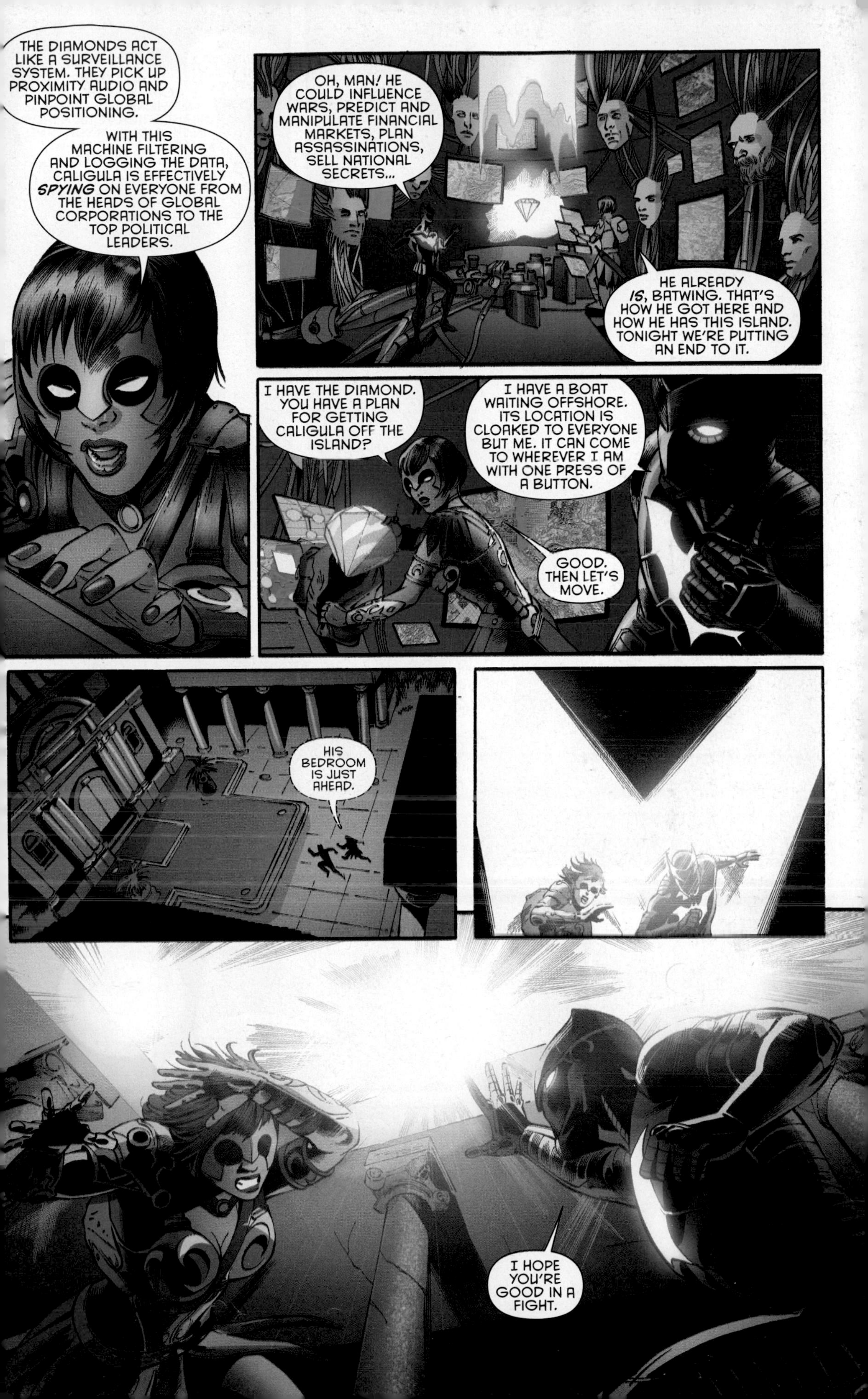
THE DIAMONDS ACT LIKE A SURVEILLANCE SYSTEM. THEY PICK UP PROXIMITY AUDIO AND PINPOINT GLOBAL POSITIONING.
WITH THIS MACHINE FILTERING AND LOGGING THE DATA, CALIGULA IS EFFECTIVELY SPYING ON EVERYONE FROM THE HEADS OF GLOBAL CORPORATIONS TO THE TOP POLITICAL LEADERS.
OH, MAN! HE COULD INFLUENCE WARS, PREDICT AND MANIPULATE FINANCIAL MARKETS, PLAN ASSASSINATIONS, SELL NATIONAL SECRETS...
HE ALREADY IS, BATWING. THAT'S HOW HE GOT HERE AND HOW HE HAS THIS ISLAND. TONIGHT WE'RE PUTTING AN END TO IT.
I HAVE THE DIAMOND. YOU HAVE A PLAN FOR GETTING CALIGULA OFF THE ISLAND?
I HAVE A BOAT WAITING OFFSHORE. ITS LOCATION IS CLOAKED TO EVERYONE BUT ME. IT CAN COME TO WHEREVER I AM WITH ONE PRESS OF A BUTTON.
GOOD. THEN LET'S MOVE.
HIS BEDROOM IS JUST AHEAD.
I HOPE YOU'RE GOOD IN A FIGHT.

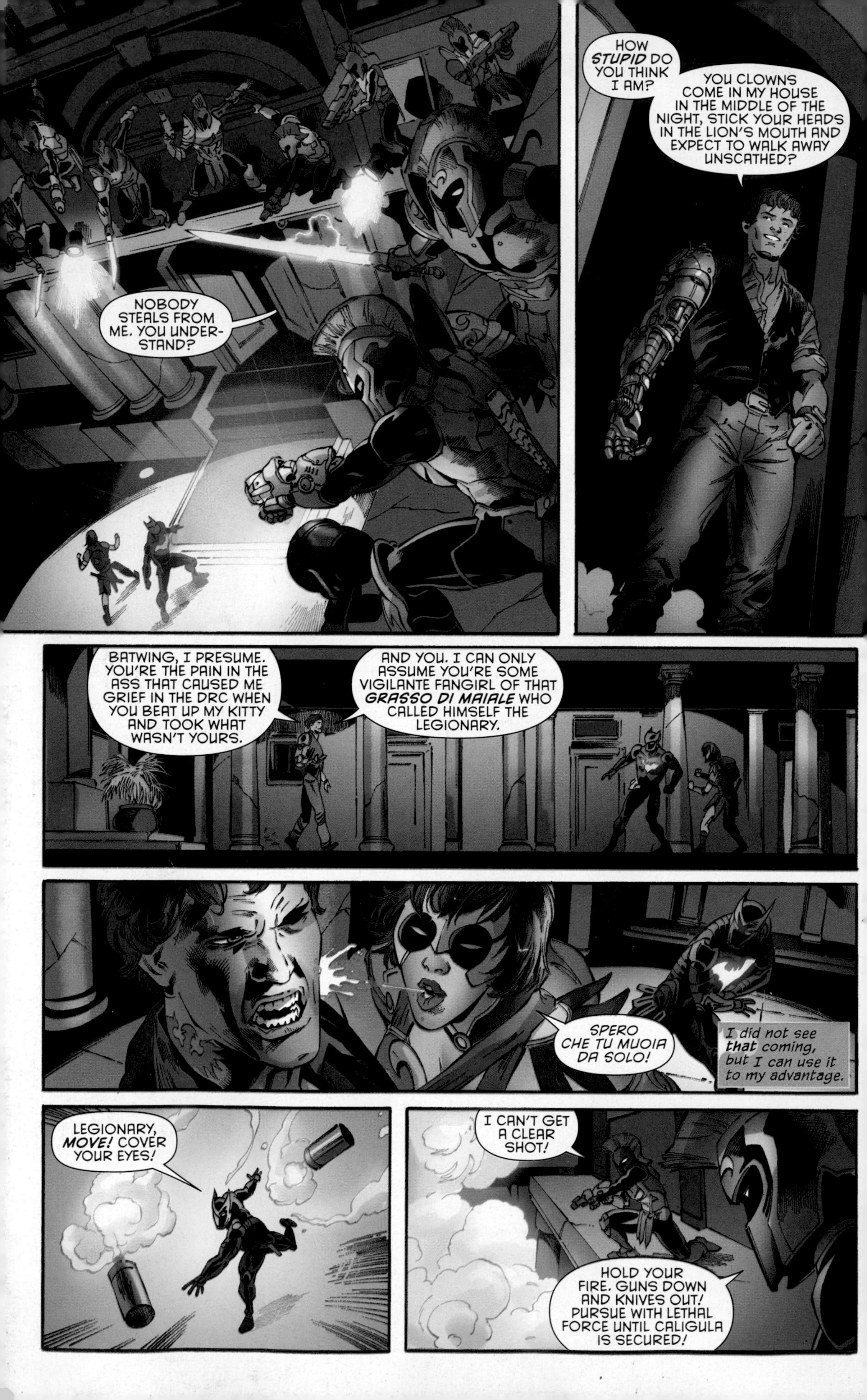
NOBODY STEALS FROM ME. YOU UNDER-STAND?
HOW *STUPID* DO YOU THINK I AM?
YOU CLOWNS COME IN MY HOUSE IN THE MIDDLE OF THE NIGHT, STICK YOUR HEADS IN THE LION'S MOUTH AND EXPECT TO WALK AWAY UNSCATHED?
BATWING, I PRESUME. YOU'RE THE PAIN IN THE ASS THAT CAUSED ME GRIEF IN THE DRC WHEN YOU BEAT UP MY KITTY AND TOOK WHAT WASN'T YOURS.
AND YOU. I CAN ONLY ASSUME YOU'RE SOME VIGILANTE FANGIRL OF THAT *GRASSO DI MAIALE* WHO CALLED HIMSELF THE LEGIONARY.
SPERO CHE TU MUOIA DA SOLO!
I did not see **that** coming, but I can use it to my advantage.
LEGIONARY, ***MOVE!*** COVER YOUR EYES!
I CAN'T GET A CLEAR SHOT!
HOLD YOUR FIRE. GUNS DOWN AND KNIVES OUT! PURSUE WITH LETHAL FORCE UNTIL CALIGULA IS SECURED!

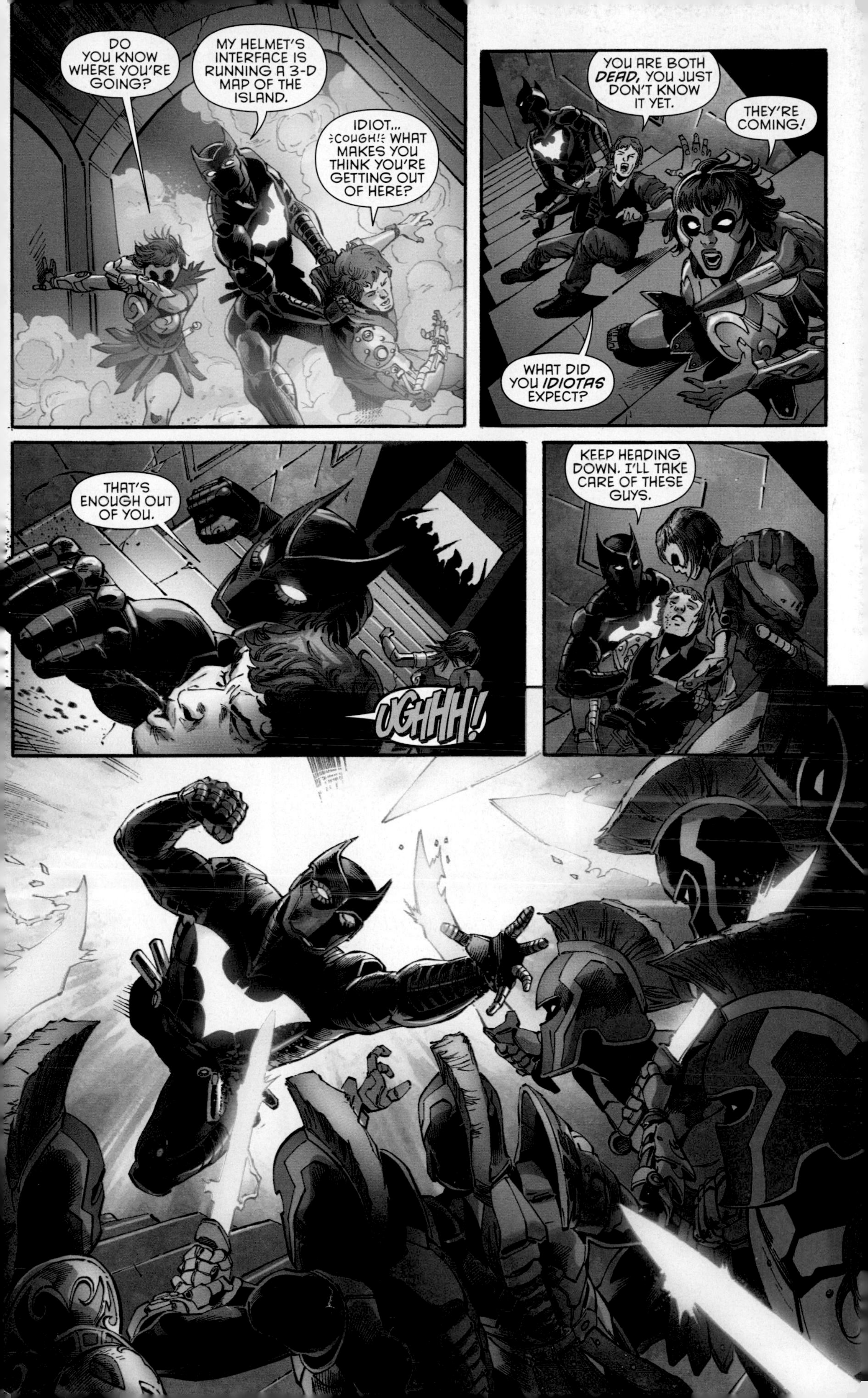
DO YOU KNOW WHERE YOU'RE GOING?
MY HELMET'S INTERFACE IS RUNNING A 3-D MAP OF THE ISLAND.
IDIOT... *COUGH!* WHAT MAKES YOU THINK YOU'RE GETTING OUT OF HERE?
YOU ARE BOTH *DEAD*, YOU JUST DON'T KNOW IT YET.
THEY'RE COMING!
WHAT DID YOU *IDIOTAS* EXPECT?
THAT'S ENOUGH OUT OF YOU.
UGHHH!
KEEP HEADING DOWN. I'LL TAKE CARE OF THESE GUYS.

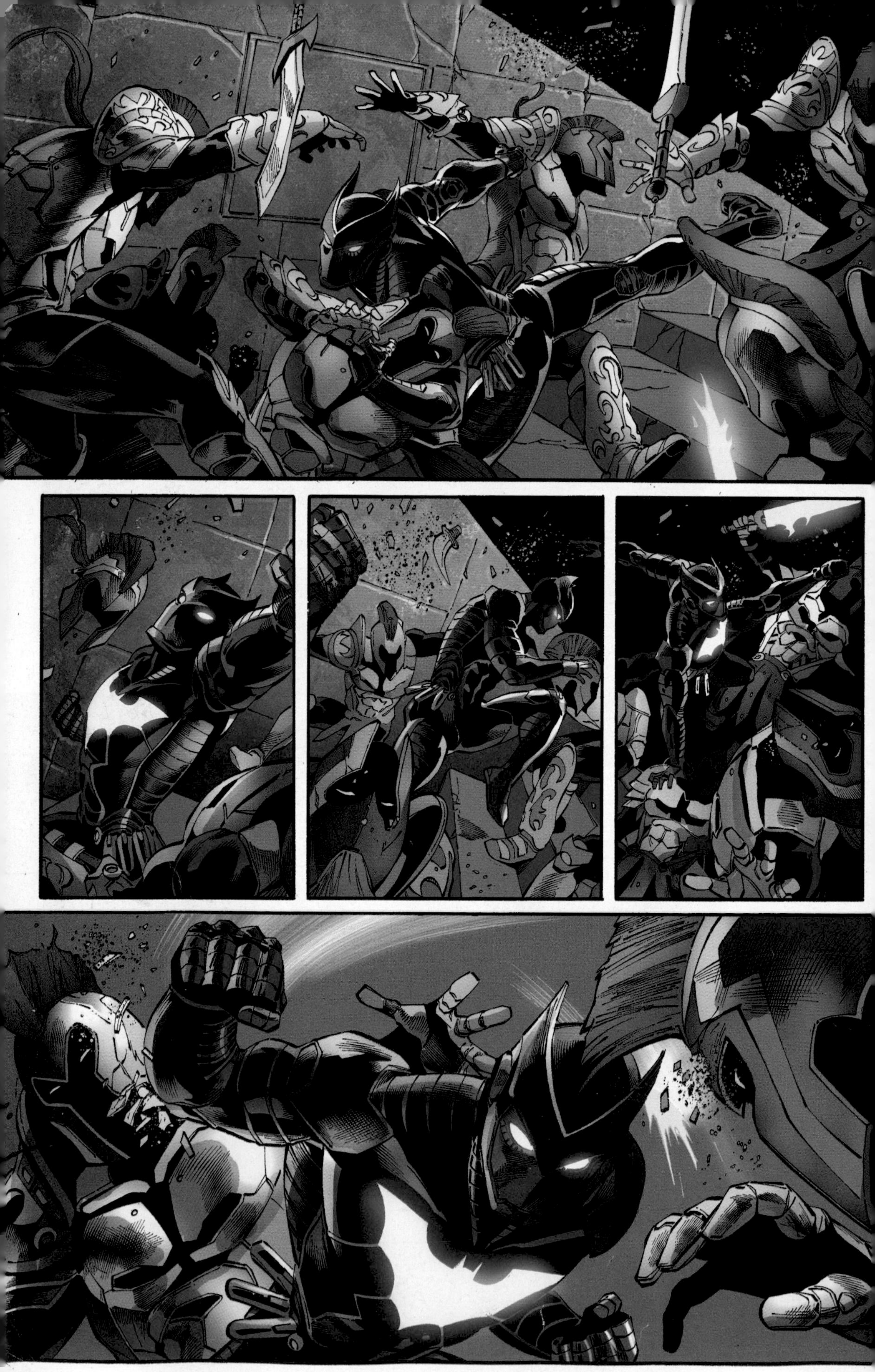

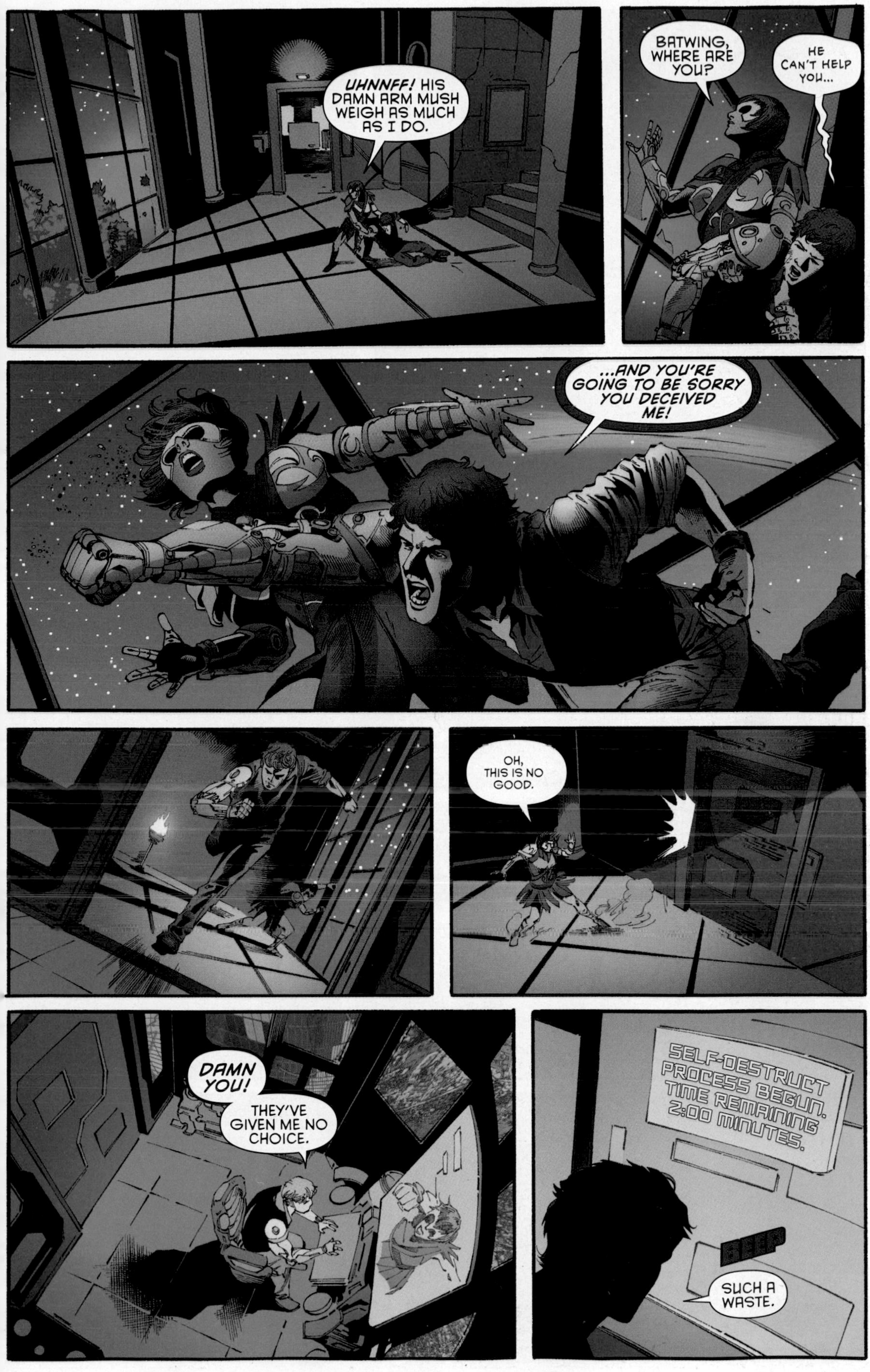
UHNNFF! HIS DAMN ARM MUSH WEIGH AS MUCH AS I DO.
BATWING, WHERE ARE YOU?
HE CAN'T HELP YOU...
...AND YOU'RE GOING TO BE SORRY YOU DECEIVED ME!
OH, THIS IS NO GOOD.
DAMN YOU!
THEY'VE GIVEN ME NO CHOICE.
SELF-DESTRUCT PROCESS BEGUN. TIME REMAINING 2:00 MINUTES.
BEEP
SUCH A WASTE.

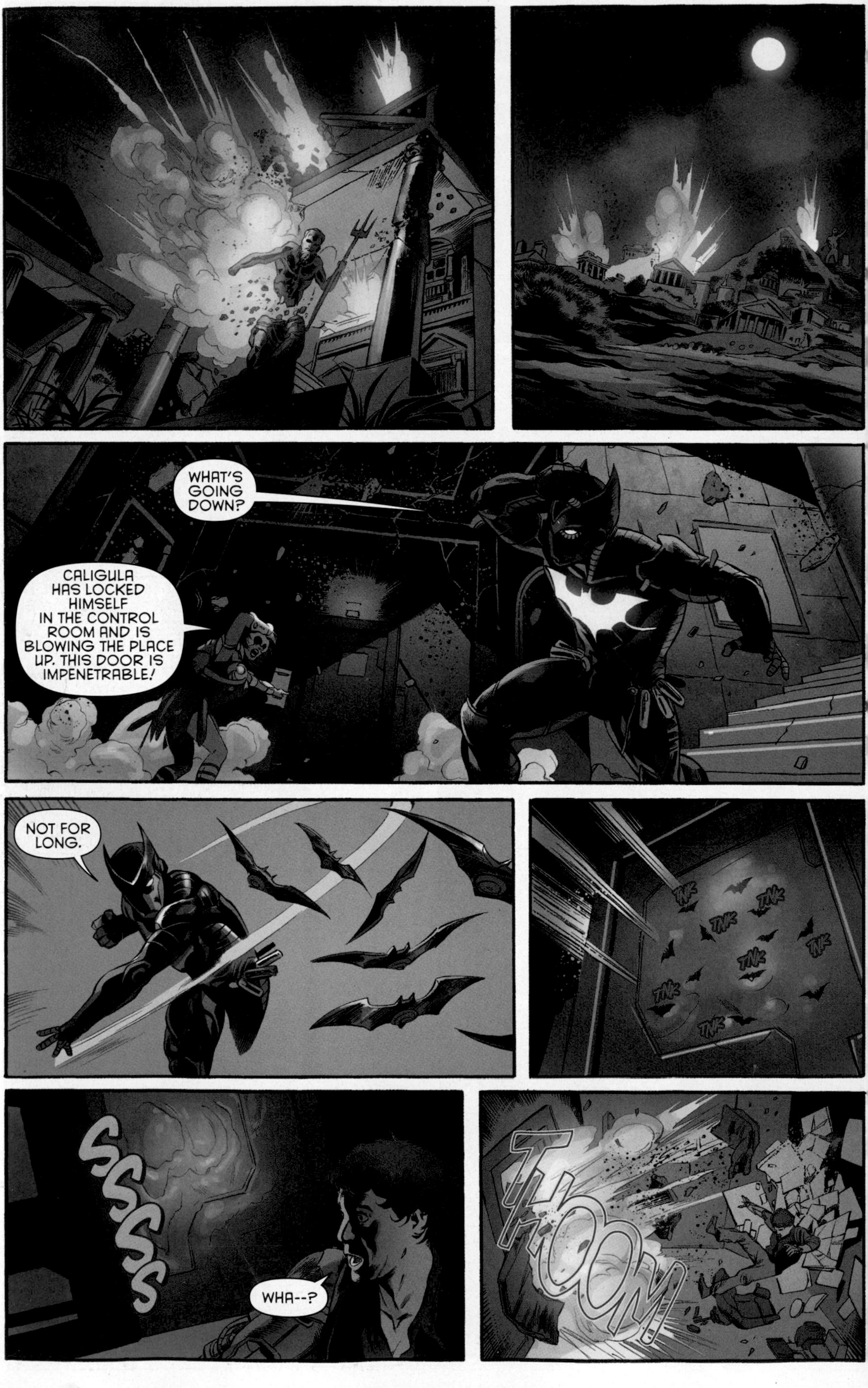
WHAT'S GOING DOWN?
CALIGULA HAS LOCKED HIMSELF IN THE CONTROL ROOM AND IS BLOWING THE PLACE UP. THIS DOOR IS IMPENETRABLE!
NOT FOR LONG.
TNK
TNK
TNK
TNK
TNK
TNK
TNK
SSSS
WHA--?
THOOOM

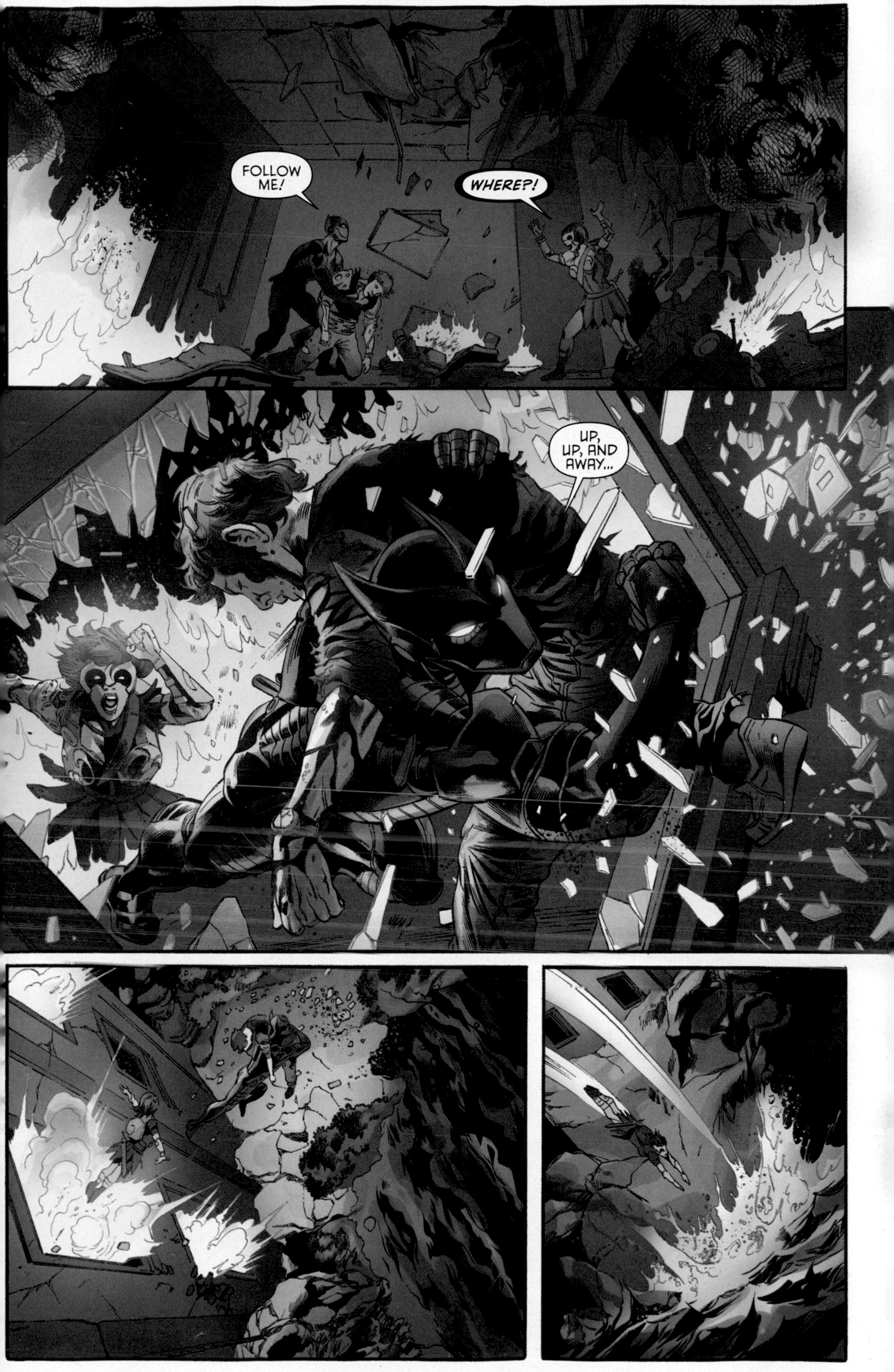
FOLLOW ME!
WHERE?!
UP, UP, AND AWAY...

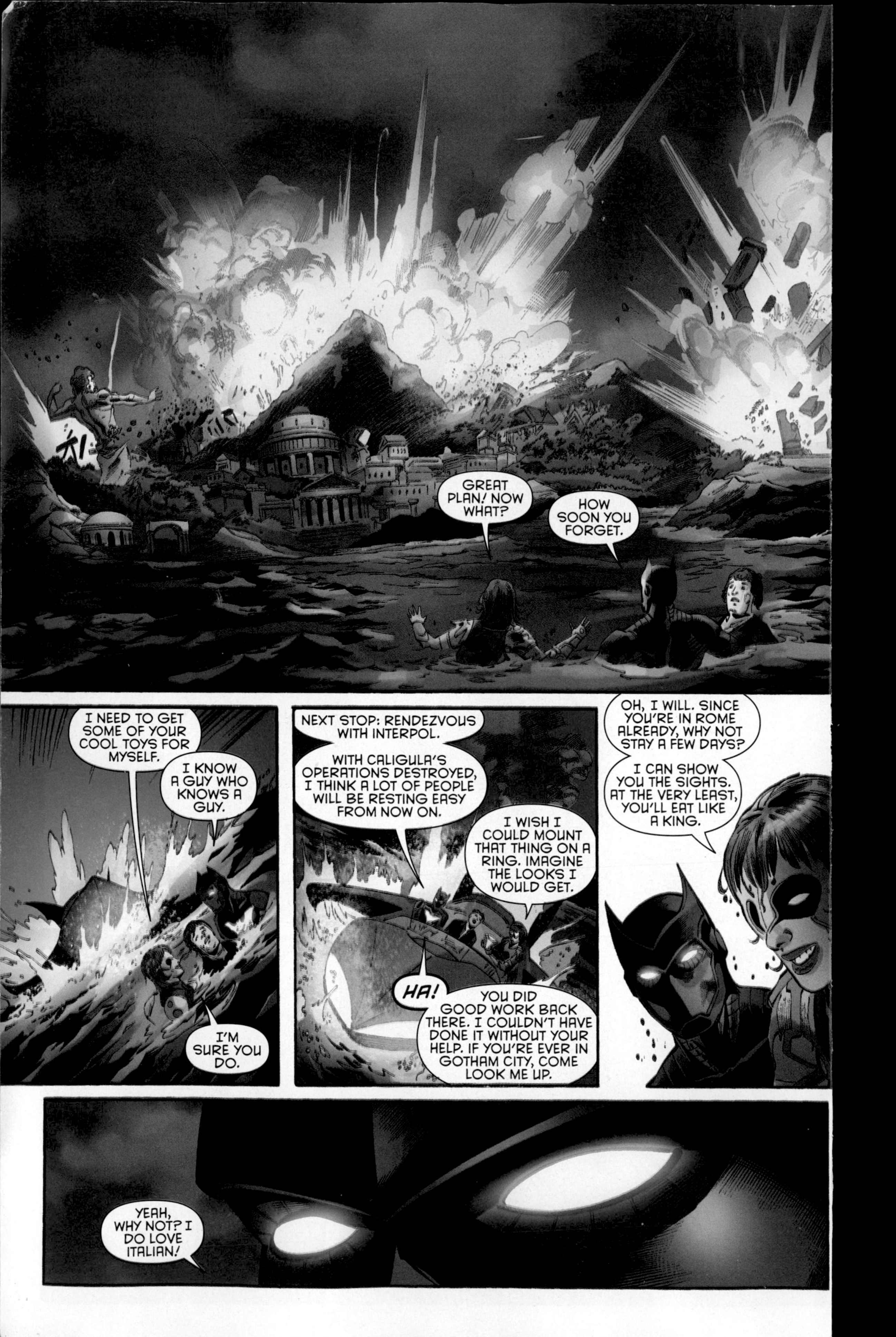
GREAT PLAN! NOW WHAT?
HOW SOON YOU FORGET.
I NEED TO GET SOME OF YOUR COOL TOYS FOR MYSELF.
I KNOW A GUY WHO KNOWS A GUY.
I'M SURE YOU DO.
NEXT STOP: RENDEZVOUS WITH INTERPOL.
WITH CALIGULA'S OPERATIONS DESTROYED, I THINK A LOT OF PEOPLE WILL BE RESTING EASY FROM NOW ON.
I WISH I COULD MOUNT THAT THING ON A RING. IMAGINE THE LOOKS I WOULD GET.
HA!
YOU DID GOOD WORK BACK THERE. I COULDN'T HAVE DONE IT WITHOUT YOUR HELP. IF YOU'RE EVER IN GOTHAM CITY, COME LOOK ME UP.
OH, I WILL. SINCE YOU'RE IN ROME ALREADY, WHY NOT STAY A FEW DAYS?
I CAN SHOW YOU THE SIGHTS. AT THE VERY LEAST, YOU'LL EAT LIKE A KING.
YEAH, WHY NOT? I DO LOVE ITALIAN!

BATWING

LUCAS FOX DESIGNS BY EDUARDO PANSICA

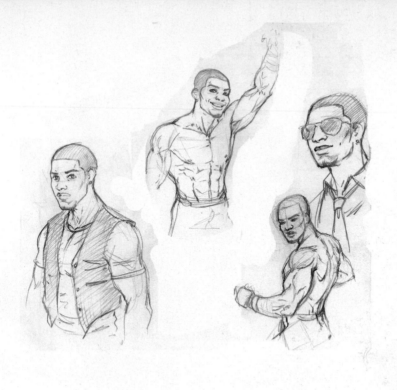

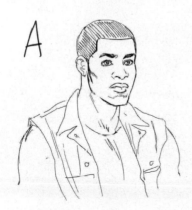

A
B
C
D

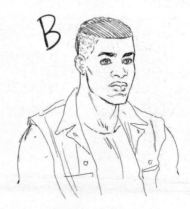

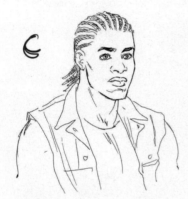

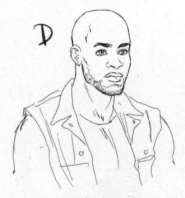

Full cover spread art for BATWING #19 by Fabrizio Fiorentino

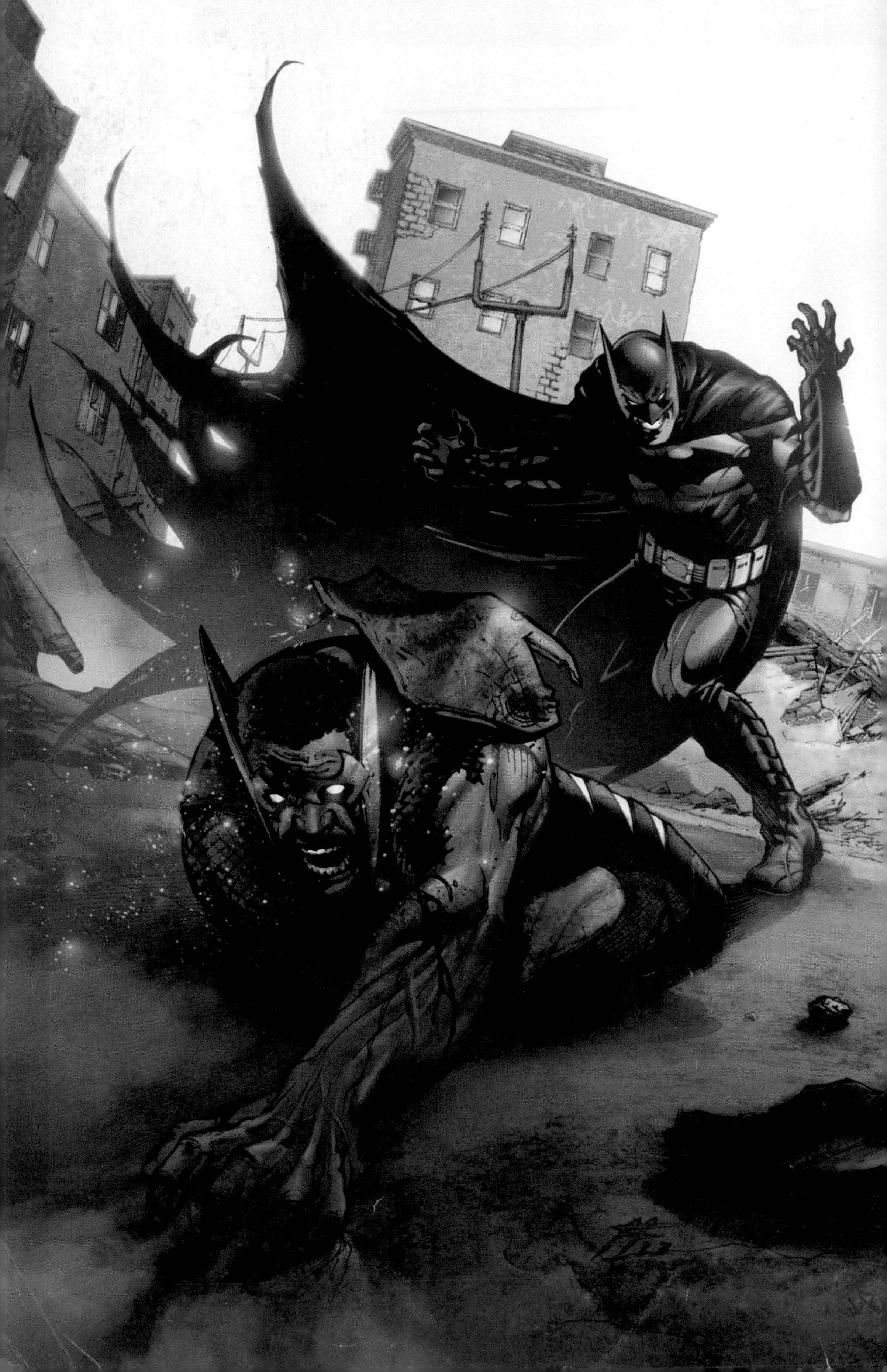

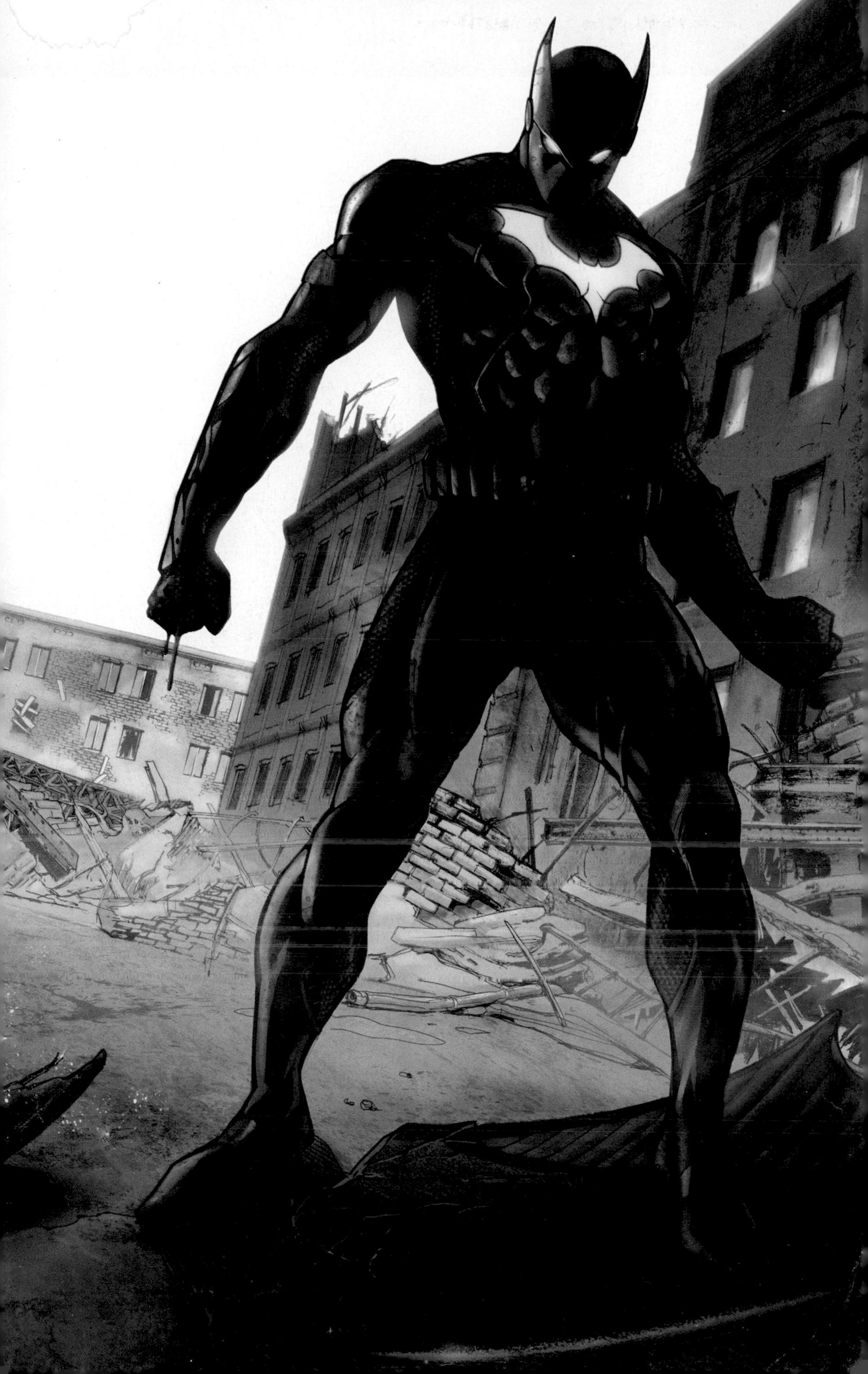

BATWING

CHARACTER DESIGNS BY EDUARDO PANSICA

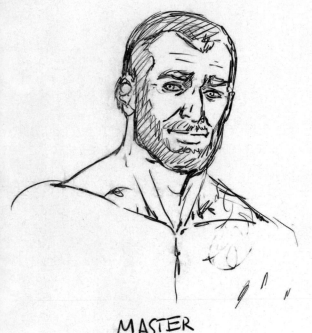

MASTER TORRES
RUSSEL